Graham McCann 1992
King's College,
Cambridge.

Michel Foucault

Michel Foucault

DIDIER ERIBON

Translated by Betsy Wing

faber and faber
LONDON · BOSTON

First published in the USA in 1991
by Harvard University Press, Cambridge, Massachusetts
This edition first published in Great Britain in 1992
by Faber and Faber Limited
3 Queen Square London WCIN 3AU

Originally published in French in 1989
as *Michel Foucault* by Flammarion

Printed in England by Clays Ltd, St Ives plc

A CIP record for this book is available from the British Library

ISBN 0-571-14474-8

2 4 6 8 10 9 7 5 3 1

For Olivier Séguret

Contents

~~~

Contents

Preface

〰

Death conceals no mystery. It opens no door. It is the
end of a human being. He is survived by the things he
has given other human beings, by the things remaining
in their memory.

Norbert Elias

Writing a biography of Michel Foucault may seem paradoxical. Did he not, on numerous occasions, challenge the notion of the author, thereby dismissing the very possibility
of a biographical study? When I started this book, several of his friends
and closest relatives brought this up. But although it may seem relevant, it also seems to me that this objection takes care of itself. Foucault
did indeed question the notion of the author. But what does that
mean? He demonstrated that in our societies the circulation of discourses had to submit to restrictive forms imposed by notions of author, work, and commentary. Even so, Foucault could not isolate
himself from the society in which he lived. He, like everyone else, was
forced to fulfill the "functions" he described. So he signed his books
and made connections among them with a collection of prefaces, articles, and interviews, endeavoring to demonstrate the coherence of his
oeuvre or to show the dynamics of his research from one stage to the
next. He played the commentary game, participating in conferences
devoted to his work, answering objections and criticism, good and bad
readings. Michel Foucault, in short, is an author. He produced an
oeuvre, which has been subject to commentary. Seminars, meetings,
and debates about his work are still being organized in France today,
and all over the world texts are being collected into complete editions
of his "writings and sayings." There is much discussion about whether
or not the tape recordings of his courses at the Collège de France should
be published. Why, then, should biography be the one forbidden form?
Because Foucault always refused to release the facts of his life, as some
have claimed? That is untrue. He provided a lot of information in sev-

eral interviews; he approved the publication of an Italian edition of interviews *(Colloqui con Foucault)* attempting, in large part, to retrace his intellectual itinerary; and in 1983 he proposed that he and I do a more complete and "formally composed" book of interviews as part of a collection in which several scholars and intellectuals would describe their training and how their work came to be.

No doubt the real reason that some object to a biography of Foucault is their feeling that discussion of homosexuality would be controversial. Invariably, throughout my research, the question arose: "Will you mention homosexuality in this book?" Some were afraid the topic would be misunderstood. Others were amazed that in 1989 anyone might hesitate to discuss it openly. Obviously, this book is destined to elicit contradictory reactions from those who think I have said too much and those who would like more details or description—about American life, for instance. My preference lies closer to the second point of view, but I also had to consider the feelings of those who hold the other. I made no attempt to conceal facts, but my intention was not to write a sensational book. The balance was not easy to achieve. I wanted to resist the subtle forms of repression and censorship that await all writers. I wanted to resist them especially because this was a book about Foucault, whose entire oeuvre can be read as a revolt against the powers of "normalization." Yet are display and exhibitionism not also ways of acknowledging the strength of these forces and of the part voyeurism plays in them? To avoid this double pitfall, I decided to tell the facts when telling them was necessary to an understanding of some particular event, some particular aspect of Foucault's career, his work, his thought, his life—or his death. I passed over them in silence when they were connected only with the secret territory that every individual creates in his or her own life. However, this point is worth noting: Foucault himself gave interviews to homosexual reviews both in France and abroad in which he expressed himself at length. Those prepared to be indignant about my "revelations" should know that many of them are only quotations and translations of his own words.

Foucault was fond of quoting René Char: "Develop your legitimate strangeness." This book, inspired by admiration for a man and an oeuvre whose brilliance have illuminated intellectual activity in France and abroad for almost thirty years, is written under the sign of Char's injunction.

The investigation offered its own difficulties. First there were the obstacles that inevitably arise in such an inquiry: the occasional lapse of memory in witnesses, and the slow resurfacing of these memories in a succession of encounters and discussions. From time to time these produced contradictory accounts whose avenues of intersection required further tracing. There was also the problem of records that were lost or buried in archives, access to which required a thousand official authorizations or unofficial collusions. To collect all these documents and speak to all the witnesses I had to travel—from Tunis to Poitiers, Lille to San Francisco, Clermont-Ferrand to Uppsala or Warsaw. I had also to move through extremely diverse cultural territories: from the historian of science, an emeritus professor at the Sorbonne, to the director of *Libération*; from the Swedish diplomat to the avant-garde writer; from a former secretary general at the Elysée to leftist leaders who founded the University of Vincennes; and so on. Then the written evidence had to be compared with the testimony gathered from relatives, friends, colleagues, students, and enemies.

But there were also very special difficulties concerning Foucault himself. He was a complex, many-sided character. "He wore masks, and he was always changing them," said Georges Dumézil, who knew him better than almost anyone else. I have not attempted to reveal "the" truth about Foucault. Under one mask there is always another, and I do not think there is any truth of personality that it would be possible to discover beneath these successive disguises. No doubt there are several Foucaults—a thousand Foucaults, as Dumézil said. I have presented them as I saw them, and often the Foucault that emerges is quite different from the one I knew from 1979 to 1984. But I have been wary of making judgments or of establishing a preferential order for those personas.

The major obstacle was less obvious, more insidious. Simply to establish the facts it was necessary first to free oneself from the mythologies surrounding Foucault, which clung so tightly to his character that sometimes they obscured evidence from documents and accounts. Foucault began to take center stage in 1966, after the publication of *Les Mots et les choses* (The order of things), but his notoriety swiftly coincided with his political activity during the 1970s. And much of what was written about him thereafter bears the mark of this latterday persona of the "committed philosopher," which seems to have changed retrospectively everything Foucault had formerly been.

Let me be clear about my purpose here. Although this account of Foucault strives to reestablish historical facts as against the sedimented layers of legend, it does not seek to efface the innovative power, the richness, and the fruitfulness of Foucault's oeuvre. On the contrary, it aims to restore these qualities to it in all their brilliance. There have been numerous readings of Foucault's oeuvre over forty years. These have been forgotten, stuck away on dusty shelves and neglected. They have vanished. It is no disservice to Foucault's work to sever it from a single, mutilating version. To return its history to it in order to restore its multiple forces can only enhance it.

Recounting a life is an interminable task. If one spent twenty years at it, there would always be something left to discover. If one wrote ten volumes, a supplement would still be required. It was impossible, for example, to catalogue here all the petitions signed by Foucault from 1970 to 1984. To report on every one of his militant actions day by day was inconceivable. Claude Mauriac devoted several hundred pages of his ten-volume journal, *Le Temps immobile*, to this subject, but he was present at only some of them. Nor was it possible to record all the lectures Foucault delivered on campuses all over the world, to list all the interviews he gave to newspapers, reviews, and magazines, or to name everyone who met him. Many people found their relationship with Michel Foucault enormously important. But because I was writing a biography of Foucault, I had to focus on those who mattered to him, rather than on those for whom he mattered.

I have also been selective about events, texts, and periods. I gave more space to one event rather than to another when it seemed to me more significant; I quoted one text at greater length than another when I felt that it better expressed Foucault's thought at the period in which he wrote it, or when it had become hard to obtain or had not been published in French.

In each period treated, I have tried to reconstruct the intellectual landscape in which Foucault developed. Clearly, a philosophy does not spring up fully formed with its concepts and discoveries in a solitary mind dedicating itself to the exercise of thought. An intellectual project and its development can be undertood only in reference to a theoretical, institutional, and political space—what Pierre Bourdieu would call a "field." I have therefore tried to amass and combine here the testimony of the philosophers who accompanied or intersected with Foucault in his career, who saw his work develop, who followed its evolution. I met with and questioned for hours, and often several times, Henri Gouhier, Georges Canguilhem, Louis Althusser, Gérard Lebrun, Jean-Claude Pariente, Jean-Toussaint Desanti, Gilles Deleuze, Jacques Derrida, Jules Vuillemin, Michel Serres. Others provided me with accounts, stories, information, or essential documents: chiefly Georges Dumézil, Paul Veyne of course, Claude Lévi-Strauss, Pierre Bourdieu, Paul Rabinow, Robert Castel, Jean-Claude Passeron, Mathieu Lindon, and Maurice Pinguet. The many others who helped me are listed at the end of the volume. They are extremely numerous because this book was to be, above all, a collective history—not the portrait of an epoch, as biographies are frequently described, but sketches of several epochs, of several cultural registers: the Ecole Normale Supérieure on the Rue d'Ulm during the postwar years, French literature during the 1960s, the structuralist controversy, the far left after 1968, the Collège de France as a specific institution in French university life, and so on.

On several occasions I was present at or involved in the events that I describe. I have systematically avoided speaking in the first person. Except in very rare instances—two, I believe—when it was difficult to do otherwise, I have substituted for my own account those of others who were present or were equally knowledgeable.

This book is a biography, and not, therefore, a study of Foucault's oeuvre. But surely the reason for writing a biography of Foucault is that he wrote books. I have tried to present the major works against the background in which they took form. I have faithfully reproduced the texts and avoided commenting on them. On the other hand, because it is part of their history, I have discussed the reception of his books at some length. Sometimes this history consists of successive receptions, as is the case for Foucault's thesis, *Folie et déraison*.

As a history of these histories this project is, perhaps, closer than may first appear to the spirit of Foucault, who wrote of Ludwig Binswanger: "Original forms of thought are their own introduction: their history is the only form of exegesis they tolerate, and their fate the only form of criticism."

L'éclair me dure.

The lightning still is with me.
René Char

Translator's Note

Works by Foucault are translated in parentheses at their first occurrence. Thereafter the French titles alone are used.

Part I

⁕

PSYCHOLOGY IN HELL

I

"The City Where I Was Born"

In a somewhat preposterous setting—the theater where Avenue Montaigne meets the Champs-Elysées—a small crowd assembled in a large room very early on the morning of January 9, 1988. Despite the voluntarily discreet, even half-secret nature of the gathering in order to avoid attracting too big a crowd, there were more than a hundred scholars assembled from almost every part of the world. They quietly took their seats, and a small man rose. Notwithstanding his eighty-four years, his voice was steady and assured as he began to read his statement: "The number of those present, the diversity of participants, and the pertinence of questions raised mark this meeting as an important event in the collective enterprise of evaluating and examining the works of Michel Foucault . . ." Georges Canguilhem paused briefly for a breath at the end of his sentence and continued: "Like all philosophers who leave behind a work that is interrupted, bereft of its author, Michel Foucault has become an object exposed to examination, to comparison, and even to suspicion. Certainly this was true when he was alive. But his scathing replies to often routine objections were not merely a defense; usually they were also a dazzling illumination of his forays into the unconscious of realms of knowledge, the questions he had and the answers he found."[1]

Nearly four years had passed between Michel Foucault's death on June 25, 1984, and this colloquium, opened and presided over by the eminent scholar who had served on the three-member jury when Foucault defended his thesis, *Folie et déraison* (Madness and folly).[2] During these years Foucault's name had not left the spotlight.

In the fall of 1986 Gilles Deleuze's soberly titled *Foucault*[3] evoked much comment. At that time several reviews published special issues on Foucault;[4] and, since news makes news, all the papers devoted space to Foucault's work: the first page of *Le Monde*, eight pages in *Libération*, six pages in *Le Nouvel Observateur*, and so on. In an interview a few days before his book appeared, Deleuze stated outright: "Foucault's thought seems to me one of the greatest of modern philosophies."[5]

In 1970 Foucault had written: "Some day this will be a Deleuzian century." In 1986 Deleuze was perhaps trying to modify the formulation, to say that, on the contrary, this was a Foucaldian century and Foucaldian it would remain; in other words, that Foucault has left a deep imprint upon this century, our world—an imprint so deep that, unlike the figures traced in the sand at the end of Foucault's *Les Mots et les choses (The Order of Things)*, it will not be effaced by the next rising tide. Or by the advent of death.

"SUCH IS THE CITY where I was born: decapitated saints, book in hand, watch to assure that justice is just and chateaux strong . . . That is where I inherited my wisdom."[6] This was how Michel Foucault liked to describe Poitiers, where he spent his childhood and adolescence—a provincial city curled around its romanesque churches and its fifteenth-century *palais de justice*, where the statues have in fact lost their heads. A city straight out of one of Balzac's narratives. A beautiful city—stifling, no doubt, but beautiful. Its ancient center, perched on a promontory, seems to defy the passage of time and the upheavals that come with it.

Perhaps it was to stave off the passage of time that the Foucault family passed down the same first name: Paul Foucault the grandfather, Paul Foucault the father, Paul Foucault the son. But Mme. Foucault did not yield entirely to the traditions imposed by her husband's family. Her first son had to be named Paul. So be it. But she added to it a hyphen and the name Michel. On official papers and school records his name is simply Paul Foucault. The one most closely concerned, the boy himself, would soon use only the other: Michel. For Mme. Foucault he would always be Paul-Michel, which is how she still referred to him shortly before her death. Even today the family speaks of him as "Paul-Michel." Why did he change his name? "Because he had the same initials as Pierre Mendès France, P. M. F." was Mme. Foucault's answer. That was what her son had told her. But to his friends he gave an entirely different reason: he did not want to have the same name as the father whom he hated as an adolescent.

Paul Foucault—*le nom du père*. A surgeon at Poitiers and professor of anatomy at the medical school, he was the son of a surgeon at Fontainebleau. He married Anne Malapert, the daughter of a surgeon at Poitiers and professor at the medical school. They lived in the big white house, of no particular distinction but near the center of the city, that Dr. Malapert had built in 1903. This house faces both Rue Arthur-Ranc and Boulevard de Verdun, which descends steeply from the upper city toward the Clain valley. Dr. Paul Foucault and his wife had three children: Francine, the eldest; Paul, born fifteen months later, on October 15, 1926; and a second son, Denys, born several years later. The three children led the life of the respectable, provincial bourgeoisie. It was a wealthy family. Mme. Foucault owned a house twenty kilometers from the city, at Vendeuvre-du-Poitou, a superb structure surrounded by a park and known by the villagers as "the chateau." She also owned land, farms, fields. Dr. Foucault was a highly regarded surgeon who spent his days operating in the two clinics in Poitiers. He was a person of some standing in the city. In short, there was no lack of money in the Foucault establishment. A nurse was in charge of the children, a cook in charge of the house; there was even a chauffeur. The children received a good but conservative education, even though Mme. Foucault subscribed to one of her father's maxims: "The important thing is to take charge of one's own affairs." She avoided controlling or directing her children's reading in any way. As for religion, apparently it was not one of the family's obsessions. Everyone went to mass on Sunday at Saint-Porchaire, in the center of the city. But Mme. Foucault neglected to do so more than once, and on these occasions her mother, the children's grandmother, took them. Paul-Michel was an acolyte and choirboy for a while; tradition required it. But in an interview much later, Michel Foucault described his family as somewhat anticlerical. No doubt respect for the proprieties coexisted with a certain detachment from faith.

Paul-Michel's early schooling in the shadow of the Jesuits was therefore entirely a matter of chance—or of history, which is often the same thing. The Lycée Henri-IV, which included kindergarten and the elementary grades, was located on Rue Louis-Renard in an old building that had belonged to the Congregation. It was a public school, but it backed against a chapel that was more like an abbey in its size and imposing appearance. Dr. Foucault's son was less than four years old when he first entered the square courtyard of the institution. Above the inner portal centuries of history looked down on the children passing beneath: effigy kings—Henri IV, "founder," and Louis XIV, "benefactor"—were engraved in the stone. Paul-Michel was not yet legally old enough to be admitted to the school, but he did not want to be separated from his sister. When Mme. Foucault discussed the situation with the teacher, the latter kindly responded: "You can bring him to us; we'll put him in the back of the room with some colored pencils." And on May 27, 1930, there he was, in the back of the classroom, with his colored pencils. "But he took advantage of it and learned to read," Mme. Foucault said. He had two years of "playschool," until 1932, and remained in the elementary school until 1936. Then he moved on to the secondary level, the lycée proper. At the beginning of the school year in 1940 he left the Lycée Henri-IV for Saint-Stanislas. He had had a bad year.

Until then Paul-Michel had had few problems in school. He was not outstanding in math, but his grades in French, history, Greek, and Latin largely compensated for this deficiency, and he regularly carried off prizes for excellence. What happened in the tenth grade[7] that made his grades slip so badly? Mme. Foucault's explanation was that the headmaster had suffered a stroke and could no longer manage his school in the new wartime circumstances. Conditions had, indeed, changed. The population of Poitiers was swollen by successive waves of refugees, and the city's schools had to make room for pupils and teachers arriving from Paris. Lycée Henri-IV took in part of Lycée Janson-de-Sailly from Paris. The tranquil, confident serenity of provincial education was seriously disrupted, and so were the established hierarchies. Michel Foucault later described to a friend his sense of utter confusion when, having always been a top student, he saw newcomers surpass and supplant him. Several of Foucault's friends from this period have another explanation: the French teacher, Guyot, took an immediate dislike to him. Guyot wasted no love on the children of the bourgeoisie. He was very "Third Republic," a radical and a Voltairean who scarcely concealed his scorn for the children of notables. He was completely prepared to detest the children from the more elegant parts of Paris who landed in his class. And the few representatives of this group from his own city of Poitiers met with even more contempt. Foucault felt the ground slip out from under him. His grades dropped precipitously in all subjects except translation from Latin. At the end of the year the headmaster decided that he must retake his exams in October in order to pass. This verdict was unacceptable to Mme. Foucault. She enrolled her son in a religious secondary school, the Collège Saint-Stanislas, then located at the corner of Jean-Jaurès and l'Ancienne Comédie. This was not the most highly regarded religious institution in the city. Saint-Joseph, run by the Jesuits, had a far better reputation; it drew most of its students from the upper middle class and landed gentry of the region. Saint-Stanislas, run by the Frères des Ecoles Chrétiennes—commonly referred to as the Ignoramus Brothers—was a notch below: most of its students were the sons of substantial merchants and small manufacturers, and the quality of teaching was poorer. When Paul-Michel Foucault entered the school in September 1940, the city had been occupied by the Germans for several weeks. The free zone was twenty kilometers from Poitiers. On the other side of the line was almost another world, and one needed a pass to get there. Eleventh-grade students were too young to be conscripted into compulsory work service in Germany. At most they were required to join the "rural service," involving six weeks of agricultural work during summer vacation, when their chief task was to pick off potato beetles.

Today everyone who attended Saint-Stanislas in that period remembers an extraordinary history teacher, Father de Montsabert. He was a Benedictine monk from Ligugé Abbey and the priest at Croutelle, a small nearby village. Traveling always on foot, his pilgrim's staff in hand, dressed in ample and muddy monk's garb, he was a familiar sight on the road between Poitiers and Ligugé. People in cars would stop to pick him up despite his disgusting filth. "Once I gave him a ride," said Mme. Foucault, "but he left the car full of fleas." He was eccentric but also very learned. Everywhere he went he carried a mendicant's kit bag, bulging with books and slung over his shoulder like a bandolier. His course was a high point of school existence. One of his former students reminisced in 1981:

> His courses were unforgettable. He had an astounding knowledge of events and people to start with, and he delivered sharp and incisive judgments, occasionally tinged with ribaldry. He would let himself get carried away by his subject, by his own hotheaded thought and picturesque images, until, inevitably, he would set off an explosion of

laughter that rapidly degenerated into a complete madhouse. Feeling totally overwhelmed and incapable of restoring order, he would leave the room in tears like a child, repeating "I can't take it, dear boys, I can't take it." But as soon as we promised that we wouldn't start up again, he would come back and quietly go on with his class, and we would be completely silent. Then his subject and eloquence would once more carry him away, the pitch would rise, and by some extraordinary phrase he would set off our laughter all over again.

According to Mme. Foucault, this priest was the only teacher to have any influence on her son. Paul-Michel had been interested in history since early childhood. He had passionately devoured Jacques Bainville's *Histoire de France* and been particularly fascinated with Charlemagne. At age twelve he was giving history lessons to his brother and sister. In short, Father de Montsabert's teaching was guaranteed to please him. Indeed, this sort of apprenticeship to history, studded with anecdotes and witticisms, filled all the students with enthusiasm. The former student quoted above observed that "history taught like this could not help but stick in your mind."[8]

Paul-Michel completed secondary school at Saint-Stanislas and always ranked high when the end-of-year prizes were awarded: in eleventh grade, for example, he carried off third prize in French composition, second prizes in history of French literature, Greek, English, history, and Latin translation, and first prize in Latin literature. But in almost every subject he was outstripped by one of his schoolmates, a friend named, incredibly, Pierre Rivière, who today serves in the government as a member of the Conseil d'Etat. Did Foucault have a good laugh on his respectable friend thirty years later when he exhumed from its archives the fantastic memoir of a "Nineteenth-century parricide" and published it with a commentary under the title *Moi, Pierre Rivière, ayant égorgé ma mère, ma soeur et mon frère . . . (I, Pierre Rivière, Having Slaughtered My Mother, My Sister, and My Brother . . .)*? In any case, though classroom rivals, the two boys were very close. Both were thirsty for knowledge and avid readers. An excellent source of books was the eccentric Abbé Aigrain, known as Poitiers's Pico della Mirandola. A professor at the Catholic university at Angers and a music critic for several reviews, he had a remarkable library. Students would visit him, and he would recommend and lend books to them, mostly history and philosophy. "Both Foucault and I were very regular visitors to Abbé Aigrain," Pierre Rivière recalls; "the abbé's library meant a lot to us, because what we read there was not on any school syllabus." Not on a syllabus—how alluring! The young Foucault may have had a similar resource in René Beauchamp, a family friend and one of the earliest Freudians, who did a great deal to introduce psychoanalysis in France.

Foucault's twelfth-grade results were excellent, and in 1942 he entered the final year of lycée, the *classe de philo.*[9] Canon Duret, who was to have been his teacher, was an eminent figure whom university professors did not hesitate to consult. All the students looked forward to the year they would spend with him. But Duret belonged to the Resistance and was arrested by the Gestapo the very first day of school. He was never seen again. The teacher who replaced him became ill several days later. As a result, a monk named Dom Pierrot from Ligugé Abbey took over as philosophy teacher. Dr. Foucault knew several monks from the abbey well, having served with them on the eastern front during the First World War. Mme. Foucault therefore asked them to send someone to Saint-Stanislas to teach philosophy. Dom Pierrot stuck as closely as possible to the syllabus. His job was to prepare the students for the *bac,* or baccalaureate exams, and he had no intention of doing anything else. But he also liked to talk with the students outside class hours. After Dom Pierrot's term as replacement was over, Paul-Michel bicycled out to Ligugé to see him. They talked about Plato, Descartes, Pascal, Bergson. Dom Pierrot remembered "young Foucault," as he called him, well: "I could class all the young philosophy students I have known in two categories: those for whom philosophy would always be an object of curiosity and who had a predilection for understanding the great systems, great works, and so on; and those for whom it would be more a question of personal anxiety, a vital anxiety. The first bear the stamp of Descartes, the second the stamp of Pascal. Foucault belonged to the first category. You could feel a formidable intellectual curiosity in him."

Because the instruction in philosophy had been so disrupted at Saint-Stanislas, Mme. Foucault asked a professor at the university to send her a student to give her son private lessons. Louis Girard, then in his second year of philosophy studies, went to the Foucaults' house at 10 Rue Arthur-Ranc three times a week. "The philosophy I was imbibing at the university was a vague sort of Kantism," he recalled, "all laid out in a nineteenth-century style, in the neo-Kantian style of Emile Boutroux, and this is what I pulled out for him. I did it with some gusto because I was only twenty-two, but I had not studied much philosophy myself." He remembers Foucault as "very demanding. I later had pupils who seemed to me more gifted, but none capable of grasping the essential so quickly and of organizing their thought with such rigor."

At the end of the school year—Father Lucien, a professor from the seminary, having taken over as philosophy instructor before joining Canon Duret in his tragic fate—Foucault won second prize in philosophy. First prize went to Pierre Rivière. Foucault took first in geography, history, English, and natural sciences.

Despite the fact that two of its philosophy teachers were deported by the Germans, Saint-Stanislas was no bastion of the Resistance. Pétain's portrait hung on the walls, as was required in all educational institutions. The students were required to gather in the courtyard to sing "Maréchal, nous voilà" (Here we are, Marshal) and were scolded roundly when they did not put enough spirit into it. Some still refer to an "ambient Vichyism" in describing the school, even though apparently some Resistance networks managed to use it occasionally as a meeting place, where identification papers or demobilization certificates were exchanged. Several pupils were arrested.

Foucault later described this difficult period in an interview:

> What strikes me now when I try to recall those impressions is that nearly all the great emotional memories I have are related to the political situation. I remember very well that I experienced one of my first great frights when Chancellor Dollfus was assassinated by the Nazis in, I think, 1934. It is something very far from us now . . . I remember very well that I was really scared by that. I think it was my first strong fright about death. I also remember refugees from Spain arriving in Poitiers . . . I think that boys and girls of this generation had their childhood formed by these great historical events. The menace of war was our background, our framework of existence. Then the war arrived. Much more than the activities of family life, it was these events concerning the world which are the substance of our memory. I say "our" because I am nearly sure that most boys and girls in France at this moment had the same experience. Our private life was really threatened. Maybe that is the reason why I am fascinated by history and the relationship between personal experience and those events of which we are a part. I think that is the nucleus of my theoretical desires.[10]

At that time students took their baccalaureate exams in two parts: French, Latin, and Greek at the end of twelfth grade, and philosophy, foreign language, history, and geography the next year. Foucault did rather well on the first exams, in June 1942. On the second part, in

June 1943, he scored high in history and natural science but achieved only average results in philosophy.

Now the question arose what to do next. Dr. Foucault wanted his son to follow in his own footsteps: Paul-Michel was to be a doctor. But Paul-Michel had decided long before that he would have to disappoint his father. His passion was for history and literature; he could not stand the idea of studying medicine. His announcement of his decision brought a stormy discussion with his father. But Mme. Foucault, faithful to her father's adage about "taking charge of one's own affairs," interceded on Paul-Michel's behalf: "Please don't insist. The boy works hard. Let him do what he wants." Dr. Foucault did not insist long, and he had his consolation when his second son entered medical school. (Today Denys Foucault is a surgeon in the Paris region.) Paul-Michel was therefore able to embark on his chosen path: preparing for the entrance exams at the Ecole Normale Supérieure (ENS) in Paris on Rue d'Ulm. This involved two years of further study in preparatory courses: the first year known as the *hypokhâgne*, and the second as the *khâgne*. In ordinary times Foucault would have taken these courses at one of the well-known Parisian schools, reputed for their high rate of success in the entrance exams. But it was wartime, and Mme. Foucault found it very hard to send her seventeen-year-old son to the capital. He enrolled once again in a public lycée in Poitiers, after three years at Saint-Stanislas. He had terrible memories of those three years. He hated the general atmosphere and the teaching. He hated religion and monks. "He described it with a lot of outrage and hostility," said one of his close friends from that time.

At the beginning of the school year in 1943, then, Foucault entered the *hypokhâgne* at the Académie de Poitiers to prepare for the entrance exams to the Ecole Normale. There were thirty altogether in the *khâgne* and *hypokhâgne* classes, and for two years Foucault would follow with great interest the courses given in history by Gaston Dez and in philosophy by Jean Moreau-Reibel. Moreau-Reibel had studied at the Rue d'Ulm and had taught at the lycée at Clermont-Ferrand while teaching in the University of Strasbourg system during the war, when its *faculté des lettres* had sought refuge there. At first the students were thrown off by his long-winded, rambling, and disorganized delivery. Moreau-Reibel's disorganization did not escape the inspector general who reported on his course on March 2, 1944:

> The lesson I attended was part of a series on "the social will and values," a rather obscure title with correspondingly confused develop-

ment. Moreau-Reibel is a fluent speaker and lets himself get carried away, perhaps, by this facility. A more vigorous, more rigorous construction would be preferable; the main ideas seem to be drowned in their development. Insufficient clarity of detail. Too many allusions to theories that are insufficiently defined. Moreau-Reibel would do better if he were harder on himself and if he improvised less.

Lucette Rabaté remembers her frustration over the first classes in September 1943. Bit by bit, however, the students began to understand their professor's teachings better. Foucault began to be caught up in the game; he became more and more interested in the discipline that this somewhat muddled teacher was presenting and began to read the authors he discussed: Bergson, whom Moreau-Reibel particularly liked, Plato, Descartes, Kant, Spinoza. And, Lucette Rabaté recalls, since Moreau-Reibel was fond of conducting his class in the form of a dialogue, he would choose as an interlocutor the one best able to answer: Paul-Michel Foucault. "The others were slightly lost."

The other teacher important for Foucault was Gaston Dez. He had collaborated on the Mallet-Issac manual for beginning secondary school students, he regularly wrote articles for the newsletter of an antiquarians' association, and in 1942 he had contributed to an anthology titled *Visages de Poitou.* His teaching method was radically different from that of his colleague in philosophy: he dictated his course. Very slowly, he dictated. And since there is no syllabus, he touched on only a tiny portion of the vast body of knowledge upon which the candidates could be examined. The students therefore tried to get hold of the courses given in preceding years. Foucault not only procured but copied and was willing to lend them.

Obviously, the period 1943–1945 was difficult and full of turmoil. In winter the lycée classrooms often lacked heat. Some boarding students took the risk of sneaking out at night to steal wood from the militia stationed nearby. To protect the students under suspicion, Rabaté and Foucault went to the headmaster and signed a statement that they were the ones who had supplied the wood. And that was where the matter rested. "Luckily," Rabaté recounts, "they didn't ask us where we got the wood. I don't know what we would have said then." Despite the often difficult conditions, a sort of student merriment prevailed among the classmates. They attended the "classical matinées" presented every month in the city theater. Either the acting was terrible or the students needed desperately to have fun. Tragedies always provoked gales of laughter. "All during *Andromaque,*" Rabaté remembers, "Foucault made jokes and laughed." A false hilarity, perhaps, but in any case, she adds, "We avoided talking about important things; we avoided tackling political questions because the students came from very different backgrounds: among our classmates, for example, there was a girl whose father and brother died in deportation, and another whose father was shot after the Liberation. So everyone was rather cautious with everyone else." She remembers Foucault as a loner: he worked all the time and mixed little. "One day, a little before the exams, I went to the university offices with him to ask for some information. We walked for about fifteen minutes, and he said to me: 'This is the first break I have taken this year.'" A fifteen-minute break!

Most serious, most dangerous, most frightening were the bombings. The Poitiers station and the railway were British targets. During air raids the students ran for cover in the shelters. In July 1944 several sections of town nearest the station, including Rue Arthur-Ranc, had to be evacuated as a precautionary measure. So the Foucault family moved to Vendeuvre for the summer. School had ended very early that year: on June 6, 1944, the janitor ran through the corridors shouting "They've landed! They've landed!" Allied troops had just established a beachhead in Normandy. The students burst out of the classrooms in an explosion of joy. Obviously, no one could even think of school. A few days later war was raging throughout the region, and teaching was suspended in all the schools. The following year was hardly less disrupted.

The students had, however, prepared for their exams, and fourteen candidates from the Académie de Poitiers presented themselves at the Hôtel Fumé on Rue de la Chaîne to take the exams in the law school offices from May 24 to June 5, 1945. The French exam was canceled twice because of various irregularities: the first time because a professor at the Sorbonne had revealed the subject to his students a few days before the exam; the second, because the official forms had not arrived everywhere at the same time. Thus all the candidates had to take the six-hour exam three times. The grades for the written exam were announced on July 16. Two students from Poitiers qualified for admission to the Ecole Normale Supérieure. But Foucault was not one of them. Only one hundred students could move on to the orals, and he placed hundred-and-first on the writtens. Paul-Michel had worked like a dog, but it was not enough. He was dreadfully disappointed. But he was not discouraged. He had every intention of trying again the following year. But this was the end of his schooling in Poitiers. The school year of 1945–46 marked a turning point in his life: he moved to Paris.

POITIERS: STIFLING. The word crops up in everything people say about this period. "I think it must have been horrible to have spent one's entire childhood in that atmosphere," says a friend of Foucault's who came to Poitiers in 1944. Others who wanted to escape it described it as "a narrow, petty city." Foucault, then, left Poitiers in the autumn of 1945. But he never totally broke his connection with the city of his birth, simply because he never totally broke with his family. It is plain that he was not very fond of his father. Moreover, Dr. Foucault seems not to have devoted much time to his children. He would work all day and well into the evening, and thus was rarely in the household. Any rupture, therefore, was with his father. Michel Foucault once recalled the relationship as "one of conflict on particular points, but representing a focus from which it was impossible to free oneself" even after leaving the family.[11] On the other hand, throughout his life he remained very attached to his mother. During his student years he returned to Poitiers every vacation, and afterward he continued to visit his parents regularly. After Dr. Foucault's death in 1959, when his mother moved out to Piroir, her house in Vendeuvre, he visited her every year during the vacations. "He always gave me his August," she said. Often he also joined her at Christmas or for a few days in the spring. He had a rather small, out-of-the-way apartment on the ground floor where he liked to work. Usually he came alone. Very rarely he would come with a friend. Mme. Foucault remembered Roland Barthes visiting. In 1982 Michel Foucault thought about buying a house nearby. He bicycled all over the countryside with his brother, stopping in villages and visiting any house that happened to be for sale. He finally chose a pretty little house in Verrue, a few kilometers from Vendeuvre. The curé had lived there. "La cure de verrue. Wart cure," Foucault called it. His pun on *verrue/verruca* and *cure/curé* always made him laugh. He bought the house and began to make necessary repairs. But he would not have time to live there.

2

~~~

The Voice of Hegel

In Paris, behind the Pantheon, next to the church Saint-Etienne-du-Mont, there was another Lycée Henri-IV, one of the most prestigious schools in France. Year after year it took in the elite of the students preparing for the exams for entrance at the Rue d'Ulm. A professor from the University of Poitiers put it to Mme. Foucault baldly: "Did you ever hear of anyone getting into Normale Sup who came from one of this city's establishments?" Things were settled quickly: Paul-Michel would try again, but this time he would have all the trump cards.

In the fall of 1945 he arrived in Paris to enter this sanctuary, whose lofty tower and repeated successes in gaining its students admission to the Rue d'Ulm dominated the Latin Quarter. The young "provincial"—that was how his classmates saw him—wore outlandish clothes and weird wooden-soled shoes. Moreover, young Foucault was not enthusiastic about moving to the capital. Life in Paris just after the war was far from easy and full of material problems (such as food shortages). Living conditions made the prospect of his new existence far from seductive. Mme. Foucault had been unable to buy or even to rent an apartment. Maurice Rat, a family friend from Vendeuvre who taught literature at the Lycée Janson-de-Sailly, put him up for a few days, after which he moved into a room rented from the headmistress of a school on Boulevard Raspail. This arrangement gave him an extraordinary status among the other students. At that time, Emmanuel Le Roy Ladurie recalls, students in the preparatory classes in Paris were divided into two basic categories: day students, the sons of the Parisian bourgeoisie, who returned home every evening; and boarders from the provinces who lived on the school premises.[1] Foucault's parents could afford to spare the fragile and unstable adolescent the shock of a communal life, which he claimed to despise above all. Sometimes he had difficulty properly heating the few square feet in which he lived, but at least he was alone. The image of an unsociable, enigmatic, and with-drawn boy, which appears in all accounts, was reinforced by this choice. Moreover, his activities in Paris during this year were rather limited: at the most he occasionally went to the movies with his sister when she too moved to the city. They were crazy about American films, which they had been deprived of by the war. The rest of the time he worked like a madman to pass his exam.

There were fifty preparing for this exam in the "K-1" class at "H-IV," and only thirty-eight students of literature would be admitted at the Rue d'Ulm. There were just as many students in "K-2," the other *khâgne* class. And the other great lycée in Paris, the nearby rival Louis-le-Grand, certainly intended to get its traditional contingent of students in as well. How many of the boys who stood with Michel Foucault at the gates of Henri-IV at the beginning of the year would be on the final list of those admitted the next summer? A group of excellent professors buckled down to ensure their effective preparation. Le Roy Ladurie, who entered the *hypokhâgne* that same year, describes the history teacher, who also taught Foucault: André Alba flaunted his "dyed-in-the-wool, comfortably anticlerical republicanism" and seduced the pupils on the left and far left, that is, a large majority. The man seemed to be a "badly wounded veteran of 1914–1918; an impressively deep scar made a line across his forehead." In fact, "this gash came from a childhood injury."[2] You could practically "see his brain quiver," said his former students.

Foucault also took a course from M. Dieny, who taught ancient history. From him the students first heard of a certain Georges Dumézil, whose reputation was just beginning to emerge beyond a specialized community. There was also Jean Boudout, who taught French literature with considerable erudition. He was equally good discussing the Middle Ages or the twentieth century—at least, up to the poetry of Apollinaire, since at this time there was very little teaching of contemporary authors.

But the teacher who most deeply impressed this group was the one responsible for preparing the class for the philosophy exam: Jean Hyppolite, whom we shall encounter more than once on Foucault's road. Jean d'Ormesson, who had been at the lycée two years previously, described this renowned master teacher as "hunched behind his lectern," speaking in a manner that was "cheerful, cluttered, dreamy, shy, drawing out his sentences with pathetic sighs, brilliantly eloquent in his very denial of it." He was determined to explain Hegel "through [Valéry's] 'La Jeune Parque' and [Mallarmé's] *Un Coup de dés jamais n'abolira le hasard"*; d'Ormesson "understood absolutely none of it." [3] No doubt many others felt the same way. But the students found him fascinating, and after the dull classes to which Foucault had been subjected in Poitiers, this torrent of rather grandiloquent, esoteric, and inspired rhetoric seemed dazzling and brilliant. Philosophy held great fascination for these times. It was 1945, and, as d'Ormesson wrote, "immediately after the war, and for several years thereafter, philosophy carried incomparable prestige. I don't know if I can describe, now, at this distance, what it represented for us. The nineteenth century was, perhaps, the century of history; the midtwentieth century seemed dedicated to philosophy . . . literature, painting, historical studies, politics, theater, and film were all in philosophy's hands." [4]

Hyppolite provided commentary both on Hegel's *Phenomenology of Spirit* and on Descartes's *Geometry*. But it was the course on Hegel that struck his listeners and became engraved in their memories. Foucault's passion was history, but now, perhaps for the first time, he felt the pull of philosophy. This was, in fact, philosophy providing the narrative of history, recounting its patient progress toward the advent of Reason. It embraced all history, and the history had meaning. There is no doubt that Jean Hyppolite was the one who initiated Foucault into the field that would become his destiny. Foucault himself never ceased to proclaim his debt to this man, whom he was to rediscover several years later at the Ecole Normale and whom he would succeed at the Collège de France. Upon Hyppolite's death in 1968, Foucault paid this homage: "*Khâgne* students from immediately after the war remember M. Hyppolite's course on *Phenomenology of Spirit:* in this voice that kept on stopping, as if meditating was part of its rhythm, we heard not just the voice of a teacher, but also something of Hegel's voice and, perhaps, even the voice of philosophy itself. I do not think it was possible to forget the force of that presence or the proximity that he patiently invoked." [5]

The voice of Hegel, the voice of philosophy! Hyppolite, an inspired and brilliant teacher, aroused intense enthusiasm among his young students. And in so doing he inscribed himself in the great tradition of *khâgne* professors, whose best-known incarnation remains the optimistic philosopher Emile Chartier, famous as Alain. In his study on *khâgne* students and students at the ENS between the two wars, Jean-François Sirinelli called these men *éveilleurs* (awakeners), rightly stressing the extremely important role played by teachers of a very special sort in stimulating the students of this thoroughly French institution, the "preparatory class for the *grandes écoles*." [6]

But the debt that Foucault later proclaimed to his former teacher went far beyond simple gratitude for having discovered his vocation in late adolescence. When he completed his thesis in 1960, Foucault invoked several people who had inspired him when he was writing the book known now as *Histoire de la folie à l'âge classique* (History of madness in the classical age).[7] Those whom he thanked were Georges Dumézil, Georges Canguilhem, and Jean Hyppolite.[8] In Foucault's first lecture at the Collège de France, ten years after publication of this book, he paid even more emphatic tribute to his teacher. Some see these closing remarks to an official speech as a mere observance of academic convention: tradition dictated that Foucault praise his deceased or retired predecessor. But Foucault devoted the entire conclusion of this lecture to Hyppolite, whereas he could have contented himself with a few words, a few remarks. What is more, he said he placed his own future work "under his sign."[9] In 1975, seven years after Hyppolite's death, Foucault sent his widow a copy of *Surveiller et punir (Discipline and Punish)* with the following dedication: "For Madame Hyppolite, in memory of the man to whom I owe everything."

It may seem astonishing that Foucault always accorded his former professor so much importance, especially since Hyppolite taught at Henri-IV for only the first two months of the 1945–46 school year. Hyppolite was a contemporary of Jean-Paul Sartre and Maurice Merleau-Ponty, and their friend. He was born in 1907, Sartre in 1905, and Merleau-Ponty in 1908. They were students together at the Ecole Normale Supérieure on Rue d'Ulm, Sartre entering (with Raymond Aron, Paul Nizan, and Georges Canguilhem) in 1924, Hyppolite in 1925, and Merleau-Ponty in 1926. But one can scarcely compare the stature of the three men. Hyppolite was not a "philosopher" in the sense that Sartre and Merleau-Ponty were; that is, he was not a creator, a producer in the realm of ideas. However, his influence was far more important than it might at first seem. Hyppolite had translated *Phenomenology of Spirit*, and he taught it at a time when Hegel's name was scarcely mentioned in philosophy courses in France. From that point on Hyppolite was commentator and spokesman for the German philosopher, especially of his youthful works, written in Jena. His two-volume translation of *Phenomenology*, published in 1939 and 1941, provided the public (which until then had for the most part ignored it) with access to a work that was to become one of the central references for the study of philosophy in France. And his thesis, *Genèse et structure de la "Phénoménologie de l'esprit,"* defended and published in 1947, was considered an event. Roland Caillois, in a review for *Les Temps modernes* in 1948, stressed the work's importance: "There is no lack of thinkers persuaded that Hegelianism is the great question: the question of the life or death of philosophy. Philosophy itself is what is in question. That is why Jean Hyppolite's thesis deserves our careful consideration. It is not simply the work of a scrupulous historian . . . It also concerns a crucial problem: is the philosophical undertaking legitimate?" [10] Indeed, at the end of the war there was "no lack of thinkers" ready to raise a statue to Hegel. The place of Hegelianism in France had entirely changed in the space of a decade. "In 1930," according to Vincent Descombes, "Hegel was a Romantic philosopher, long since refuted by scientific progress (this was Léon Brunschvicg's opinion). In 1945, Hegel became the acme of classical philosophy and the origin of what became most modern." [11]

Hyppolite, of course, did not act alone in this reversal. As early as 1929 Jean Wahl had drawn attention to Hegel in *La Conscience malheureuse dans la philosophie de Hegel*, in which he presented a "mystical Hegel," as Caillois put it. And in 1938 Henri Lefebvre published an issue of *Cahiers de Lenine* on Hegel's dialectic. So there were many stages in what Elisabeth Roudinesco has called a slow "rumination," comparing the introduction of Hegelianism in France, with its successive advances and resistances, to that of psychoanalysis. [12] Moreover, the two movements intersected at a major point in their respective breakthroughs when Alexandre Kojève began his seminar at the Ecole Pratique des Hautes Etudes. The members of his audience from 1933 to 1939 have been listed frequently: Alexandre Koyré, Georges Bataille, Pierre Klossowski, Jacques Lacan, Raymond Aron, Maurice Merleau-Ponty, Eric Weil, and André Breton. [13] In 1947, the year Hyppolite defended his thesis, Raymond Queneau, who was also a member of this select audience, published the notes he had taken at Kojève's lectures as *Introduction à la lecture de Hegel*. The movement surrounding Hegelianism was so strong that in 1948 Georges Canguilhem could write: "In a period of world revolution and world war, France discovered, in the strict sense of the word, a philosophy contemporary with the French Revolution and one that is to a great extent its full realization." [14]

Jean Hyppolite was thus one of the key figures in the triumph of Hegelianism in postwar France—a triumph reinforced by the vogue of existentialism, to which Hyppolite claimed close connections. He recalled this in particular in December 1955 during a lecture at the

Maison de France at Uppsala, whose director at the time was Michel Foucault. The theme of the conference was "Hegel and Kierkegaard in contemporary French thought."[15] That, in fact, was the crux of this Hegelian explosion: Hegel was no longer read as the "professor's professor," the "creator of systems," but as the author of a work with which one compared its descendents: Feuerbach, Kierkegaard, Marx, Nietzsche. In short, Hegel was now read as the one who instituted philosophical modernity. Merleau-Ponty put it well in comments on a February 1945 lecture by Hyppolite on existentialism in Hegel: "All the great philosophical ideas of the past century—the philosophies of Marx and Nietzsche, phenomenology, German existentialism, and psychoanalysis—had their beginnings in Hegel; it was he who started the attempt to explore the irrational and integrate it into an expanded reason which remains the task of our century." He went on: "As it turns out, Hegel's successors have placed more emphasis on what they reject of his heritage than on what they owe to him." Merleau-Ponty concluded that there was no more urgent work to be done than "re-establishing the connection between, on the one hand, the thankless doctrines which try to forget their Hegelian origin and, on the other, that origin itself."[16]

This "discovery" of Hegel was of major importance in terms of its connection with a particular branch of its lineage, in an era concerned with filiation: Marxism. Hyppolite himself took note of the twofold development in another lecture at the Maison de France in Uppsala, in December 1955: "We were latecomers to the Hegelianism that had invaded all of Europe except France, but we came to it via *Phenomenology of Spirit*, the least known of the youthful works, and via the possible relation between Marx and Hegel. There had, indeed, been socialists and philosophers in France, but Hegel and Marx had not yet entered French philosophy. Today that has happened. Discussion of Marxism and Hegelianism is on the agenda."[17]

This radical transformation of the philosophical arena had tremendous consequences. With it Marxism won its *droit de cité* before blazing forth as "the untranscendable horizon [*l'indépassable horizon*] of our times," as Sartre described it in *Critique de la raison dialectique*. In any case, it represented the horizon for a good many intellectuals during the three decades following the Second World War.

Hyppolite thus embodied access to everything that fascinated Foucault's generation: Marx, but also Nietzsche and Freud. And basically,

Foucault was not too far from Merleau-Ponty when in 1970, in his first lecture at the Collège de France, he evoked the memory of his teacher:

> Our age, whether through logic or epistemology, whether through Marx or through Nietzsche, is attempting to flee Hegel . . . But truly to escape Hegel involves an exact appreciation of the price we have to pay to detach ourselves from him. It assumes that we are aware of the extent to which Hegel, insidiously perhaps, is close to us; it implies a knowledge in that which permits us to think against Hegel, of that which remains Hegelian. We have to determine the extent to which our anti-Hegelianism is possibly one of his tricks directed against us, at the end of which he stands, motionless, waiting for us. If, then, more than one of us is indebted to Jean Hyppolite, it is because he has tirelessly explored, for and ahead of us, the path along which we may escape Hegel, keep our distance, and along which we shall find ourselves brought back to him, only from a different angle, and then finally be forced to leave him behind once more.[18]

More than twenty years had gone by between the time when Merleau-Ponty assigned philosophy the task of linking ungrateful philosophies to their Hegelian source, and this year, 1970, in which Foucault talked about how Hyppolite had accomplished this in the presence of a generation of apprentice philosophers whose formation he had greatly influenced.

In his speech in October 1968 paying homage to Hyppolite shortly after his death, at a ceremony organized by Louis Althusser at the Rue d'Ulm, Michel Foucault further declared:

> All the problems we have, those of us who yesterday were his pupils, all these problems—he is the one who set them up, he is the one who articulated them separately . . . he is the one who formulated them in *Logique et existence*, which is one of the great books of our time. He taught us, just after the war, to think about the relations between violence and discourse; he taught us, yesterday, to think about the relations between logic and existence; and now, at this very moment, he has proposed that we think about the relations between the contents of knowledge and formal necessity. Finally, he has taught us that thought is an endless practice, that it is a certain way of bringing nonphilosophy into play, but all the while staying as close as possible to it, there, where existence is first formed.[19]

Foucault wrote yet another tribute to Hyppolite, for a collective volume that he edited and whose contributors were Martial Guéroult,

Michel Serres, Georges Canguilhem, Jean Laplanche, Suzanne Bache-lard, and Jean-Claude Pariente. Not surprisingly, his contribution, now famous, was titled "Nietzsche, la généalogie, l'histoire."[20]

☙

THIS "VOICE OF HEGEL" suddenly resounding in the ears of fifty boys at the Lycée Henri-IV in the fall of 1945 produced a real intellectual—or, one should say, existential—shock. But "Hippal," "Master Hippal," as Foucault liked to call him afterward, was summoned to the University of Strasbourg, where Georges Canguilhem was teaching. His lycée students had scarcely two months in which to hear him, and off he went, leaving them to marvel. Foucault would have to wait several years before meeting him again at the Sorbonne and the Ecole Normale. Hyppolite was replaced by Dreyfus-Lefoyer, a dull man who knew perfectly well that he had to bear comparison with the brilliant predecessor who had kept his classroom spellbound with the epic of philosophy. The fifty students went from admiring their teacher to poking fun at this "gnome," whom several described as "ugly as sin." He was incapable of producing anything from his notes except long hours of boredom. His favorite references were the neo-Kantian Emile Boutroux and the nineteenth-century philosopher Jules Lachelier. Nothing could have been further from the philosophical modernity that was reinventing itself at the time. And the students never stopped baiting him. One day Dreyfus-Lefoyer literally fell to pieces: "I know I am not as good as Hyppolite," he exclaimed, his voice cracking with emotion and impotent rage, "but I am doing all I know how to get you through the exam."

Foucault was now caught up in philosophy and devoted himself to it passionately. His grades made great leaps forward: at the end of the first trimester he was twenty-second in the class (with this comment, however: "Is much better than his grades—will have to free himself of a tendency to be obscure—a rigorous mind"). He was still twenty-second at the end of the second term; but he was first at the end of the year. His teacher's assessment was the highest praise: "One of the elite of students."

"One of the elite" in philosophy, but also in history. He was seventh in the first trimester, with this evaluation: "Good work. Very encouraging results"; and at the end of the year he was first. All the teachers concurred in the matter of Foucault. "An active mind," M. Boudout, the French teacher, noted in his report book; "he gives evidence of literary taste." In Latin composition Foucault moved from thirty-first, "passable results," to tenth, "excellent student." He was fourth in Greek. The headmaster summed up these assessments in the report book with the final judgment: "Deserves to succeed."

3

Rue d'Ulm

This time he had no trouble taking the hurdle. The written exam was a mere formality, and one fine day in July 1946 Foucault presented himself before the two men who administered the philosophy oral, in the Salle des Actes of the Ecole Normale Supérieure on Rue d'Ulm. The examiners were Pierre-Maxime Schuhl, a professor at the University of Toulouse, and Georges Canguilhem, an eminent figure in academic philosophy in France, who taught the history of science at the University of Strasbourg. It was Foucault's first encounter with this little man, whose gruff bearing contrasted with a southern accent that implied a warm, affable nature. But it was far from the last. Foucault had an appointment that day not only with the Rue d'Ulm and the promises that that venerable institution seemed to offer those it took in; in some ways he also had an appointment with his destiny. He was meeting one of the individuals destined to play a key role in the path it took, in its history. Foucault would meet Canguilhem again several years later, when he passed the orals for the *agrégation*, the degree that would qualify him for teaching in a lycée. Both of these early contacts remained bad memories for him. It was not until he had to choose a member of the jury for his thesis, *Folie et déraison*, that he really got to know Canguilhem. That episode would mark the beginning of a deep friendship and profound respect between the two men. But for Foucault in 1946 Canguilhem was simply one of the two individuals upon whom the results of the exam depended. The professor had an impressive presence, "his eyes wide open, almost staring, as if to pick up everything," as one of his students describes him.[1] He had a reputation for terrifying candidates. Foucault was not yet twenty years old, and he had less than an hour to convince his judges that he deserved to enter the Ecole Normale.

Several days later a jostling crowd of candidates, along with their relatives or friends, stood at the door of the ENS on Rue d'Ulm to read the list of those admitted. There was almost insane tension. For these nineteen- or twenty-year-old boys, who had worked with everything they had for two or three years, staking all on this day, it was more than a moment of truth; it was almost a matter of life or death. The ghosts of Jean Jaurès, Léon Blum, Edouard Herriot, Jules Romains, and Jean-Paul Sartre hovered overhead. Everyone felt that in this one instant he was risking his social and intellectual existence. It was all or nothing. Little rectangles of white paper were posted on the concierge's window: first, Raymond Weil; second, Guy Palmade; third, Jean-Claude Richard. Fourth: Paul Foucault . . . Foucault scarcely glanced at the names that followed. He was completely taken up in his own joy, and there would be time enough later to find out which of his fellow students had also been promoted. Maurice Agulhon, Paul Viallaneix, Robert Mauzi, and Jean Knapp were among those with whom he would spend the next few years, and some of them would later play a role, large or small, in his career.

That fall thirty-eight students moved into the old buildings of the Ecole Normale Supérieure, which resembled some sort of republican convent. Six of the "conscripts" from the Lycée Henri-IV took up residence in a "pad" on the ground floor. They formed a long rectangle from the door to the window: Jean Papon, Guy Degen, Guy Verret on one side, Robert Strehler, Maurice Vouzelaud, Michel Foucault on the other.

A new life was beginning for Foucault, a life he would have trouble enduring. He was a solitary, unsociable boy, whose relationships with others were very complex and often conflict-ridden. He was never at ease with himself and was somewhat unhealthy. Obviously, he was even less at ease with the lack of privacy the school imposed—all the more since the Rue d'Ulm in itself was a pathogenic milieu, a center where the most absurd, the most eccentric behavior came out, as much on a personal as on an intellectual or political level. The Ecole Normale represented above all an order to be brilliant, to stand out. *Normaliens* would stop at nothing to play the part of the exceptional individual, to strike a pose of future fame. Thirty or forty years later, many recalled their years at the ENS with rancor or disgust. "Everyone showed himself in his worst light," says Jean Deprun, today a professor at the Sorbonne. "Everyone had his own neurosis," adds Guy Degen, who roomed for several years with Foucault. Foucault never adapted to

communal life or to the sort of sociability required by the internal organization of the Ecole. He confided once to Maurice Pinguet that his
years at the Rue d'Ulm had been "sometimes intolerable." Foucault
withdrew into his solitude, leaving it only to scoff at the others with
a ferocity that soon became notorious. He subjected those whom he
particularly disliked to constant putdowns and laughing scorn. He gave
them insulting nicknames, going after them doggedly in public, particularly during the "pot" in the school cafeteria where they all ate two
meals a day together. He argued with everybody. He got angry. He
exuded in every direction a formidable level of aggression and, in addition, a pronounced tendency toward megalomania. Foucault liked to
make a production of the genius he knew he had. He was soon almost
universally detested. His fellows thought him half mad and passed
around stories about his odd behavior. One day someone teaching at
the ENS found him lying on the floor of a room where he had just
sliced up his chest with a razor. Another time he was seen in the middle
of the night chasing one of the other students with a dagger. And when
he attempted suicide in 1948, for most of his schoolmates the gesture
simply confirmed their belief that his psychological balance was, to say
the least, fragile. In the opinion of someone who knew him very well
during this period, "all his life he verged on madness." Two years after
entering the ENS, Foucault found himself at the Hôpital Sainte-Anne
in the office of Professor Delay, a prominent psychiatrist. His father,
Dr. Foucault, took him for this first encounter with institutional psychiatry. This was also the first time he had come so close to that elusive
line dividing, less completely perhaps than one might think, the "madman" from someone who is "well," the mentally ill from the mentally
sound. At any rate, this painful episode gave Foucault a privilege en-
vied by many: a room in the ENS infirmary, where he was isolated
with the peace and quiet he needed to work. He would return to this
infirmary room, this time for the sake of convenience, while preparing
a second time for the *agrégation*, in 1950–51, and again later, when he
gave his courses. Meanwhile there were several attempts at or stagings
of suicide: "Foucault was obsessed by this idea," according to one of his
friends. Another student once asked him: "Where are you going?" and
heard the astonishing answer: "I'm going to the BHV [the Hotel de
Ville Bazaar] to buy some rope to hang myself with." The doctor at the
Ecole, citing his patient's right to privacy, would say only that "these
troubles resulted from an extreme difficulty in experiencing and accepting his homosexuality." And in fact, after returning from his fre-

quent nocturnal expeditions to pickup hangouts or homosexual bars, Foucault would be prostrate for hours, ill, overwhelmed with shame. Dr. Etienne was called upon frequently to keep him from committing the irreparable.

Living with one's homosexuality was not easy in that period. Dominique Fernandez, who entered the ENS in 1950, describes the pathetic situation of homosexuals during those years. It was a "time of shame and clandestine actions," when the pleasures of the sin impermissible in broad daylight had to be repressed, pushed back into the shadowy zones of nocturnal existence. Fernandez sums up the feelings he experienced as he left childhood behind: "I could see that I would grow up apart from others, interested by things I could never talk about to anyone around me; that this situation would be a source of endless torment; but also that it was the sign of a secret and wonderful choice. A mixture of pride and fear at entering a freemasonry that risked public condemnation kept my adolescent years in a turmoil."[2] Describing the library that he wanted to put together at any cost on the subject of his "condition," he writes: "In 1950, and throughout the ten or fifteen years that followed, the books I accumulated concerned only trauma, neurosis, natural inferiority, misery as a calling. The self-portrait I was able to sketch from these texts was of some inferior being condemned to suffer."[3] How many were victims of this repressive violence? How many had to lie, sometimes to themselves? Among them was Michel Foucault. Many of his schoolmates learned only later that he was homosexual; others said they only suspected it or discovered it by accident or knew it because they themselves were. But whether or not they knew the deeper reasons for his troubles, all remembered Foucault as precariously balanced on a tightrope between sanity and madness. All took this to be the explanation for his obsessive interest in psychology, psychoanalysis, and psychiatry. "He wanted to understand whatever was connected to the private and the privative," is one's remark. "His pronounced interest in psychology doubtless stemmed from elements in his own life," says another. And another: "When *Histoire de la folie* came out, everyone who knew him saw immediately that it was connected to his personal history." Someone close to him at this time remarks: "I always thought he would write about sexuality some day. He had to give sexuality a central position in his work, since it was central in his life." Or: "His last books in some ways constitute the personal ethics he imposed upon himself by force of will. Sartre never wrote his Ethics, but Foucault did." Or: "When he went back to ancient Greece in *Histoire de la sexualité*, Foucault found his own archaeological pedestal." In short, everyone agreed that Foucault's work, his research itself, was firmly rooted in the situation that he experienced so dramatically during his years at the Ecole Normale. Obviously, one cannot pretend that Foucault's entire work is explained by his homosexuality, as certain American academics do, imagining, moreover, that this would be enough to discredit it. Sartre's answer to vulgar Marxism might be useful here: of course Paul Valéry is a *petit-bourgeois*, but not all *petits-bourgeois* are Paul Valéry. Quite simply, it is possible to see how an intellectual project is born in an experience that should perhaps be described as primary; how an intellectual adventure is created in the struggles of individual and social life—not to remain stuck in them, but to think them through, to go beyond them, to problematize them by ironically turning the question back on those who level it. Do you really know who you are? Are you so sure of your reason? of your scientific concepts? of your categories of perception? Foucault read the psychiatrists. He worked with psychologists. He could have become one of them. Did his homosexuality perhaps bar him from taking this route? Fernandez writes: "This was the age of psychiatry and psychoanalysis. Medical doctors, successors to the priests and police, now rendered sentences on the homosexual condition that were even more highly valued because they came from an apparently scientific authority and emanated a certain paternal benevolence. Each time a psychoanalyst wrote: 'I never met a happy homosexual,' I took this judgment to be a truth beyond doubt and huddled deeper into the consciousness of my woes."[4] Until the day when the "pariah" revolted, when insubordination raised its voice. For Foucault this insubordination had to take the double detour of literature and theory. On the one hand, there was his fascination with writers who dealt with "transgression," the "limit experience" (*expérience limite*) of excess and expenditure (Bataille's *dépense*); the exaltation he would feel on reading Bataille, Maurice Blanchot, and Klossowski and on discovering the "possibility of a mad philosopher," whose fiery words turned dialectics and positivism to ashes as he described it in "Préface à la transgression."[5] On the other hand, there was his examination at a historical level of the scientific status of psychological disciplines, the medical gaze, and then the established human sciences as a whole. "Whenever I have tried to carry out a piece of theoretical work," he said in 1981, "it has been on the basis of my own experience, always in relation to processes I saw taking place around me. It is because I thought I could recognize in the things I saw, in the institutions with which I dealt, in my relations with others, cracks, silent shocks, malfunctionings . . . that I undertook a particular piece of work, a few fragments of autobiography."[6]

Foucault's malaise may also explain his desire for exile, to flee the impasses that he felt enclosed him. At any rate, this seemed clearly the case to those who mentioned reasons for his departure for Sweden in 1955. Foucault would have to wait for the 1960s and the decolonization of minds that began at that time before he could free himself, bit by bit, from the normative snares of repression. Perhaps he did not free himself enough; Dominique Fernandez severely reproaches both Barthes and Foucault for having kept silent about their homosexuality even after silence was no longer imposed upon them. For Roger Martin du Gard, a Nobel prize winner, to have wished to conceal himself to the extent of not publishing a novel with homosexual characters might be "legitimate prudence." But Barthes! In 1975 Barthes devoted a single, extremely neutral paragraph of his *Barthes par Roland Barthes* to the "Goddess H.": "The pleasure potential of a perversion (in this case, that of the two H's: homosexuality and hashish) is always under-estimated."[7] "What cowardice!" is Fernandez' comment, and he applies the same verdict to Foucault: "He, too, never decided to bear personal witness."[8] This is far from the truth. But obviously those who had lived through the earlier situation often had a hard time following the "cultural revolution" effected after 1968. One example is emblematic: in 1981, disoriented by the obtrusive militancy of "gay movements," André Baudry decided to scuttle the review *Arcadie* and the movement bearing the same name, whose driving force he had been since 1954. For three decades *Arcadie* had embodied the hope of making homosexuality "acceptable" by dint of discretion, respectability, and what he called "dignity." Everything had been concealed with pseudonyms. One can see how, called upon suddenly to say out loud to the whole world things they had had to keep quiet for so many years, more than one individual would have felt rather disoriented. In Jean-Paul Aron's wish, at death's door, to announce on the front page of *Le Nouvel Observateur* that he had AIDS and, at the same time, publicly to "confess" his homosexuality, we hear a moving echo of these troubled consciences.[9] When Aron criticized Foucault for having hidden the nature of his illness, he reproached him at the same time for having wanted to escape making that "confession" also. But was it not precisely the very idea of "confession" that Foucault loathed? This loath-

over
ginero
interpret

ing left its mark in all the effort expended in his last books to reject, refuse, and defuse the order to say, to speak, to make someone speak— as if a historical perspective and a theoretical investigation also had their origins in the brutal experiences of daily life.

Foucault's classmates are unanimous in describing him not only as disconcerting and strange, but also as, already, a passionate worker. He read all the time but was not content just to read; he took notes on cards, which he organized methodically and meticulously in boxes. He even dug up some bound manuscript notes taken by students in Bergson's classes on the history of philosophy. The other students considered him exceptional in his culture, his capacity for work, and his interest in a wide range of subjects. He read everything: the classical philosophers, of course, Plato, Kant . . . and Hegel, on whom he wrote and defended a paper, "La constitution d'un transcendantal historique dans la *Phénoménologie de l'esprit* de Hegel," for his *diplome d'études supérieures*, an intermediate degree, necessary for continuing on for the *agrégation*, which would certify him to teach. He read Marx, of course, because everybody did. Somewhat later he would also read Husserl and especially Heidegger. Alphonse de Waelhens published a commentary on the latter in 1942, but Foucault plunged into the study of German so that he could read the original texts. Reading Heidegger would be of great importance to him: "I began by reading Hegel, then Marx, and I set out to read Heidegger," he said at the end of his life, recalling the years of his training. "I still have here the notes I took when I was reading Heidegger. I've got tons of them! And they are much more important than the ones I took on Hegel or Marx. My entire philosophical development was determined by my reading of Heidegger. I nevertheless recognize that Nietzsche outweighed him . . . My knowledge of Nietzsche certainly is better than my knowledge of Heidegger. Nevertheless, these are the two fundamental experiences I have had. It is possible that if I had not read Heidegger, I would not have read Nietzsche."[10]

His passion for Nietzsche would come somewhat later. For the moment he was very interested in psychoanalysis and psychology. He read Freud—long one of his favorite authors, a preferred subject of conversation, a major focus of his interest. But he read also Krafft-Ebing and Marie Bonaparte. He made much of a book that left an impression on this whole generation: Georges Politzer's *Critique des fondements de la psychologie*, published in 1938 but out of print. The students had only one copy and passed it around fervently. There were other works that were important for him: *The Individual and His Society* and *The Psychological Frontiers of Society* by Abram Kardiner, whose notion of a "basic personality" and whose arguments concerning the relationship between individual behavior and the cultures in which these are inscribed would nourish his later reflections. Foucault was also interested in Margaret Mead and in the division of the sexes in primitive societies; and in the Kinsey report on sexual behavior. He read Gaston Bachelard, the aesthetician and philosopher of science, of course, who had a great influence on him. But he was also a voracious reader of literature. He read Kafka, enthusiastically discovered by this whole generation, and he read him in German because he wanted to become familiar with the language. And Faulkner, Gide, Jouhandeau, Genet. Imagine the storm raised by Genet's novels in the early 1950s and the delight caused by Sartre's long commentary, in which he described how, from Proust to Genet, homosexuality had gone from being experienced as a curse of nature to being lived as a defiant choice flung in the face of the world. Foucault also read Sade with great delight, going so far as to proclaim loudly his scorn for anyone not an initiate.

Students at the Ecole Normale rarely attended classes at the Sorbonne; generally they went there only to take their exams for the *licence* (more or less the equivalent of an American bachelor's degree). Foucault was no exception, but he did go to hear Daniel Lagache and Julian Ajuriaguerra discuss psychiatric science. He also attended some sessions of Henri Gouhier's course on seventeenth-century philosophy. And, of course, he would rediscover Jean Hyppolite's teaching starting in 1949, the year Hyppolite was appointed to the *faculté des lettres* at the Sorbonne.

Above all, Foucault attended the few teaching sessions offered at the Rue d'Ulm. He went regularly to hear Jean Beaufret, to whom Martin Heidegger had written his "Lettre sur l'humanisme." Beaufret discussed Kant's *Critique of Pure Reason* but also talked a great deal about Heidegger. He was one of Heidegger's most faithful disciples and helped introduce him in France. Beaufret's performances made rather an impression on Foucault; he talked about him frequently with his friends. There was also Jean Wahl's course, in which he explicated Parmenides for three students: Jean-Louis Gardies, Jean Knapp, and Foucault. Then there was the course given by Jean-Toussaint Desanti, a fervent Communist who was putting great effort into reconciling

Marxism and phenomenology. That was one of the big problems for postwar French philosophy. A book along these same lines by Tran Duc Thao had considerable repercussions in philosophical circles. Desanti was a brilliant professor; he exerted enormous influence on the ENS students and helped make membership in the Communist party attractive.

But Merleau-Ponty's course was certainly the one that most impressed the young students. Existentialism and phenomenology were at their peak of glory, and students at the ENS—like everyone else—were fascinated by Sartre, who so dominated his period. But they admired Merleau-Ponty even more. He was more academic, more rigorous, less "in vogue," and, above all, took more risks in his attempts to open philosophy up to contributions from the human sciences. Foucault never missed a single lecture given by Maurice Merleau-Ponty at the ENS in 1947–48 and 1948–49. Though primarily about the union of soul and body in Malebranche, Maine de Biran, and Bergson, they also dealt with language.[11] Merleau-Ponty was fascinated by problems of language and tried to expose the students to Saussure's work. He had a great many students because this was the only place in Paris where they could hear the author of *Phénoménologie de la perception*. At that time his appointment was to the University of Lyons, but Merleau-Ponty would be given a chair in child psychology at the Sorbonne at the beginning of the 1949 school year, and his faithful audience rushed to his courses in the university amphitheaters. Merleau-Ponty discussed "consciousness and the acquisition of language" and also the connection between "human sciences and phenomenology." His lectures were published in the *Bulletin de psychologie* almost as soon as they were given, and there is no doubt that Foucault took advantage of them.[12] The course on "human sciences," for example, given in 1951–52, in which Merleau-Ponty expounded at length the theories of Edmund Husserl, Kurt Koffka, and Kurt Goldstein, certainly would have been of the greatest interest to Foucault, who began to teach at that very time and on exactly the same subjects.

Another figure who made a great impression on the young students on the Rue d'Ulm was a schoolmate who was appointed philosophy *caïman*[13] in 1948—that is, he was given the responsibility of preparing candidates for the *agrégation*. He took the place of Georges Gusdorf, who left to teach in Strasbourg. The new *caïman*'s name was Louis Althusser, and in those days—as would be the case until the mid-1960s—his name meant nothing to anyone outside the Latin Quarter. But he would have considerable influence on the small circle of his students. Althusser passed the *agrégation* in 1948 at the age of thirty. He had been accepted at the ENS much earlier, in 1939, but was drafted and then taken prisoner. He spent five years in a stalag. At the end of the war he went back to school and passed the *agrégation* along with Gilles Deleuze and François Châtelet, placing second only to Jean Deprun. Although Althusser's pedagogical abilities were highly praised, he soon felt the effects of severe psychological problems and frequently had to leave the ENS for several weeks at a time. So in fact he gave very few classes. But he formed personal relationships with the students in his charge, and one after another they visited him at length in his office. He listened to them and gave them advice and technical tricks—very useful for going before the jury of a competition as codified and ritualized as the *agrégation*.

Foucault would become close friends with Althusser. When he became ill, Althusser advised him to refuse hospitalization. But also, above all, it was largely through Althusser's influence that Foucault would join the Communist party. When he first took over as *caïman*, Althusser was not yet a Communist. He even participated in the meetings of the Catholic group at the ENS. He had been a very devout Catholic and a student of Jean Lacroix and Jean Guitton and was still on excellent terms with them. Althusser swung toward Marxism and communism at a time when almost the entire Ecole Normale and a large proportion of French intellectuals were doing so.

It has often been remarked that in France philosophy and intellectual questions are always strongly shaped by political authority. That has undoubtedly never been truer than it was in the years following the Liberation. And the Ecole Normale, far from standing aloof from the phenomenon, drove it to fever pitch. As early as 1945, but especially starting in 1948, the Communist party was firmly entrenched at the Rue d'Ulm. Emmanuel Le Roy Ladurie reports that according to Jean-François Revel, who was at the Ecole just after the war, the Communist influence was still limited in 1945. But as the cold war wound into high gear, and with the launching of the insurrectionary strikes of 1947, everyone was called upon to "choose sides," and the ENS was speedily politicized; it took the "workers' side," and therefore the side of the Communist party.[14] Paul Viallaneix recalls being present at "veritable conversion phenomena," where people he had known to be apolitical during the *khâgne* years plunged passionately and furiously into revolutionary activism. The warnings of Jacques Le Goff, who had spent some time in Czechoslovakia, did nothing to damp the Marxist ardor of his schoolmates—an enthusiasm so great that historians today ponder the phenomenon of this "Communist generation" at the Ecole Normale.[15] How many were Communist? It is hard to be precise, because "belonging" could vary from a distant, informal affinity all the way to the most frenzied, sectarian militancy. Le Roy Ladurie, who entered the ENS in 1949 and almost immediately became the secretary of the cell, claims that one of every four or five, or "forty or fifty students out of a total of two hundred," were party members, although only about twenty came to meetings. Among the Communists at the Rue d'Ulm, a few names stand out—Michel Crouzet, Pierre Juquin, Maurice Caveing.

Why did so many intellectuals become members of the Communist party? First, it must be said that its popularity was not confined to intellectuals; during these years 5 million people in France, or more than 25 percent of the electorate, voted for the Communists in national elections. And then, as Maurice Agulhon put it,

> people who did not live through this period cannot imagine the extent, the persistence, the force, and we might as well say it, the shamelessness of Communist propaganda on the subject of the Resistance: "There were more of us," the party claimed, "we did the most, were the only ones effective, the only genuine participants in the patriotic struggle, our list of martyrs is the longest; we were proudly known as the Party of men shot by the firing-squad . . ." The party was the fierce guardian of patriotic integrity. Let's admit it: our critical faculties had been overcome. Besides, it is not one's critical faculties that are the most developed at eighteen or twenty, especially when a vague remorse for not having fought in the Resistance tugs in the opposite direction, resulting in a desire to make up for it by joining the politics that claim to continue this movement.[16]

Thus it is not surprising that the *normaliens* were members en masse of the party, even if not quite in the numbers it claimed. Long presenting itself as the gathering place for intellectuals, the "party of intelligence" pictured itself as controlling, dictating, or enlisting everything that happened in research or thought. The reality was far from that, but one of every four or five students at the ENS over almost ten years is quite a lot of people.

The life of the school was pervaded by politics and extremely heated arguments. The climate of "intellectual terror" maintained by members of the Communist party was especially overbearing. Anyone not following the line was excommunicated and denounced. Le Roy Ladurie, the secretary of the cell, was one of the most virulent. He was a real inquisitor, giving orders and judging everything all the time, especially the students' orthodoxy.

There was also a small socialist group, but it seemed rather old-fashioned; Jean Erhard, now the mayor of Riom, Marcel Roncayolo, and Guy Palmade were among its members. There were others who belonged to the ephemeral Rassemblement Démocratique Révolutionnaire (RDR), launched by Sartre and David Rousset in 1948 and somewhat prematurely dubbed the "students' party"; in fact few students joined it. The Christians formed the "groupe tala" (from vont-à-la messe, "they go to Mass") and were divided between a left wing and a tiny minority on the right. The more numerous "progressive Christians" were attracted by the Communist party. They defended the idea of a missionary church that should direct its attentions to the poor. Starting in 1947, his second year at the Rue d'Ulm, François Bédarida was "prince tala," the head of the Catholic group. Though very young, he had participated in the Resistance and had a close connection to the progressive Christians involved with the Catholic newspaper *Témoignage chrétien*. He was seduced by communism because, as he says today, "progressivism, meaning communism, was very much in the air at the time." A pro-Communist Christian. This was also the situation of Roger Fauroux, who is presently minister of industry, after serving as head of the Ecole Nationale d'Administration.

A "handful" of *normaliens* on the other side, the vilified right, felt that the atmosphere of the Rue d'Ulm was stifling in its "leftist conformity." Looked upon as "strange beasts" and systematically referred to as "fascists" by everyone else, these few students—Jean d'Ormesson, Jean Charbonnel (who would become a minister under General de Gaulle), and Robert Poujade (who today is mayor of Dijon)—were militant members of de Gaulle's party, the Rassemblement pour la France. According to Charbonnel, they were exceedingly interested in the Gaullist intellectual review *Liberté de l'esprit*, for which both Claude Mauriac and Maurice Clavel wrote.[17]

In 1948 Louis Althusser joined the Parti Communiste Français (PCF). In a letter to Maria-Antonietta Macciocchi, he explained his reasons for doing so:

As a lycée student and later, I was a militant member of Action Catholique. In the 1930s the church had set up its own youth organizations to confront the influence of "socialist" ideas. It did us a sacred service. Our chaplain talked to us, the children of the petit bourgeois, about the "social cause," which gave us a head start. It was one of "history's tricks" that most of my Catholic schoolmates of that period became Communist. The Popular Front, the war in Spain, the war against fascism, and the Resistance all showed us the "social cause" close up, and we learned its real name: class struggle. In 1948 I became a teacher of philosophy and joined the French Communist party. Ever since that time I have . . . pursued my profession and tried to be a Communist. Being a Communist in philosophy means being a Marxist-Leninist philosopher. It is not easy being a Marxist-Leninist philosopher.[18]

Not until 1968 and after did Louis Althusser become the Marxist-Leninist philosopher who "reread" *Capital* and mobilized around himself the disciples of a thus renewed "revolutionary theory." But already his influence was strong enough to induce some students to follow him into the party. Foucault was one of these; he joined in 1950.

In 1950. That means that Foucault had spent four years at the ENS without doing something a good number of his schoolmates were doing. However, he had wanted to join ever since his first year at the Rue d'Ulm, in the spring of 1947. Maurice Agulhon remembers how this attempt ran into trouble. Foucault wanted to become a militant in the party cell but not in the students' syndicate. This seemed unthinkable to the Communists responsible for examining his membership request, and consequently they rejected him. Foucault was therefore not politically engaged, at least not through any organizational framework, throughout his student career. He had close connections to the party, according to Jacques Proust, who saw a lot of him in those days; but at the same time he was very critical of the party's dominant intellectual personalities, such as Roger Garaudy. Moreover, at the time Foucault was more Hegelian than Marxist. He worked extensively on *Phenomenology of Spirit* for his diploma, and he shared this interest with Althusser, who several years before had also defended a thesis on Hegel, as did his friend Jacques Martin (to whom *Pour Marx* is dedicated) and also Jean Laplanche.

The year 1950 was not just the year Foucault joined the Communist party. It was also the year he flunked the *agrégation*. And yet he had chosen to take four years for preparing his exam instead of the usual three. In the spring of 1950 he sat the written exam, in which he had to ponder the problem "Is man part of nature?" and then discuss the work of Auguste Comte. He did not do too badly and found himself listed—along with 73 other candidates out of 219 who had taken the exams—among those admitted to the oral. What he did not know was that he was ranked only twenty-ninth; this ranking was a serious obstacle to becoming one of the fifteen top students finally awarded the *agrégation.* There were two stages to the oral at that time: first a "little oral," which consisted of a lecture on a subject chosen at random; then a "big oral," with four different tests, a lecture, and three discussions of texts (French, Latin, and Greek). The first oral was an eliminating exam. And Foucault succumbed at this stage of the competition. He encountered a subject that he was not enthusiastic about: hypothesis, a traditional subject to which the proper responses were all mapped out in advance. But Foucault plunged into a long discussion of hypotheses in Parmenides and completely neglected the notion of hypothesis in the sciences. Down came the verdict: Michel Foucault was not one of the twenty candidates accepted for the second series of oral exams. The jury, composed of the dean of the Sorbonne, Georges Davy, Pierre-Maxime Schuhl, and the inspector general Bridoux, criticized him for not having cited Claude Bernard. Foucault later explained ironically, "I forgot to mention the rabbit pee," referring to a famous experiment by Bernard that the jury expected him to mention. The report by the president of the jury, written in Davy's hand, spoke volumes: "A candidate who is certainly cultivated and distinguished and whose failure can be considered as an accident. But, having already placed badly in the written, he made the mistake on the oral, and on a standard subject, of being more concerned with demonstrating his erudition than with treating the subject proposed." Among those receiving the *agrégation* that year were Pierre Aubenque, Jean-Pierre Faye, Jean-François Lyotard, and Jean Laplanche; the failures included Michel Tournier and Michel Butor.

Foucault's failure nevertheless stirred up a lot of fuss. Everyone had been convinced that he would rank with the highest. He was considered one of the most brilliant students at the Ecole, and no one understood how he could have flunked that way. Some even suggested that he had been refused for political reasons. Such interpretations were quite common at the time. For example, in 1951 *La Nouvelle Critique* reported that a member of the philosophy jury had said: "This year no Communists will pass." One thing is certain: Foucault was grievously affected by his failure, to the extent that Althusser asked Jean Laplanche and his young wife to keep an eye on him to keep him from doing "something stupid." Foucault went through another period of crisis, but he was soon back at work preparing for the next year's exams. He teamed up with Jean-Paul Aron, who was not enrolled at the ENS but took courses there, and with whom he had become friends. Foucault prepared dozens of lecture outlines on every possible subject. He knew that the oral was his difficult hurdle. By June 1951 he was ready to face the written exams again. For seven hours he had to write about "experiment and theory: what philosophical consequences result from how they are defined and how their relations are conceived." He wrote for another seven on "perceptive activity and intelligence." Finally, he had to spend six hours imagining that Bergson and Spinoza met "in the somnolent world of pure memory" and "engaged in a dialogue on time and eternity with the intention of defining the sort of consideration that philosophy must give these two notions." He came through it all very well and again found his name on the list of those admitted to the oral. This time the jury was composed of Georges Davy as president, Jean Hyppolite, and Georges Canguilhem, who had become inspector general of secondary education, as vice-president. Canguilhem wanted to bring the subjects given the candidates more up to date. Overcoming considerable opposition, he succeeded in getting topics such as "sexuality" included. "They all read Freud. And, in any event, that's all they talk about," he emphasized to the somewhat recalcitrant Davy. And that was precisely the subject that fate assigned Foucault. Jean Deprun, who attended the lecture because Foucault already enjoyed a certain notoriety among students at the ENS, remembers a very classical, three-point exposé: sexuality as nature, sexuality as culture, and sexuality as history. History here was understood in the sense of individual history, because Foucault was very strongly influenced by his reading in psychology and psychoanalysis.

This time Foucault was accepted. He tied for third place with one of his schoolmates, Jean-Paul Milou. Yvon Brès, a student in the same year as Foucault, was first. He went up to Foucault afterward and apologized for having come out ahead of him, which he felt was unjust. The jury's report took note of Foucault's obvious uneasiness: "A candidate who is certainly cultivated and distinguished but who seemed to be approaching the *agrégation* this second time fearfully, perhaps with prejudice," wrote Dean Davy. After the results were announced Foucault, furious that he was not first, complained to Canguilhem about the subject assigned him to discuss.—Really! What an idea! he fumed. Examining candidates for the *agrégation* on sexuality!

Theoretically the *agrégation* competition led to teaching on the secondary level, and in this period it usually opened the way to teaching at a university, after some time spent teaching at a lycée, which the *normaliens* considered an inevitable purgatory. Because Foucault had been exempted from military service on account of his very fragile health, this was a matter of some urgency. The new graduates were supposed to request a lycée post, and they met with the inspector general to do so. Foucault therefore went to talk to Canguilhem—to tell him he did not want to teach. Because he had ranked very high, he had some hope of entering the Fondation Thiers, a very special institution created in 1893 by Adolphe Thiers' sister-in-law. Each year several students—only boys—were accepted, with a monthly stipend so that they could write their theses under good conditions. The status of the foundation was somewhat modified after the war. Because the money in its endowment was greatly devalued, it was put under the supervision of the Centre National de la Recherche Scientifique (CNRS). This state body paid a monthly allowance to the boarders, who then had to pay half of it back to the foundation for providing bed and board. The boarders were given the title of CNRS research attaché while they were at the foundation. For a long time there had been five new recruits each year, in literature, law, or medicine. In the fall of 1950 six had been admitted, among them Robert Mauzi, Paul Viallaneix, and Jean-Louis Gardies. In 1951 there were ten. Foucault's fellows included Jean Charbonnel, Pierre Aubenque, Guy Degen, and Jean-Bernard Raimond.

How did one get into this strange house, this huge nineteenth-century building, located in what is now the Place du Chancelier-Adenauer, in the sixteenth arrondissement near the Porte Dauphine? First, one had to be recommended by the director of one's university. Then one had to apply to the foundation director, who at the time was the Hellenist Paul Mazon. Finally, because the foundation, despite its supervision by the CNRS, was still administered by the academies composing the Institut de France, one had to visit the representatives of each of the academies making up the administrative council. The Académie Française was represented by Georges Duhamel. Jean Charbonnel, who arrived at the foundation the same year as Foucault, described his own visit to Duhamel: "When I went to introduce myself to him, as was the current custom, he said to me, in his little Mauriac voice: 'Listen, young man, I don't know whether or not you'll ever enjoy fame and glory, but I can tell you that one of the moments in which I felt I experienced this was when one of my grandsons came home shouting: 'I had grandfather in my dictation!'"[19] Every applicant heard the same story from the novelist.

After this series of procedures and visits, the happy few could finally move into "this majestic house," as Charbonnel described it. It was "quaint and outmoded but dedicated to the cult of intelligence, and, all in all, it was charming. It had a valet, pretty furniture, a billiard table, a piano, and a large garden. The decor was sumptuous, but our resources were modest . . . We entered modern science then the way one enters religion. We had to make a vow of poverty and . . . of celibacy."[20] During Foucault's visit to Paul Mazon, he mentioned two subjects for research: "the problem of human sciences in post-Cartesian philosophers" and "the notion of culture in contemporary psychology." "The first seemed particularly interesting to me," Mazon wrote in his report at the end of Foucault's stay at the foundation. "It dealt with how Cartesianism had evolved under foreign influences, Italian and Dutch, and what the results of this evolution had been in Malebranche and Bayle."[21] Foucault in fact had gone to see Henri Gouhier to ask if he would be willing to direct his secondary thesis on Malebranche. The principal thesis, as Mazon mentioned, was supposed to deal with the problem of culture as it is analyzed by contemporary psychology. And he set to work as furiously as ever. This was when he developed the habit of going to the Bibliothèque Nationale every day—a habit he maintained for years, until he left for Sweden, and one he resumed upon his return to France. The BN is no doubt the one place in which Foucault spent the most hours of his life.

But Foucault would spend only one year at Fondation Thiers, not the three the rules allowed. It was very hard for him to stand the communal life that he had already found so abhorrent at the Rue d'Ulm. Here, of course, everyone had his own room and hence could live in relative independence. But it was still a boarding institution, where one had to live with about twenty other people. All meals had to be taken with this group. Foucault again made himself universally detested. He attacked everybody, carried on, provoked arguments. Conflict prevailed in all his relations with the other students. It came to a head over an amorous adventure with one of the other students that went awry. Foucault was suspected of having stolen mail from the letter boxes. He did not particularly want to stay, nor did the place particularly want him to.

At the beginning of the 1952 school year, he found a new place to go for a while. He became an assistant lecturer at the University of Lille.

4
~~

The Carnival of Madmen

When Foucault first arrived on the Rue d'Ulm, Georges Gusdorf was philosophy *caïman*. Although he is known today for his works on the history of Western thought, he had not then published anything to speak of. Gusdorf was very interested in psychology, and with his friend Georges Daumézon he organized in 1946 and 1947 an introduction to psychopathology for his students. They were able to see patients at Hôpital Sainte-Anne, and there was a lecture series at the ENS that included not only Daumézon but also psychiatrists such as Lacan and Ajuriaguerra. Gusdorf went even further in offering his students experience. Every year he took a group of *normaliens* to visit the psychiatic hospital directed by Daumézon at Fleury-les-Aubrais, near Orléans. There they spent a week listening to analyses by the doctors and their assistants. And they strolled around inside the hospital enclosure. Fleury-les-Aubrais, with its pavilions dispersed over a large wooded area, did not seem at all like a prison.

When he succeeded Gusdorf, Althusser also took students to Sainte-Anne. There they attended lectures by another topnotch psychiatrist, Henri Ey. With Daumézon and Ey, Foucault found himself very early in contact with currents of reform in psychiatry. He associated with people involved in the group and review named *Evolution psychiatrique*, who were trying to reconsider the knowledge and practice of their discipline in a very liberal vein. And what he saw of psychiatry at that time had no "repressive" or "punitive" character.

From his very first years at the Ecole Normale, Michel Foucault began to be keenly interested in psychology. After obtaining his *licence* in philosophy at the Sorbonne in 1948, he began studying for one in psychology. He therefore took courses from Daniel Lagache, who taught general psychology and social psychology at the *faculté des lettres*. He also had to take courses for the certificate in psychophysiology given in the *faculté des sciences*. There, however, he was less assiduous, teaming up with André Vergez and Louis Mazauric to spell one another in attending class and taking notes. In 1949 Foucault obtained both this *licence* and an additional diploma from the Institut de Psychologie de Paris, for which he again studied with Lagache.

Daniel Lagache is one of the great names in psychology in the postwar period. He was part of the class of 1924 at the Rue d'Ulm along with Aron, Canguilhem, Nizan, and Sartre. He passed the *agrégation* in philosophy but chose to pursue clinical psychology. He taught for a long time at Strasbourg before being appointed in 1947 to the Sorbonne, where his inaugural lecture on the "unity of psychology," in which he tried to integrate psychoanalysis with clinical science, caused a great stir. The lecture was published in 1949. During this same period he began to give courses at the Institut de Psychologie.

Foucault ardently attended Lagache's courses, because psychology was the route he had chosen. He even contemplated studying medicine. He asked Lagache if it was necessary to be a medical doctor to specialize in psychology. The question did not surprise Lagache. Didier Anzieu, whose own orientation was toward psychoanalysis, explains: "At the time, a lot of philosophers who were turning in the direction of psychology, psychiatry, or psychoanalysis were wrestling with that problem." Anzieu did not go into medicine. Jean Laplanche seems to have been one of the few who did. Foucault also would remain on the threshold. Lagache advised him, as he usually did anyone who asked him, not to study medicine. "If we were in the United States, you would certainly have to do it," he told him, "but in France, no." Foucault tried to take advantage of the interview to ask the great psychiatrist questions about his own psychic problems. But Lagache refused to be a student's professor and his psychotherapist at the same time. All he would do was provide Foucault with the address of another psychoanalyst, a recommendation that would remain a dead letter for the time being. Later Foucault would plunge briefly into the adventure of "therapy," for three weeks at most. This was one of the questions that continued to haunt him throughout the years: should he or should he not go into analysis?

Foucault did not stop his scientific training after passing the *agrégation*. During his year at the Fondation Thiers he began studying for a diploma in pathological psychology at the Institut de Psychologie, which he received in 1952. His curriculum included courses with Professors Poyer and Delay, among other things "clinical instruction" with presentations of patients in the great amphitheater at Sainte-Anne. There was also a course in "theoretical psychoanalysis" by Professor Benassy, also at Saint-Anne because the Institut de Psychologie did not have its own building. Pierre Pichot, who oversaw the practicums required for this degree, remembered Foucault, whom he did not much like. Pichot, who wanted to familiarize his students with testing technique, thought he was too much the *normalien*, too theoretical and quite resistant to the experimental nature of psychology. In one of his very first articles, written in 1953, Foucault made some rather vicious allusions to his problems with adherents to a purely "scientific" psychology. He recalled being asked, upon his arrival in this den of experimental psychology, "Do you want to do scientific psychology or psychology like Merleau-Ponty's?" Foucault remarked with irony: "What deserves our attention is not so much the dogmatism with which "real psychology" is defined as the disorder and fundamental skepticism presumed by the question. It takes an astonishing biologist to ask if you want to do biological research that is scientific or biological research that is not!" He added: "Research must be held accountable for the choice of its rationality; its basis—which we know is not the established objectivity of science—must be questioned." [1]

For a very long time, however, Foucault was fascinated by psychological techniques and experimentation; he even bought the material necessary to give Rorschach tests. Admittedly, he had been to a good school; Lagache was one of the earliest initiates and helped introduce the method in France. When the French Rorschach organization was founded, he became its honorary president. Foucault, while at the ENS, enjoyed subjecting his schoolmates to this "test" involving their spontaneous reactions to inkblots on different-colored cards. On the basis of their responses Foucault proposed an interpretation of the underlying personality of whoever went along with the game. "That way, I'll know what's on their minds," he told Maurice Pinguet, who managed to elude the experiment. A great number of students from the ENS remember being tested in this way by Foucault, who remained fascinated by Rorschach tests for many, many years. Whether he was in Clermont-Ferrand or Tunis he devoted many long class hours to something that his companions considered mere amusement.

Rorschach tests also fascinated Jacqueline Verdeaux, who would play a major role during Michel Foucault's years of training. She had known his family for a very long time; her parents were long-standing friends of the Foucaults. During the war her father had sent her with her brother to the safe refuge of Poitiers. Verdeaux eventually became the assistant anesthetist of Dr. Foucault, who continued to serve as a surgeon in the city while supervising the makeshift hospital set up in the Jesuit school to take in the wounded after Germany's sweeping invasion of northern France. When German troops arrived in Poitiers the young woman left the city. A few years later, when peace was restored, Mme. Foucault asked if she would look after her son when he moved to Paris. Foucault dined regularly with Georges and Jacqueline Verdeaux at 6 Rue de Villersexel, a little street off the Boulevard Saint-Germain, not far from the Assemblée Nationale. Jacqueline worked with her husband, who had just defended his dissertation with Jacques Lacan. They had established an electroencephalographic laboratory at Sainte-Anne. Jean Delay had found them a few rooms in the hospital attic, where they set themselves up with André Ombredane, a former student of Georges Dumas. Ombredane, who had just translated a book on psychiatric nosology, asked Jacqueline, who had studied German, if she would be willing to submit the translation to a rather well-known Swiss psychiatrist, Roland Kuhn. At the same time Ombredane loaned her Kuhn's *Maskendeutungen im Rorschachschen Versuch* (Phenomenology of the mask). Jacqueline Verdeaux read the book and left for Turgovie, in Munsterlingen, on the shores of Lake Constance. She showed Ombredane's translation to Kuhn and also made a personal request: she herself wanted to translate his *Maskendeutungen*, which she had found fascinating. He agreed and suggested that she also translate a book by another psychiatrist, Ludwig Binswanger, who lived three kilometers away and was the director of Bellevue Clinic in Kreuzlingen. He was the nephew of Otto Binswanger, who had directed the clinic in Jena where Nietzsche had been treated. Verdeaux visited Binswanger and was amazed by the organization of this "asylum," where opulent-looking buildings were scattered around vast grounds, brightened by colorful beds of roses. He asked her many questions before making up his mind, then finally went to search his bookshelves for the text he would like to see published first in French, *Traum und Existenz*, which would be published in French as *Le Rêve et l'existence (Dream and Existence)*.

Binswanger had long before developed the notion of something he called "existential analysis." He had been friends with Freud, Jung, Jaspers, and Heidegger, and the last had made a particularly strong impression on him. Consequently, when Verdeaux returned to Paris and asked her friend Foucault to help her with the translation because the text was teeming with philosophical terms, he was not at all disconcerted. Foucault and Verdeaux together worked out the French translation. They met every day at the Ecole Normale, where Foucault now—in 1952—had an office, because at Althusser's request he had begun to give classes there. They debated the best way to transpose certain notions from one language to another. One evening, after a day of work, Verdeaux took her young collaborator to visit Gaston Bachelard, an avid reader of Binswanger's work, who later kept up a correspondence with him.

Verdeaux and Foucault traveled to Switzerland several times in 1952 and 1953 to meet Kuhn and Binswanger and to show them the translation in various stages. They spent a lot of time discussing Heideggerian vocabulary. Eventually they decided to render *Dasein* not with the usual *être-là* (being-there), but simply with *présence*. When the translation was finished, Verdeaux said to her collaborator: "If you like the book, do a preface for it." Not one to shrink from difficulty, Foucault promptly set to writing.

Not long afterward, while spending Easter vacation in Provence with her husband, Verdeaux received a rather large envelope. "Here is your Easter egg," was the brief note accompanying Foucault's text. Jacqueline Verdeaux was at first astounded at its length: the introduction was longer than the work itself. But as she read it she became more and more excited, deciding it was "fantastic!"

Together they went back to see Binswanger, to show him both the translated text and the introduction. The psychiatrist was extremely pleased with both. Then they had to convince the editor, who was understandably hesitant about publishing this bizarre composite: such a long introduction by someone unknown and such a short book by someone equally unknown, at least in France. But Verdeaux fought hard and finally won. The book was published in 1954 by Desclée de Brouwer in the series Textes et Etudes Anthropologiques.

Foucault had placed an excerpt from René Char's "Partage formel" at the beginning of the text: "When I reached manhood, I saw rising and growing up the wall shared between life and death, a ladder longer all the time, invested with an unique power of evulsion: this was the dream . . . Now see the darkness draw away, and LIVING become, in the form of a harsh allegorical asceticism, the conquest of extraordinary powers by which we feel ourselves confusedly crossed, but which we express incompletely, lacking loyalty, cruel perception, and perseverance."[2] The introduction also concluded with long quotations from "Partage formel," which Foucault felt provided the best key to understanding dreams.

Foucault's style in the introduction is flamboyant and strong. What attracted him in Binswanger's work was the way he had reconciled and gone beyond the contributions of Freud and Husserl. Above all, however, Foucault was proposing his own vision of the dream: "In every case death is the absolute meaning of the dream," he wrote, and the dream of death "appears as what existence can learn that is most fundamental about itself." Whence the idea that "the dream has absolute primacy for an anthropological understanding of concrete man." But Foucault saw also the necessity—"an ethical task and a historical necessity"—for going beyond this primacy, and with this he concluded his text.[3] Foucault cited the psychologist Eugène Minkovski's works, Bachelard's *L'Air et les songes*, Melanie Klein, and Lacan, whom he had just begun to read. He had, for example, strongly recommended to Jean-Claude Passeron, who was beginning to work on "the concept of specularity" for his diploma, that he get hold of Lacan's text on the "mirror stage" published in *L'Encyclopédie française*.

On their first trip to Switzerland in 1952, Verdeaux and Foucault visited Kuhn at the Munsterlingen hospital the day before Mardi Gras. On this date the patients traditionally prepared costumes and masks; then doctors, nurses, and patients went in disguise to the village hall. At the end of the evening they all threw their masks into a huge fire where the figure of Carnival was sacrificed. Foucault was much struck by this strange ceremony: "This is not a carnival of madmen; it's a carnival of dead men," he confided to his friend.

Foucault and Verdeaux, whom he referred to as "my wife," also visited Binswanger during his vacation in Ticino, in the southern Alps, on the shore of Lake Maggiore. The two colleagues met in Florence and, after spending a few days in Venice, took a car to reach the psychiatrist's summer residence, visiting churches and museums along the way. "He loved painting," Verdeaux recalled of Foucault. "He is the one who made me understand Masaccio's frescoes in Florence." On the other hand, she remembers equally well that Foucault detested nature. Whenever she showed him some magnificent landscape—a lake sparkling in the sunlight—he made a great show of walking off toward the road, saying, "My back is turned to it." They spent a few days with Binswanger, who took them several times for tea with one of his friends, Szilazyi, a Heideggerian philosopher cited by Foucault in his "Introduction." They talked about Heidegger, phenomenology, psychoanalysis. And the great question was, is psychoanalysis a science? Binswanger spent his entire life struggling to prove that it is.

The time spent with Binswanger, both the man and his work, was to play a very important role for Foucault. Foucault would, of course, break away from this form of "phenomenological psychiatry," but Binswanger's analyses revealed to him a sort of underlying reality to madness. "Reading what has been defined as 'existential analysis' or 'phenomenological psychiatry' was undeniably important to me," he later said.

> This was the period in which I was working in psychiatric hospitals and looking for something different from the traditional grids imposed by the medical gaze, some counterbalance. Most certainly, these superb descriptions of madness as fundamental, unique, incomparable experiences were decisive for me. Moreover, I believe [R. D.] Laing was also impressed by all of this. For a long time he, too, took existential analysis as a reference. (He was more Sartrean, I was more Heideggerian) . . . I believe existential analysis helped me limit and better define what it was about academic psychiatric knowledge that was heavy and oppressive.[4]

Foucault's introduction to Binswanger's text is the best reflection of his intellectual orientation during this period. But beyond that, it is an essential text for grasping his preoccupations, the problems he set and would set for himself—for grasping, perhaps, the genesis of his work at its point of origin. In 1983, in an early version, published in the United States, of his preface to *L'Usage des plaisirs* (*The Use of Pleasure*; Vol. II of *L'Histoire de la sexualité*), Foucault would recall everything he owed to Binswanger and how he moved on from these ideas:

> To study forms of experience in this way—in their history—is an idea that originated with an earlier project, in which I made use of the methods of existential analysis in the field of psychiatry and in the domain of "mental illness." For two reasons, not unrelated to each other, this project left me unsatisfied: its theoretical weakness in elaborating the notion of experience, and its ambiguous link with a psychiatric practice which it simultaneously ignored and took for granted. One could deal with the first problem by referring to a general theory of the human being; and treat the second altogether differently by turning, as is so often done, to "the economic and social context"; one could choose, by doing so, to accept the resulting dilemma of a philosophical anthropology and a social history. But I

wondered whether, rather than playing on this alternative, it would not be possible to consider the very historicity of forms of experience.

And after a long development laying out the path of thought enabling him to think in terms of a "history of the forms of experience," he added: "It is easy to see how reading Nietzsche in the early fifties has given access to these kinds of questions, by breaking with the double tradition of phenomenology and Marxism." [5]

Foucault also worked as a psychologist with Jacqueline Verdeaux at Hôpital Sainte-Anne, where his status was somewhat vague. He was a *stagiaire*—a trainee—which means little more than that he had no official functions and was not paid. But during this time he first lived at the Fondation Thiers and then became a lecturer at the University of Lille, so it was not to earn his living that he did this "training" at the electroencephalographic laboratory. He helped Verdeaux perform tests and experiments. Measurement was all-important. They measured brain waves, skin resistance in the palm of the hand, the rhythm of respiration. The subject of the experiment had to sit harnessed to an armchair, strung with electrodes on head, feet, and hands. This apparatus allowed the psychologist to register the whole body's nervous reactions. Foucault sometimes served as a subject; more often, however, he helped in preparing and reading the experiments. Robert Francès, a psychologist and musicologist, came to the laboratory to set up some tests on musical hearing. And what a surprise it was for Jean Deprun, whom Francès had asked to be his guinea pig, to discover Foucault among the experimenters and technical aides!

The laboratory was obviously not meant for pure research or for amusing experiments. It was under the authority of Jean Delay and an integral part of the hospital services. Georges and Jacqueline Verdeaux were, above all, responsible for diagnosing and keeping track of patients interned at Sainte-Anne.

In an interview in 1982, Foucault described this work:

There was no clear status for psychologists in a mental hospital. So as a student in psychology . . . I had a very strange status there. The *chef de service* was very kind to me and let me do anything I wanted . . . I was actually in a position between the staff and the patients, and it wasn't my merit, it wasn't because I had a special attitude, it was the consequence of this ambiguity in my status which forced me to maintain a distance from the staff. I am sure it was not my personal merit, because I felt all that at the time as a kind of malaise. It was only a few

years later, when I started writing a book on the history of psychiatry, that this malaise, this personal experience, took the form of an
historical criticism or a structural analysis.

When asked whether Hôpital Sainte-Anne gave an employee a particularly negative impression of psychiatry, Michel Foucault answered:
"Oh no. It was as typical a large hospital as you could imagine, and I
must say it was better than most of the large hospitals in provincial
towns that I visited afterwards. It was one of the best in Paris. No,
it was not terrible. That was precisely the thing that was important.
Maybe if I had been doing this kind of work in a small provincial hospital, I would have believed its failures were the result of its location or
its particular inadequacies."[6]

Foucault worked as a psychologist not only in a psychiatric hospital
but also in a prison. In 1950 the Ministry of Health asked Georges and
Jacqueline Verdeaux to open an electroencephalographic laboratory at
the prison in Fresnes, site of the general hospital for the French prison
system. The laboratory had two functions: to examine sick prisoners at
their doctors' request, to detect possible brain injuries, latent epilepsy,
neurological troubles; and to carry out a series of tests designed to
steer prisoners toward prison schools such as the printing press at
Melun. Jacqueline Verdeaux went there every week and took her friend
Foucault along. For two years she taught him to perform admission
tests and to decipher the results while he worked as her assistant.
Together they discussed the cases, writing up notes for each person
examined.

Foucault, then, spent this period steeping in the professional atmosphere of experimental psychology. His apprenticeship had now left a
strictly academic framework, and Foucault found himself in the "field,"
as an ethnologist would say. He was confronted with the reality of illness and with the presence of people who were ill. He was immersed in
the reality of two forms of internment: that of "madmen" and that of
"delinquents." And he himself was among those who "looked," "examined," "decided," even if his uncertain and poorly defined status gave
him some distance in relation to the psychologist's profession that he
was learning.

5

Stalin's Shoemaker

Before receiving his appointment at Lille, Foucault had already begun to teach psychology at the Ecole Normale Supérieure; Louis Althusser had asked him to teach as soon as he had completed the *agrégation*. From the fall of 1951 through the spring of 1955 Foucault gave a course on Monday evenings in the little Salle Cavaillès. He had a rather large attendance for the ENS, between fifteen and twenty-five people; usually no more than five or six attended a class. A large audience, therefore, and very enthusiastic. "It's fantastic," Jean-Claude Passeron proclaimed one day as he left one of Foucault's lectures. Paul Veyne now says: "His course was famous. It was like going to a show." And Jacques Derrida: "I was struck, like many others, by his speaking ability. His eloquence, authority, and brilliance were impressive." Certain of Foucault's great themes of this period would appear in lectures and reappear in texts. In 1953 he wrote an introduction to a history of psychology from 1850 to 1950 at the request of Denis Huisman, who wanted to bring Alfred Weber's *Histoire de la philosophie* up to date. His first book, *Maladie mentale et personnalité* (Mental illness and personality), was written at almost the same time.

Foucault continued tradition, taking his students to Sainte-Anne to attend the patient presentations. Jean-Claude Passeron, for example, attended Daumézon's discussions. And Jacques Derrida retained a sharp memory of these rather pathetic sessions: "Foucault took three or four of us at a time. We went into Daumézon's office, where he was having his students practice their clinical technique. A patient was brought in, and a young doctor questioned and examined him. We were present for that. It was very upsetting. The doctor would then leave and, after writing down his observations, would deliver a sort of lecture for Daumézon."

During this period Foucault became the center, not to say the head, of a small band of Communist students at the Ecole. The group was composed of Paul Veyne, Jean-Claude Passeron, Gérard Genette, Maurice Pinguet, Jean Molino, and Jean-Louis Van Regemorter, who was thought of as the young professor's henchman. All of them were three or four years younger than Foucault and more or less worshiped him. They were Communists but did not really toe the line. The other Communist students at the Ecole, who were orthodox, called them the "groupe folklorique"—a bunch of weirdos—or "the Marxist Saint-Germain-des-Prés." They discussed things for hours on end in the ENS entrance hall or courtyard. And "le Fouk's"—as they called Foucault (*Fuchs* means "fox" in German)—spent a great deal of time with them whenever he was at the Rue d'Ulm. He had fixed up an office in the former record library above the Salle Dussane. He called this space the "psychology laboratory," but about the only equipment was a mouse in a shoebox. "There's the laboratory," he would laugh, showing his visitors the box. The shelves along the walls were still full of dusty 78s, useless following the advent of LPs. Students and friends would visit him there, and he spent long hours chatting with his confidant at the time, Maurice Pinguet, who years later wrote a fine book, *La Mort volontaire au Japon*.

Like the members of the "groupe folklorique," Foucault belonged to the Communist party. Afterward he had very little to say about this temporary affiliation. For example, this is how he described the political situation during this period, in his interviews with Ducio Trombadori in 1978:

> What could politics represent for those who were twenty when the war was over, for those who had been more subjected to this tragedy than participated in it? What could politics mean when it was a question of choosing between Stalin's U.S.S.R. and Truman's America, or else between the old SFIO [the French Socialist party] and the Christian Democrats, and so on? Many young intellectuals, of whom I was one, considered a bourgeois-type professional future—professor, journalist, writer, whatever—to be intolerable. Experience itself had demonstrated the necessity and urgency of creating a radically different society from the one we knew. This was a society that had put up with Nazism, that had prostituted itself to it, and then had gone over en masse to de Gaulle. Confronted with all that, a large part of the youth of France reacted with total rejection.[1]

Foucault did not intend, with these remarks, to explain why he had belonged to the Communist party, but instead why he was interested in Nietzsche and Bataille, and why he turned his back on the traditional forms of philosophy that Hegelianism and phenomenology represented for him. And when his interlocutor expressed surprise at this reply and really stressed the Marxist culture of the period, Foucault replied:

> For many of us, young intellectuals, interest in Nietzsche or in Bataille did not represent a way of distancing oneself from Marxism or communism. On the contrary, it was the sole route of communication, the only way to get through to what we thought we should expect from communism. This requirement that we totally reject the world in which we had had to live was certainly not satisfied by Hegelian philosophy. On the other hand, we were also seeking other intellectual routes to reach precisely that point at which something entirely different seemed to take shape or exist: that is, communism. That was how, without really knowing Marx, rejecting Hegelianism, feeling uncomfortable because of the limits of existentialism, I decided to join the Communist party. This was 1950. To be a "Nietzschean Communist"! Something really close to impossible to live with and even a little ridiculous, if you like. Even I knew it was.[2]

It seems clear that Foucault substantially reconstructed his intellectual and political itinerary, for it was certainly not his fascination with Nietzsche that made him join the Communist party. According to witnesses from the period, it was not until around 1953 that Nietzsche began to have an important influence on him. Maurice Pinguet described Foucault's discovery of Nietzsche on the beaches in Italy, during summer vacation in 1953. "Hegel, Marx, Freud, Heidegger—this was his frame of reference in 1953, when the encounter with Nietzsche took place. I can still see Michel Foucault, reading his *Untimely Meditations* in the sun, on the beach at Civitavecchia."[3] Paul Veyne confirmed this, saying that in 1983 he had spoken at length with Foucault and noted these conversations in his journal. Foucault had specifically told him that 1953 was the year he began to read Nietzsche. And he had also told him: "When I was in the Communist party, Marxism as a doctrine made good sense to me."

Moreover, "Nietzscheism" is totally absent from the texts that Foucault published during this period, whereas Marxist vocabulary and subject matter are frequently present, even if Foucault cannot be defined as a Marxist pure and simple. One need only refer to the first edition of *Maladie mentale et personnalité* (to which we shall return shortly). It should be noted, though, that Foucault never belonged to the Communist party in the same way that a great many of his schoolmates did. He rarely attended cell meetings. "I remember, however," Maurice Pinguet writes, "that he was there one night, upstairs above the little café on the place de la Contrescarpe. All of a sudden he launched into some vehement remarks opposing the coal-steel pact." [4] But Foucault never took part in militant activity. No one ever saw him selling the Communist party newspaper, *L'Humanité*, or handing out tracts or attending demonstrations. Except once, according to Jean-Louis Gardies, who, one day when *L'Humanité* was seized, joined up with Foucault and several others in front of the newspaper's headquarters to go and distribute copies of it in the Latin Quarter. "But," he added, "neither he nor I was cut out for this. We did not have the souls of militants." It is, above all, not possible to class Foucault, either politically or intellectually, with those who designated themselves as "Stalinists." Emmanuel Le Roy Ladurie, who was one of the most eminent among them, noted in his memoir that "Michel Foucault fell, far less than others in this period, into the excesses of Stalinism." [5]

Jean-Claude Passeron and Alexandre Matheron, however, recall that Foucault participated in a series of lectures at the Maison des Lettres on Rue Férou, near Place Saint-Sulpice. "The Communist philosophy students at the time had formed a work group," according to Matheron, "to which a certain number of philosophers who were party members (Desanti, Vernant, etc.) agreed to speak. And Foucault, who was then a lecturer at Lille and gave classes at the Rue d'Ulm, came one day to talk about Pavlov," in the context of a discussion about psychiatry, which would become chapter 7 of *Maladie mentale et personnalité*. Of course, Passeron adds, his talk did not fit into the straight-line Marxist orthodoxy of the period, but nonetheless Foucault did quote Stalin in it. In fact his lecture ended with a reference to something Stalin had said about a poor alcoholic shoemaker who beat his wife and his children, to explain that cases of mental pathology are the fruit of poverty and exploitation and that only a radical transformation of the conditions of existence would be able to put an end to this. Should this be seen as a "wink" in the direction of the "groupe folklorique," who were present at the lecture, as Passeron suggests? Or perhaps it was quite simply a reflection of the fact that it was unthinkable to omit Stalin's name in a lecture organized by the party, no matter what the subject was; even if Foucault benefited from a rather special status: no one reproached him for his absenteeism from cell meetings or even—something far more serious—his making fun, with Jean-Louis Van Regemorter, of the articles in *L'Humanité* on the Soviet Union.

All the evidence indicates that Foucault was not an ardent militant. One might even say that he was a rather distant one. How, then, should we explain the following strange conversation in 1971, reported by Claude Mauriac in his journal? Foucault said to Jean-Claude Passeron: "Do you remember when we were ghostwriters at *La Nouvelle Critique?* And that famous article we were always talking about: 'Il faut régler son compte à Merleau-Ponty' [The score must be settled with Merleau-Ponty] was the phrase we used. I don't think that article was ever written. But we are the authors of plenty of other pages in *La Nouvelle Critique.*" Mauriac joined in: "I ask were they, by any chance, signed Kanapa?"[6] After this volume of *Le Temps immobile* came out, the idea became firmly established, like a kind of incontestable truth, that Foucault had written some articles signed by Jean Kanapa. Kanapa was the editor-in-chief of *La Nouvelle Critique* and a Stalinist apparatchik whom Sartre, in 1954, called a "cretin" in *Les Temps modernes.* Moreover, Foucault never denied this version of the facts. He did not tell Mauriac that things happened otherwise. He just made it clear, according to Mauriac's account in a later volume of *Le Temps immobile*, that "I did not write 'the' texts by Kanapa. At most two or three of them. Truthfully, one should say . . ." Foucault's sentence was left unfinished, because here Mauriac interrupted him, precisely to point out that he had not reacted to what was reported in the earlier published volume and had let it pass.[7]

Tracking down the details of this story made things even less clear. Quite simply, Kanapa was apparently not a man who used ghostwriters for his articles. Pierre Daix, who was a member of the editorial board of the review, made this abundantly clear. Kanapa wrote his articles with a great deal of care and allowed no one to interfere. At the very most "he might be made to change some expression or other, but it took hours of discussion." Jean Kanapa's son, Jérôme, met Foucault during the 1970s, and Foucault knew who he was but did not allude to this episode. Furthermore, Jérôme Kanapa told his father about meeting Foucault, but Jean Kanapa never mentioned any connection or any past encounter with the philosopher. As for Desanti, he burst out laughing when asked about this: "That can't be anything but a hoax by Foucault." There might be another answer—that Foucault did write for *La Nouvelle Critique*, not Kanapa's articles, but rather articles signed with a pseudonym. But none of the members of the editorial board or people who worked with it closely at the time—whether Annie Kriegel, Jean-Toussaint Desanti, Francis Cohen, Victor Leduc, or Gilberte Rodrigues (who was editorial secretary and Kanapa's constant collaborator)—had any memory of seeing Foucault or hearing him mentioned. Not one could be found who believed it possible that he had worked for the review. Michel Verret, a philosophy student at the ENS in the class of 1948 who wrote regularly for *La Nouvelle Critique*, thoroughly agreed. It seemed unthinkable to him because, as he pointed out, the use of pseudonyms was reserved for administrative officials, high-ranking civil servants, or members of the military. He himself generally signed his own articles, such as the one praising Louis Aragon's *Communistes* and defending the German-Soviet pact, written and signed with Alexandre Matheron and François Furet. Another key Communist figure at the ENS, Maurice Caveing, ruled out any notion of Foucault's having written in this manner for the party's intellectual journal. He added that, at any rate, to have done so would hardly have comported with Foucault's own temperament. Michel Crouzet, who was the cell secretary, admitted that he too knew nothing about it. There still remained the person to whom Foucault was speaking in the conversation reported by Mauriac: Jean-Claude Passeron. But he said he had never written for *La Nouvelle Critique* in any capacity whatever, and he thought it unlikely that Foucault did so. He spoke only of some brief notes that students at the Ecole Normale might make, drafts that could be useful for articles signed by the main writers at the review. As for the brief unsigned texts that appeared at this time at the end of issues of *La Nouvelle Critique*, recording events in the Latin Quarter or at the Ecole Normale, Passeron denied that Foucault could have written any of them. Althusser categorically asserted the same thing, and it does seem that the one person who would have known what was going on would have been Althusser. "I think," he explained, "that Foucault meant to say: we were responsible for 'Kanapism.'"

So, what then? Claude Mauriac does not claim today that what he wrote corresponds to historical reality. He simply states that Foucault did indeed say these words in his presence. And Jean-François Sirinelli, questioning Foucault in 1981 for a study of the Communist students at the Ecole Normale after the war, said that Foucault told him in passing that the students wrote for *La Nouvelle Critique* and seemed to include himself in the group. The mystery remains unsolved.

Only two things are certain. One is that Foucault wrote an article about Descartes for *Clarté*, the Communist students' journal, at the request of Michel Verret, its editor-in-chief. But this "stunning" article (according to Alexandre Matheron, who was a member of the editorial committee) was considered too difficult "for the mass of the students."

It was therefore not published, despite Matheron's and Verret's favorable opinions. The other is that Foucault's membership was very "marginal." That is what he said to Sirinelli in the 1981 interview. It was also rather short-lived, he added. As for this claim, Foucault's Communist sojourn was longer than he would later be willing to say: three months, six months, eighteen months, depending on who asked. Foucault left the party in 1953. There were numerous reasons, of course, for his departure. First of all, he must have felt very uncomfortable in a party that rejected and condemned homosexuality as a bourgeois vice and a sign of decadence. Foucault felt that his homosexuality set him apart. There were others at that time who were excluded from their cells for this reason. This interpretation is strengthened by a privileged witness, Althusser himself. His unhesitating answer to the question why Foucault left the Communist party was "because of his homosexuality."

Foucault gave another reason also: his distress over the affair known as the "Doctors' Plot." In 1952 Stalin's doctors were accused of plotting against the life of the "brilliant and beloved father of the people." The denunciation reeked of anti-Semitism. But all the members of the PCF, including Foucault, went out of their way to give credence to the official Soviet version. In an interview with Ducio Trombadori Foucault recounted how this story had affected him:

> When I left the PCF, it was after the famous plot by Stalin's doctors in the winter of 1952, and it came about because of a persistent feeling of uneasiness. Shortly before Stalin's death the news was spread that a group of doctors had made an attempt on his life. André Wurmser called a meeting of our student cell, to explain how the plot unfolded. Even though we were not convinced, we all tried our hardest to believe what we had been told. This too was part of what I would describe as a disastrous attitude, but one I shared. That was my way of being in the party. Being obliged to stand behind a fact that was the total opposite of credible was part of that exercise of "ego dissolution," part of the search for some way to be "other." Consequently, we gave some credit to what Wurmser said. Three months after Stalin's death, however, we learned that the doctors' plot had been sheer invention. What happened? We wrote to Wurmser, asking him, more or less, to come and see us, to explain what the plot was all about. We never had an answer. You will say it was something they did all the time, nothing out of the ordinary . . . The fact is that from that moment on I moved away from the PCF.[8]

Since Stalin died on March 5, 1953, the disaffection described by Foucault can be dated from the summer or fall of that year. Jean-Paul

Aron told an anecdote demonstrating that Foucault was still a member of the PCF in April 1953. In April the same André Wurmser held a meeting in Lille, this time to denounce Picasso's portrait of Stalin on the cover of *Lettres françaises*, the PCF's cultural journal, edited by Louis Aragon. Michel Simon and Foucault were present at this meeting. Wurmser told his listeners that "this portrait, condemned by Thorez, is self-destructing, dying through its error, or through what amounts to the same thing, its harmfulness." According to Aron, Foucault "began" to be "shaken up" by that sort of reasoning.[9] Began! In any case, he was still going to meetings at which Wurmser was the speaker. And since he joined in 1950, it is clear that he remained in the Communist party for about three years.

Foucault took even longer to break away from Marxism. Michel Simon remembers having heard Foucault say in 1954, before a group of Communist students, that "Marxism is not a philosophy, but an experience along the path leading to a philosophy." And Etienne Verley, a Communist at the ENS, participated with Foucault in a meeting organized by Althusser to form a group responsible for creating a manual of Marxist psychology. According to Verley, this meeting took place just after the publication of *Maladie mentale et personnalité*, that is, in the spring of 1954.

This much we can say: Foucault had left the PCF and turned his back on Marxism before he left for Sweden in the summer of 1955. But he remained very close to Louis Althusser. "When I left the Communist party, he did not see me as anathema; he did not want to break off his relations with me."[10] This relationship with Althusser was, no doubt, extremely important for both men. In 1964, when *Lire le Capital* came out, Althusser paid homage to Foucault, speaking of "the masters teaching us to read the works of knowledge—for us these were Gaston Bachelard and Cavaillès, and today they are Georges Canguilhem and Michel Foucault." Althusser, "le Tus" or "le vieil Alt" as Foucault called him, had been enthusiastic about his student's first books. He himself had not yet published anything when *Folie et déraison* and *Naissance de la clinique (The Birth of the Clinic)* appeared in 1961 and 1963. He wrote warmly to Foucault, speaking of "pioneering work" and "liberation." But this *caïman* from the Rue d'Ulm who was just beginning to publish his work was not indifferent to Foucault's attacks on Marxism in *Les Mots et les choses* in 1966. When Foucault spoke ironically about the children's pool being tossed by theoretical storms, everyone understood his reference to the courtyard of the Ecole Normale.[11] When *Reading Capital* was published in English in 1970, it contained a note concerning Foucault—apparently a warning: "He was one of my students, and something of my research entered into his, including certain of my formulations. But in his thought and his writing, the very meaning of terms borrowed from me has been transformed into something profoundly different from the meaning I attributed to them."[12] Despite their theoretical disagreements, firmly and discreetly demonstrated, Althusser and Foucault would remain friends. Foucault would always have a very high opinion of Althusser and the greatest respect for him. And there were no words too harsh for him to use to blast those who ridiculed his professor when the wind changed and Marxism went out of style.

If Foucault could say that he had been a "Nietzschean Communist," it is because he was still within the theoretical space defined by phenomenology and Marxism when he discovered the great contemporary writers who would fascinate him, with whom he would identify, whom he would quote at every opportunity: Georges Bataille and Maurice Blanchot. Thanks to these two writers he did in fact break the ties still holding him inside the established space of philosophy and politics—despite the fact that the discovery of these authors in this period was through Sartre, whose *Situations I* in 1948 had devoted long commentaries to them. "We came to Bataille and Blanchot *through* Sartre, and we read them *against* Sartre," Jacques Derrida explains. In any event, as Foucault would frequently remark later, they would provide the real access to "Nietzscheism." He also discovered René Char and the work of Samuel Beckett. In 1953 *En attendant Godot* was playing, "a breathtaking spectacle."[13]

Thus began the period of Foucault's fascination with literature, which would last until the end of the 1960s, when it gave way to a more political perspective. Foucault once described the 1950s to Paul Veyne: "At that time, I dreamt of being Blanchot," and said he had been a passionate reader of Blanchot's columns, published regularly in the *Nouvelle Revue française (NRF)* starting in January 1953. In October 1953 Blanchot wrote a long article on Beckett's *L'Innommable*, analyzing the dissolution of the "I" and of the author in that text.[14] It was perhaps through Blanchot that Foucault discovered *L'Innommable*, which he later frequently quoted, as in his inaugural lecture at the Collège de France, though without attribution to the author. In 1953 Blanchot also wrote a preface to the translation of Karl Jaspers' *Strindberg and Van Gogh*. Foucault had long been an attentive reader of

Jaspers and often mentioned Jaspers' *Psychologie générale* in his first articles. In *Strindberg and Van Gogh*, Jaspers broadly outlined a history of the forms of madness: "It is tempting to speak of a specific affinity between hysteria and the spirit prevailing before the eighteenth century, an affinity that would exist today between schizophrenia and the spirit of our times."[15] In his preface, titled "La Folie par excellence," Blanchot wrote: "What science explains causally is not understood for all that. Understanding seeks what eludes it; it moves powerfully and constantly forward toward the moment when understanding is no longer possible, when the fact, in its absolutely concrete reality, becomes the obscure and the impenetrable."[16] Blanchot is unquestionably one of the fundamental sources for an understanding of Foucault's work in these years.

As for Char's poems, innumerable traces may be found in Foucault's writings, from the very first to the last: as early as his introduction to Binswanger's text in 1953; then in the preface to *Folie et déraison* in 1961. Here Foucault declared: "The only rule and method I have kept is one contained in a text by Char, where the most urgent and restrained definition of truth may also be read: 'I shall take from things the illusion they produce to preserve themselves from us and leave them the part they concede to us.'"[17] The preface also ends with a quotation from Char, though without attribution: "Pathetic companions who scarcely murmur, go with your light extinguished and return the jewels. A new mystery sings in your bones. Develop your legitimate strangeness."[18] René Char was quoted again in 1984 on the cover of Foucault's last books, *L'Usage des plaisirs* and *Le Souci de soi* (*The Care of the Self*). Paul Veyne said that Foucault knew some of Char's poems by heart at the beginning of the 1950s and was always quoting "Le Requin et la Mouette." A few years later, in Sweden, Foucault would ask visiting students and friends to recite poems by Char to gain admission to his premises.

Oddly, however, Foucault, who knew or intersected with so many people later, never met his idols. Bataille died shortly after Foucault's return to France. And he never had any connection with either Blanchot or Char. In his *Michel Foucault tel que je l'imagine*, published after the philosopher's death, Blanchot said that they spoke together only once. "I never had any personal relationship with Michel Foucault. I never met him, except once in the courtyard of the Sorbonne during the events of May 1968, perhaps in June or July (although people tell me he wasn't there), where I said a few words to him, but he was unaware of who was speaking to him." [19] Blanchot reviewed *Histoire de la folie* in the *NRF* when it was published and, two years later, *Raymond Roussel*. Foucault analyzed Blanchot's work in a long article in 1966, "La Pensée du dehors." Their only dialogue, then, occurred through articles and books. "We missed each other," said Blanchot. [20] But, deep down, was that perhaps what they wanted?

Nor did Foucault ever meet René Char. He never even telephoned him, said Paul Veyne, who was close to both. Veyne and Foucault, one day in 1980, "plotted" to get Char into the Collège de France. The plot did not go very far, because they almost immediately realized that the poet had passed the age of retirement. René Char, for his part, had great respect for the philosopher and admired his *Histoire de la folie*. He even dedicated one of his last poems "to Michel Foucault" when the latter died. But this poem, "Demi-jour en Creuse," had not been written for Foucault. It is dated June 21, 1984, four days before his death. Char simply offered the original manuscript to Veyne, who lived close by in the countryside in the south of France. It was a present to console him for his pain on the death of his friend. But when Paul Veyne read:

> A pair of foxes overturns the snow
> Trampling the edge of their nuptial earth;
> At night harsh love reveals a bitter thirst
> On every side in drops of blood.

he was moved to tears and told the poet: "We used to call Foucault 'le Fuchs.'" Char then added the dedication, and the poem was read at Foucault's funeral in Vandeuvre-du-Poitou. There was no close connection between Char and Foucault other than this postmortem coincidence, contrary to already well-entrenched legend. "I would find it pleasant to believe [in such a connection]," Paul Veyne says, in a work now in preparation on René Char. But "it is only fair to cut it short." [21]

6

Discords of Love

In the early 1950s the University of Lille had only three or four phi-losophy professors. French universities were not yet staffed as they would be fifteen or twenty years later. But since none of these three had a taste for psychology or wanted to teach it, Raymond Polin, Olivier Lacombe, and Yvon Belaval decided to recruit someone who would take it on, and take it off their backs. They specified their ideal candidate: a philosopher interested in psychology rather than a clinical psychologist. One day in Paris Polin mentioned the problem to one of his colleagues, Jules Vuillemin, who suggested Foucault. Vuillemin, who would play an important role in Foucault's career, was a friend of Louis Althusser's and taught at the Rue d'Ulm, where he had met Foucault. He also gave courses at the other *école normale supérieure* for boys, at Saint-Cloud, where he had met Polin, who taught there as well. Polin, already favorably disposed, contacted Foucault and met with him. When Foucault explained that he was preparing a thesis on "the philosophy of psychology," the professor was delighted.

Foucault was therefore appointed an assistant in psychology at the University of Lille and assumed the post in October 1952. But he never lived in the city. Like the full professors, he scheduled all his classes on two or three days and made the trip each week, staying in a little hotel near the train station.

The university occupied a huge gray stone building in the center of the city, on Rue Auguste-Angelier, behind the Palais des Beaux-Arts. The facade was decorated with a pediment and the entrance hall opened onto two rows of columns. It was an imposing, pompous, and sinister place. And there Foucault taught psychology and its history. He explained the theories, covered all the authors, discussed psycho-pathology as well as Gestalt theory and Rorschach tests. His students were somewhat disconcerted when he lectured on a fairy tale by way of introduction to psychoanalysis. But next he lectured on Freud at great length and recommended that his audience read *Five Psychoanalyses*. Then he devoted equal time to "existential psychiatry" and the work of Kuhn and Binswanger. He concluded the year by talking about the Soviet physiologists working in the Pavlovian tradition. "What I heard was very clearly Marxist in orientation," says Gilles Deleuze, who attended one of Foucault's courses entirely by chance. Deleuze was teaching at the lycée in Amiens and had come to visit his friend Jean-Pierre Bamberger in Lille; it was Bamberger who took him to hear Foucault. That was their first meeting: Bamberger invited them both to dinner at his home. The evening was not a huge success—Deleuze and Foucault did not click. And it would be several years before their paths crossed again.

Foucault had a free hand in teaching. Polin merely asked him at the beginning of the year what subjects he intended to cover and then allowed him full scope to see his program through. This worked best. Relations were apparently somewhat strained between the section professors and their lecturer in psychology. Nonetheless, Foucault's teaching was effective enough to earn him the official appreciation of the dean in April 1954: "Young, extremely dynamic lecturer. Organized the teaching of scientific psychology in a talented manner. Truly deserves promotion." He was indeed young for a lecturer—only twenty-six when he was appointed, and he would be only twenty-nine when he left to go to Sweden.

In Lille Foucault rediscovered several friends from his years at the Rue d'Ulm. Michel Simon, a philosopher of the class of 1947, had an appointment at the Lycée Faidherbe in Lille; Jean-Paul Aron taught at the Tourcoing lycée. In 1954 Marcel Neveux, who had been a *khâgne* student with Foucault at the Lycée Henri-IV, also got a job at the Lycée Faidherbe. These youngsters developed a habit of having lunch together, when they discussed politics at length—Neveux and Simon were members of the Communist party—but also literature. Simon liked Stendhal; Foucault and Aron preferred Balzac. All three remember Foucault loudly defending another author, Jacques Chardonne. "*Claire* is a masterpiece," he told his friends again and again.

At the end of this sojourn in Lille, from October 1952 to June 1955, Foucault began to talk a lot about Nietzsche and the book he wanted to devote to his new philosophical passion. But before being smitten by Nietzsche, his interests centered essentially on psychology.

Foucault the psychologist? Foucault the philosopher of psychology? The list he handed in as proof of what he had worked on during the 1952–53 school year—work in progress, work accomplished, and work projected—shows his perspective clearly. The following list, in Foucault's hand, is in the archives at the University of Lille:

WORK FOR THE YEAR 52–53:
1. *Maladie mentale et personnalité.* Work completed (in press, [Presses Universitaires Françaises]).
2. "Eléments pour une histoire de la psychologie," Article for new edition of *Histoire de la philosophie* by A. Weber. Completed. In press.
3. *Psychiatrie et analyse existentielle* (secondary thesis). Work completed (in press, Desclée).
4. Translation of *Gestaltkreis* [Cycle of structure] by von Weizsäcker. For July publication.
5. Introduction to *Traum und Existenz* [Binswanger]. Study that should come out in July at Desclée.

The two undated sheets containing this list appear to have been written at the end of the 1952–53 school year, that is, in May or June 1953, or, at the latest, when school opened in the fall, that is, September or October of the same year. The publication dates indicated, however, were not the actual ones: *Maladie mentale et personnalité* was published in 1954, as was Binswanger's *Le rêve et l'existence* with Foucault's "Introduction." But the translation of von Weizsäcker's *Gestaltkreis*, titled *Cycle de la structure*, and the article on the history of psychology did not come out until 1957. The third item on the list was never published, and no one has ever heard of this "secondary thesis," despite Foucault's notation that it was "in press." In his introduction to Binswanger Foucault indeed mentioned "another work" that would "try to situate existential analysis within the development of contemporary reflection on men,"[1] but this "sequel" never saw the light of day. Moreover, he did not defend his secondary thesis until 1961, when he had completed the principal thesis, *Folie et déraison;* and it focused not on psychology and psychiatry, but on Kant's *Anthropology.* Clearly, one must take this list with several grains of salt. Foucault may have counted the introduction to Binswanger twice to lengthen the list artificially, and this text is indeed a general study on the theme "psychiatry and existential analysis," written "in the margins of *Dream and Existence.*"[2]

Even minus one of the works listed at Lille as completed, the number of texts written in such a short time is still impressive and demonstrates Foucault's enormous capacity for work. He read, he wrote, he taught. In this respect he would change little.

Moreover, other ideas for books, besides the one for the work on Nietzsche, would soon arise. And when he left for Sweden he took with him two other projects. Jacqueline Verdeaux had taken the young philosopher to visit Colette Duhamel, who worked at the Table Ronde press, and Duhamel commissioned him—them?—to do two small projects. One was supposed to focus on the history of death, the other on the history of madness.

At the end of July 1951, at the Abbaye de Royaumont, converted several years before into a cultural center, a ten-day musical festival was held. One evening a young composer, Pierre Boulez, was among the participants. When he sat down at the piano and played a Mozart sonata, the audience was much impressed. Boulez was already highly regarded in musical circles in Paris. Foucault and Jean-Paul Aron were present, having come with Louis Althusser and several students from the Ecole Normale. Once they had passed their written exams, Althusser was in the habit of taking his students to this ideal spot for working, to give them the best possible conditions in which to prepare the oral for their *agrégation.* Foucault was there in the summer of 1951, preparing his final exams for the second time. Aron had also flunked, and although he was not enrolled at the ENS, he was admitted to the group because of his friendship with Foucault. He tells of this first meeting between Boulez and Foucault in *Les Modernes:*

> There was a young man with a lot of people around him who was discussing literature in a fierce tone of voice. He spoke particularly of Gide, who had died the preceding year, and insulted him. I asked who this bad-tempered young man was—sharp as a knife, sure as a prophet, and bad-mannered to boot. I was told his name was Boulez and that he was famous in his own milieu; that, still in the cradle, he had published a *Livre pour quatuor* and two piano sonatas, that [Olivier] Messiaen said he was the best of the best. It is true that in the explosion of the Paris school that, after 1945, claimed succession from Vienna and drew off toward France the lifeblood of European music, [Karlheinz] Stockhausen and [Iannis] Xenakis among others, Boulez, at twenty-seven, had good reason to feel he was among the chosen . . . As is natural in a period of questioning, he invoked new guides: Char and Mallarmé. Soon he dedicated two major scores to

them: in 1955 *Le Marteau sans maître*, on an old poem by Char; and in 1960 *Pli selon pli*, on Mallarmé's famous poem. This contact had major repercussions on Foucault's itinerary. He always had a soft spot for music. He got at it through words. Boulez was his mediator before he became friends with Jean Barraqué, who died prematurely, and with Michel Fano, Gilbert Amy, members of Boulez's band, which later fell apart because of the vicissitudes of the musical world.[3]

In fact Aron considerably exaggerates Boulez's role in Foucault's formation; no doubt his agenda, inspired more by rancor than by concern for the truth, required it. Boulez was not connected with Foucault until the end of the 1970s, almost thirty years later, and even then it was never a close relationship. Foucault was behind Boulez's election to the Collège de France in 1975, but when Foucault called him with this proposal they had not seen each other for twenty years. And it was Le Roy Ladurie who wrote the official report for his candidacy. In 1978 Boulez would organize a colloquium in which Barthes, Deleuze, and Foucault participated. And in 1983 Boulez and Foucault would publish a dialogue on music in the Beaubourg museum review.[4] But in the early 1950s they rarely saw each other. Any picture of an old friendship between Boulez and Foucault is pure and simple fiction, even if it constantly turns up everywhere. Moreover, Boulez has never done anything to promote this idea: "We saw each other, we intersected, rather than met," he says today, speaking of that period. He remembers very well the scene at Royaumont that Jean-Paul Aron recounts— but it was almost the only such meeting. He scarcely saw Foucault again, except perhaps through Jean Barraqué, and then rarely, fleetingly. If he read *Le Rêve et l'existence* when it came out, it was because Barraqué lent him his copy. The composer who was of such enormous importance for Foucault was not Boulez, but Barraqué, another of Messiaen's pupils, and one often presented as Boulez's rival early in his career.

Jean Barraqué was born in 1928. When he was twenty he began to attend Messiaen's course on musical analysis at the Paris Conservatory. From 1951 to 1954 he was trained at the Groupe de Recherche sur la Musique Contemporaine alongside Boulez and Yvette Grimaux. In 1952 he completed his Piano Sonata, and apparently during this year he also met Foucault. It seems that at first they were friends; then, little by little, the friendship developed into a tempestuous and passionate relationship between lovers.

From 1952 to 1955 a small circle formed around them that included

Michel Fano and his wife. Foucault would look for them after Messiaen's class—a liturgical event for these young musicians—and they would go out for lunch or dinner together. Their discussions were rarely on serious subjects. They were all jokes, witticisms, laughter, games. "Our life was permanent theater," according to Michel Fano, who also recalls that Foucault was not particularly attracted by this new music they embodied. He preferred Bach. Jacqueline Verdeaux, with whom Foucault regularly attended concerts, also remembers this preference. But the relationshp between the young musician and the young philosopher would make a deep impression on their work. They seemed to have a similar view of the world. Music, for Barraqué, "is tragedy, pathos, death. It is the whole game, the trembling to the point of suicide. If music is not that, if it does not overtake and pass the limits, it is nothing."[5] Foucault gave Barraqué Hermann Broch's *The Death of Virgil* to read. The French translation was published at the beginning of 1955, and Barraqué wrote several compositions inspired by this book: *Le Temps restitué*, a first version of which was completed in 1957; then *Discours*, in 1961, and *Chant après chant* in 1966. Subsequently he began work on a lyric piece, *L'Homme couché*, still on themes by Broch, which was interrupted by his death. Foucault was also the one who gave him the poems by Nietzsche that he inserted in *Séquence* in 1955:

> You stop frozen
> You look behind, how long.
> Are you mad then
> To flee the world . . . before winter?
>
> The world, an open door
> To a thousand silent, cold deserts.
> One who has already lost
> What I lost stops nowhere.
>
> All pale you stop,
> Doomed to wander in midwinter
> Like the smoke in never-ending search of colder skies . . .

The music he was discovering through Barraqué would also deeply influence Foucault. In an interview published in *Ethos* in 1983, he said: "I had a friend who was a composer and who is dead now. Through him I knew all the generation of Boulez. It has been a very important experience for me."[6] When he wrote "à propos de Boulez" in 1982 to celebrate the tenth anniversary of the Fall Festival of Paris, Foucault spoke of Barraqué in every line, even though he was never named. For example, the entire beginning of the article evokes the figure of Barraqué, not that of Boulez as one might think:

> You ask me what it was like to have been privileged by a friendship to see a bit of what was going on in music almost thirty years ago now? I was there only as a passerby bound by affection, a certain turmoil, curiosity, the strange feeling of being present at something I felt almost incapable of being contemporary with . . . I am no more able to talk about music now than then. I know only that because I could see—and usually through someone else's mediation—what was happening with Boulez, I was able to feel myself a foreigner in the world of thought in which I had been trained, to which I belonged, and which, for me, as for many others, was still the obvious one . . . In a period when we were being taught to privilege sense, lived experience, the carnal, originating experience, subjective contents, or social significations, encountering Boulez and music was to see the twentieth century from an unfamiliar angle: that of a long battle about the formal. It was to recognize how in Russia, in Germany, in Austria, in Central Europe, work on formal structures through music, painting, architecture, philosophy, linguistics, and mythology had flown in the face of old problems and overturned ways of thinking.[7]

Music, then, breaking his adherence to the cultural values in which he had until then been comfortable, triggered for Foucault a more general distancing that would permit his escape from the influence of phenomenology and Marxism. This was what he meant when he replied to Paolo Caruso in 1967 that music had played as important a role for him as the reading of Nietzsche. And he mentioned on that occasion, to fill in a bit, that he had given Nietzsche's poems to Jean Barraqué, "one of the most brilliant and least understood musicians of the current generation."[8]

During the two or three years that his relationship with Barraqué lasted, Foucault was immersed in this somewhat exalted climate of artistic innovation, in this stimulating atmosphere of questioning in which personalities began to assert themselves and works began to take shape. But his ties with Barraqué dissolved rather quickly after his departure for Sweden. Foucault was still deeply in love. He wrote almost every day to the musician, who had stayed behind in France. The correspondence, preserved in the Barraqué archives and still unpublished, shows how violent his emotions were. His letters are written in an impassioned style and are superb exercises in the literature of love.

The first letters proclaim his desire not to stay away from Paris. On August 29, 1955, three days after his arrival in Uppsala, he wrote that his only hope was to get far enough along on his thesis that he could return to France. We have only one life, he said in substance, and perhaps it is the same one. We have twice as little right to lose it, twice as little right to waste it. A few days later he wrote again to Barraqué to tell him that, if he wanted, he could return to France for good in May.

In December 1955 and January 1956 Foucault spent his winter vacation in France. Part of the time was spent with his parents in Poitiers, and then he returned to Paris. But when he saw Barraqué again, things began to go rather badly. A few weeks later, after *Séquence* was performed at the Petit Marigny on March 10 and 11, 1956—a performance that Foucault was very upset about missing—Barraqué wrote to him breaking off their relationship: "I want nothing to do with December any more; I don't want to be the actor or spectator of this debasement. I have come out of that vertigo of madness." And in reply to a letter he had written, Barraqué received this advice from a friend: "You are setting false problems for yourself, or, to be more precise, problems that do not concern you. They are Foucault's problems, not yours. He is a philosopher; you are a musician. Don't let that man destroy you after having destroyed himself. I don't think he is likely to destroy you, because you are strong."

In May 1956 Foucault made one last attempt. He said he was returning to France for the vacation and proposed to Barraqué that they spend the summer together as they had vowed to do. The answer was no. Nonetheless, Barraqué never forgot Foucault. One of the rare photos of the musician shows him ten years later, in 1966, in his Paris apartment. On the shelves of his bookcase there is a newspaper spread out with a large photo of Foucault, published on the occasion of a review of *Les Mots et les choses*. No doubt he retained many memories of things his former friend had said. It is impossible not to hear Foucault's distant voice in Barraqué's statement in an interview in 1969: "Once someone told me something Genet said: 'Genius is rigor in despair.'"[9]

∿

BY THE MIDDLE OF 1955, when he prepared to leave France for several years, Foucault had written two long articles for collective volumes and an "Introduction" to *Le Rêve et l'existence*, and he had published his first book: *Maladie mentale et personnalité*. A rather modest work, it appeared in 1954 in the series Initiation Philosophique, edited by Jean Lacroix at Presses Universitaires de France. In fact it was Louis Althusser, who had a connection with the Catholic Lacroix, who commissioned it. In keeping with the series format, the book was no more than 114 pages long.

"We wanted to demonstrate," Foucault wrote at the beginning, "that mental pathology requires different analytical methods from organic pathology and that it is through a device of language that the same sense can be imputed to 'ills of the body' and to 'ills of the spirit.'"[10] This statement must be taken as criticizing the theories of Kurt Goldstein, who at that time was the inspiration for both Maurice Merleau-Ponty and Georges Canguilhem. Foucault then dwelt at some length on "existential analysis," which he treated with a bit more sympathy, and which, in his view, had caused psychiatry to take a great leap forward. On the other hand, he criticized psychoanalysis rather severely, reproaching it for having "unrealized" the "relations between man and his environment." He then devoted an entire chapter to Pavlov and Pavlovism. This is a truly political marker, for in those days Pavlov symbolized every attempt to construct the "materialist psychological science" demanded by the Communist party. *La Raison. Cahiers de psychopathologie scientifique*, a review founded by Marxist psychologists (with an editorial board headed by Henri Wallon, whose editor-in-chief was Louis le Guillant), was a clear expression of this tendency, directed in large part against psychoanalysis. The table of contents of the first issue, in January 1951, listed the translation of a text by Pavlov, "Psychiatrie et l'enfance," and an article by Sven Follin, "L'Apport de Pavlov à la psychiatrie." The editorial of the first issue, reprinted in *La Nouvelle Critique* in April 1951, was full of praise for the "remarkable work of Pavlov and his successors" and sentences such as this: "Man is a social being, and his social life can never be foreign to what happens to him and particularly to his illness." It then defined "social life" as "the material and ideological realities," that is, "more expensive bread, lower salaries, more certain war."

Foucault's formulations in his book were astonishingly close to those of this editorial. Here, for example, is what he wrote in the chapter "La Psychologie du conflit" after presenting Pavlov's theses: "When conditions in the environment no longer allow the normal dialectics of excitation and inhibition, a defensive inhibition is instituted . . . Illness is one of the forms of defense."[11] This amounts to saying that "it is not because one is ill that one is alienated, but because one is alienated that one is ill." A few pages earlier, mentioning case studies proposed by Kuhn and Binswanger, as if to reinscribe them in a Marxist perspective, he had written: "If illness finds a privileged mode of expression in this network of contradictory forms of conduct, it is not because the elements of contradiction are juxtaposed as a paradoxical nature of the human unconscious; it is simply that man has a contradictory experience of man; the social relations determined by the present economy, in the guise of competition, exploitation, imperialist wars, and class struggle, provide man with an experience of his human environment that is constantly haunted by contradiction." Whence his definition of mental illness as "the result of social contradictions in which man is historically alienated."[12] Whence, also, the necessity for orienting therapies in new directions: one can "suppose that when the day comes that the patient is not subjected to a fate of alienation, it will be possible to envisage the dialectics of the illness within a human personality." And Foucault's conclusion: "There is no healing other than one realized by new relations with the environment . . . True psychology must rid itself of psychologism, if it is true that, like all science, it must have disalienation as its goal."[13]

Here, for the first time, Foucault used the term *archaeology*, in reference to what psychoanalysis called "archaic stages" in the evolution of the individual: "Psychoanalysis believed it was possible to write a child psychology by making an adult pathology . . . Every libidinal stage is a potential pathological structure. Neurosis is a spontaneous archaeology of the libido."[14]

Foucault did not want this book reissued. And in 1962, after *Folie et déraison* was published, he would provide a new version, titled *Maladie mentale et psychologie (Mental Illness and Psychology)*, with an entirely different ending. Pavlov was jettisoned, replaced by a summary of the long work he had written in Sweden, which he had just defended as his doctoral thesis. The second part of the book, previously titled "The Real Conditions of Illness," would become "Madness and Culture." And the chapters of this second part, "The Historical Meaning of Alienation" and "The Psychology of Conflict," became "The Historical Constitution of Mental Illness" and "Madness, a Global Structure."[15] But this new edition was such a mongrel that Foucault also forbade its reissue, and he would try, but without success, to prevent its being translated into English. Foucault completely renounced this book. When he mentioned his "first book" later in interviews, he always meant *Histoire de la folie*, locking the 1954 work and its 1962 version away in the dungeons of history . . . and in library catalogues.

In 1954, when the book appeared, Foucault frequently discussed problems of psychology with Jean Hyppolite, who that year became the director of the Ecole Normale. Hyppolite, like many other philosophers at that time, reflected a great deal on the subject. The theme of alienation that lay at the heart of Foucault's work was in fact one that dominated philosophical discussion. Hyppolite was so fascinated by psychiatry that for an entire year he attended Professor Baruk's consultations at the Charenton asylum. In a lecture in 1955 he stated: "I have been confirmed in my idea that the study of madness—alienation in the deepest sense of the term—was at the center of an anthropology, of a study of man. The asylum is the refuge for those who can no longer be made to live in our interhuman environment. Thus it is a way of understanding this environment indirectly, as well as the problems it constantly poses for normal men." [16] Hyppolite also attended Lacan's seminar, which had begun in 1951 in the psychiatrist's apartment with only a few listeners but had moved in 1953 to Hôpital Sainte-Anne and was therefore open to a wider audience. On two occasions in 1954, Lacan and Hyppolite engaged in public discussion, on Hegelian philosophy and on linguistics. These were important moments for the development of Lacan's theory of maturity. [17] According to Maurice Pinguet, Foucault went "every week" to hear the psychiatrist, who was then not yet famous. But in his interviews with Ducio Trombadori, Foucault seemed to say that he did not attend Lacan's seminars. In fact, on the original tape he says that he did not attend enough to be up to really understanding Lacan, at the moment when he was being asked the question, in 1978. One thing is certain: Foucault knew Lacan's name as early as 1953, read him, and quoted him. None of these facts is surprising, since he frequented Sainte-Anne at that period. And when he published *Folie et déraison* in 1961, he listed Lacan, along with Blanchot, Roussel, and Dumézil, among those who had influenced him.

To give this interest in psychiatry and psychoanalysis some concrete form, Hyppolite attempted to form a team of thinkers that would include both philosophers and psychologists. A meeting for that purpose was held at the Ecole Normale on February 5, 1955. Yvon Brès recalled the date because it was the day the Mendès France government fell. In attendance were André Ombredane, Robert Francès, and Foucault.

But Foucault was on the verge of leaving France. He did not know it yet, perhaps, but he was about to carry out the program he had set for psychology in his article for the collective work *Des chercheurs français s'interrogent*, written at the same time as *Maladie mentale et personnalité* but with an entirely different tone. To counter positivist psychology, which claimed to have attained scientific status because it had prolif-

erated tests and investigative methods, he recalled that this technologi-
cal refinement was, on the contrary, only "the sign that it has forgotten
man's negativity," that is, the analysis of the contradictions that had
been its point of departure and its "country of origin." It had forgotten
that "if mental pathology has always been and still remains one of the
sources of psychological experience, it is not because illness reveals
hidden structures . . . in other words, it is not because man more easily
recognizes here the face of his truth, but, on the contrary, because he
discovers here the dark side of this truth and the absolute fact of its
contradiction. Illness is the *psychological truth* of health, to the very extent that it is its *human contradiction*." [18] This psychological science, so
forgetful of its origins, must be made to recall its "eternally infernal"
vocation. Foucault concluded: "Psychology will be saved only by a return to hell." [19]

7

Uppsala, Warsaw, Hamburg

And when did *you* get your baccalaureate?" Georges Dumézil asked, in a parody of the medieval ritual of title display. Then, having determined that his diploma was appreciably earlier (by more than thirty years) than that of his interlocutor, he said to the younger man: "I propose we call each other 'tu.'" Michel Foucault raised his glass of schnapps (there wasn't any mead): "Tack ska du ha," "Thanks be unto you." He was twenty-nine, and Dumézil, the great specialist in Indo-European mythology, was almost sixty. But in Sweden the familiar form is used among members of the university, whatever the speaker's age or rank. The "elder" must simply take the initiative.

This scene took place in Uppsala, seventy kilometers north of Stockholm, in the spring of 1956. It was the first meeting between the well-known scholar, a professor at the Collège de France, and the future philosopher of *Histoire de la folie*. However, it had been Dumézil's intervention, before they even knew each other, that brought Foucault to the little Swedish university city at the end of August. In fact, this trip had its origins back in 1934. In 1934 Foucault was barely eight years old, but Dumézil had just published his third book, *Ouranos-Varuna*. Sylvain Lévi had invited him to present his work at the Institute of Indian Civilization, where discussions were held every Thursday. Eminent academics in history, philology, and linguistics were present, among them Jules Bloch, Marcel Granet, and Emile Benveniste. Benveniste at the time was very hostile to Dumézil's theses, and in fact Dumézil himself renounced them several years later. The debate took a rather lively turn during this confrontation. At the end, when the students left the room, Raoul Curiel, who would become a highly regarded archaeologist, stopped to chat with Dumézil about several of the points figuring in the afternoon's dispute. Since both were Freemasons, they "recognized" each other quickly and went on to form a close, long-lasting friendship.

Dumézil had returned from a long period abroad. He had lived for six years in Turkey and two in Sweden, where from 1931 to 1933 he had served as French instructor at the University of Uppsala. He kept in touch with his friends from the Great North, and after the Second World War he returned frequently to Sweden, where his work had made a spectacular breakthrough. Consequently, it is not surprising that twenty years after Dumézil's first stay in Uppsala, Paul Falk, who directed the Romance Language Institute, wrote to him asking if he knew anyone who might be good for the job of French instructor. This was 1954, and Dumézil was puzzled. He did not know any of the new generation of students at the Ecole Normale, and he was on the verge of replying when Raoul Curiel mentioned a young philosopher he had just met. "He is the most intelligent person I know," he told Dumézil—who, trusting him, wrote to Falk that he had turned up the man for the spot. And he wrote a note to Foucault: don't ask me how I know your name, was the gist of the message. Let me just tell you that there is a position awaiting you in Sweden if you want it. They did not have a chance to meet, because Dumézil went off "on the prowl," as he liked to put it, in Wales. But things were settled, and Foucault went to take up his appointment on August 26, 1955.

"I have suffered and I still suffer from a lot of things in French social and cultural life. That was why I left France in 1955," he would say much later to explain his departure. He added: "At this time Sweden was supposed to be a much freer country. And there I had the experience that certain kinds of freedom may have, not exactly the same effects, but as many restrictive effects as a directly restrictive society."[1] And in fact, although he had wanted to get far away from France to escape the malaise, the pain of existence, he was suffering, his three years in Uppsala were rather hard on him. A chief reason was the climate. He had great difficulty adjusting to the glacial cold of Scandinavian winters: "I am the twentieth-century Descartes," he told his freeze-mates, "I'm going to die here. Luckily, there's no Queen Christina to top it all off." Then, there was the nightfall at three in the afternoon in November and at two in December. The phenomenon was deeply disorienting to anyone not accustomed to it, provoking a persistent gloom. Third, although the University of Uppsala was one of the most prestigious universities in northern Europe, its atmosphere was disastrously small-town, like the city itself: 70,000 residents and

6,000 or 7,000 students. The atmosphere was extremely rigid, even stuffy; Lutheran puritanism weighed heavily. Shortly after he arrived there, Foucault wrote Jean Barraqué: "Life in Uppsala is painfully like university life." If he had dreamed of finding an open-mindedness that did not yet exist in France, he must have been quickly disillusioned. Homosexuality was no more accepted in Uppsala than in Paris, perhaps even less. Foucault felt ill, but he stayed.

A few months after his arrival he met one of the very great scholars, Georges Dumézil. Every year since 1947, Dumézil had returned to Sweden to work for two or three months after completing his lectures at the Collège de France. The university put a small apartment at his disposal. Foucault saw him very often and at great length during his three years in Uppsala, and thereafter a close friendship, complicity even, existed between them. Foucault, already a profound admirer of Dumézil's work, developed an equally great admiration for the man. He became something of a model for Foucault: a model of rigor and patience in his work; a model as well in the diversity of his interests and his meticulous attention to archives. Dumézil was undoubtedly of major importance in the development of Foucault's thought, and Foucault never kept his debt a secret. In the preface to *Folie et déraison* he wrote: "In this somewhat solitary task, all those who helped me deserve my gratitude. And M. Georges Dumézil above all, without whom this work would not have been undertaken."[2] This could be taken simply as an appropriate acknowledgment, because Dumézil was the one Foucault had to thank for the conditions allowing completion of this book. But after the book was published he spoke again of his profound intellectual debt in an interview in *Le Monde* on July 22, 1961. In reply to a question about who had influenced him, he mentioned Blanchot, Roussel, and Lacan and then added: "But also, and principally, Dumézil." His interviewer was astonished: "How could a historian of religions have been able to inspire work on the history of madness?" And Foucault explained: "By his idea of structure. I tried to discover, as Dumézil did for myths, structured norms of experience the scheme of which could be found with modifications on different levels."[3] Foucault would acknowledge his debt even more forcefully, in his inaugural lecture at the Collège de France: "I believe I owe a great deal to M. Dumézil, since he is the one who urged me to work at an age when I still thought that writing was a pleasure. But I also owe a great deal to his work . . . He is the one who taught me to analyze the internal economy of a discourse in a manner that was entirely different from the methods of traditional exegesis or those of linguistic formalism. It was he who taught me how to describe the transformations of a discourse and its relations to an institution."[4]

A strong intellectual influence, therefore, but also an indestructible friendship that would last for almost thirty years, "cloudless and untorn," as Dumézil would say, interrupted only by the philosopher's death. This friendship would play a crucial part in Foucault's university career, particularly his election to the Collège de France.

The two men first met on the premises of the Maison de France in Uppsala. Foucault, the French instructor, was also responsible for running this small but venerable cultural institute. It had the same function as its counterparts elsewhere: to make the French language and culture known through lectures, discussions, and recreational activities. In Uppsala the Maison de France was completely contained in an apartment on the fifth floor of a nineteenth-century bourgeois apartment building, at 22 St. Johannesgatan, a patrician street. It was a stone's throw from the Fyrisån River, which divides the town in two: on one bank the university section, and on the other the residential section. The building's facade was in red stone at ground level, in pink stone for the floors above. A lion surmounted the entrance portal. The fifth-floor apartment was divided in half: several public rooms—a library, a record collection, and a meeting hall—constituted the Maison de France proper; and two "private" rooms were reserved for the director's use. Here Foucault lived throughout his stay in Sweden.

Despite the dreariness of the town—a tiny Nordic Cambridge—Foucault gradually settled into his new life and established as agreeable an existence as was possible. Early on he had met a young French biologist, Jean-François Miquel, who had arrived at the same time. They shortly decided to take all their meals together. And soon there was a third thief to join them: Jacques Papet-Lépine, a physicist studying storms and lightning, who was writing a thesis with the superb title: *Contribution mathématique à une théorie du coup de foudre* (but *coup de foudre* means more commonly falling love!). They took turns cooking on St. Johannesgatan. Often they were joined by the Italian instructor, Costanza Pasquali, whom they called "Mimi," and by Peter Fyson, the English instructor, a specialist in European poetry and a great opera lover. This little crowd took itself twice a week to the Forum, a restaurant that they particularly liked. One day Maurice Chevalier joined them there at their invitation. Foucault and Miquel had been to hear the singer give a recital in Stockholm. After the show they went to speak to him in his dressing room, and the next thing they knew, they were sitting down to dinner with him. To return his hospitality, Foucault and Miquel invited the star to Uppsala, where they showed him around the town and took him to dinner at the Forum.

There too they celebrated the comings and goings of their spiritual master, Dumézil, once he had made an appearance in their little universe. It turned into a real communal life, and, for the first time, Foucault accepted it. He did more than that; he created it around himself. For he was certainly the center of this circle of friends. The Maison de France quickly became a convivial place where they all met after work or over the weekend.

Two new people joined them soon after this group became established, making a thundering entrance into the communal life, spreading a wind of joyful disorder. Foucault could not have been happier, so delighted was he with their presence. The first was a young Swedish student whose father worked at the Swedish embassy in Paris. Educated at the Lycée Janson-de-Sailly, he had come to Uppsala to study law and intended to join the diplomatic corps. Which he in fact did, becoming an eminence in Swedish foreign policy, particularly as ambassador to Hanoi at the height of the war in Vietnam. Today Jean-Christophe Oberg is ambassador to Poland. At the time, however, the eighteen-year-old became Foucault's secretary at the Maison de France. The following year he brought a French friend, a young woman named Dani, whom Foucault immediately adopted and adored. Oberg let her gradually take his place as secretary at the Maison de France. Foucault had a wonderful time with them. One day he and Oberg went to Stockholm to buy a car. They returned with a magnificent beige Jaguar, which dumbfounded polite society in Uppsala. People were accustomed to more austerity and were especially taken aback to see an instructor—the bottom rung in a very strict university hierarchy—make such a display of wealth. But in fact Foucault had plenty of money (his family continued to support him), and he was by no means the ascetic monk people often portrayed him as later. He ate with gusto in restaurants, he liked to drink, and his friends from this period describe some of the memorable times he was "plastered," such as the day when, as he stood up to propose a toast at the end of dinner, he fell on the floor, dead drunk. He was known to disguise himself as a chauffeur and take Dani to run errands in town. His Jaguar became legendary among all the Uppsalans who knew him. Everyone describes him as driving like a madman. Dumézil remembered finding themselves in the ditch once.

They all remembered numerous incidents of this sort, accidents that luckily were never really serious, despite all that snow and ice.

But for Foucault Uppsala was, above all, work. His professional activities divided into three categories. First, he had to perform his job as instructor in French, which he did marvelously well. Dumézil was much impressed by his success. Foucault's public lectures, given at six every Thursday evening, drew a large and enthusiastic audience in the large central building of the university. The entire cultivated society of the town crowded in, and it was said that the ladies all brought their marriageable daughters along. The series was quite unorthodox the first year: Foucault discussed "the concept of love in French literature from the marquis de Sade to Jean Genet." One can imagine the stir this created in the university community. The following years Foucault turned to less daring themes: "contemporary French theater" and finally, in 1957–58, "religious experience in French literature from Chateaubriand to Bernanos," even though the latter could also set a few teeth on edge in a strictly Protestant country.[5]

Foucault taught six hours a week (with an additional four hours of "conversation"). Three hours were intended for beginners and students from all disciplines who wanted an introduction to French. Three hours were devoted to literature. Of these three, one was the famous public lecture. The two remaining hours were devoted to seminars intended solely for students who were specializing in French. In 1956 these seminars focused on "French theater of the seventeenth century," and specifically on Racine and *Andromaque*—no doubt this is where the pages in *Histoire de la folie* dealing with Orestes' insanity came from—or on "contemporary theater." But whereas the public lectures drew audiences of a hundred or more, and the president of the Alliance Française spoke of the "intellectual joy" she derived from them, the courses for students drew far fewer, and very few of those understood anything of what this combination French instructor/philosopher was saying. The teachers may have appreciated their young colleague, but some of his students experienced Foucault's teaching as a long hermetic discourse. Imagine eighteen- or twenty-year-olds with only a rudimentary knowledge of French being dealt dizzying interpretations of Sade's work or of madness in Racine! A few students from this period still sound angry when they talk about those lectures: "It was enough to turn you off French"; "Going to class was really painful." Others are still reeling from the encounter in a very different way and speak of Foucault with tremendous admiration. But the class size for these courses and seminars became considerably reduced as the year went by, because the students were so put off. Foucault's colleagues felt embarrassed, but there was not much they could do. Foucault himself was somewhat bothered by it and annoyed. But that did not prompt him to switch methods. In fact, he was interested only in the rare student who could follow him. He had his usual store of sarcasm for all the rest.

But Foucault's activity was not limited to teaching. He was also supposed to enliven the Maison de France. When he arrived in Uppsala, Foucault outlined his program to a reporter from the local newspaper *Uppsala Nya Tidning* (his first interview!), and in February 1956 he laid out his projects at greater length in a report submitted to the embassy. Whereas only a few students had come to the Maison de France at the beginning of the semester, thirty to thirty-five now came regularly. But this number still seemed small to him, in relation to the total number of students, and therefore he suggested: (1) increasing student interest in the Maison de France by having more recreational sessions (film showings, recitals of recorded music), which meant asking the French foreign ministry for material (records, books, record player); (2) setting up a sort of club for the students: a room had been turned into a study room and subscriptions to papers and reviews had been increased. The Maison de France would be open several nights a week, and, as much as possible, Swedish students would be invited to discussions in French after lectures and recreational events; and (3) developing the library. In Foucault's view, the Maison de France ought to reach an audience in Uppsala broader than that of the university's Romance Language Institute. Although it might be true, he said, that French culture had lost its influence in scientific circles or in non-philosophical disciplines, this fact was perhaps not beyond remedy. Hence he proposed to start classes in elementary French at the Maison de France for students or young research scholars, whatever their speciality, who might need French for their work or travels.

It is clear that Foucault was far from indifferent about his administrative or managerial functions. He was even less indifferent about his functions as leader. He organized evening gatherings in this House of France that he wanted to turn into one of the cultural poles of Uppsala's existence. He showed films and commented on them. Dumézil liked to tell about a brilliant improvisation Foucault did on a film adaptation of Sartre's *Mains sales*. At four in the afternoon, Foucault still did not know what film he was going to get. Yet that evening he carried off a brilliant discussion of it before a captivated audience. Then there was theater—not theater for analyzing, but a theater of acting. With Oberg he organized a small troupe who publicly performed plays—in French, of course: Eugène Labiche's *La Grammaire*, Jean Giraudoux's *Cantique des Cantiques*, Alfred de Musset's *Les Caprices de Marianne*, and Jean Anouilh's *Le Bal des voleurs*. Foucault directed; Oberg and a few other students acted. The plays were first presented in Uppsala; then they "toured" Stockholm and Sundvall. On these tours Foucault carried the bags and took care of costumes. There were many trips to Stockholm anyway because Foucault also lectured frequently at the French Cultural Institute in the capital. He went by car or, when there were too many in the group accompanying him, by train. He nicknamed the train the "soûlographe" (the old boozy), which was how they were when they arrived. Erik Nilsson, one of Foucault's close friends at the time, recalls: "We never stopped laughing." Nilsson was doing his military service in Uppsala and had gone to the Maison de France to borrow books. The group quickly adopted him, and he participated often in the theatrical events. Foucault took a great liking to the young man and a few years later dedicated *Folie et déraison* to him.

Foucault was supposed to receive speakers invited to Uppsala by the French embassy. It was his pleasure to welcome his former professor, Jean Hyppolite, and some writers who would become famous such as Marguerite Duras and Claude Simon; or politicians such as Pierre Mendès France. He was also obliged to receive Albert Camus, who was awarded the Nobel Prize in literature in 1957. The laureate's traditional lecture in Uppsala took place in a somewhat strained atmosphere: two days before, in Stockholm, an Algerian had reproached Camus for his silence concerning colonialism. Then came the famous reply: "I have always condemned terror, I must also condemn a terrorism that is blindly practiced on the streets of Algiers, for example, one that might strike my mother or my family. I believe in justice, but I will defend my mother before I will defend justice."[6] In Uppsala things went better, because the students did not ask any political questions. But the incident in Stockholm was on everybody's mind. And Oberg was very surprised that Foucault did not voice any reservations about Camus's remarks or bring the matter up during the reception at the Maison de France: the Foucault he had known up to this point was resolutely anticolonialist and agreed more with Mendès France. But perhaps the director of the Maison de France was supposed to remain neutral, forbidding himself to let his real feelings show.

There were also two visits from Roland Barthes, at Foucault's invitation. They had met at the end of 1955, when Foucault returned to Paris for Christmas vacation. Robert Mauzi, a former fellow student at the Rue d'Ulm and still a friend, had introduced them. Barthes had not yet published much: only *Le Degré zéro de l'écriture* in 1953. At the time Foucault himself had only one book to his name, *Maladie mentale et personnalité*.

An immediate friendship mixed with reserve developed between Barthes and Foucault. They dined frequently in the restaurants of the Latin Quarter; they went to nightclubs on the Boulevard Saint-Germain whenever Foucault was in Paris. But from the beginning the friendship was poisoned by a certain intellectual and personal rivalry that would make their relations difficult. The two men had very different natures, and there were many points of friction, so that over the years there were more disagreements than reconciliations. All the same, Foucault helped Barthes be elected to the Collège de France in 1975, more perhaps out of faithfulness to an old friendship than through a real admiration for his work, according to those who knew both. Foucault himself delivered the speech in praise of the applicant, even though it seems he was not behind Barthes's candidacy. Pierre Nora remembered Foucault saying to him one day: "I'm very annoyed; I have to see Barthes, who wants to be a candidate for the Collège de France. I haven't seen him for a long time. Could you come with me?" Everything went well, and Nora left them alone after ten minutes. Foucault wrote two reports presenting Barthes to his colleagues. At the end of one he tried to respond to criticisms arising in the Collège de France that the candidate was too "fashionable": "his audience can, indeed, be thought of as being, as one says, in fashion. But what historian could be made to believe that a fashion, an enthusiasm, a passion, even exaggerations, do not betray, in any given moment, the existence of a fertile center in a culture? Those voices, those few voices somewhat outside the university, that we hear and are currently listening to—do you believe that they are not part of our history today, and that they do not have to become part of our histories?"[7] Foucault's voice was heard, and Barthes was elected. After this important episode a calmer and unshadowed friendship developed. But it was brief. Barthes was struck by a van on Rue des Ecoles on March 26, 1980. Foucault delivered the traditional eulogy at the Collège de France before the assembled professors, one Sunday in April 1980. "A few years ago," he said,

> when I proposed that you welcome him among you, the originality and importance of a work pursued for more than twenty years with acknowledged brilliance permitted me not to resort to my friendship for him in support of my request. I did not have to leave it out, for the work was there. But from now on there is only the work. It will continue to speak; others will make it speak and will speak about it. So,

this afternoon, allow me to bring to light friendship alone. Friendship that should, at least, be like the death it detests in not talking too much. You knew him when you elected him. You knew that you chose the rare balance of intelligence and creation. You chose, knowingly, someone who had the paradoxical power of understanding things as they are and of inventing them with amazing freshness. You consciously chose a great writer and an astonishing professor, whose teaching, for those who took his courses, was not a lesson but an experience . . . Destiny decreed that the stupid violence of things—the only reality he was capable of hating—put an end to all that, right at the very doorstep to this House where I had asked you to admit him. The bitterness would be unbearable if I did not know how happy he was to be here, and if I did not feel I had the right to bring, from him to you, across our sorrow, a faintly smiling sign of friendship.[8]

FOUCAULT TOOK HIS OFFICIAL FUNCTIONS in Uppsala very seriously. Indeed, he wore himself out performing them. In his report to the minister of foreign affairs, Inspector General Santelli wrote on January 26, 1956: "It is very hard work, which he performs conscientiously and with a dedication that is obvious in his appearance. He does not look well, and I have the impression that M. Foucault is overworking himself and not taking the necessary rest." A year later M. Gouyon, the cultural adviser, sent the following assessment: "M. Foucault has very brilliantly made his influence felt, both in Uppsala and in Stockholm, where the Institute and the School of Civics argue over his extremely brilliant lectures. But there is some reason to fear that, a victim of his success and his constant availability, he might literally kill himself on the job. The creation of a position at the Institute (whether Foucault takes this appointment and is relieved of his functions in Uppsala or the future appointee, on the contrary, relieves him of his work in Stockholm) is an absolute necessity for him" (May 6, 1957). And on March 25, 1958, the cultural adviser M. Cheval sent this report on the director of the Maison de France in Uppsala: "M. Foucault is a very brilliant representative of French culture abroad. He is a magnificent success at Uppsala, where he has been able to gain the confidence of both professors and students. He is indispensable in this position, and one wonders who could replace him if (and this seems, alas, predictable) he ends by tiring of the Nordic climate. In any event, M. Foucault is one of the very few to whom one could entrust a more important foreign post and have no apprehensions."

But for Foucault the most important time he spent in Uppsala was the time spent in writing his thesis. It was there that he started *Folie et déraison*, and when he left in 1958 the manuscript was almost complete, according to the reports of several of his friends. With *Maladie mentale et personnalité*, Foucault had wanted to define what alienation represented in contemporary psychiatric thought and to propose a critique of medical and psychological theories in the light of a Marxism tinged with Binswanger's thought. During this period, as we have seen, he worked in psychiatric hospitals. A number of doctors suggested that he write a history of their discipline, but he was more interested in madmen than in psychiatrists. Specifically, he was interested in the relationship between doctors and patients—that is, in the relationship between reason and what it talked about: madness. Then there was the commission from Colette Duhamel to do a work on the history of madness. So everything came together, and the treasure that existed in the great library at Uppsala, the Carolina Rediviva, caught his attention. A real treasure! In 1950 a Dr. Erik Waller had presented the library with a collection of 21,000 documents—letters, manuscripts, rare books, bits of scrawl—from the sixteenth century to the beginning of the twentieth. Above all there was Waller's considerable collection on the history of medicine—almost everything of importance that had been published before 1800 and a good portion of what had been published after. The catalogue of this "Bibliotheca Walleriana" was published in 1955. A stroke of luck. When Foucault discovered this veritable mine, he began exploring it systematically and using its material for his thesis. Every day at ten, after having worked for an hour with one of his secretaries, Jean-Christophe or Dani, he left for the Carolina. He remained in the library until three or four in the afternoon, writing pages and pages, and at night he kept right on writing. Always to music. Not an evening went by that he did not listen to the *Goldberg Variations*. Music for him meant Bach or Mozart. He wrote and rewrote, copying his pages out neatly, endlessly reworking them: on the left a pile of papers to do over, on the right the growing pile of revised pages.

As the book began to take shape, Foucault considered defending his thesis in Sweden. He hoped to find there a more understanding group of examiners than the ones he dreaded facing in the French university system. At the Carolina he had met Stirn Lindroth, who held the chair in the history of ideas and science at the University of Uppsala. They shared certain interests: Lindroth had worked on medicine and philosophy in the Renaissance, on Paracelsus. They chatted, and Lindroth invited Foucault to dinner. Foucault asked him to read what he was writing and brought him a few chapters, an enormous stack of hand-written pages on very thin paper. But Lindroth was a dyed-in-the-wool positivist and not particularly open to grand speculation; he was simply frightened by the style and content of the pages he had been given. All he saw there was a "convoluted" literature, and he did not imagine for a moment that this book, bits of which he had just read, could be presented to obtain a doctorate. He wrote Foucault to inform him of his impressions—extremely unfavorable. Foucault tried to explain and to clarify the project, but to no effect. Here are the few explanations he offered in a letter dated August 10, 1957:

> Your letter has been very useful in making me aware of the flaws in my work, and I am very grateful to you for this. My first mistake, I should tell you right away, was in not having warned you sufficiently that this was not a "fragment of a book" but only rough work, a first draft that I intend to work on again in the future, in any event. I willingly concede that the style is unbearable (one of my flaws is not being naturally clear). Of course, I intend to get rid of all the "convoluted" expressions that managed to escape me. I submitted this attempt to you, in spite of its style, to have your opinion, which I value highly, on the quality of the information and the principal ideas. It is clear that this latter point caused difficulties. There too, I was wrong in not defining my project, which is not to write a history of the developments of psychiatric *science*, but rather a history of the *social, moral, and imaginary* context in which it developed. Because it seems to me that up until the nineteenth century, not to say up until now, there has been no objective knowledge of madness, but only the formulation, in terms of scientific analogy, of a certain experience (moral, social, etc.) of Unreason. Hence this decidedly unobjective, unscientific, unhistorical method of dealing with the question. But perhaps this undertaking is absurd and doomed in advance.
>
> Finally, my third great mistake was to prepare first the pages dealing with medical theories, whereas the realm of "institutions" is unclear and would have helped me to be more clear in other areas. Since you are willing to allow me to do so, I shall show you what I did over the vacation on the subject of institutions . . . There we are in a realm that is far easier to define and one providing the social conditions of the beginnings of psychiatry.

Lindroth did not feel any more enlightened, and Foucault did not defend his thesis in Uppsala. It is true that he seems to have been swamped by his materials, and that he had a lot of trouble putting his book together. Dumézil, who supervised his work and constantly asked him for news about it, and who also read and commented on the pages already written, had advised him against trying to defend his thesis in Sweden. "Publish it in France," he told him. He knew the sort of reservations the Swedes had; he knew them better than anyone. He knew also that Professor Hasselroth was right in telling Foucault, speaking of his colleagues, "You will never get them to accept that." According to Jean-Christophe Oberg, Foucault never really seriously considered defending his thesis in Sweden. Jean-François Miquel, on the other hand, said that Lindroth's rejection was one of the main reasons for his departure. In any case the Swedes remained insensitive to Foucault's nascent work. In a recent controversy in Sweden the unfortunate Lindroth was condemned for having ignored signs of such genius. Perhaps the tradition of the history of science prevented this thoroughly Germanic professor, who had some reservations about "literature," from understanding the book's significance. But the fact remains: Foucault would have to wait several years to defend his thesis. When he left Sweden, a country that he considered thoroughly unfriendly, his work was finished as far as documentation was concerned. But a great deal of writing and organizing remained to be done.

Part of another book was perhaps worked out during Foucault's stay in Uppsala. A few kilometers from the little city stood Linnaeus' house, a wooden house, lost in some of the most beautiful countryside one could ever hope to see. Foucault often took his group of friends on pilgrimages to this mecca of the history of sciences. The chapter on Linnaeus in *Les Mots et les choses* certainly owes a great deal to those long, exhausting walks.

Foucault had many other opportunities to manifest his interest in science. The University of Uppsala boasted two Nobel prizewinners in chemistry: Theodor Svedberg and his student Arne Tiselius, in 1926 and 1948, respectively. Foucault became friends with them, and Svedberg took Foucault down into the third underground level in Uppsala's laboratory center and spent a week explaining how the cyclotron functioned. Foucault's comment was: "But why didn't I study science instead of philosophy?"

Why did Foucault decide to leave Uppsala? His first contract provided for a two-year stay, and it had been renewed for another two. According to Gunnar Bröberg, the reason was rather simple: his teach-

ing obligations had been increased to twelve hours a week. Consequently, it would have been impossible for Foucault to work on his
thesis. Moreover, because he knew that he could not defend it in Sweden, he preferred resigning at the end of his third year. The university
directory announced Michel Foucault's courses for the beginning of
the term in October 1958. The Thursday lectures were supposed to
deal, once again, with "religious experience in French literature from
Chateaubriand to Bernanos." They never took place. Foucault left
Uppsala, taking with him, according to numerous witnesses, a rather
unpleasant memory, despite the friendships he formed (he would keep
up his connection with Jean-François and Christina Miquel, with Jean-
Christophe Oberg, and especially with Erik Nilsson) and despite the
almost completed thesis. The next stage of his journey would be Poland.

~

FOUCAULT HAD PLENTY OF TIME to work out the particulars of his
departure for Warsaw during a long visit to Paris in 1958. It was a
rather odd, almost impromptu visit, decided one May evening while
Foucault and Jean-Christophe Oberg—in tuxedos—were attending a
reception at a chateau near Uppsala. They had been invited by the
heiress to one of the great Swedish fortunes, who had fallen in love
with the young French instructor. During dinner Oberg went off alone
to listen to the news on the radio. When he came back he told Foucault, "Something is going on in France." Which was putting it mildly.
General de Gaulle, borne along by the supporters of a French Algeria,
was on the verge of returning to power. There was hardly a moment's
hesitation before they decided to go. They returned to Uppsala just
long enough to change their clothes, and off they went to France in the
Jaguar. Oberg describes the escapade:

> Michel and I left on Wednesday, May 28, 1958. We spent the night in
> a little hotel in Denmark, in Tappernöje. The next morning, May 29,
> we took a ferry from Gedser, Denmark, to Grossenbrode, Germany.
> We spent the second night in Belgium at La Calamine in a very small
> hotel, the Select. Then we kept on toward Paris, arriving on May 30
> around three in the afternoon. Paris was in complete turmoil—for
> no apparent reason, since the game was already over. We headed to-
> ward the Champs-Elysées via Rue de Bassano, which the police had
> blocked near the George-V metro stop. We left the Jaguar on Avenue
> Marceau, slipped through the police cordon, and began to walk along
> the Champs-Elysées, where we were quickly caught up in a wave of

demonstrators. I found myself perched on the roof of a car heading toward the Arc de Triomphe, while Michel followed, surrounded by youths who were waving the blue-white-and-red flag. The Place de l'Etoile was also blocked by police, and the car had to turn around. That gave me a chance to jump to the ground, but Michel had disappeared into the crowd. We found each other back at the Jaguar and went off to eat together on Saint-German-des-Prés. Then we separated. I went to the Swedish embassy, where my parents were waiting for me, worried because they did not know where we were or whether we had got to Paris, and Michel went to meet his brother, with whom he was living.

Foucault stayed in Paris for a good month. When he returned to Uppsala it would be simply to pack his bags, after a meal washed down with plenty of wine in the company of the small group with which he had spent the past three years.

Why Warsaw? Once again, the hand of Dumézil must be seen behind this appointment. He had friends everywhere—particularly, in this case, on the Quai d'Orsay, where Philippe Rebeyrol, a former student at the ENS, worked as chief of the service in charge of teaching French abroad. With him as intermediary, the French government had just negotiated a cultural convention with the Polish government that provided for the creation of a French cultural center in the University of Warsaw itself. This arrangement implied the presence of a native instructor with an office and library at his disposal, who would also organize cultural events. At the time this was rather exceptional, and it was considered a great diplomatic success, made possible by improved East–West relations after periods of great strain.

But it was not enough merely to create the post of French instructor; it was also necessary to find someone qualified to fill it. This risked being a delicate task. Dumézil asked Philippe Rebeyol to give the post to Foucault. He did so, chiefly because he had complete confidence in Dumézil's judgment, and secondly because the official assessments of Foucault's work in Sweden had been especially laudatory.

In October 1958, therefore, Foucault flew to Warsaw and presented himself to Etienne Burin des Roziers, who had recently been appointed French ambassador to Poland. "I remember a smiling young man," he said, "nice, relaxed, happy to take on a job whose interest, importance, and great difficulty he understood from the start."[9]

Foucault was lodged at first in a seedy room at the Bristol Hotel, near the university, which was a cluster of buildings on Krakow Avenue. He then moved to an apartment that was also very close to where he worked. He worked on his thesis on the one hand and, on the other, fulfilled the university and administrative functions entrusted to him. His first task was to give this "Center of French Civilization" a material existence. Tables and chairs had to be ordered, as well as books and reviews. Foucault also gave classes and lectures at the university, where he was connected with the Romance Language Institute in the faculty of modern philosophy. He repeated the course on French contemporary theater that he had broken in at Uppsala. He immediately seduced his students and colleagues with his intelligence, his seriousness, and his kindness. Today the exquisite courtesy that he showed on every occasion is still talked about. He also struck up a friendship with the president of the Academy of Sciences, Professor Kotarbinski, a figure of major importance in the Polish university but one regarded by the authorities as a "bourgeois philosopher," since he took his inspiration from the theories of the Vienna Circle.

Bit by bit Foucault's role changed. The embassy's cultural adviser, Jean Bourilly, asked for several leaves of absence to prepare his doctoral thesis, and because Foucault and Burin des Roziers got along famously, Foucault served as de facto cultural adviser for almost a year. In that capacity he gave a series of lectures on Apollinaire during a tour that took him from Gdansk to Krakow, presenting the exposition that Professor Zurowski created for the fortieth anniversary of the poet's death.

"He put himself into this role [of cultural adviser] with a great deal of good grace and, it seemed to me," Burin des Roziers went on, "not at all disliking it, sacrificing himself, putting in an appearance at cultural events in the four corners of Poland, observing with a certain amount of indulgence and amusement the somewhat vain rites of diplomatic mumbojumbo." As a result, when Jean Bourilly announced that he wanted to quit the post for good because his thesis was finished and he expected to be appointed to a chair at the Sorbonne, the ambassador proposed that Foucault replace him. But Foucault set several conditions for his acceptance: "He thought," said Burin des Roziers, "that the Quai d'Orsay was on the wrong track in the way it set up corps of agents for our foreign cultural activity. Somehow, these agents were to be polyvalent, as if a cultural adviser or a French instructor was equally qualified for service in South America, in Scandinavia, in the Slavic countries, or in the Far East. To stick with Poland, Michel Foucault was willing to stay as headman only if allowed to recruit, as he was confident he would be able to, young Slavists who would act as aides in Warsaw, Krakow, and throughout the territory."[10]

This project never came to anything, because Foucault had to leave Poland in a hurry. The story is rather muddled but apparently quite a commonplace in Eastern Europe. He met a boy, with whom he began to spend some happy hours in this gloomy, stifling country. But the young man was working for the police, who were trying to infiltrate the Western diplomatic services. One morning Burin des Roziers informed Foucault that he had to leave Poland. "When?" asked Foucault. "In the next twenty-four hours," the ambassador replied.

Once again, Michel Foucault left with a glowing report, extravagant praise, written by Jean Bourilly:

> A clear, precise and penetrating intellect, with a wealth of great culture, Michel Foucault possesses a sense of authority. He is capable of fulfilling important foreign functions most satisfactorily, whether in a teaching position or in a position that includes administrative responsibilities. In his direction of the Centre d'Etudes at the university, a post he took on in 1958–1959, he had to confront numerous difficulties, which involved material conditions (the absence of any location for the center or apartment for himself for many months) as much as they involved the specific nature and aims of the activities of the center itself. He was, nonetheless, able to guarantee a propitious beginning for this new Franco-Polish organization.

ᐁᐁ

FOUCAULT WENT BACK TO SEE Philippe Rebeyrol on the Quai d'Orsay and told him that he would like very much to go to Germany. He had taken up German while at the ENS so that he could read Husserl and Heidegger, and then he had become fascinated by Nietzsche. It is easy to see why Germany could have been particularly attractive to him. So he would follow in Sartre's and Aron's footsteps; before the war each of them had spent a year in one of the great German cities. Rebeyrol proposed several possibilities, including Munich and Hamburg. There was a thick network of French cultural institutes in Germany. Foucault chose Hamburg.

Foucault's functions in Hamburg were almost identical with the ones he had already performed in Uppsala and Warsaw. They involved directing the Cultural Institute, receiving lecturers (it was there that he would meet Alain Robbe-Grillet), and giving courses in the Department of Romance Languages at the University of Hamburg.

His students remember that his courses dealt, as was to be expected, with French literature and that he discussed contemporary theater (because it was one of his favorite subjects), Sartre, and Camus—after a lingering look at the eighteenth century. Because his course was listed as a supplementary one and required no exam, only ten or fifteen attended. These students were truly passionate about literature, however, and this situation was more to his liking than the one he had experienced in Uppsala, especially because he taught only two hours a week.

In fact, essentially, he was dealing with the French Institute, located at 55 Heidemer Strasse. Foucault spent the year 1959–60 in the director's apartment, which occupied almost the entire third floor. Other than the director, the Institute consisted of four professors who gave French courses in the city or on the premises. Among them were Jean-Marie Zemb, who is today a professor at the Collège de France, and Gilbert Kahn, the nephew of Léon Brunschvicg and a friend of Simone Weil's.

As in Uppsala, Foucault devoted part of his time to theater, with a small troupe organized by Gilbert Kahn. At his suggestion, Cocteau's *L'Ecole des veuves* was produced in June 1960. He discussed Cocteau at great length with some of the students who had become his friends, such as Jurgen Schmidt and Irene Staps, two pillars of the theatrical group.

And then, not surprisingly, he spent a lot of time at the university library. He had completed his principal thesis, *Folie et déraison*, and it was during his stay at Hamburg that he went to Paris to show it to Jean Hyppolite, whom he had chosen as his "thesis director." Foucault was now concentrating on his secondary thesis, a translation of Kant's *Anthropology*, for which he intended to write a long, historical introduction. When his two theses were in their final stages and ready to submit to the ordeal of a defense, Foucault would find a position in French higher education—not with the title of "professor," because for that the defense had to have taken place, but as a *chargé d'enseignement* in a vacant chair, with a rank that corresponded approximately to what is now called *maître de conférence* in France. Such an offer came from Clermont-Ferrand, and Foucault decided to end, at least temporarily, his exile from France.

Never again would he hold the same sort of administrative or cultural posts as the ones he was about to leave, although on several occasions there was a serious possibility of his doing so. In 1967, when Etienne Burin des Roziers became ambassador to Italy, he phoned Foucault—then in Tunisia—to propose that he become his cultural adviser. Foucault found the offer tempting, but the project was cut short because the Collège de France was already on the horizon. Earlier, in 1963, he had accepted responsibility for the French Cultural Institute in Tokyo, but the dean of the faculty at Clermont-Ferrand had begged the minister not to steal this professor, who was indispensable to the smooth operation of his institution. Much later, in 1981, when the left came to power in France, there was talk of naming Foucault as cultural adviser in New York; but the discussions never came to anything.

There would be other ways in which Foucault would continue his work as "ambassador of French culture throughout the world," as the administrative reports referred to him: as a professor in Tunis, as a lecturer in dozens of countries, and, above all, through his books and their enormous international success.

FOUCAULT HAD LEFT FRANCE IN 1955 feeling that his life from then on would be marked by travel, not to say exile. He seemed to be obsessed with being always somewhere else. But was he never to live in France again? Yes, perhaps, but he would use this country, with which he had such conflicting relations, as a strategic base to organize stays of varying length in other parts of the world. When he returned to Sweden in 1968 for a series of lectures, he said in an interview that when he left France in 1955, he had firmly intended to spend the rest of his life "between two suitcases," to traipse around the whole world, "and especially never again to touch a penholder . . . The idea of devoting my life to writing seemed completely absurd to me then, and I never dreamed of it. It was in Sweden, during the long Swedish nights, that I contracted this mania, this filthy habit of writing for five or six hours a day." He felt then that he was "a sort of world tourist, useless and superfluous." And he added (this was in March 1968): "I still feel that I am just as useless, the difference being that I am no longer a tourist. Now I am glued to my work table." [11] Michel Foucault, in 1955, a tourist to whom the idea of writing had never occurred? This seems, perhaps, an exaggeration; he had already published several texts. But it is true that throughout his life he did consider that he had never really chosen to be a writer. This theme would come up again and again in conversation with his friends while he was working on his last books—with so many problems, hesitations, and regrets, and perhaps a certain weariness deep within, a desire to drop it all. "I started writing by chance. And once one has begun, one is a prisoner of this activity; it is impossible to escape." He was certainly tempted to flee this body of constraints. But it is probably not all that easy to escape roles into which one has poured one's entire existence.

Foucault left France in August 1955. In the summer of 1960, not yet thirty-four, he moved back. Two important things happened during his absence. First was the absence itself. As a result Foucault remained on the outside of all the political changes occurring in France at the time of the Algerian War and de Gaulle's return to power. He was isolated from all the upheavals preoccupying the left—the emergence of a strong movement unionizing the students, the appearance of political movements that were outside Communist influence, mainly in university settings. Many phenomena helped trigger the events of May 1968. During the years Foucault spent abroad, hidden fissures were produced that would end up violently shaking French society several years later. But then, once again, Foucault would be absent. During the struggles tearing France apart over the Algerian War, he was in Sweden, Poland, and Germany. While March, April, and May 1968 were ripping apart the social, political and institutional framework of the country, he was in Tunis.

The second important event was that Foucault began, wrote, and completed his thesis, *Folie et déraison. Histoire de la folie à l'âge classique.* The work was supposed to be called "L'Autre Tour de folie," in reference to a quotation from Pascal with which Foucault began his preface. But since it was a thesis that had to be subjected to a defense, Foucault finally opted for a more academic title.

The book begins:

Pascal: "Men are so necessarily mad, that not to be mad would amount to another form of madness." And Dostoevsky, in his *Diary of a Writer:* "It is not by confining one's neighbor that one is convinced of one's own sanity."

We have yet to write the history of that other form of madness, by which men, in an act of sovereign reason, confine their neighbors, and communicate and recognize each other through the merciless language of non-madness; to define the moment of this conspiracy before it was permanently established in the realm of truth, before it was revived by the lyricism of protest. We must try to return, in history, to that zero point in the course of madness at which madness is an undifferentiated experience, a not yet divided experience of division itself. We must describe, from the start of its trajectory, that "other form" which relegates Reason and Madness to one side or the other of its action as things henceforth external, deaf to all exchange, and as though dead to one another.

In order to explore this "uncomfortable region," Foucault announces at the outset that it will be necessary to "renounce the convenience of terminal truths," that is, lose one's fondness for the concepts developed by contemporary psychopathology: "What is constitutive is the action that divides madness, and not the science elaborated once this division is made and calm restored." Medical categories isolate the madman in his madness. The madman and the man of reason no longer communicate. "As for a common language, there is no such thing; or rather, there is no such thing any longer; the constitution of madness as a mental illness, at the end of the eighteenth century, affords the evidence of a broken dialogue, posits the separation as already effected, and thrusts into oblivion all those stammered, imperfect words without fixed syntax in which the exchange between madness and reason was made. The language of psychiatry, which is a monologue of reason *about* madness, has been established only on the basis of such a silence." Then comes the superb and often-cited declaration defining Foucault's project: "I have not tried to write the history of that language, but rather the archaeology of that silence." [12]

Writing the archaeology of that silence involved excavating all of Western culture. Because "European man, since the beginning of the Middle Ages, has had a relation to something he calls, indiscriminately, Madness, Dementia, Insanity," one must acknowledge that the Reason-Madness connection constitutes "one of the dimensions of its originality," and that it is defined by the depths threatening it. Foucault intends to draw us into these depths, into this "realm . . . where what is in question is the limits rather than the identity of a culture." A "history of these limits" must be written, a history "of those obscure acts, forgotten of necessity as soon as they are performed, by means of which a culture rejects something that will represent the Exterior for it; and throughout the course of its history, this empty hole, this blank space with which it isolates itself, designates it just as much as do its values . . . To question a culture on the extremities of its experience is to question it on the confines of history, on a breach that is like the very birth of its history." [13]

At this point Foucault anchors his work in the Nietzschean tradition: "At the center of these extremities of experience in Western culture erupts, of course, the experience of tragedy itself—Nietzsche having demonstrated that the tragic structure on which the history of the Western world is based is none other than the rejection and forgetting of tragedy and its silent fallout." But there are "many other experiences centering on" this experience, each of which traces on the frontiers of our culture "a limit that implies, at the same time, an originative division." Foucault wants to become the archaeologist of all those threatening but rejected experiences—repressed, forgotten, and always present. He proposes to carry out a series of studies "in the light of a great Nietzschean inquiry" in an attempt to discover and recount other divisions upon which our culture has been constructed. He mentions two: first, "the absolute dividing off of the dream, that man cannot keep himself from consulting on the subject of his own truth—whether the truth of his destiny or of his heart—but that he consults only from the other side of a basic rejection, derisively constituting and repressing the dream as hallucination"; then, "the history, and not just in terms of ethnology, of sexual prohibitions: to speak of the constantly shifting and obstinate forms of repression in our own culture, and not to write a chronicle of morality or of tolerance, but to reveal how the limits of the Western world and the origins of its morality are its tragic division from the happy world and from desire." But there remained one vital task: "to speak of the experience of madness," to rediscover it before its capture by knowledge and scientific discourse, and, even more vital, to let it express itself, to let it speak itself with "those words, those texts that come from beneath language and were never made to attain speech." [14]

This was the project that Foucault announced in the ten-page preface dropped from the 1972 edition. But what about the book itself? Obviously, it is impossible to reconstruct all the analyses, which run to more than six hundred pages of print in French. So rich, so teeming, so involved are these analyses, sometimes disconcerting as well as contradictory; they move from one register to another, discussing the economic level (much in evidence in Foucault's books of a historical nature) as readily as the juridical or artistic level to make his argument. But it is worthwhile to extract a few things he said in the course of this vast demonstration, in order, above all, to hear Foucault's voice. The style is rather different from what it will become.

When madness still had an established place in society, that is, in the middle of the Renaissance, there was already a split forming between two forms of madness. There was the madness of the paintings of Bosch, Breughel, or Dürer on the one hand, troubling, obsessive, and threatening, seeming to reveal the deep secret into which the truth of our world of appearances would vanish. It was a madness like that in Erasmus' *In Praise of Folly*. Reason was in a dialogue with this folly, which was however a madness already set at a distance, caught in the universe of dicourse, one evoked only to direct its critical powers against human illusion and its pretension. On the one hand a profoundly tragic madness and on the other a madness, a folly, that was almost tamed, whose violence subsided under the humanist's ironic gaze. The gap is already there, and it will only grow deeper with the passing centuries. This is, perhaps, the point of divergence between two paths: the path of critical consciousness that will lead to medical science, and the path taken by those tragic figures who are supposed to remain silent yet who reemerge in the works of Goya, Van Gogh, Nietzsche, and Artaud. In any case, and in spite of everything, madness is still present and familiar at the time the rupture is already occurring.

In the seventeenth century madness finds itself rejected and banished. Foucault calls this development "the classic event," and it has two "aspects."[15] On the one hand, madness is challenged by a sovereign act of reason, which excludes it and condemns it to silence, with Descartes's paradigmatic words, "but so what? they are madmen," in the first *Meditation*, when he evokes and then dismisses what foundations there might be for a possible doubt concerning the truths that thought believes are obvious to perception. A man may well be mad without jeopardizing the rights of thought. On the other hand, madness is locked up, put away. In this case there are economic, political, moral, and religious motives exerting their full force: in this "great confinement" spanning the seventeenth century, the poor, the idle, beggars, and vagabonds, later to be joined by the debauched, those with venereal diseases, libertines, and homosexuals, would all find themselves behind the walls of the Hôpital Général with the insane. "Perhaps," wrote Foucault, "this is where, for centuries, the kinship between unreason and guilt would be formed, one that today the insane person experiences as destiny and the doctor discovers as a truth of nature."[16] Somehow we have moved from madness to unreason, from the period in which madness had its own specificity to the period in which it is based in the group of those confined, those who must be "corrected." For this confinement organizes punishment and chastisement rather than medical treatment for the ones sent into it, all together.

But in thus defining the features of what was to be condemned, and in radically banning it from society, the "great containment" did not play a merely negative role. It also "constituted a realm of experience," by bringing together, "in an area uniting them, figures and values among whom earlier cultures had perceived no resemblance at all; imperceptibly it shifted them in the direction of madness, preparing an experience—ours—in which they stand out as being already integrated into the set of those belonging to the mentally deranged." [17]

On the other hand, unreason is located and isolated as a concrete presence. It can become an "object of perception." And Foucault undoubtedly sees this as a crucial moment:

> What was the horizon against which it was seen? Clearly, against that of a social reality. Starting in the seventeenth century, unreason is no longer the world's great obsession; it also ceases to be a natural, adventurous dimension of reason. It comes to be seen as a human phenomenon, a spontaneous variety in the realm of social species. What formerly was an inevitable danger inherent in things, in man's language, in his reason and his world, now assumes the figure of a character—or rather, of characters. The men of unreason are types recognized and isolated by society: the debauched, the dissipated, the homosexual, the magician, the suicide, the libertine. Unreason begins to be measured according to a certain gap dividing it from social norms . . . This is the essential point: madness, abruptly invested in a social world, now puts in a privileged and almost exclusive appearance. Almost from one day to the next, it has been provided with a limited sphere in which everyone can recognize and denounce it— the madness formerly seen prowling at every border, surreptitiously inhabiting the most familiar places. From this point on, it can be exorcised all at once by dealing with each of the figures in which it is embodied, to maintain order and as a police precautions.

And at this point Foucault asks the question: "Is it not important to our culture that unreason could become an object of understanding only to the extent that it first had been an object of excommunication?" [18]

But the figure of madness would gradually, once again, win for itself a particular place within this constellation formed by unreason. For, in the end, the value of internment from an economic point of view was called into question and the conclusion was reached that it was better politics to return to the work force all those who were capable of operating in it. How could poverty be treated by incarceration? Madness, in this development, would once again find itself separated from its other housemates in this entity called Unreason. It alone ended up occupying those places of confinement that it had shared with them. The insane found themselves alone with the doctors who tended them. This was the birth of the asylum, the medicalization of internment. The conditions were now provided for madness to be constituted as "mental illness." Henceforth lunatics were loosed from their chains, but one must beware of naively accepting the positivist mythology that sings the virtues of this liberation and takes credit for it: "The asylum of the age of positivism, which it is Pinel's glory to have founded, is not a free realm of observation, diagnosis, and therapeutics; it is a juridical space where one is accused, judged and condemned, and from which one is never released except by the version of this trial in psychological depth, that is, by remorse. Madness will be punished in the asylum, even if it is innocent outside of it. For a long time to come, and until our own day at least, it is imprisoned in a moral world." And Foucault adds: "It is thought that Tuke and Pinel opened the asylum to medical knowledge. They did not introduce a science, but a personality, whose powers borrowed from science only their disguise, or at most their justification . . . If the medical personage could isolate madness, it was not because he knew it, but because he mastered it; and what for positivism would be an image of objectivity was only the other side of this domination." [19]

Medical science, however, was singing its victories in vain; it had not, for all that, won the struggle. Because, for Foucault, the asylum constructed by Philippe Pinel did not serve to protect the modern world from madness. Madness may no longer be set up as night confronted by the light of day, but as an observable reality whose truth can be told by the normal human being. But in return it must be acknowledged that this truth is bound to madness: "In our time man has no truth except in the enigma of the madman, who he both is and is not: each madman both bears and does not bear within him this truth of man, which he exposes in the consequences of his humanity." In short: "Man and madman are bound by an impalpable connection of truth that is both reciprocal and incompatible." And then, above all, at the moment at which unreason seems doomed to disappearance, the voice of those who again pick up its torch must be heard. It is a torch of darkness and night, of infinite negation. Such was the case for Goya; "this madness so foreign to the experience of its contemporaries . . . does it not transmit—to those able to receive it, to Nietzsche and Artaud—those barely audible voices of classical unreason, in which it was always a question of nothingness and night, but amplifying them now to shrieks and frenzy? But giving them for the first time an expression, a *droit de cité*, and a hold on Western culture, which makes possible all contestations, as well as *total* contestation? But restoring their primitive savagery?" Then there was Sade, for whom, as for Goya, "unreason continues to watch by night." But "in this vigil it joins with fresh powers." Through Goya and Sade, "the Western world received the possibility of transcending its reason in violence and of recovering tragic experience beyond the promises of dialectic." [20]

Foucault concludes with this proclamation: "Ruse and new triumph of madness: the world that thought to measure and justify madness through psychology must justify itself before madness, since in its struggles and agonies it measures itself by the excess of works like those of Nietzsche, of Van Gogh, of Artaud. And nothing in itself, especially not what it can know of madness, assures the world that it is justified by such works of madness." [21]

Part II

The Order of Things

8

The Talent of a Poet

Begun during the long Swedish night" and completed "in the obstinate, hot sun of Polish freedom," [1] *Folie et déraison* turned into a monstrous manuscript: 943 pages, according to Georges Canguilhem—not counting appendixes and bibliography. The preface, written after the text itself, was dated "Hamburg, February 5, 1960." In this period the award of the highest French degree, a *doctorat d'état*, required the presentation of two theses, and *Folie et déraison* was to constitute the principal thesis. The annotated translation of Kant's *Anthropology*, preceded by a long introduction, would serve as the secondary thesis.

Even before moving back to France, Foucault had sought a "patron" who would be willing to play the role of "research director," in this case someone to be simply the *rapporteur* sponsoring him for his defense, because there was nothing left to direct. Both theses were already finished. While on a brief visit to Paris he went to see Jean Hyppolite to ask if he would perform this role. Hyppolite, who was at that time director of the Ecole Normal Supérieure, agreed to do so for the secondary thesis, because he was well acquainted with German thought and the history of philosophy. This was his field. But for the principal thesis, which he read "with admiration," [2] he thought his former pupil should work with Georges Canguilhem. Canguilhem had been teaching the history of science at the Sorbonne for several years, and Hyppolite considered him in a better position to be the academic supervisor of this vast portrait of madness through the ages, which bore little resemblance to a classic thesis in philosophy. He thought it would interest Canguilhem, who had himself defended a thesis in medicine titled *Le Normal et le pathologique*. Foucault therefore went to find the man who had already officiated at the first two rites of passage opening his way to an academic career: the entrance exams for the ENS and the oral for the *agrégation*. This time they met in the vestibule of an amphitheater at the old Sorbonne where Canguilhem was about to give a lecture. Foucault outlined what he wanted to do: to demonstrate how the advent of classical rationalism had instituted the division that made madness a thing apart, and how psychiatric knowledge had invented, molded, and carved out its object—mental illness. Canguilhem listened and commented laconically, in a single sentence, pronounced in the gruff voice he liked to use: "If that were true it would be known." But he read the work and experienced "a real shock." Convinced that he was looking at truly first-rate work, he immediately agreed to serve as its *rapporteur*. He simply suggested that Foucault change or tone down some of the formulations he thought were too peremptory. Foucault, however, was apparently very attached to the form he had given his book and refused to change anything in it. The thesis was defended and the work published in the form in which Canguilhem first read it.

This is, perhaps, the place to take a closer look at the individual who would question and judge Foucault once more, at this final hurdle on the institutional track leading to the rank of "university professor." Foucault regarded "Cang," as he was called at the ENS, with some hostility following their first two encounters, but he ended up reading his works all the same and finding them useful. How could he have ignored them completely, when Althusser never missed a chance to call his students' attention to this herald of the philosophy of science during a period in which the existentialists prevailed? Foucault therefore overcame his personal annoyance and read *Le Normal et le pathologique* and the articles that Canguilhem published from time to time in specialist reviews. Canguilhem was, above all, a professor and, as Desanti describes him, "an organizer of the philosophical tribe." He published very little at a time, over a considerable period—one carefully defined article after another, gradually constructing what would only later form the volumes that became rather famous in academic circles: *La Connaissance de la vie*, *Etudes d'histoire et de philosophie des sciences*, *Idéologie et rationalité dans les sciences de la vie*. In the preface to *Folie et déraison*, Foucault cited Canguilhem as one of his masters, and he would render homage again in his inaugural lecture at the Collège de France, in December 1970. But basically, Canguilhem's influence on him made itself felt primarily between these two events. Thus *Naissance de la cli-*

nique shows more of his influence than does *Folie et déraison*. Foucault seems to acknowledge this in a June 1965 letter to Canguilhem:

> When I began to work, ten years ago, I did not know you—not your books. But the things I have done since I certainly would not have done had I not read you. You have had a great impact on [my work]. I cannot describe to you precisely how, nor precisely where, nor what my "method" owes to you; but you should be aware that even, and especially, my counterpositions—for example, on vitalism—are possible only on the basis of what you have done, on this layer of analysis introduced by you, on this epistemological eidetics that you invented. Actually the *Clinique* and what follows it derive from this and, perhaps, are completely contained within it. Some day I shall have to come to grips with exactly what this relationship is.

To "come to grips with exactly what this relationship is" and, perhaps, to understand the influence this discreet professor had on an entire generation of philosophers, one must refer to the long preface written by Foucault for the American edition of *Le Normal et le pathologique*, in 1977. In this text he emphasizes Canguilhem's role in the debates sweeping French thought during the 1960s and 1970s: "This man, whose austere work—a work that is limited by choice and meticulously devoted to one particular area of the history of sciences, which, in any case, is not seen as a particularly spectacular discipline—found itself somehow present in the debates in which he had been careful never to play a part himself."[3] He would, however, play a part in it once, just once: when he commented on *Les Mots et les choses*, in a very vigorous article that received much attention.[4] He wrote it, Canguilhem recalls today, "because I was annoyed at the Sartreans' criticism of Foucault." After Foucault's death Canguilhem would pay homage to his departed friend in a magnificent article reconstructing the coherence of Foucault's thought, from *Histoire de la folie* to the final volumes of *Histoire de la sexualité* (*The History of Sexuality*).[5] In January 1988 he presided over the colloquium in Paris, "Foucault philosophe," that attracted scholars from all over the world.

Georges Canguilhem was born in 1904 at Castelnaudary, in southwestern France. He was a member of the famous class of 1924 at the ENS that included Aron, Sartre, and Nizan. After having passed his *agrégation* in philosophy, he started to study medicine. He defended his thesis in 1943—that is, in the midst of war in occupied France. The University of Strasbourg, where he was teaching, had withdrawn to

Clermont-Ferrand for the duration. Canguilhem continued to teach there and at the same time worked actively in the Resistance. After France was liberated he again taught in Strasbourg before becoming the inspector general of national education. During this period he aroused profound hostility among the secondary school teachers whose pedagogical competence he was responsible for evaluating. His fits of anger and his abrupt manners made him feared, even detested. There are many unkind stories still going around today about things he did and said while performing his job as "inspector"—the title alone is enough to create mistrust. But in 1955 he was appointed to the Sorbonne, where he succeeded Gaston Bachelard, and it was most certainly from that point on that he began to have a real influence on the French philosophical landscape. That influence was almost invisible; in fact it remained in the shadows until Foucault made such a point of it. Throughout his life Canguilhem had reflected on the problems of scientific practice, taking the route marked out by Bachelard but concentrating on the life sciences rather than physics. He was especially interested in the relationship between ideology and rationality, in the process of discovery, in the role of error in the search for "truth," the very notion of which he also questioned. By so doing, as Foucault demonstrates very well in his 1977 text, he inscribed himself in the tradition of conceptual philosophers, embodied by Bachelard, Jean Cavaillès, and Alexandre Koyré, who fundamentally (and as if from the dark beginnings of time) confronted the opposite philosophical tradition of experience and sense, as it was embodied in Sartre and Merleau-Ponty, the existentialists and phenomenologists.

Canguilhem, then, served as a rallying point. His name became something of a militant password for all those who were trying to escape the well-trod paths of a philosophy of the subject—that is, for all those who, from the 1950s until the 1980s, attempted to inject new life into the theoretical discourse of philosophy, sociology, or psychoanalysis. Canguilhem, we might venture, is a sort of precursor of structuralism; or rather, he acclimated many young scholars to what would become structuralism, by laying out for them what could be called a structural history of science.

⚡

AT THAT TIME, to be defended a thesis had to be printed. And the dean of the faculty that was being asked to award the title of doctor had to authorize this printing. Canguilhem therefore took on the task of writing in Foucault's behalf the "report: to obtain the printing permit as a principal thesis for the doctorate of letters." On April 19, 1960, he summarized the thesis and expressed high praise for it in several closely spaced, typed pages, which he kept afterward in his personal files. The following excerpt gives some indication of his opinion: "The significance of this work is clear. Since M. Foucault has never lost sight of the wide variety of ways in which madness has been useful to modern man, from the Renaissance until today, its mirroring in the plastic arts, in literature, and in philosophy; since he has sometimes untangled and sometimes enmeshed numerous vital leads, his thesis presents itself as a work that is simultaneously analytic and synthetic, whose rigor makes its reading not always easy, but always rewarding to the mind." Canguilhem added:

> As for documentation, M. Foucault has, on the one hand, reread and looked at a considerable number of records once again, and, on the other, he has read and made use of many records for the first time. A professional historian cannot help but like the effort by a young philosopher to gain access to primary documents. On the other hand, there is no philosopher who could reproach M. Foucault for having given up autonomy of philosophical judgment by being submissive to the sources of historical information. M. Foucault's thought, in implementing his considerable documentation, has preserved from beginning to end a dialectical rigor that derives in part from his sympathy with a Hegelian view of history and his familiarity with *Phenomenology of Spirit*. The originality of this work consists, essentially, in its taking up once again, on a higher level of philosophical reflection, material that up to now has been left by philosophers and by historians of psychiatry up to the sole discretion of those psychiatrists interested in the history or prehistory of their specialty, most often for reasons of method or convention.

Canguilhem ended his report with a formulation corresponding to official requirements: "I believe that I can conclude, therefore, convinced as I am by the importance of M. Foucault's research, that his work deserves to be presented for the defense before a jury of the *faculté des lettres*, and I propose that the dean authorize its printing."

It goes without saying that authorization was granted. An editor still had to be found, but Foucault had made his own choice long ago. His dream was to be published at Gallimard, where the great names of the preceding generation, specifically Sartre and Merleau-Ponty, had been published. He submitted his manuscript to Brice Parain, a member of

the editorial committee that read submissions for Gallimard, on Rue
Sébastien-Bottin, and a friend of Georges Dumézil's. These two men
had met at the Rue d'Ulm after the First World War, during a time
when all the classes were mixed together at the ENS, following the
restoration of peace and the demobilization of the army. From 1941 to
1949 Parain had edited several of Dumézil's works. But every series he
had launched had been short-lived because sales were too small.[6] It
was, perhaps, in response to these failures that Parain had become suspicious of anything resembling academic work. In the early 1950s he
turned down a collection of articles by an ethnologist who at the time
had published only one book, whose title in English became *Elementary Structures of Kinship*. This was, of course, Claude Lévi-Strauss,
who several years later got these essays published at Plon with a title
destined to be known far and wide: *Structural Anthropology*.[7] Similarly,
despite Dumézil's kindly patronage (Dumézil was always there, at
every step of Foucault's career), Parain rejected the work submitted by
the young philosopher. "We don't publish theses," was the substance
of his explanation, to Foucault's great frustration. Later Foucault
would frequently tell his friends: "They didn't want my book, because
it had footnotes." However, the detour via Gallimard was not completely futile. Another reader for the press had been consulted: Roger
Caillois. He had been Dumézil's student in the fifth section of the
Ecole Pratique des Hautes Etudes. Caillois was on the jury for the
prestigious Critics' Prize, and he decided to have another member of
the jury read this impressive manuscript. He wanted his opinion:
would such a work stand a chance of winning? Maurice Blanchot did
not have time to read the whole book, but he read enough to judge its
importance. He expressed his enthusiasm to Caillois and, when the
volume came out the following year, expressed it again publicly.

Blanchot's favorable impression was not enough for the book to be
awarded the Critics' Prize, just as Caillois's opinion had not been
enough for Gallimard to accept it. Never mind that. Foucault would
find a solution. Jean Delay had already offered to publish it in a series
he edited at Presses Universitaires de France, but Foucault really
wanted his book to escape the thesis ghetto. He had been impressed by
how Lévi-Strauss had been able to demolish the frontier separating the
specialist academic audience from the broader, cultured one. After
Gallimard's rejection, Lévi-Strauss had gone to Plon, where he then
published *Tristes Tropiques* in 1955 and *Anthropologie structurale* in 1958.

Foucault happened to know Jacques Bellefroid, the literary adviser at Plon, very well. He had met him in Lille. Bellefroid at the time was in Lycée and was very close to Jean-Paul Aron. Since then Bellefroid had moved to Paris, where he had begun an editorial and literary career. He suggested that Foucault submit his manuscript to the editor who had introduced the work of Lévi-Strauss. Foucault recounted this episode more than twenty years later: "On the advice of a friend, I took my manuscript to Plon. A few months later I went back to get it. They said that to return it to me they were going to have to find it first. Then one day it turned up in a drawer and they even realized that it was a book of history. They had Ariès read it; that was how I came to know him."[8]

Philippe Ariès was the editor of a series called Civilisation d'Hier et d'Aujourd'hui. Plon had wanted to modernize by promoting influential collections: thus Eric de Dampierre was put in charge of sociology and published, among other things, translations of Max Weber; Jean Malaurie launched the series Terre Humaine; and Ariès dealt with history. Already published in his series were Louis Chevalier's *Classes laborieuses, classes dangereuses* and a book he had written himself, *L'Enfant et la famille sous l'Ancien Régime*. Then one day, as he wrote in his memoirs, "a thick manuscript arrived: a philosophy thesis on the relations between madness and unreason in the classical age, by an author I didn't know. I was dazzled when I read it. But I had to go through hell and high water to talk them into it."[9] The breeze of openmindedness that blew through Plon had proved to be short-lived, and the new managers of the press looked with disfavor upon these series that, though influential, were clearly unprofitable. Ariès went to battle— and won. *Folie et déraison* would therefore be published by Plon.

Foucault was forever immensely grateful to Ariès, who would seem to have had every reason to be hostile. There was nothing banal about the meeting between these two personalities. They were like night and day, like the devil and Christ. Ariès was a Catholic who had long been a monarchist, and he still held rightist (not to say extreme rightist) ideas. It is hard to imagine anyone more traditionalist than this historian with no university appointment, this marginal man, kept at a distance by academic institutions. Yet perhaps Ariès, who defined himself as a "Sunday historian," was precisely the most capable of recognizing the innovative force pervading this work so resistant to the academic classifications to which it had just been subjected.

When Ariès died, Foucault wrote: "Philippe Ariès was a man whom it would have been hard to dislike: he insisted on attending his parish mass but was careful always to wear earplugs so he wouldn't have to face the liturgical botherations of Vatican II." And he added these comments about the historian's books:

> He studied demographic facts each in its turn, not as a biological background to a society, but as a means of behaving toward himself, toward his posterity, toward the future; then childhood, which for him was a figure of the life that outlined, actualized, and shaped the attitude and sensibility of the adult world; and finally death, which men ritualize, make a production of, exalt, and sometimes, as they do today, neutralize and nullify. "History of mentalities" was a phrase he himself used. But reading his books suffices to show that he has written a "history of practices," of the practices that take the form of humble and stubborn habits, as well as of the practices that can create magnificent art; and he has tried to define the attitude, the way of doing, being, acting, or feeling that could be at the root of both kinds of practice. In his attention to the silent gesture that lives on through the ages, as well as to the singular work of art sleeping in a museum, he has established the principle of a stylistics of existence. By this I mean the principle of a study of the forms with which man manifests himself, invents, forgets, or denies himself, in his destiny as a living, mortal being.[10]

This appreciation, written in February 1984, expresses Foucault's feelings in the special vocabulary of the work he was just then completing on the art of self-control, on the aesthetics of the self, a work that would come to an end four months later on the eve of his own death in two volumes titled *L'Usage des plaisirs* and *Le Souci de soi*. But it is easy to see why there could have been a lasting, though initially strange, relationship between the two men. It is especially apparent that Foucault had a sincere and enduring admiration for Ariès, and he doggedly reiterated the "personal debt" he "owed" him.[11]

〜

SATURDAY, MAY 20, 1961. Michel Foucault concluded his defense: "To speak of madness one must have the talent of a poet."[12] He had dazzled the jury and audience by the brilliant presentation of his work. "But you, sir, have it," was Georges Canguilhem's response. Between the time the two men had met in the vestibule of an amphitheater at the Sorbonne to discuss this defense, and this spring afternoon on which the applicant completed the ritual, slightly more than a year had gone by. As required, Foucault had set forth the broad outlines of his research for the members of his jury before they subjected him to the business of close questioning. The session had begun at half past one in the Salle Louis-Liard: a place reserved for important theses. It was impressive in its solemnity, with a raised dais and a long wooden podium on top of that, running its full length. The ancient paneling, the rows of overhanging seats on both sides as in an Italian-style theater, the dull, fuzzy light—it was almost dark—contributed to this effect. There was a considerable crowd; of course, not yet the mob that would push in to hear his inaugural lecture ten years later at the Collège de France. But the room was full; there were almost a hundred people, each of whom had come knowing this was going to be an event.

Henri Gouhier headed the jury. He is a historian of philosophy, a professor at the Sorbonne since 1948, and had been chosen as president because he, of all the members of the jury, had been "tenured professor longest at the highest rank." That was the rule. Gouhier was an affable, open man, a scholar with many interests and always meticulous in whatever he did. He was well known for his work on Descartes, Malebranche, and Maine de Biran, but also for books such as *Auguste Comte et la naissance du positivisme*. He was also known for his passion for the theater, manifested in 1952 in an essay, "Le Théâtre et l'existence," and in 1958 in another, "L'Oeuvre théâtrale." During this period he also wrote a theater column in the review *La Table Ronde*. With him on the jury were Georges Canguilhem, of course, and Daniel Lagache, with whom Foucault had studied psychology and who now held the psychopathology chair at the Sorbonne. Canguilhem and Lagache were old accomplices. Not only did they both teach at the Sorbonne; they had met at the Rue d'Ulm, and they had taught together during the war. Lagache had been drafted as a forensic surgeon in 1939. Taken prisoner, he escaped and joined the University of Strasbourg at Clermont-Ferrand. Here he met up again with Canguilhem, who attended his classes and his presentations of patients. When Canguilhem published his medical thesis, Lagache reviewed it for the *Bulletin de la faculté des lettres de Strasbourg;* his article was reprinted a few months later in the *Revue de métaphysique et de morale*.[13] He defended his *thèse d'état*, *La Jalousie amoureuse*, in 1946 and was appointed to the Sorbonne the next year. In 1953, despite their differences, he helped found the Société Française de la Psychanalyse with Jacques Lacan. In 1958 he published *La Psychanalyse et la structure de la personnalité* and began the vast project of putting together a "vocabulary of psychoanalysis," for which he would enlist two young collaborators: Jean Laplanche and Jean-Bertrand Pontalis.

Gouhier, Canguilhem, Lagache. The candidate could expect a formidable encounter with this trio of eminent specialists. After all, the tradition of defense derives as much from initiation rites, including obligatory ordeals and requisite traps, as from intellectual debate.

But the audience would have to wait before reveling in pronouncements and exchanges about *Folie et déraison*. First Foucault had to respond to questions on Kant's *Anthropology*, because the defense had to begin with the "secondary thesis." There he had to take on Jean Hyppolite and Maurice de Gandillac, a professor at the Sorbonne, a great expert on the Middle Ages and Renaissance, and the translator of many German texts. Foucault explained what he had wanted to do and pointed out that, to understand this text by Kant, which had been written, rewritten, and transformed over a period of almost twenty-five years, it was necessary to create a hybrid structural and genetic analysis. A genetic analysis would determine the ways in which the final work had been elaborated, what its successive sediments were. A structural analysis would determine the status of this work within the global and internal organization of the Kantian system, and the relationship between the *Anthropology* and the "critical" development laid out by Kant. Both in this oral exposition and in the text of his thesis, Foucault made abundant use of a vocabulary that was to become famous. He spoke of writing the "archaeology of the Kantian text"; his questions concerned the "layers" of his "underlying geology."

This "secondary thesis" was never published. Only the translation of Kant's text would come out at Vrin in 1963. Indeed, in response to certain criticisms from the jury, Foucault claimed that it was not intended for publication but was merely an anchoring device for a general investigation of the possibility of a philosophical anthropology. Foucault would prefer to let his long introduction lie sleeping in the Sorbonne archives, where it is still to be found. But it by no means remained a dead letter. For this essay may well be the point of origin of many passages in *Les Mots et les choses*.

For the moment, however, these pages were no more than the "minor thesis," the hors d'oeuvre to the ceremony. Next would come the *plat de résistance:* the "major thesis."

After a few minutes of intermission the show continued. The president of the jury turned the floor over to the candidate. Foucault's voice rose: tense, nervous, unfolding in rhythmic, staccato sequences. Every statement was as polished as a diamond. The origin of his research, he explained, had been an idea for a book that was more about madmen than about their physicians. But this book was impossible to write because the voice of madness had been stifled and reduced to silence. Therefore, it was necessary to collect the signs of a constant debate between reason and unreason, to make something speak that had no language yet, no words to speak itself. This had necessitated immersion in archives—whence the evidence, discovered in the dust-laden documents, that "madness was not a fact of nature" but a "fact of civilization." Madness is always, in any given society, "an *other* behavior," "an other language." Consequently, there can be no history of madness "without a history of the cultures that describe it as such and persecute it." Foucault added that to carry out his investigation successfully he had first had to disabuse himself of the concepts of contemporary psychiatry, since medical science intervenes only as "one of the historical forms of the relationship between reason and madness." Foucault concluded by stating the problem, which was to see what was at risk for a culture in its debate with madness.

After this preliminary statement, discussion began. The objections raised by Lagache have been frequently mentioned since. Today people usually speak with irony about how little this representative of the French tradition in psychiatric medicine understood when confronted, at the beginning of the 1960s, by an individual intent on dynamiting scientific certainties and the psychopathological institution. In his preliminary report Canguilhem had already predicted and stressed this point in many ways: "Calling back into question the origins of psychology's scientific status will not be the least of the surprises provoked by his study." Lagache did in fact raise many objections and express numerous reservations. But the notes taken by Henri Gouhier during the discussion also indicate that from beginning to end he remained extremely cautious. His criticisms dealt primarily with details, his remarks were never aggressive, and basically he never really disputed, much less condemned, Foucault's project. Ultimately his remarks were limited to calling into question the lack of specifically medical, psychiatric, or psychoanalytic information in the book, and also to emphasizing that the author had been unable to detach himself completely, as he claimed, from contemporary concepts. But he does not seem to have overtly denounced Foucault's global vision, which nonetheless must have been completely foreign to him.

It was the president of the jury, Gouhier, who was the most contentious during this memorable session. This was not a result of hostility toward either the candidate or his work. It was simply a matter of intellectual and professional scruples. "I had been asked to participate in the jury as a specialist in the history of philosophy," he explains today. "And that is the role I had to play." Gouhier, then, had a very specific function to fulfill in implementing the ritual, and he played his role to the hilt. With immense erudition he questioned and commented on every aspect of the work, pointed out and corrected historical inaccuracies, and challenged certain interpretations of texts or works. "It is necessary to know if one is providing the philosophy of a text or if one is philosophizing about a text," he flung at the candidate. Although he appreciated his interlocutor's talent, elegance of style, and eloquence, he raised a multitude of objections and cited a myriad of references in contradiction of Foucault's findings. He particularly criticized the discussion of the scriptures: "I am unsure of your interpretation," he said. "The texts that you cite from the scriptures and from St. Vincent de Paul's comments on them do not say that Jesus went mad, but that he wanted to take upon himself the appearance of certain passions, that he wanted to be taken for mad." He went on: "I believe it is wrong to have discussed the 'madness of the Cross' in a chapter about the insane, because there is always the idea of a higher wisdom." Gouhier also argued about the theme of the *danse macabre;* he rejected Foucault's view that the grinning depiction of madness took the place of the depiction of death in literature or pictorial art. "One can see why: for you there is a philosophical continuity—madness is still death. And you transpose this into continuity in the history of art." But for Gouhier this was not at all the case; for example, he challenged Foucault's interpretation of Bosch's paintings. Gouhier also expressed surprise at certain omissions: "You cite Shakespeare, but you should also cite John Ford, Penthea's madness in *The Broken Heart.*" He challenged what he saw as a wrong reading of Diderot's *Neveu de Rameau;* what the candidate claimed Diderot's characters said involved a manipulation of the text. Far more important, in Gouhier's view, Foucault had also manipulated the text of Descartes. For example, concerning the hypothesis of "evil genius" in the *Meditations:*

> The evil genius symbolizes the hypothesis of an absurd world in which I would see that 3 plus 2 equals 5, whereas this would be wrong. But I cannot see any way in which this symbolizes madness. The idea is produced by associating the notion of malice with the notion of omnipotence. The psychology of this figure was outlined at the beginning of the fourth Meditation: *it is the idea of omnipotence, suggested by imagery tinged with Machiavellism,* that is one of the first principles of existence. You see there a threat of unreason. No, it is

simply the possibility of another reason. That is the metaphysical foundation for this hypothesis.

Gouhier also refused to see in Descartes's words "Mais quoi, ce sont des fous" (But after all, they are madmen) the act creating the great division that would isolate reason from unreason. Gouhier stressed Descartes because he understood that the discussion of him was central to Foucault's argument. But he also reproached Foucault for "thinking allegorically": using "personifications that allow a sort of metaphysical invasion into history and somehow transform narrative into epic, history into allegorical drama, giving life to a philosophy." In conclusion, the president of the jury said to the candidate: "I do not understand what you meant when you defined madness as the absence of work." Foucault acknowledged the validity of this remark in a long article reprinted as an appendix to *Histoire de la folie*, where he characterized the statement as "something I said somewhat unwittingly."[14]

The ceremony was over. Speaking through its president and before the assembled audience, the jury awarded the candidate the title of doctor of letters, with "very honorable mention." A few days later Gouhier wrote an official report reviewing the defense. The text is worth including in its entirety, because it summarizes the earliest reactions to Foucault's work:

On May 20, M. Michel Foucault, an instructor at the Faculty of Letters and Human Sciences at Clermont-Ferrand, presented his doctoral thesis:
—Kant: *Anthropology*, introduction, translation, and notes. Minor thesis. Respondent: M. Hyppolite.
—*Folie et déraison. Histoire de la folie à l'age classique.* Principal thesis. Respondents: M. Canguilhem, first reader; and M. Lagache, second reader.
Also present on the jury were M. de Gandillac (for the minor thesis) and the president (for the principal thesis).
The two works presented by Foucault, though very different, nonetheless received quite similar praise and criticisms. It is obvious that M. Foucault is extremely well-read and possesses a strong personality and rich intellect. The defense only confirms these judgments. His two expositions are remarkable for their clarity, their ease, the elegant precision of a thought that knows where it is going, advances unhesitatingly, and is, one feels, in control of itself. But apparent here and there is a certain indifference to the drudgery that always accompanies the most elevated work. The translation of the

Kant text was correct but not sufficiently subtle. The ideas were seductive but were rapidly developed on the basis of just a few facts: M. Foucault is more philosopher than exegete or historian.

The two judges of the minor thesis concluded that it juxtaposes two pieces of work:

1. a historical introduction that is the outline for a book on anthropology and, as M. Hyppolite remarked, one inspired more by Nietzsche than by Kant;

2. the translation of Kant's text, which now serves only as a pretext, should be revised. M. de Gandillac advised the candidate that he should separate the two pieces, giving the introduction its full scope as a book in its own right and publishing separately a truly critical edition of Kant's text.

The three examiners who dealt especially with the principal thesis all recognized the work's originality. The author sought within consciousness for the idea that men in each age have formed of madness, and he defines several mental "structures" in the "classical age," that is, in the seventeenth, eighteenth, and early nineteenth centuries. It would be impossible to recount here all the questions raised by his work. Let us simply mention the following: Canguilhem asked whether this was a dialectics or a history of structures. M. Lagache questioned whether the author had really been able to free himself from the concepts elaborated by contemporary psychiatry to define his structures and to draw his historical portrait.

The president induced the candidate to explain the underlying metaphysics of his research: a certain "valorization" of the experience of madness in the light of cases such as that of Antonin Artaud, Nietzsche, and Van Gogh.

The impression to be retained from this defense is that of a curious contrast between the indisputable talent that everyone recognized in the candidate and the many reservations expressed from the beginning to the end of the session. M. Foucault is, of course, a writer, but M. Canguilhem criticized the rhetoric of certain parts, and the president thought he was too concerned about creating an "effect."

There is no doubt about his erudition, but the president mentioned instances revealing a spontaneous tendency to go beyond the facts. One has the impression that criticisms of this sort would have been even more numerous if the jury had been able to include an art historian, a literary historian, and a historian of institutions. M. Foucault's competence in psychology is real. M. Lagache found, however, that the psychiatric information was somewhat limited and the pages on Freud a bit cursory.

Hence, the more one thinks about it, the more one can see that these two theses have provoked numerous and serious criticism. Nonetheless, the fact remains that we are in the presence of a principal thesis that is truly original, by a man whose personality, whose intellectual "dynamism," whose talent for exposition all qualify him for higher education. That is why, despite reservations, this degree was awarded unanimously with highest honors.

Henri Gouhier, May 25, 1961

"Despite reservations," as the president of the jury wrote in his report, *Folie et déraison* also received a medal from the Centre National de la Recherche Scientifique (CNRS). Every year a gold medal was awarded for a work as a whole, a silver medal for postdoctoral work, and twenty-four bronze medals for the best thesis in each discipline. The bronze medal in philosophy was awarded to Foucault. And since Foucault now had the title of "doctor," he could be named as a "tenured professor" at the University of Clermont—which was done in the fall of 1962. It remained then for the book to find its readers, taking a strange and chaotic route to do so. It also had to find the category—or categories—to which it belonged, through commentaries that would come and settle upon it, turning this "event,"[15] this sudden appearance, into the starting point for a thousand other events as the readings gradually multiplied, proliferated, and diverged.

9

The Book and Its Doubles

During the 1970s Foucault complained on several occasions about the reception of *Folie et déraison* when it was published. "When I began to be interested in subjects that were sort of the lowest depths of social reality, a few poeple, such as Barthes, Blanchot, and the English antipsychiatrists, focused on it with interest. But I must say that neither the philosophical community nor the political community was interested. None of the reviews institutionally earmarked to register the slightest convulsion in the philosophical universe paid any attention."[1] Here Foucault was attacking *Les Temps modernes* and *Esprit*, for which he never had any great liking. And it is true that neither of these reviews mentioned his book. It is also true that the work went unnoticed by the broad cultured public. But did Foucault really hope to reach this public? In 1977 Foucault developed these remarks further to explain the reasons for what he considered the quasi-silence surrounding his book. He blamed the leaden mold that the power of the Communist party and Marxist ideology forced onto the behavior of intellectuals, and hence on their capacity for seeing the critical force of a book that escaped this rigidly limited framework.[2]

But was this disappointment—perhaps retrospective—justified? In any case, it is hard to go along with Foucault's claim that only a few, marginal individuals had been able to measure the importance of his work. In addition to the articles by Blanchot and Barthes, mentioned by Foucault, there were an article by Michel Serres and a long commentary signed by Robert Mandrou in *Annales* (where he was editorial secretary).[3] Mandrou's article was followed by a "Note" by Fernand Braudel, in which this pope of the new historical research gave his blessing to the book.[4]

After the official (and confidential; the reports were not shared even with the candidate) judgments written by Georges Canguilhem and Henri Gouhier when the thesis was defended, these good reviews heralding the book's publication were the first public reaction to Foucault's work. It is useful to quote a few passages from them, because Foucault was still an unknown and these readings were not filtered through any deforming, already constituted image. Michel Serres made the connection between Foucault's book and Dumézil's work: "In effect," he wrote, "the history of madness will never be understood as a genesis of psychiatric categories, as a search for premonitions of positive ideas in the classical age . . . Rather, what are described are variations of the structures that can be applied to this double family of spaces, ones that have in fact been applied to it: the structure of separation, of relationship, of fusion, of foundation, of reciprocity, of exclusion." But Serres was not unaware of the other inspiration for the book:

> This architectural rigor would be in vain if, beyond the structural comprehension, a more secret vision, a more fervent attention was not revealed. The work would be precise, but not quite true. That is why, at the very heart of the logical argument, at the heart of the meticulous erudition of historical inquiry, a deep love circulates—not in the least a vaguely humanist love, but one almost religious—for this obscure population in which the infinitely close, the other oneself, is recognized. This book, therefore, is also a cry . . . Consequently, this transparent geometry is the pathetic language of men who undergo the greatest of tortures, that of being cornered, of disgrace, of exile, of quarantine, ostracism, and excommunication."

In short, "this is the book of every solitude." Nor did Serres forget to celebrate Nietzsche's shadowy presence: "Michel Foucault's book is to classical tragedy (and more generally to classical culture) what the Nietzschean approach was to Hellenic tragedy and culture: it shows the latent Dionysian elements in Apollonian enlightenment."[5]

Barthes, for his part, liked to imagine that Lucien Febvre would have liked Foucault's book, "because it returns a fragment of 'nature' to history and transforms madness, something we take to be a medical phenomenon, into a phenomenon of civilization." A little farther along he added: "In fact, Michel Foucault never defines madness; madness is not an object of understanding, whose history must be rediscovered; it is nothing more, if you like, than this understanding itself; madness is not an illness, it is a variable and perhaps heterogeneous sense, depending on the century; Michel Foucault never treats madness as a functional reality: for him it is the pure function of a couple formed by reason and unreason, the gazer and the gazed upon." But Barthes, too, was completely aware that Foucault's heavy volume was "something other than a book of history," that it was "something like a cathartic question asked about madness." He concluded by mentioning, along with questions of knowledge, the other theme of Foucauldian research in years to come, dwelling on the "vertigo of discourse that Michel Foucault has just shown in a dazzling light, vertigo that arises not merely from contact with madness, but rather every time that man, taking some distance, looks at the world as something other; that is, every time he writes."[6]

The articles by Barthes and Serres, with their very different styles and points of view, were remarkable, brilliantly acute and intelligent, readings of *Folie et déraison*. Of course, Barthes was one of Foucault's friends, and Serres was a colleague at Clermont. But this was not the case for Blanchot, who described the book as "extraordinary . . . rich and insistent, and almost unreasonable in its necessary repetitions," and who concluded his commentary with a mention of Bataille.[7]

Nor was it true of Mandrou or Braudel. Mandrou first pointed out a way to get into the book. Rather than entering through its "too brilliant formulations," he would advise one to slip into it, taking a detour through the introduction to *Le Rêve et l'existence*, "where the dream is studied as a means of knowledge, following processes parallel to those of wide-awake reason . . . he considers that madness, like dream, is a means of knowledge, a truth that is other and not-other. And our author finds himself up against the fact that madness no longer has any place in the contemporary world except in a lyrical formulation, from Nerval to Artaud. He takes a violent stand against this exclusion." Mandrou also made reference to Dumézil, recalling Foucault's mention of him in his interview in *Le Monde*, and he quoted this particularly Dumézilian sentence from the book: "Unreason would be the long memory of peoples, their greatest fidelity to the past." He concluded with this judgment on Foucault himself: "His book puts him in the forefront of the research that is his passion and our passion as well."[8]

This is Braudel's "note":

I am adding a few lines to the preceding review to stress the originality, the pioneering nature of Michel Foucault's book. I do not see it as merely one of those studies of collective psychology so rarely attempted by historians, though much in demand since Lucien Febvre. I see in it, and admire, a singular aptitude for approaching a problem from three or four different directions, in an ambiguity that is sometimes mistakenly reflected in practical procedures (one must play close attention to follow its line of reasoning). This is precisely the ambiguity of any collective phenomenon. Any truth of civilization plunges into the obscurity of contradictory, conscious and unconscious motivations. This magnificent book tries to pursue—apropos of a specific phenomenon: madness—what the mysterious progression of a civilization's mental structures may be; how it has to free itself from and give up on a part of itself, separating out those things it means to keep of what its own past offered and those things it hopes to repress, ignore, and forget. This difficult pursuit requires a mind that is capable of being in turn a historian, a philosopher, a psychologist, and a sociologist—never simply one of these . . . This is not a method that could be offered as an example; it is not within the reach of just anybody. Something more than talent is necessary.

Folie et déraison—a work that went unnoticed? There is even more evidence that it met with a rather kindly welcome. There is, for example, Bachelard's very nice letter after Foucault had sent him a copy of the book. On August 1, 1961, this well-known philosopher, one especially well placed to understand the intertwining of the history of sciences and a "poetic" vision, wrote to him: "I have just finished reading today your great book . . . Sociologists go to great lengths to study foreign populations. You prove to them that we are a mix of savages. You are a real explorer. I took special note of your intention (p. 624) to go exploring in the nineteenth century." He concluded with an invitation: "I am going to be obliged to leave wonderful Paris, but in October, you should come see me. I want to congratulate you in person, to tell you out loud again and again all the subtle pleasures I had in reading your pages, to express, in short, my most sincere esteem."[9]
Another reaction worth noting is that of a very young philosopher who had been one of Foucault's students at the Rue d'Ulm and had since become Jean Wahl's assistant at the Sorbonne. This was Jacques Derrida. His response had a great effect on the French philosophical landscape in years to come. Jean Wahl, who was the director of the association called the Collège de Philosophie, asked his assistant to give a lecture there. Derrida discussed *Folie et déraison*, particularly the passage concerning Descartes, since he considered that "Foucault's whole project can be pinpointed in these few allusive and somewhat enigmatic pages" and that "the reading of Descartes and of the Cartesian cogito proposed to us engages in its problematic the totality of this *Histoire de la folie* as regards both its intention and its feasibility."[10] This was Derrida's famous lecture "Cogito et histoire de la folie,"

given on March 4, 1963. He mentioned at the outset the delicacy of undertaking discussion of a book so "powerful in its inspiration and in its style," and he added that it was "even more intimidating for me in that, having formerly had the good fortune to study under Michel Foucault, I retain the consciousness of an admiring and grateful disciple." Then: "The disciple's consciousness, when he starts, I would not say to dispute, but to engage in dialogue with the master, or, better, to articulate the interminable and silent dialogue which made him into a disciple—this disciple's consciousness is an unhappy consciousness." He then referred to "the interminable unhappiness of the disciple" who is unable to engage in this dialogue without having it be "taken—incorrectly—as a challenge." [11] It might have been wrong to hear it so, but it was very hard to do otherwise; the lecture was rather sharp in tone, sometimes harsh. Despite the admiration he felt for this "monumental" book, the "disciple" was not particularly inclined to spare the master. Derrida, like Henri Gouhier during the thesis defense, refused to see Descartes's "But after all, they're madmen" as a brutal assertion of ostracism, tossed out when he met up with madness. This, in his view, was a very "naive" reading of the Cartesian text. But it was also a dangerous reading, which claimed to reinscribe a text in a "historical structure," in a "total historical project," and which would in turn work violence "with regard to rationalists and sense, 'good' sense." [12] After taking a few rhetorical precautions, Derrida risked the following formulation: "Structuralist totalitarianism here would be responsible for an internment of the cogito similar to the violences of the classical age." [13]

What must Foucault have felt when he heard these remarks? Because he was present in the room! It would seem, according to what several witnesses have said, that for the moment his legendary touchiness lay dormant and that he did not hold this argumentative attack against his former student. The text of the lecture was published a few months later in *Revue de métaphysique et de morale*, which Jean Wahl also headed. [14] Foucault does not seem to have taken umbrage either on this occasion or when Derrida reprinted the text in 1967 in *L'Ecriture et la différence*. Foucault even sent him a very friendly letter to acknowledge receipt of the volume. The incident did, however, produce a delayed explosion. And it is very hard to know why. Was Foucault in the end exasperated at seeing this lecture reprinted in a book, whereas up to now it had been addressed to a rather limited audience? There is yet another possible explanation, offered here merely for what it is, a hypothesis, for Foucault's apparently abrupt change of behavior. When

L'Ecriture et la différence was published, both Foucault and Derrida were on the editorial board of the review *Critique*. An article by Gérard Granel arrived in the review's office, full of praise for Derrida's collection and equally full of venom toward Foucault, who took offense and asked Derrida to prevent the article's publication. Derrida refused to intervene, preferring, as a member of the editorial committee, not to pronounce judgment on material that concerned him. The article was published. And Foucault shortly afterward wrote an extremely violent response to Derrida's 1963 lecture. The reply, titled "Mon Corps, ce papier, ce feu," was published in September 1971 in the review *Paideia;* and Foucault reprinted it in 1972 at the end of *Histoire de la folie.* Foucault sent the new edition of his book to Derrida with a brief inscription: "Sorry to have answered you so late." Nine years later! The end of Foucault's text has the ring of a declaration of war. Roles have been reversed; now it is the teacher's turn to judge his former student:

> I agree on one fact at least: it is not as a result of inattention that classical interpreters, before Derrida, and like him, have erased this passage by Descartes. It is systematic. Derrida, today, is the most authoritative representative of this system, its final radiance. In it discursive traces are reduced to textual traces; events occurring there are elided and kept only as markers for a reading; voices behind the texts are invented so as not to have to analyze the ways in which the subject is implicated in discourses; the original is allocated to what is said and not-said in the text, so as not to put discursive practices back into the field of transformations in which they are carried out.

Foucault pronounced this final verdict: "I am not going to say that there is a metaphysics, *the* metaphysics or its closure, concealed in this "textualization" of discursive practices. I am going to go much further. I am going to say that it is a minor pedagogy, one thoroughly historically determined, that manifests itself in a way that is highly visible. This pedagogy teaches the pupil that there is nothing outside the text . . . This pedagogy gives the teacher's voice that unlimited sovereignty which allows it to repeat the text indefinitely." [15] Here we see Derridan "deconstruction" reduced to functioning as the "restoration" of tradition and authority. A duel to the death has never been forbidden in the republic of letters. From that moment on there was a radical and absolute break between the two philosophers, and it lasted for ten years. It took Derrida's arrest in Prague in 1981 (accused of "drug trafficking," whereas he had gone to participate in a seminar organized by dissidents) for them to renew their connections. There was considerable sentiment in France concerning this arrest, and while the government was interceding with the Czech authorities, French intellectuals called increasingly for protest. Foucault was among the first signatories, and he spoke on the radio in support of Derrida's action. When Derrida returned to Paris several days later, he telephoned Foucault to thank him. They met again on several occasions after this.

In addition to the reviews accorded *Folie et déraison* soon after its publication there was an interview with Foucault in *Le Monde* as well as an article in the *Times Literary Supplement*.[16] But all the same, the book is difficult reading. Even those who gave it a kind welcome emphasized its complexity, its occasional oversubtlety, indeed its hermetic quality. Foucault himself, when the book was reissued in 1972, would tell Claude Mauriac: "If I had this book to write again today, I would be less rhetorical."[17] Sales, of course, were not overwhelming. There had been an initial printing of 3,000 copies in May 1961, followed by another 1,200 in February 1964. But at the same time a drastically abridged pocket edition appeared, which is the one that most people read during the eight years that would elapse before the reprinting of the complete text.

The abridged edition, unfortunately, was the one translated into English in 1965, with the title *Madness and Civilization*. This publication in English demonstrated the immediate interest of "antipsychiatrists" in Foucault. The book, ironically, was published in a series called Studies in Existentialism and Phenomenology, edited by Ronald Laing. David Cooper wrote the preface for it. Laing and Cooper were in the process of inventing "antipsychiatry" in London in the 1960s. A group of psychiatrists, clinicians, and psychoanalysts compared their experiences. In their view, schizophrenia in the broad sense was the consequence of full-scale repressive apparatus imposed by the family and society. This "original violence" was followed by a relegation of schizophrenics to psychiatric institutions. As they saw it, classic psychiatry represented ultrarepression. The antipsychiatrists were influenced by Nietzsche, Kierkegaard, and Heidegger but also, and above all, by Sartre, to whom Laing and Cooper devoted a book. Cooper was the first to attempt an experiment in a traditional psychiatric setting. He worked in a hospital on the north side of London, and he began by grouping all his patients together in one pavillion. But the experiment quickly came to an end because of the hostility of the hospital milieu. At this point the antipsychiatrists founded the Philadelphia Association so that they could create novel places to accommodate patients. They then opened several "households," among them the celebrated

Kingsey Hall, opened in 1965. At the same time the psychiatrists developed a leftist political program that resulted, for example, in an international congress devoted to "the dialectics of liberation." Laing and Cooper were among the organizers, but Gregory Bateson and Herbert Marcuse also participated.[18] In any case, Foucault's book caught the attention of Laing and Cooper, and they turned a different light on it, giving it an entirely different interpretation from earlier readings, as well as from Foucault's original conception. The fact that the book had had no political impact when it came out, as Foucault complained during the 1970s, was largely a reflection of the fact that it had not been written from a political perspective. Robert Castel made this forcefully clear in his 1986 article on the fate of *Histoire de la folie:*

> The role of flagbearer that fell to Michel Foucault in a movement protesting certain institutional practices is one that is inscribed, first of all, in a historical process. It had not been an immediate result of his work . . . *Histoire de la folie* had an earlier fate, that of an academic work asking academic questions. This is not meant to be pejorative, nor does it question the work's originality. But its novelty was, first of all, inscribed within the framework of an epistemological questioning that bore all the markers of its contemporary intellectual arena. The university tradition continued by Foucault (that of Brunschvicg, Bachelard, Canguilhem) questioned scientific discourses' claim to truth and the conditions under which such discourses might exist outside the threshold of reflexivity that is the basis for the development of the classic history of sciences as an interlocking of pure intellectual projections.

Castel added: "It was only in a nonpractical register that Foucault's analyses were able to have some impact on the way one could see psychiatry and madness in the beginning of the 1960s." Castel provided a very good summary of the first reactions to the book and of the various levels on which Foucault was undoubtedly inspired:

> It was possible, therefore, to read *Histoire de la folie*, in the middle of the 1960s, simultaneously as an academic thesis that was a continuation of the work of Bachelard and Canguilhem, and as an evocation of the dark powers of the forbidden—in the manner of Lautréamont or Antonin Artaud. It was this paradoxical montage that provided the unique status of this work. To some it was fascinating, to others irritating, or both at once. But believing in the theses of the work did not imply any precise political option, or any project for practical change.[19]

Therefore, it was not until after 1968 and the development of "sector-based struggles," as they were described at the time—concerning prisons, psychiatry, and so on—that the book was literally taken over by social movements, which imposed an entirely different reading of it, giving it a political significance that it did not have when it was first published. Foucault was perfectly aware of this. When he revised the work in 1972 he left out the preface written in 1960, and, after hesitating for a long time over writing a new one that would position him in relation to the antipsychiatrists, he finally decided to replace it with a very short "nonpreface," and justified his refusal to update his introductory remarks by the fact that an author did not have to prescribe the correct usage for a book. "A book," he said in this wonderful text,

is produced, a minute event, a small, handy object. From that moment on it is caught up in an endless play of repetitions; its doubles begin to swarm, around it and far from it; each reading gives it an impalpable and unique body for an instant; fragments of itself are circulating and are made to stand in for it, are taken to almost entirely contain it, and sometimes serve as refuge for it; it is doubled with commentaries, those other discourses in which it should finally appear as it is, confessing what it had refused to say, freeing itself from what it had so loudly pretended to be.

Consequently, it is better not to try "to justify this old book or to reinscribe it today; the series of events to which it belongs and which form its true law is far from being closed."[20] Is there a better way of saying that books change? and that, in any case, this one had changed?

Likewise, the reception from the French medical-psychiatric profession had changed. When Foucault first came on the scene, he was not unanimously condemned. Foucault himself described it: "There were diverse reactions among the physicians and psychiatrists. Some, with a liberal and Marxist viewpoint, demonstrated a certain interest; on the other hand there were others, more conservative, who totally rejected [my work]."[21] As we have seen, Foucault as a student had been in contact with progressive psychiatric milieus, which had been trying ever since the end of the war to give new life to psychiatric discourses and practices. According to Robert Castel, "the most progressive psychiatrists of the period all had, or thought they had, their own formula for renewing their practices. They claimed, by putting "sector politics" in place, to be bringing off a "third psychiatric revolution" (the first being Pinel's, the second Freud's), which would reconcile psychiatry with its century by breaking down the asylum walls and reorganizing help for the mentally ill within the community, on the level of needs expressed by the population."[22] This idea was incompatible with Foucault's theses. He saw such progressive optimism as a new avatar of a positivism still intent on denying the fundamental otherness of madness, and on reducing it to silence. However, most of the doctors connected with the group Evolution Psychiatrique seem to have been sympathetic to *Folie et déraison*. Condemnation would come when the book began to serve as a "toolbox," as Foucault liked to put it, for movements rightly looking in it for instruments to use in a radical critique of psychiatric institutions. From that point on, those who had been sympathetic to Foucault's efforts revised their judgment. When, several years later, the antipsychiatric wave swept out from England, the people whose views and practices it was challenging hardened into hostility and targeted the book that was being held up to them as having dynamited their certainties and attitudes. This was true of Lucien Bonnafé, a member of the Communist party, whom Foucault mentioned as having reacted positively to his book when it first came out. Bonnafé would participate in the annual meeting of Evolution Psychiatrique in Toulouse on December 6 and 7, 1969, which literally excommunicated the "ideological conception of *Histoire de la folie*." Foucault was not present. Henri Ey, there on the front lines, declared:

> This concerns a psychiatricide position that is of such great importance for the very idea of man that we would very much have desired Michel Foucault's presence among us, both to pay our just respects of admiration for the systematic methods of his thought and to challenge the notion that "mental illness" may be considered as the fantastic manifestation of madness or, more exceptionally, as the spark of poetic genius, because it is something other than a cultural phenomenon. If there are some of us who, worried by the vulnerability of their own positions or seduced by Foucault's brilliant paradoxes, had hoped not to have to face up to this debate, for myself, I regret the absence of this face-to-face encounter. Michel Foucault, whose invitation I saw to, regrets it as much as we do, as he expressed it in a letter, excusing himself because he was unable to be in Toulouse at this time. So we will go on just as if he were here. Physical presence is not very important in a debate of ideas, precisely when the confrontation is one only of ideas.[23]

The wrath of Professor Baruk also descended upon Foucault. This eminent specialist endlessly—in books, articles, conferences, and lectures—denounced Foucault's disastrous role, which he saw only as that of instigator, founding father of antipsychiatry, for a whole flood of "incompetent" people who were working to destroy the humanistic and liberating medicine set in place by Pinel.[24]

Foucault accepted the way his book had been intercepted and used. After 1968 he would draw closer to antipsychiatric movements, sometimes even very close, although he was often annoyed by the infantilism of some of their most extreme adherents. This coming together took place, essentially, in the wake of another of Foucault's preoccupations, as founder of the Groupe d'Information sur les Prisons (GIP) in 1971. But he never became involved in militant activism concerning asylums to the same extent that he was on the question of penal institutions. He never really took part in the antipsychiatric movements but was content to go along with them from some distance, at the most to encourage them.[25] All the same, he did associate with antipsychiatrists such as Cooper and Franco Basaglia. In 1976 he had Cooper invited to the Collège de France to give a series of lectures, and in 1977 he participated with him in a debate organized by Jean-Pierre Faye and sponsored by the review *Change*.[26] He supported the translation into French of the books of Thomas Szasz, took part in a group founded by radical Italian psychiatrists for the critique of institutions, and wrote a piece for the collective volume *Crimini di pace* to support Basaglia in his problems with the Italian justice system. Other contributors to this volume included Sartre, Erving Goffman, Noam Chomsky, and Robert Castel.[27] In any event, although, as Castel put it, he responded *a minima* to solicitations concerning antipsychiatric action,[28] Foucault nonetheless admitted playing some part in this struggle. Taking stock in 1977, he was able to credit the category "local and specific struggles" with "important results obtained in psychiatry."[29]

This interception of the book had several results. In the first place, it can be seen, as Robert Castel sees it, as "an impoverishment" of the book. The fact that *Folie et déraison* functioned on a wide range of levels is what made it possible to describe it as a "structural history." It related elements of different orders—economic, institutional, political, philosophical, scientifc—and they consequently took on meaning. Now it was reduced to nothing more than a denunciation of oppressive forces: "The breadth of theoretical detours and the subtlety of analyses of situations close up around several simplified formulas, and the argument in the hands of epigones becomes repetitive: everywhere and always there is nothing but repression, violence, the arbitrary, confinement, police control, segregation, and exclusion."[30] A weakening then, but also, perhaps, an anchoring device for the unity that Foucault gave his work in this period and in the years to come, attaching it to the notion of "power" and to the dyad "knowledge-power." After 1970 this was the unifying category that he gave his oldest works: "All of that," he told Ducio Trombadori, "emerged like something written in invisible ink that began to appear on the paper when the right reagent was added, which was the word POWER."[31]

10
~~

The Dandy and the Reforms

Foucault's thesis did have to not wait for publication to find attentive readers. The manuscript was first handed around among a
group of friends, and Louis Althusser was naturally among the
earliest. He read, liked, and approved it. He loaned the work to Jules
Vuillemin, who was then director of the philosophy department at the
University of Clermont-Ferrand. Althusser and Vuillemin had known
each other for a long time. As was mentioned earlier, both had entered
the Ecole Normale Supérieure in 1939 and met again after the war,
and when Althusser took on the job of *caïman* he invited Vuillemin on
several occasions to give lectures. Foucault got his job at Lille thanks to
this friendship. Vuillemin was a good friend of Maurice Merleau-
Ponty. Until the early 1950s he was closely connected with existentialism and Marxism. There are signs of this double influence in the
titles of the two theses he defended in 1948: "Essai sur la signification
de la mort" and "L'Etre et le travail." During this period he also published some articles on aesthetics in *Les Temps modernes.* Vuillemin had
changed substantially since that time, although he remained close to
Merleau-Ponty. For one thing, his intellectual interests has shifted; he
began to deal closely with the philosophy of science, with mathematics
and logic. No doubt he had also changed politically, but the mutual
respect binding Althusser and Vuillemin did not suffer from their radically divergent evolutions. In the years before 1968, the French university had not yet been cut in two by political and ideological intolerance
as it would be later.

In 1951 Vuillemin was appointed to a post at Clermont-Ferrand,
thanks to Merleau-Ponty. The author of *Humanisme et terreur* wanted
his disciple and friend to succeed him in his position at Lyons, which
he was leaving to go to the Sorbonne. But university rivalries pre-

vented realization of this plan. Merleau-Ponty then went personally to the Ministry of Education to ask that a chair be found for Vuillemin. Shortly afterward the director of higher education met with Vuillemin to tell him: "There is a position for you in Clermont-Ferrand, a chair in psychology. But there is one condition: you have to live there." Vuillemin accepted and moved to the capital of the Auvergne. He arrived at the same time as several other professors sent there by the ministry, which was intent on waking up a rather sleepy university. The historian Jacques Droz and the Hellenist Francis Vian were part of the shipment. For several years Vuillemin was in charge of teaching psychology. He was then assigned to teach philosophy and was later made head of the entire section. A rigorous academician, obsessively conscientious, and aspiring above all to high-quality teaching, he surrounded himself with a brilliant team, turning his philosophy department into a sort of experimental laboratory. He repeatedly went fishing for young colleagues in the tank on the Rue d'Ulm. Among his catches were Michel Serres, Maurice Clavelin, Jean-Claude Pariente, and Jean-Marie Beyssade, all of whom had great careers. Serres, Clavelin, and Beyssade are teaching today at the Sorbonne and at Nanterre. Pariente is still teaching at Clermont and is president of the jury for the *agrégation*. Vuillemin also wanted Althusser to come, but his friend preferred the protected environment of the ENS, for reasons to do with his psychological health, which was fragile. In 1960 Vuillemin's choice fell upon Michel Foucault. He had just read the manuscript of *Folie et déraison* and he wrote to the author in Hamburg, asking if he would take charge of the psychology courses at Clermont. Foucault immediately answered yes. He wanted to find a way to get back to France after his long sojourns abroad, and he was all the more willing to accept because he would not be obliged to be "in residence"; he could therefore live in Paris. The remaining formalities were got through very quickly and easily. To be appointed to a position in higher education, one first had to have been registered on a *liste d'aptitude*.[1] Georges Bastide submitted the report on Foucault's candidacy on June 15, 1960: "Michel Foucault has already produced several minor works: translations of German works, essentially popularizing the history and method of psychology. This is all, moreover, respectable work. But certainly the theses of this candidate constitute his best books." He concluded: "We are registering M. Michel Foucault on the *liste large* (should his classification be psychology? or history of science?). That should be discussed." In support of Foucault's candidacy, Canguilhem added to

Bastide's report the one he himself had just written to obtain the printing permit for *Folie et déraison*, and Hyppolite wrote a letter of recommendation. And so, all the business having been dealt with briskly, Foucault could be appointed to Clermont, "starting October 1, 1960," as "instructor in philosophy, replacing the chaired professor M. Cesari, who is on extended leave," according to the ministry's official notice. On May 1, 1962, after the death of this professor, he would be promoted to "the vacant chair, with tenure." All the official papers designated his field as "philosophy" because psychology had not yet attained status as an independent academic discipline; like sociology, it was attached to philosophy departments. But it was certainly psychology that Foucault was supposed to teach. The dean's report requesting that he be given the tenured position in 1962 was quite specific: "His specialty is psychopathology."[2] And throughout his years at Clermont-Ferrand, Foucault would be officially responsible for teaching psychology, even if in reality he shirked much of it (though less than one might think).

This was the beginning of a new life for him. From the fall of 1960 to the spring of 1966 he made the trip between Paris and Clermont every week of the school year. All his classes were scheduled on one day, so he had to spend only one night in a hotel. It was a six-hour trip, and the trains afforded rather rudimentary conditions of comfort. The ride on the "Bourbonnais" was so rough that the teachers who came from Paris—called "sputniks"; "turbo-profs" were not yet invented—invented a little game that involved managing to drink one's coffee without spilling it. Foucault devised the dodge of blocking it with his teaspoon, and excelled in this risky maneuver.

In those days the University of Clermont was completely contained in a large white stone building on the Avenue Carnot, not far from the Lycée Blaise-Pascal, where Bergson had taught. The building dated from 1936, and, *époque oblige*, it looked like a miniature Palais de Chaillot. The interior facades had a rather grim look; as soon as one entered the courtyard, everything became dark and somber, as if covered by the black dust that seemed to have settled on most of the city, with its black stone cathedral, its whitish houses decorated with black trim in volcanic rock from nearby Volvic. The first time he saw the houses, Foucault said they looked like "funeral announcements." The philosophy faculty was on the ground floor and occupied a corridor of at most ten rooms, which served as offices and classrooms. This corridor had "belonged" to philosophy forever. Georges Canguilhem remembered having worked there during the war. But in 1963 the whole crew of philosophers had to abandon their territory and emigrate to a sort of prefabricated barracks, one of those hideous "temporary" constructions fated to endure. It is still there today, sheltering the administrative services. In this sinister blockhouse Foucault's students heard the outline of what would become *Les Mots et les choses*. He did not have many students, but there were more than the mere ten registered in philosophy. The ranks were swelled to thirty by students who wanted to take courses in psychology to obtain a diploma in, for example, nursing or social work.

During Foucault's first two years at Clermont he and Vuillemin became quite close friends. They took long walks together in the streets of the old city and often ate together, either just the two of them or with other members of the philosophy department. Ten people for lunch or dinner was not unusual. Vuillemin and Foucault got along terrifically, and they took to the little group of philosophers at Clermont, where friendly relations and warm companionship prevailed, like fish to water. Nevertheless there were many things to separate the two professors. Vuillemin was oriented to the philosophy of science; he looked to the Anglo-Americans and was particularly interested in the writings of Bertrand Russell, in logic and mathematics. During this period he published the two volumes of his *Philosophie de l'algèbre*. Politically, too, there was a rather wide gap between them: Vuillemin gradually evolved toward the right, and Foucault remained more or less a man of the left. They often argued, and Foucault frequently concluded their exchanges by saying: "Basically, you are an anarchist of the right and I am an anarchist of the left." What could this conservative interested in logic and this leftist who wrote about Blanchot, Roussel, and Bataille have had in common? Both Foucault and Vuillemin demanded rigor, and their intellectual respect for each other took priority over all their differences. On many points they were on the same wavelength.

This would be a lasting attachment with important consequences for Foucault's career. In 1962 Vuillemin left Clermont. Merleau-Ponty had suddenly died of a heart attack, and Vuillemin was summoned to succeed him at the Collège de France. Foucault had a hand in the appointment. He asked Dumézil to support his colleague at Clermont and thus was able to win approval from those whom the mythologist's influence could mobilize. Vuillemin was elected over Raymond Aron, who had to wait several years before he could renew his candidacy. One year after Vuillemin's appointment, Jean Hyppolite entered the

Collège de France. The two philosophers were soon working with the approaches and ways of thinking that in 1969 would promote Foucault's acceptance in the prestigious institution on the Rue des Ecoles, the holy of holies, the glory of French academia. And Dumézil lent his support. By this time the events of May 1968 had hardened oppositions between Vuillemin and Foucault. But Vuillemin, though violently hostile to the student revolt, refused to place political disagreement ahead of his respect for Foucault's work.

In fact there was nothing substantive before 1968 that would have caused a breach, or even real disagreement, between them. They frequently argued over politics, but, so far was each from being militantly involved, neither even belonged to a party. Politics was far from providing the structure of their existence or thought. One should beware above all of projecting the image of a later Foucault onto the Foucault of that period. His colleagues from that time are in general agreement in placing him "more to the left," but they describe him primarily as someone who maintained a distance from any militant involvement, despite his very real interest in politics. They were very surprised by his swing to the far left and by the radical positions he took during the 1970s. "I never managed to believe it really," says Francine Pariente, who was his assistant from 1962 to 1966. There was nothing to make them suspect that he would evolve in this direction.

Some people who knew him well during these years attach a different political label to him: they claim that Foucault was a Gaullist. Jules Vuillemin challenges this idea. He talked enough with Foucault to be certain that it has no foundation. But some people may have believed this because Foucault remained on very good terms with Etienne Burin des Roziers, who left his post as ambassador in Warsaw to become secretary-general at the Elysée shortly after Foucault left Poland. This was an extremely important political position, a sort of prime ministership in the shadows. Foucault did not miss an opportunity to go behind the scenes of power and pay a call on his friend in the presidential palace, on the Rue Faubourg-Saint-Honoré. "When he visited me sometime during 1962," wrote Burin des Roziers, "the future of our higher education was his dearest project. He eagerly accepted a meeting with Jacques Narbonne, in the heart of the general secretariat, who was in charge of dossiers pertaining to the university."[3] Narbonne did in fact meet with Foucault and asked his opinion about possible reform in the universities. But this remained an informal exchange and led to no report, official or otherwise.

These contacts with Gaullist power went rather further in later years—as when Foucault was being considered for appointment as assistant director of higher education in the Ministry of Education. The appointment seemed assured, and several rectors of education districts sent letters congratulating him on his new promotion—prematurely. Foucault's nomination collided with head-on refusal. In the front lines of the opposition were the very influential dean of the Sorbonne, Marcel Durry, and his no less influential wife, Marie-Jeanne Durry, who was head of the Ecole Normale Supérieure in Sèvres. Their objection was based on the "special" nature of the proposed individual, meaning, of course, his homosexuality. "Just imagine having a director of higher education who is homosexual!" Foucault's detractors exclaimed, and did not hesitate to recall the unfortunate episode in Poland. Foucault did not get the post.

This anecdote reveals the sort of man Foucault was in those days—an academic in the most classic sense of the word, one who did not find the political and administrative functions of assistant director of higher education at all repugnant. Moreover, in this same period he was not only on the jury for admission to the ENS on the Rue d'Ulm but also on the jury for exit exams at the Ecole Normale d'Administration, the most official, most establishmentarian of the elite schools. It is also abundantly clear from this episode that Foucault's homosexuality must have played a role in the distance he always kept from institutions, or that institutions always kept from him. Foucault's entire philosophical and political itinerary was, perhaps, at stake here. What would Foucault have been like as an upper-level administrator in a ministry? or as director of the ORTF (Office de Radiodiffusion Télévision Française), a job he was offered a few years later?

So why raise it?

But we cannot write history in the conditional. Let us return to the real history of those years. In 1965 Foucault took part in elaborating the university reforms that Christian Fouchet, the national education minister, had begun. This reform had been one of Gaullism's great projects, and especially of Prime Minister Georges Pompidou, and it had unleashed a storm of passions for years. "The Fouchet-Aigrain reform," wrote Jean-Claude Passeron,

> began to take effect in 1963. It involved principles of specialization in scientific and professional tracks, revision of curricula and programs, and control of the number and flow of students by a selection process at the university entrance level. As this filtered down in 1964, it set in motion a debate that was joined immediately by the teachers' unions and UNEF [the national students' union], groups such as the

Club Jean Moulin, and reviews (a special issue of *Esprit* in May–June 1964)—and went on growing. Therefore, starting in 1965 the Fouchet project was the crux of the debate that made the university so central in contemporary events.[4]

Christian Fouchet had established a commission to study the problems of higher education as a whole. This group, known as the "Eighteen-Man Commission," met from November 1963 to March 1964, defining the major principles of reform. All that remained was to apply them. For that purpose, in January 1965 the Commission on the Teaching of Literature and Science was created to prepare the concrete details of the reform. The members of this new commission included professors at the Collège de France: Fernand Braudel, André Lichnérowicz, and Jules Vuillemin (who resigned after the first meeting); several deans: Georges Vedel of the law faculty in Paris, and Marc Zamansky from the faculty of science. The director of the ENS, Robert Flacellière, was also there along with university professors from every discipline. Among them was Michel Foucault. How did he land in that spot? On the suggestion of Jean Knapp, the minister's technical adviser, who had been in the same class as Foucault at the Rue d'Ulm. In 1962 Knapp was cultural adviser in Copenhagen, and he had invited Foucault to give a lecture on *Folie et déraison*. France's ambassador to Denmark at the time was Christian Fouchet, so he had heard about the strong impression made by Foucault's talk. When Fouchet was appointed minister of education he named Knapp as one of his advisers, and the latter suggested Foucault's name for the commission. There is nothing surprising about all that. The importance of solidarity and networks among *normaliens* is a commonplace in French academic, cultural, and political life. Foucault accepted but asked that Jules Vuillemin also participate. The commission met approximately once a month, in the library of the offices of the ministry, from January 22, 1965, until February 17, 1966, and Foucault assiduously attended all the work sessions. The commission reports contain traces of some of his remarks. For example, on April 5, 1965, concerning the content of secondary school teaching: "M. Foucault asks that in the organization of instruction, stress be laid upon disciplines of a formative nature rather than on instruction prefiguring instruction in higher education. He hopes the fundamentals will be gone into more deeply." Or his opinion about the *agrégation*: it "provides no information concerning the research aptitude of candidates. Essentially, it is a test of intellectual sharpness." However, he was "in agreement that it should remain in the form of a competition." The minister of education was present at the final meeting. The report of the meeting contains no evidence that Foucault demonstrated any major disagreement with the general direction of the reform or with the details of implementation worked out by the commission; and François Chamoux, a Hellenist who served on the commission, confirmed this impression. More than that: Foucault wrote several reports laying the ground for the commission's work. One of these, written with Chamoux and dated March 31, 1965, pondered several problems concerning the organization of the faculties, and specifically the system of the doctoral thesis, which was judged to be unwieldy and out of date. Foucault and Chamoux proposed replacing it with a system of publications spread out over time: "The completion of the principal thesis would not run the risk of being, as it sometimes is today, the crowning achievement of so long an effort that the author is exhausted for the rest of his days." Another report, written by Foucault alone, dealt with the curriculum in philosophy. Foucault laid out a detailed plan of what should be taught in various years of higher education. He also suggested a two-stage program for the final two years of secondary school: students would begin philosophy studies in the *première* (twelfth grade) with psychology, and would continue them in the *terminale*, when they would be exposed to philosophical problems in the strict sense and to contemporary contributions from the human sciences (psychoanalysis, sociology, linguistics).

Concurrently with the commission meetings at the ministry, many meetings were held at universities all over France to open up the discussion as widely as possible. The debates were intense. There was apparent consensus in the scientific disciplines, but the reform project encountered much opposition in the others. Henri Gouhier remembered Foucault recalling his colleagues to reality during a meeting at the Rue d'Ulm, attended by representatives from all the universities of France: "Don't forget," he interjected, "the way we are going we will end up with one university per department." Foucault therefore took very seriously his part in implementing the reforms. Throughout this year he talked a great deal to his students about the discussions going on in Paris. Often before beginning his lecture, he would ask them: "Do you want to know how far we've got with reforms?" And for a good twenty minutes he would explain what was at stake, the problems raised, the answers they had come up with.

The reform took effect in 1967. The national students' union had denounced its broad outlines as early as December 1964. In March 1966 the union of teachers in higher education organized a three-day strike protesting the conclusions reached by the commissions and the ministry. According to reports in *Le Monde*, this demonstration received wide support. Did the Fouchet reform play a major role in triggering the events of May 1968? This explanation, though frequently offered, is certainly too simple to account for such a complex phenomenon. Certainly it is rather amusing to think of Foucault's having participated in developing this reform. But the fact of that participation renders totally ridiculous any claim that Foucault's works published in the 1960s created the revolutionary line of thought so closely bound up with the events of May 1968.[5] When he wrote *Les Mots et les choses*, Foucault was hardly preparing a revolution or thinking of barricades. He was in the offices of a Gaullist minister, discussing the future of secondary and higher education in France.

There is one political label that everyone agrees upon: Foucault was violently anticommunist. After leaving the Communist party, and especially following his stay in Poland, Foucault had developed a fierce hatred of anything even remotely reminiscent of communism. Academic life in Clermont provided him with an occasion for manifesting this hatred. When Jules Vuillemin was elected to the Collège de France, Foucault suggested that Gilles Deleuze might replace him at the University of Clermont-Ferrand. Foucault and Deleuze had not seen each other since their dinner in Lille ten years earlier. But Deleuze had just published a book that clearly caught Foucault's attention. At the time Deleuze was a rather classical historian of philosophy, although the originality that would burst forth in his later work could already be seen dawning. His *Nietzsche et la philosophie* was much admired in professional circles, and it fascinated Foucault. Vuillemin welcomed Foucault's suggestion and wrote to Deleuze, who was recovering from a serious illness in the country, in the nearby Limousin. Shortly thereafter Deleuze turned up in Clermont, where he spent the day with Foucault and Vuillemin. The meeting went well, the philosophy department unanimously approved Deleuze's candidacy, and Vuillemin also secured unanimous approval from the faculty council. Nevertheless, the appointment eluded this candidate and his overwhelming majority. There was another applicant, supported by the Ministry of Education. Roger Garaudy, a member of the political bureau of the Communist party, would be given the chair. He had been the guardian of Marxist orthodoxy for a considerable time while Stalinism was in its heyday. Why would the minister intervene in his favor and force him upon Clermont, whose faculty wanted nothing to do with him? Rumor had it that Georges Pompidou had expressly requested the appointment. What deal had been struck? The answer remained a mystery. The dean of the faculty made an official protest, to no avail. Garaudy was appointed and moved to Clermont—and paid by having to face Foucault's intransigent hostility. After Vuillemin's departure and the failure of Deleuze's candidacy, Foucault tried to leave Clermont, but only after launching a war of attrition against Garaudy, a war that was all the more effective because Foucault had taken over from Vuillemin as director of the philosophy section. He seized every occasion and every pretext to vent his hatred. It was fierce and unflagging hatred. Garaudy tried to sort things out. One evening he rang the doorbell at Foucault's apartment in Paris and asked to speak to him. Foucault tried to slam the door in his face, but Garaudy persisted, holding the door open with his foot. The confrontation ended in a stream of insults.

Foucault's hostility was motivated on two levels. First, he considered the new professor "intellectually nil." "He is no philosopher," he told anyone willing to listen; "we don't need him here." That was his "official" reason, the one he gave in all his public vituperations. To his friends, however, he explained that this pitiful representative of French-style Stalinism inspired a profound disgust in him. Garaudy had been a high-level party official while Foucault was a Communist party member. So Foucault had accounts to settle with Garaudy. And he would settle them.

Garaudy had to put up with all the sarcastic remarks and all the imprecations that his director's genius could invent against him. He had to bear Foucault's fits of rage as well. If he spelled something wrong in a bibliography he could expect an immediate summons from Foucault, followed by a denunciation of his incompetence. Life in the philosophy department was peppered with incidents of this sort. The conflict came to a head when Garaudy made a rather bad mistake assigning a research topic to a student: he asked her to translate Marcus Aurelius' *Meditations* from the Latin. But the *Meditations* are written in Greek. Michel Serres was a witness because he shared an office with Garaudy. When he told Foucault the story, Foucault literally exploded, called Garaudy every name in the book, and even threatened to drag him before the administrative tribunal for professional misdemeanor. And the

Stalinist apparatchik, who as an activist must have experienced many other attacks, succumbed in the face of Foucault's increasingly violent, repeated assaults. He asked to be transferred to "any other equivalent post." Two years after the ministry's power move, Garaudy left Clermont to teach in Poitiers. Foucault was jubilant. He had vanquished an enemy. And simultaneously won a friend. His relationship with Deleuze, who had instead received an appointment at Lyons, dates from this time. They regularly got together whenever Deleuze went to Paris. Although they never became extremely close, it was a strong enough friendship that Foucault lent his apartment to Deleuze and his wife several times when he was not there.

Foucault also became friends with Michel Serres during these years in Clermont. Serres worked on Leibniz and possessed a knowledge of science that was unusual among philosophers. He discussed many parts of *Les Mots et les choses* with Foucault as they were being developed. Foucault submitted his hypotheses, discoveries, and intuitions to Serres, who examined them, made comments and criticisms. They spent hours working together this way. When Foucault left Clermont they would lose track of each other, meeting again only in 1969, at Vincennes.

FOUCAULT WAS A "DANDY" —a surprising description, perhaps, but one repeated again and again in accounts by colleagues and students— a dandy who came, once a week, to give his class at Clermont. He wore a black corduroy suit, white turtleneck sweaters, and a green loden cape. People who had known him at the ENS remembered him as a tortured adolescent, sickly and uneasy with himself. Over the next five or six years they had lost track of him. They knew only that he was abroad, preparing his thesis, getting ready to defend it. Then, after this long absence, they rediscovered a changed Foucault, a radiant man, re-laxed and cheerful, a man who had kept his taste for sarcasm and provocation but had integrated it into a character that, though enigmatic for many, at least seemed reconciled with itself and with others.

Foucault had organized his work with a mind to avoiding everything that bored him. In 1962 he recruited two assistants, Nelly Viallaneix and Francine Pariente. "Foucault's sisters," as they would soon be known at the university, took charge of courses in social psychology and child psychology, two subjects that Foucault hated teaching. He kept the course in "general psychology"; the term was vague enough that he could present whatever he liked. He warned his students at the outset: "General psychology, like anything general, does not exist." He launched into long discussions about language and the history of linguistic theories as well as psychoanalysis. One day he announced to Pariente: "This year I'll give the course on the history of law." Which he did. His work on madness was a thing of the recent past, still close at hand, but already he was en route toward his future books. From 1960 to 1966 his courses bore the marks of this tension between what had been written and what would be, between the past and the future, between published research and the gestating work. This very fact indicates that at its deepest intuitive level his thought was highly unitary despite the differentiated forms it took. He also gave a course on sexuality, starting with a discussion of Freud and the theory of infantile sexuality. He made no secret of his intention to write something on this subject along the lines of *Histoire de la folie*. In 1976, immediately after publishing *Surveiller et punir*, he came out with the first volume of a vast enterprise whose general title was *Histoire de la sexualité*. At that time he was asked many questions about moving from one field of inquiry to another and about the connections between them. But in fact these preoccupations had been cohabiting in Foucault's thought since the 1960s. His lectures, moving from sexuality to law and from law to sexuality make this perfectly plain.

Psychoanalysis was a prominent topic in Foucault's courses. Foucault had long ago renounced Marx, but he remained very attached to Freud. He always discussed *Five Psychoanalyses* and *The Interpretation of Dreams*. He quoted Lacan often and recommended that his students read Lacan's articles in the review *Psychanalyse*. As a professor of psychology, Foucault invariably offered his students a long apprenticeship in Rorschach tests, devoting one or two hours of class each week to them for several years. Similarly, he lingered over "present-day theories of perception and sensation."

But however unorthodox their content, Foucault's lectures were always pedagogically unimpeachable. There were no great inspired tirades flying out over the heads of the audience, or remarks that were too difficult for them. This was no longer Uppsala. And it was not yet what would be the lectures at the Collège de France, whose function is precisely to set forth, to be, the testing grounds for new research. At Clermont Foucault almost always followed the set program; he defined notions, presented different theories, and gave summaries synthesizing the material. The notes taken by his students make this perfectly clear: they are all organized by paragraphs, with little explanatory schemas.

His courses were academic in the best sense of the word, and, despite the distant manner he displayed in his role of professor, despite the liberties he took with university standards, he remained a rather traditional teacher. He offered his students real introductory work, simply and precisely presented. Of course, he discussed material he was using for the books he was working on. For example, his course on "contemporary problems of language" addressed many of the themes later found in *Les Mots et les choses*. But he did not mix his two activities. He never confused the two audiences for these different registers of discourse: teaching and writing.

Foucault was a fascinating teacher. He walked back and forth on the podium, talked non-stop, and only rarely consulted the bundle of note cards he had set on the desk: one quick glance and he would start talking again in his rapid, staccato rhythm. His voice seemed about to fly off at the ends of his sentences, with the melodic lift of a question, only to sink again with the confident inflections of an answer to the problems he had raised. Foucault liked to make his students uneasy. He would stop suddenly in the middle of a lecture and ask: "Do you want to know what structuralism is?" And since nobody dared answer, after letting a few minutes of silence go by he would deliver a long explanation that left his audience flabbergasted. Then he would pick up the thread of his discussion, abandoned for the past twenty minutes. The course most dreaded by the students—because they were fascinated but always somewhat uneasy—was the one he devoted to the Rorschach method. This took place in the evenings; in the morning he discussed law or sexuality, and early in the afternoon he taught psychoanalysis, language, or the human sciences. Foucault divided his students into groups of seven, putting the inevitable two or three extra ones off to the side. Throughout the course, he contrived to subject these exiles, whom he called "bedouins," to a hailstorm of questions—and gibes when the answer was wrong. His sardonic reply for a correct answer was "Candy for Miss So-and-so." It was perfectly clear to the students that their salvation lay in escaping the condition of "bedouin." But how could they avoid the dissertation topics, such as "the neurotic family, that is, quite simply, the family"? Nobody would dare venture into that swamp, and Foucault had not a single paper to grade: everyone shied off. Even more dreaded was the oral exam at the end of the year. He once asked a young woman who was already paralyzed by her timidity: "What do you want to do when you grow up?" And that was to be the question. The student began to develop an answer, and after a few minutes Foucault interrupted her. "Can you list five cases of neurosis described by Freud?" She did so, and the exam was over.

Despite everything, the students liked and admired their professor. They went to talk to him after class, they went with him to the station, had a last drink with him before they let him go. During his last year at Clermont, Foucault was applauded at the end of every lecture—something that had never happened before in the Auvergne; nor since.

Foucault's manner, his appearance, his bizarre relations with students, his evaluations, which some suspected of being dictated by his advisees, did not please all his colleagues. Foucault may have been much appreciated in the philosophy department, but not all of the rest of the faculty were friendly toward him. For some he was neither more nor less than the devil incarnate. As one can imagine, from what we know of him, he never hesitated to play up this image. In addition to the "dandy" side of him, there was his "sardonic" laugh, the "arrogance" always, everywhere, displayed also in his "eccentric" behavior (these are the words of witnesses). All of this disconcerted the small, very provincial faculty and focused on Foucault a resentment against "Parisian intellectuals." "A Parisian intellectual"—that was certainly the problem. He lived in Paris—his apartment was on Rue du Docteur-Finlay, in the fifteenth arrondissement; he frequented avant-garde literary circles, contributed to reviews such as *Critique*, *Tel quel*, and *NRF*, in which he wrote about Bataille, Blanchot, Klossowski. He seemed hardly the appropriate person to come and teach in this remote spot.

Perhaps students and professors today would be less astonished by all this. But before 1968, Foucault's presence was as shocking as it was seductive. Outside a small group of colleagues and friends, Foucault was badly thought of and severely criticized for having Daniel Defert appointed as an assistant in the philosophy department. Defert was a student at the Ecole Normale at Saint-Cloud when Foucault met him, upon his return from Germany. He had just begun a love affair with Defert that would last until his death. Daniel Defert would share Foucault's life for almost twenty-five years. And Foucault loved him, despite moments of tension and difficulty, even moments of crisis, until the end. Any number of people mentioned Foucault's torment and despair when a final rupture seemed imminent. But the relationship survived all its ordeals. Foucault described the intensity of the affair in an interview with the German filmmaker Werner Schroeter in 1981: "I am living in a state of passion with someone. Perhaps, at some given moment, this passion took a turn for love. Truly, this is a state of passion between the two of us, a permanent state with no reason to come to an end other than itself, one in which I am entirely invested, one running through me. I think there is nothing in the world, nothing, no matter what, that could stop me from going to see him again, or speaking to him."[6] When he was at Clermont this affair was just beginning, and Foucault did not hesitate to use the prerogative provided by his status as head of the department to offer an assistantship to his lover. He could not care less about scandalizing the university, and when a member of the faculty council asked him what criteria he had used in the choice of this candidate rather than another applicant, a woman who was older and had more degrees, he replied: "Because we don't like old maids here."

WAS IT BECAUSE he was fed up with teaching psychology? Was it because he was uncomfortable in this rather cramped world? Or was it simply, as one of his friends said, "because he never stayed put"? All these reasons, perhaps, combined to result in his departure from Clermont at the end of the 1965–66 school year. In any case he had already tried several times to escape this somewhat stifling university scene. In 1963 he was on the verge of being appointed director of the French Cultural Institute in Tokyo, but the dean of the faculty persuaded him to stay. On September 2 the dean had written to the ministry:

> M. Foucault's departure would cause very serious damage to our faculty. Not only would it be impossible to replace him for the beginning of classes next year, but the extremely critical situation of the philosophy department at Clermont—a situation I have reviewed for you several times—requires that the director of the section be retained for the next year. Another consideration is that M. Foucault, as a psychologist, is the only one able to carry through the reorganization of the Institute for Applied Psychology that we have undertaken. Under these conditions, I have pressed M. Foucault very strongly to decline the offer he has received. With an unselfishness for which I am very grateful, he was willing to admit the validity of the arguments I gave him.

In 1965 Foucault again intended to leave Clermont. The sociologist Georges Gurvitch suggested that he apply to teach at the Sorbonne and offered his support. But Canguilhem advised Foucault not to do so, because it seemed rather a bad situation. Foucault would have the majority of the philosophy section, which included not only philosophers but also sociologists and psychologists, against him. On the one hand, the Sorbonne did not seem ready to accept Foucault, and on the other, Gurvitch was not particularly liked by his colleagues; they were likely to reject any candidate he suggested. Foucault decided to follow Canguilhem's advice and sent him a long letter thanking him for having opened his eyes: "You did me a *great* "service" as it is curiously described, in preventing me from making the stupid mista'.e Gurvitch was urging me to make. Thanks to you, I can see it all now with blinding clarity." So Foucault remained at Clermont. But on several occasions he went to ask Jean Sirinelli, in charge of foreign French instruction, to dig up a post for him. Foucault had known Sirinelli at the Rue d'Ulm when both were giving classes there in the early 1950s. Moreover, Sirinelli was a friend of Barthes. So doing Foucault a favor posed no problem at all. Except, simply, Sirinelli could not see what audience Foucault could find at Congo-Kinshasa, whose university was still in the clutches of professors from Louvain, and he strongly advised Foucault—who seemed to want to go there—not to.

Foucault did not go to live in Brazil either. He went there for two months in 1965 at the invitation of Gérard Lebrun, who had been his student at the Rue d'Ulm in 1954, and who had since moved to São Paulo, where he still lives and teaches today. Foucault gave a series of lectures there.

But indeed Foucault refused to stay put. In 1966 he was given leave to go to Tunis. *Les Mots et les choses* had just come out, to a resounding and entirely unexpected success. In all the uproar accompanying the publication of this book, which his students at Clermont had been the first to hear of, Michel Foucault said goodby to that city.

11

~~~

Opening Bodies

ompletely absorbed in writing *Folie et déraison*, Michel Foucault had not published anything during his years in Sweden, Poland, and Germany. As soon as he returned to France, however, he produced an increasing number of books and projects for books. *Les Mots et les choses*, published in 1966 just before his departure for Tunis, was the culmination of a many-sided progression.

The projects were numerous. The first was to be a direct sequel to *Folie et déraison*. Pierre Nora, who was working then at Julliard, wanted to launch a new series called Archives, for which historians would gather and discuss documents pertaining to a given subject or period. Nora had read *Folie et déraison*, and he wrote to Foucault. At their first meeting, Nora recalled, Foucault was "dressed all in black" and wore a homburg and gold cufflinks. Above all, he remembered Foucault's accepting his suggestion and proposing to work with texts about prisoners. The project was advertised as one of the first volumes of the series: "Madmen. From the Bastille to Hôpital Sainte-Anne, from the seventeenth to the nineteenth centuries, Michel Foucault recounts the journey to the end of night.—Forthcoming." But it never came. Other projects were born and then vanished, only to return in other forms. There was the "History of Hysteria," for which he signed a contract in February 1964 with Flammarion and its New Scientific Library headed by Fernand Braudel. This great historian, as we have seen, had quickly recognized the young philosopher's talent. The manuscript was due in the fall of 1965. But Foucault speedily changed his project and signed a new contract for an entirely different book, "The Idea of Decadence." The only thing these two texts had in common was that neither ever existed.

Foucault, however, was far from idle. In 1963 he published two distinctly different works. One was a study on Raymond Roussel, published at Gallimard in the series Le Chemin, directed by Georges Lambrichs; the other was *Naissance de la clinique*. He very carefully arranged for them to be published on the same day. Perhaps he wanted to show that these two areas of concentration were equally important. Or perhaps, on a deeper level, he meant to show that in both instances he was talking about the same thing.

THE BOOK ON ROUSSEL was one of several works that, as a whole, might even be described as a "literary cycle," just as, in the 1970s, there would be a "prison cycle," with a constellation of articles, prefaces, and interviews proliferating around a book. From 1962 to 1966 Foucault published a series of articles on writers. But Roussel is the only one to whom Foucault ever devoted a book. Not only was this author not a philosopher; he was the least philosophic of the writers Foucault admired. In any case he was the most enigmatic and most esoteric, a poet and playwright who was almost unknown at the time, and whom the avant-garde novelists, under the guidance of Michel Leiris in *Biffures*, would discover as one of their precursors. Published in 1948, this first volume of Leiris' autobiography dwelt at length on memories of Roussel, whom Leiris had known very well. But how did Foucault discover Roussel? By chance, he explained, in what became the "Postscript" to the 1986 American edition of his book.

> I can recall how I discovered his work: it was during a period when I was living abroad in Sweden and returned to France for the summer. I went to the *librairie* José-Corti to buy I can't recall what book. Can you visualize that huge bookstore across from the Luxembourg Gardens? José Corti, publisher and bookseller, was there behind his enormous desk, a distinguished old man. He was busy speaking to a friend, and obviously he is not the kind of bookseller that you can interrupt with a "Could you find me such and such a book?" You have to wait politely until the conversation is over before making a request. Thus, while waiting, I found my attention drawn to a series of books of that faded yellow color used by publishing firms of the late nineteenth, early twentieth centuries; in short, books the likes of which aren't made anymore. I examined them and saw "Librairie Lemerre" on the cover. I was puzzled to find these old volumes from a publishing firm as fallen now in reputation as that of Alphonse Lemerre. I selected a book out of curiosity to see what José Corti was

selling from the stock of the Lemerre firm, and that's how I came upon the work of someone I had never heard of named Raymond Roussel, and the book was entitled *La Vue*. Well, from the first line, I was completely taken by the beauty of the style, so strange and so strangely close to that of Robbe-Grillet, who was just beginning to publish his work. I could see a relationship between *La Vue* and Robbe-Grillet's work in general, but *Le Voyeur* in particular. At that point José Corti's conversation had come to an end, I requested the book I needed, and asked timidly who was Raymond Roussel, because in addition to *La Vue*, his other works were on the shelf. Corti looked at me with a generous sort of pity and said, "But, after all, Roussel . . ." I immediately understood that I should have known about Raymond Roussel, and with equal timidity I asked if I could buy the book, since he was selling it. I was rather surprised to find that it was expensive. José Corti probably told me that day that I should read *How I Wrote Certain of My Books* [*Comment j'ai écrit certains de mes livres*]. Raymond Roussel's work immediately absorbed me: I was taken by the prose style even before learning what was behind it—the process, the machines, the mechanisms—and no doubt when I discovered his process and his techniques, the obsessional side of me was seduced a second time by the shock of learning of the disparity between this methodically applied process, which was slightly naïve, and the resulting intense poetry. Slowly and systematically I began to buy all his works. I developed an affection for his work, which remained secret, since I didn't discuss it.[1]

Raymond Roussel was born in 1877 in Paris. He began studying music but then abandoned it all, at seventeen, to shut himself up with pen and paper and throw himself into writing—letting radiate around him the blazing, solar glory he felt inside, needing, as he endlessly proclaimed, no one else's acknowledgment. The eminent psychiatrist Pierre Janet found his case fascinating and analyzed Roussel's illuminations in his book *De l'angoisse à l'extase*, comparing this literary exaltation to religious ecstasy. In 1897 Roussel published *La Doublure*, a long poem recounting the life of an understudy. Then came *La Vue*, which described a landscape visible only to someone who brought his eye close to the surface on which it is engraved. As Hubert Juin said in his introduction to *Comment j'ai écrit certains de mes livres*, Roussel faced his poem alone, and it owed nothing to the outside world.[2] He was also alone with his novels, written in accordance with procedures to which he provided a key in this posthumous work. His first novel was *Impressions d'Afrique*, in 1910; next was *Nouvelles Impressions d'Afrique*, written en route to Australia and New Zealand. He spent the trip shut up in the cabin of a ship, with all the curtains drawn, stubbornly refusing to look at the scenery. He also wrote for the theater; his plays either flopped resoundingly or else created a huge uproar, and earned him the support of the surrealists. After his death he was almost completely forgotten until Leiris relit the flame that had been so quickly extinguished. And until the "radiating glory" caught the eye of a young philosopher, exiled in Sweden but visiting Paris, who was then writing a book on madness, in which he wanted to return speech to all those who turned madness into works. Foucault must have been fascinated to discover that Roussel had been a patient of Pierre Janet, and also that in 1933 Roussel had chosen to be treated at the Binswanger clinic at Kreuzlingen. But he had taken a detour before going to Switzerland, stopping in Palermo, where he was discovered, dead, in his hotel room. Did he commit suicide, as the official version has it? Or was he killed by a transient lover, as some think? Foucault accepted the suicide theory. His book begins and ends with a ceremony imagined by Roussel: preparing for death and sending his editor a work explaining how his books were written. Foucault discussed Roussel's suicide in an article published in *Le Monde* in 1964.[3]

Aside from the connection between writing and death, made by Roussel in this strange act, biographical facts are of very little interest to Foucault in this book. Only the literary mechanisms, the processes and wordplay that Roussel produced interest him—all the machinery described in *Comment j'ai écrit* with which language could be made infinitely prolific. "Roussel invented language machines that have no other secret outside of the process than the visible and profound relationship that all language maintains, disengages itself from, takes up, and repeats indefinitely with death."[4]

Before starting *Raymond Roussel*, Foucault visited Michel Leiris, asking for information about Roussel and his work. Leiris, however, was not particularly swayed by the philosopher's analyses: "He attributed too many philosophical ideas to Roussel, who had none at all," he says today.[5] Robbe-Grillet was scarcely more enthusiastic. He wrote a long article about Roussel when Foucault's book was published, but mentioned the latter's "fascinating essay" only in a single sentence as one sign of the interest in this "direct ancestor of the modern novel." He then proceeded with his own discussion of Roussel's work.[6] Today he acknowledges that he did not much like Foucault's analyses. Blanchot, on the other hand, spoke of "Roussel's work, as Michel Foucault's book has once again made it speak for itself." He admiringly quoted a sentence from Foucault, in which he discovered the themes traversing his own inquiry echoed and reflected. "This solar cavity is the space of Roussel's language, the void he speaks from, the absence through which work and madness communicate with and exclude each other. And when I speak of void it is not meant as metaphor: it is a matter of words' being deficient because they are fewer than the things they designate, and it is thanks to this economy that they mean something."[7]

Although he celebrated Roussel, Foucault did not forget the writers he was fond of before reading the author of *Impressions d'Afrique*. For example, after Bataille's death, he wrote a very long article, "Préface à la transgression," for a special issue of *Critique*, the review Bataille had founded. Foucault is listed in the table of contents along with others whom Jean Piel had invited to pay their respects: Michel Leiris, Alfred Métraux, Raymond Queneau, Maurice Blanchot, Pierre Klossowski, Roland Barthes, Jean Wahl, Philippe Sollers, André Masson. In this article Foucault reaffirmed all the profound reasons for his interest in—his passion for—this group of writers whom he had discovered ten or fifteen years earlier:

> To awaken us from the confused sleep of dialectics and of anthropology, we required the Nietzschean figures of tragedy, of Dionysus, of the death of God, of the philosopher's hammer, of the Superman approaching with the steps of a dove, of the Return. But why, in our day, is discursive language so ineffectual when asked to maintain the presence of these figures and to maintain itself through them? Why is it so nearly silent before them, as if it were forced to yield its voice so that they may continue to find their words, to yield to these extreme forms of language in which Bataille, Blanchot, and Klossowski have made their home which they have made the summits of thought?[8]

For Foucault the strength and liberating violence of Bataille's work lay in its having dynamited traditional philosophical language by demolishing the idea of a speaking subject: "This experience forms the exact reversal of the movement which has sustained the wisdom of the West at least since the time of Socrates, that is, the wisdom to which philosophical language promised the serene unity of a subjectivity which would triumph within it, being entirely constituted by and through it." Whereas Bataille, perhaps, defined "the space given over to an experience in which the speaking subject, instead of expressing himself, is exposed, goes to encounter his own finitude and, under each of his words, is brought back to the reality of his own death."[9] This article contains hints of an archaeology of sexuality. But it is still far from the work that would become *La Volonté de savoir* (The will to knowledge), because Foucault was still thinking in terms of the forbidden and of transgression. "The discovery of sexuality, the discovery of that firmament of indefinite unreality, where Sade placed it from the beginning, the discovery of those systematic forms of prohibition which we now know imprison it, the discovery of the universal nature of transgression in which it is both object and instrument—indicates in a sufficiently forceful way the impossibility of attributing the millenary language of dialectics to the major experience that sexuality forms for us."[10]

Foucault would also write the introduction to Bataille's *Oeuvres complètes*, the first volume of which was published in 1970 by Gallimard. "Bataille," he wrote at the beginning of this short text, "is one of the most important writers of his century: *Histoire de l'oeil* and *Madame Edwarda* broke the narratives' thread to recount things that had never been told. *Somme athéologique* brought thought into the game—the risky game—of limits, extremes, heights, and transgression. *L'Erotisme* brought Sade closer to us and made him more difficult. We are indebted to Bataille for much of the moment in which we now exist . . . But no doubt we are indebted to him also for things that remain to be done, to be thought and said, and will be so for a long time."[11]

In June 1966 Foucault published an article on Blanchot, "La Pensée du dehors" (The outside's thought), again in *Critique*. In it he stated:

> The breakthrough toward a language from which the subject is excluded, the revelation of an incompatibility that has no recourse, perhaps, between the appearance of language in the subject's being and the consciousness of self in the subject's identity, is an experience making itself known today in many different areas in culture: in the very act of writing, as well as in attempts to formalize language, in the study of myths, and in psychoanalysis . . . We now find ourselves facing a gap that had long remained invisible to us: the being of language is apparent to itself only in the disappearance of the subject.[12]

His article on Klossowski should also be mentioned, because Foucault unfailingly linked these three names: Blanchot, Bataille, Klossowski. "La Prose d'Actéon" was published in March 1964 in the *NRF*. Foucault had met Klossowski through Barthes in 1963, and thereafter the two men got together often. All three dined together several times in the days before Foucault and Barthes had begun to argue; later the two met without Barthes. Klossowski read Foucault passages from a novel he was working on, *Le Baphomet*. When it was published in 1965 he dedicated it to Foucault: "because he was the first to hear it and the first to read it," Klossowski says today. During this same period Klossowski was also working on Nietzsche, writing what was to become *Nietzsche ou le cercle vicieux* and preparing his translations of *Gai savoir* and its variations for a volume intended to inaugurate Gallimard's edition of Nietzsche's *Oeuvres complètes*. This was an edition "for which Gilles Deleuze and Michel Foucault are responsible," as it says on the flyleaf. In fact the two philosophers wrote a short introduction for this volume (which was published as the fifth in the edition). Deleuze also was rather close to Klossowski at this time, and he wrote an article on him that would be reprinted in *Logique du sens*.

Foucault remained a great admirer of Klossowski, as can be seen from the letters he wrote him in 1969 and 1970 about *Cercle vicieux* and *La Monnaie vivante*. "It is the greatest book of philosophy that I have read, on a level with Nietzsche himself," he wrote of the first in July 1969. And during the winter of 1970, on the second:

> One has the impression that anything that counts in one way or another—Blanchot, Bataille, *Beyond Good and Evil* also—was insidiously leading up to this: but now we have it, it has been said . . . That was what had to be thought: desire, value, and simulacrum—a triangle that dominates us and that, no doubt for centuries of our history, has constituted us. Those who said, or say, their Freud-and-Marx, went after it fiercely: today we can laugh about it, and we know why. Without you, Pierre, we would have had no other recourse than to come to a halt, up against the wall marked once and for all by Sade, which no one but you has ever got around—which no one else, really, ever came near.[13]

In 1981, when the left came to power, Jean Gattegno, a colleague of Foucault's in Tunis and at Vincennes, was put in charge of books at the Ministry of Culture. He phoned Foucault to ask who he thought should be awarded the Grand Prix National des Lettres. Foucault replied: "Klossowski, if he will accept it." Klossowski accepted.

Foucault constantly referred to Nietzsche in texts of this period. And it was at this time that he gave his famous lecture "Nietzsche, Marx, Freud" at a colloquium on Nietzsche at Royaumont on July 4–8, 1964. He made no attempt to conceal his preference for the first among these three. During a discussion after the lecture, this odd exchange took place:

Demonbynes: Concerning madness, you said that the experience of madness came closest to absolute knowledge . . . Is that really what you said?
Foucault: Yes.
Demonbynes: You didn't mean "consciousness," or "prescience," or "premonition" of madness? Do you really think that one can have . . . that great minds such as Nietzsche can have "the experience of madness"?
Foucault: Yes, yes.[14]

A few years later, in 1971, Foucault's "Nietzsche, la généologie, l'histoire" appeared in the volume published in homage to Jean Hyppolite.

During this "literary" period Foucault also wrote about Robbe-Grillet (with whom he had become friends since their meeting in Hamburg), about the avant-garde writers grouped around Philippe Sollers and *Tel quel* (in 1963 he took part in a colloquium on the novel and on poetry organized by the review), about Roger Laporte, about Michel Butor and Jean-Marie Le Clézio, but also about classical authors. He wrote a preface to Rousseau's *Dialogues,* that work of madness, and commented on Flaubert, Jules Verne, Gérard de Nerval, and Mallarmé. The first text in this long series was an article on Hölderlin, "Le 'non' du père" ("The Father's 'No'"), which appeared in *Critique* in 1962.[15] Jean Piel had liked *Folie et déraison* very much, and he contacted Foucault to ask him for some articles. He had long known the Foucault family, having been assistant commissioner of the republic in Poitiers during the Liberation. Dr. Foucault had even operated on him. After the death of his brother-in-law Georges Bataille in 1962, Piel did not want to take sole charge of a review, and he asked Foucault to join an editorial board along with Roland Barthes and Michel Deguy. The board's meetings took place over lunch at Piel's. One of Foucault's projects was to ask Jules Vuillemin, Pierre Kaufmann, and André Green for articles on Merleau-Ponty's posthumous work, *Le Visible et l'invisible,* for an issue that was published in December 1964. The editorial board later increased in size to accommodate, among others, Jacques Derrida in 1967. Foucault's last article for *Critique,* in 1970, was titled "Theatrum philosophicum" and dealt with two books by Gilles Deleuze. It ended with these words: "In the sentry box of the Luxembourg Gardens, Duns Scotus places his head through the circular window; he is sporting an impressive moustache; it belongs to Nietzsche, disguised as Klossowski." [16]

~~

NAISSANCE DE LA CLINIQUE was published in 1963. Foucault's father died in 1959. Did this immersion in medical archives represent a way for Foucault to look back on his own past? to settle his accounts with the lost father figure? or to pay him the respect he had been unable to convey during his father's lifetime? Foucault said that this book, like the others, had its birthplace in personal experience, but he was never specific. We cannot presume to answer for him.

The preface begins with these words: "This book is about space, about language, and about death; it is about the act of seeing, the gaze." [17] This statement echoes uncannily the themes and vocabulary haunting Foucault's texts about literature. The book, however, was about the history of science. It was published in the Galien series, supervised by Georges Canguilhem for the Press Universitaires de France, and its subtitle was *Une Archéologie du regard médical*. Canguilhem did not commission the book, as has sometimes been reported: "I never commissioned anything from Foucault," says Canguilhem now. "Foucault sent it to me after he had finished it." But what possible connection was there between the literary texts and this book? Nietzsche may have served as their common origin. To anyone who seemed surprised about the coexistence of these two divergent paths of research, or to anyone who saw a contradiction between his Nietzschean inspiration and the tradition of the history of science, Foucault answered that Canguilhem himself often placed his research in a line of descent from Nietzsche—a fact that Canguilhem confirmed. But basically, in reading *Naissance de la clinique* alongside the texts on literature, one is struck less by any contradiction between research in two directions than, on the contrary, by the astonishing convergence of the two registers. Several years later the evidence of this kinship would burst forth in *Les Mots et les choses*.

Naissance de la clinique is both a direct sequel to *Folie et déraison* and a transition to the books that follow. It is a direct sequel in that it extends the analyses used to study concepts of mental medicine to medicine in general, examining how and where they were born and what made them possible. But unlike *Folie et déraison*, which covers several centuries in six hundred pages, *Naissance de la clinique* is a small book—two hundred pages—and limits its discussion to the end of the eighteenth century and the very beginning of the nineteenth. In these years, with the appearance of pathological anatomy as a field of study, medicine reorganized itself, both as a practice and as a science. But here also, Foucault applies principles of "structural history." He relates different registers—economic, social, political, ideological, cultural—to one another to illumine the transformations that affected ways of speaking and seeing as a whole and, more profoundly, affected what it is possible to say and to see at any given period, the seeable and the sayable. The reorganization of hospitals, the upheaval in medical instruction, scientific theories, and practices, and economic preoccupations—all worked toward the rupture. The turning point came when the need to dissect cadavers was recognized. To decipher symptoms at the deepest level, the doctor had to look for their source inside the body. "Open up a few corpses," said Xavier Bichat, as Foucault vividly reports, "and you will dissipate at once the darkness that observation alone could not dissipate." Foucault comments on Bichat's words with one of those magnificent phrases in which the book abounds: "The living night is dissipated in the brightness of death." From that point on, "life, disease, and death now form a technical and conceptual trinity. The continuity of the age-old beliefs that placed the threat of disease in life, and of the approaching presence of death in disease is broken; in its place is articulated a triangular figure the summit of which is defined by death. It is from the height of death that one can see and analyze organic dependences and pathological sequences." There was another change occurring, too, one that involved language. Foucault recognized Pinel's texts as part of this development, with their stated intention of producing an exact and exhaustive description of illnesses and the bodies that carried them. This double movement was not just a transformation of medical technologies, but a reorganization of all of medicine and, beyond this, of the entire perception of life and death and the very foundations of knowledge: "This structure in which space, language, and death are articulated—what is known, in fact, as the anatomo-clinical method—constitutes the historical condition of a medicine that is given and accepted as positive."[18]

This is the point at which *Naissance de la clinique* opens onto Foucault's later inquiries. It demonstrates just how the possibility of a "knowledge of the individual" was instituted. "It will no doubt remain a decisive fact about our culture," said Foucault, "that its first scientific discourse concerning the individual had to pass through this stage of death. Western man could constitute himself in his own eyes as an object of science, he grasped himself within his language and gave himself in himself and by himself, and a discursive existence only in the opening created by his own elimination: from the experience of Unreason was born psychology, the very possibility of psychology; from the integration of death into medical thought is born a medicine that is given as a science of the individual."[19] This idea leads into *Les Mots et les choses*, in the sense that Foucault saw here that he had just described the base upon which all human sciences would flourish: on man's possibility of being simultaneously the subject and the object of his own knowledge.

But, he added, let us make no mistake. This birth of positive medicine, and of the scientific way of thinking that helped medical practice escape from an empire ruled by chimera, this arrival of a new discursive knowledge is contemporary with and part of the movement that, in all of contemporary culture, put death at the heart of the individual:

> The experience of individuality in modern culture is bound up with that of death: from Hölderlin's Empedocles to Nietzsche's Zarathustra, and on to Freudian man, an obstinate relation to death prescribes to the universal its singular face and lends to each individual the power of being heard forever . . . In what at first sight might seem a very strange way, the movement that sustained lyricism in the nineteenth century was one and the same as that by which man obtained positive knowledge of himself; but is it surprising that the figures of knowledge and those of language should obey the same profound law, and that the irruption of finitude should dominate, in the same way, this relation of man to death, which, in the first case, authorizes a scientific discourse in a rational form, and in the second, opens up the source of a language that unfolds endlessly in the void left by the absence of the gods?[20]

Naissance de la clinique received little notice. But Jacques Lacan discussed it at length in one of his seminars, and in the next few days several dozen copies of the book were sold. Foucault went to dinner at the Lacans' several times, though they never became close friends. Sylvia Lacan remembered well something Foucault threw out in the conversation one evening at her home on Rue de Lille: "There will be no civilization as long as marriage between men is not accepted."

12

Ramparts of the Bourgeoisie

I n August and September 1965 Foucault was in São Paulo, where he gave Gérard Lebrun a large manuscript to read. This was practically consulting the expert: Lebrun was a specialist in Kant and Hegel but was also extremely well versed in phenomenology and the work of Merleau-Ponty. He read the manuscript Foucault showed him, and they talked about it. When the book came out a few months later, Lebrun was surprised to see a first chapter that had not been in the version he had read. In an "ouverture" that announced the themes of the book, Foucault analyzed a painting by Velásquez, *Las Meninas*. This bit of bravura, undoubtedly added at the last moment, played a large part in the book's success. It was an article that Foucault had published in *Le Mercure de France*, and he was very hesitant about putting it in, according to Pierre Nora. "He thought this article was too literary to figure in his book, but I thought, myself, that it was fine." Foucault would have liked to give his work the title that would appear for its second chapter, "La Prose du monde." But Merleau-Ponty had wanted to give this title to a text found among his papers after his death.[1] Foucault was not eager to seem too much influenced by the philosopher he had so long admired. He then thought of *L'Ordre des choses*, or maybe *Les Mots et les choses*. Foucault preferred the former, Nora the latter. And Foucault went along with his arguments. The English translation, however, would appear as *The Order of Things*, and Foucault said in several interviews that, basically, this was the better title.

〰

"FOUCAULT COMME DES PETITS PAINS" —Foucault selling like hotcakes!—announced an article in *Le Nouvel Observateur* devoted to the best-sellers of the summer of 1966.[2] Surprising as it may seem, *Les Mots et les choses* met with huge success. No one was more surprised than the author and the editor. This was an extremely difficult work, meant for a limited audience interested in the history of science.

The book was published in April 1966 by Gallimard, where Foucault had published his study on Roussel. He submitted the new book to Georges Lambrichs, and, since Pierre Nora had just left Julliard to start a Bibliothèque des Sciences Humaines for Gallimard, it was understood that *Les Mots et les choses* would be the first title in his collection. All of Foucault's books from then on came out in this series or its twin, Bibliothèque des Histoires, and right from the beginning he provided these collections with a quality and prestige that persisted until his death.

The first run of 3,500 copies was quickly sold out. In June there was another printing, of 5,000; then 3,000 in July, in September, and again in November. It kept right on the next year: 4,000 in March 1967 and 5,000 in November; another 6,000 in April 1968 and in June 1969; and so on. It is very rare for a book of philosophy to attain these numbers. To date more than 110,000 copies have been printed.

Success came first from philosophical circles, of course. In November 1966 Jean Lacroix reported in *Le Monde* that the most frequently mentioned names in theses written for the *agrégation* were Althusser and Foucault. But the success went beyond this acclaim. According to newspapers at the time, people were reading Foucault's book on the beaches, or at least they took it with them, left it lying around on the table at cafés to show they were not ignorant of such a major event. *Les Mots et les choses* had such wide repercussions that there would be echoes of it in Louis Aragon's *Blanche ou l'oubli*, as well as in Jean-Luc Godard's *La Chinoise*, in 1967, which made great fun of its vogue. Godard even said in an interview that it was against people like "the Reverend Father Foucault" that he wanted to make films. "If I don't particularly like Foucault, it is because of his saying, 'At such and such a period they thought . . .' That's fine with me, but how can we be so sure? That is exactly why we try to make films; to prevent future Foucaults from presumptuously saying things like that."[3]

～

AS WE HAVE SEEN, in 1961 Foucault preferred not to publish his introduction to Kant's *Anthropology*. The long typescript ends with a lively—though stylistically somewhat obscure—attach on contemporary attempts to establish an "anthropology," in Sartre's or Merleau-Ponty's sense of the term, and not as Lévi-Strauss used it. He challenged their "illusions" and expressed surprise that they could be left to flourish without anyone's trying to "critique" them.

However, he concluded, "we have had the model for this critique for more than half a century. The Nietzschean undertaking might be understood as finally putting an end to the proliferation of questioning about mankind. Was not the death of God, in fact, revealed in a doubly murderous act that, at the same time that it put an end to the absolute, assassinated man himself? Because man, in his finitude, is inseparable from the infinite, which he both negates and heralds. The death of God is accomplished through the death of man." It was therefore necessary to oppose the Kantian question "What is man?" along with all its spinoffs in contemporary thought, from Husserl to Merleau-Ponty, with "an answer that challenges and disarms it: *Der Übermensch*." The Overman.[4] The final pages of this "minor thesis" seem directed almost entirely against Sartre's *Critique de la raison dialectique* (published in 1960, but parts of which appeared as early as 1958 in *Les Temps modernes*) and even more certainly against the work of Merleau-Ponty. These pages would be the starting point for *Les Mots et les choses*. Moreover, they were repeated almost unchanged: "Rather than the death of God . . . what Nietzsche's thought heralds is the end of his murderer; it is the explosion of man's face in laughter, and the return of masks."[5] Gérard Lebrun has recently noted the extent to which *Les Mots et les choses* was haunted by Merleau-Ponty's negative presence. From beginning to end, Foucault's book is inspired and driven by polemics against Husserl's thought and Merleau-Ponty's interpretation of it. *Les Mots et les choses* is, first of all, a gesture of refusal, a rejection of phenomenology. A bursting "rupture"! Because this time is now long past, as Lebrun remarked in a 1988 lecture, and because the wave of phenomenology has long ago receded, *Les Mots et les choses* has obviously lost much of its "polemical flavor." "Today's readers tend to ignore or forget—depending on their age—that this is, first of all, a fighting book and a philosophical book." This essential point allows us to understand why *Les Mots et les choses* "was not seen as an attempt at a new method, but as an aggression,"[6] During the discussion following Lebrun's lecture, Raymond Bellour told of having read the proofs for this book shortly before it was published. At that stage it contained numerous attacks on Sartre that Foucault omitted from the final version.

This book that created such an uproar claimed to be "an archaeology of human sciences." It intended to locate the moment at which questioning about man, at which man became an object of knowledge, first occurred in Western culture. In superb descriptions of the forms of knowledge elaborated from the beginning of the sixteenth century to our times, Foucault demonstrated his breathtaking erudition. In essence, *Les Mots et les choses* maintains that every period is characterized by an underground configuration that delineates its culture, a grid of knowledge making possible every scientific discourse, every production of statements. Foucault designates this "historical a priori" as an episteme, deeply basic to defining and limiting what any period can—or cannot—think. Each science develops within the framework of an episteme, and therefore is linked in part with other sciences contemporary with it. Foucault focuses on three realms of knowledge that were developed in the classical episteme: general grammar, the analysis of wealth, and natural history. In the nineteenth century these three domains gave way to three others that were formed in a new grid of knowledge being instituted at that moment. These were philology, political economy, and biology. Foucault shows how the figure of man came to reside within their elaborations as an object of knowledge: the man who speaks, the man who works, the man who exists.

The birthplace of "human sciences" is in this global redistribution of the episteme. But this very vicinity precludes any possibility of their attaining real scientific status. "They are rendered incapable of being sciences," says Foucault, since it is only this situation of "vicinity" with regard to biology, economics, or philology that makes them possible, and they are only "projections" of these. However—and this is the contradiction undermining them—because they are rooted archaeologically in the modern episteme, they are obliged to claim to be scientific: "Western culture has constituted, under the name of man, a being who, by one and the same interplay of reasons, must be a positive domain of *knowledge* and cannot be an object of *science*."[7]

Within the framework of generally questioning the "human sciences," Foucault acknowledges that psychoanalysis and ethnology stand in a place apart, granting them the privileged status of "counter-sciences": they "ceaselessly 'unmake' that very man who is creating and recreating his positivity." Foucault adds: "One may say of both of them what Lévi-Strauss said of ethnology: that they dissolve man." And along with these two counter-sciences would come a third—linguistics—to disturb the constituted field of the human sciences, and to form the most general challenge to that field. "In 'exposing' it, these three counter-sciences threaten the very thing that made it possible for man to be known. Thus we see the destiny of man being spun before our very eyes, but being spun backwards; it is being led back, by those strange bobbins, to the forms of its birth, to the homeland that made it possible. And is that not one way of bringing about its end? For linguistics no more speak of man himself than do psychoanalysis and ethnology."[8]

This privileging of linguistics brings us back to problems raised constantly by Foucault ever since the early 1960s, in his articles on literature: "By a much longer and much more unexpected path, we are led back to the place that Nietzsche and Mallarmé signposted when the first asked Who speaks? and the second saw his glittering answer in the Word itself." The question of language then opens up on two horizons: attempts at formalizing thought and, at the other extreme of culture, modern literature: "That literature in our day is fascinated by the being of language is neither the sign of an imminent end nor proof of a radicalization: it is a phenomenon whose necessity has its roots in a vast configuration in which the whole structure of our thought and our knowledge is traced." And once again, in the order in which they made their entrance, Foucault discusses Artaud, Roussel, Kafka, Bataille, and Blanchot.[9]

These experiences that are both opposed to and bound up with contemporary culture—the formation of knowledge on a linguistic model and violence, excess, the cry, the "language reduced to powder" of literature—these experiences perhaps announce the end of the episteme that marked man's accession to knowledge. The final page of the book has been quoted so often that one hesitates to do so again: "One thing in any case is certain: man is neither the oldest nor the most constant problem that has been posed for human knowledge. Taking a relatively short chronological sample within a restricted geographical area—European culture since the sixteenth century—one can be certain that man is a recent invention within it. It is not around him and his secrets that knowledge prowled for so long in the darkness . . . As the archaeology of our thought easily shows, man is an invention of recent date. And one perhaps nearing its end."[10]

This flamboyant book, with its dazzling and complex style, was an immediate and resounding success. Not one newspaper or review could resist commenting on it. Foucault was even invited to appear on Pierre Dumayet's television program, "Lecture pour tous." A few excerpts from the press illustrate the response. "Foucault's work is one of the most important of our times," wrote Jean Lacroix in his philosophical column in *Le Monde*.[11] Robert Kanters called *Les Mots et les choses* "an impressive work" in *Le Figaro*.[12] And Gilles Deleuze, in *Le Nouvel Observateur*, after having painted a glowing picture of the many-faceted work, ended his article with these words: "To the question: what is new in philosophy? Foucault's books by themselves are a penetrating reply, the reply that is most acute and convincing as well. We think that *Les Mots et les choses* is a great book, about new thoughts."[13] Even earlier, in April, François Châtelet had written in *La Quinzaine littéraire:* "Michel Foucault's rigor, originality, and inspiration are such that inevitably, from reading his new book a radically new look at the past of Western culture and a more lucid idea of the confusion of its present are born."[14]

The success that greeted *Les Mots et les choses* was due in part to the cultural scene in which it appeared. In 1966 the "structuralist controversy" was in full swing. Claude Lévi-Strauss had published his *Anthropologie structurale* in 1958 as the manifesto of a new school, a new "philosophical" movement. In 1962 Lévi-Strauss had made things plain: he attacked Sartre rather harshly at the end of *La Pensée sauvage*, reducing his adversary's philosophy to the level of a contemporary mythology. For the first time in twenty-five years Sartre's undivided domination of French cultural spheres was seriously challenged. Think of how many saw this dispute as a liberation! Pierre Bourdieu, for example, in the preface to *Le Sens pratique*, speaks of the exaltation that Lévi-Strauss's work produced, especially the "new way to conceive of intellectual activity" that it imposed on an entire generation.[15] Lévi-Strauss's books had had an impact in every cultural sphere; all the more because he had brought Roman Jakobson's linguistics back with him from the United States, providing his friend Lacan with some essential links for the theory he was forming. Lacan's series Ecrits would be published in 1966. Since the beginning of the 1960s, every issue of every intellectual review not dedicated entirely to it had contained at least some mention of structuralism: structuralism and Marxism, structuralism against Marxism, structuralism and existentialism, structuralism against existentialism. Some promoted it; some opposed it; some were determined to come up with a synthesis. Everybody, in every area of intellectual life, took a position. Rarely had culture bubbled and seethed with more intensity.

The stage was thus set for a new and passionate battle about the "death of man." Foucault gave several interviews that attracted much attention, including one published in *La Quinzaine littéraire* on April 15, 1966: "We have experienced Sartre's generation," he said, "as a generation that was certainly brave and generous, one that had a passion for life, politics, and existence. But as for us, we have discovered something else, another passion: the passion for concepts and for what I will call 'system.'"

Question: What were Sartre's interests as a philosopher?
Answer: Roughly, faced with a historical world that bourgeois tradition, no longer able to keep its bearings, wanted to consider as absurd, Sartre wanted to demonstrate that, on the contrary, there was *meaning* [*sens*] everywhere . . .
Question: When did you stop believing in "meaning"?
Answer: The break came the day that Lévi-Strauss demonstrated—about societies—and Lacan demonstrated—about the unconscious—that "meaning" was probably only a sort of surface effect, a shimmer, a foam, and that what ran through us, underlay us, and was before us, what sustained us in time and space, was the system.

Foucault then defined this system, referring to the work of Dumézil and Leroi-Gourhan (whose name he did not mention, but everyone knew that was whom he meant), then mentioning Lacan again:

. . . Lacan's importance comes from the fact that he showed how it is the structures, the very system of language, that speak through the patient's discourse and the symptoms of his neurosis—not the subject . . . Before any human existence, there would already be a discursive knowledge, a system that we will rediscover.
Question: But then, who secretes this system?
Answer: What is this anonymous system without a subject, what thinks? The "I" has exploded—we see this in modern literature—this is the discovery of "there is." There is a *one*. In some ways, one comes back to the seventeenth-century point of view, with this difference: not setting man, but anonymous thought, knowledge without a subject, theory with no identity, in God's place.

In another interview two months later, Sartre was still in Foucault's line of sight: "*La Critique de la raison dialectique* is the magnificent and pathetic effort of a nineteenth-century man to conceive of the twentieth century. In this sense, Sartre is the last Hegelian, and even, I would say, the last Marxist." [16]
In these interviews Foucault showed very clearly the theoretical

space in which he himself situated his book. The same names were always brandished like banners: principally Lacan and Lévi-Strauss, but Dumézil as well, and "contemporary literature." How Foucault linked contemporary literature with works about prehistory, ethnology, or Roman mythology was also clear. Sometimes he would add Bertrand Russell and "analytical reason," formal logic, information theory, Canguilhem and the history of science, Althusser and his "brave attempts" to dust off Marxism with a Christian slant as served up by Teilhard de Chardin. In short, Foucault was evidently moving straight on into the "structuralist" galaxy.

Reactions were not long in coming. The Marxists went on the counteroffensive and excommunicated Foucault's book from party circles. He was not forgiven for his statement that "Marxism exists in nineteenth-century thought in the same way a fish exists in water; that is, it stops breathing anywhere else." Jacques Milhau wrote in *Cahiers du communisme*: "Michel Foucault's antihistorical prejudice holds up only because it is underpinned by a neo-Nietzschean ideology that serves too well, whether he is aware of this or not, the designs of a class whose only interest is to mask the objective choice of a path toward the future." [17] Jeannette Colombel's attack in *La Nouvelle Critique* was more moderate. She particularly reproached Foucault for neglecting temporality and history and for privileging the status quo by his vision of "apocalypse" and the announcement of "man's dissolution." "Foucault presents the world as a spectacle and as a game. His is an invitation to a magical attitude . . . Structuralism understood in this way would contribute to maintaining the established order." [18] But as soon as one left the milieu of "political" Communists for that of the party's "intellectual" reviews, the criticism became more professional: *Les Lettres françaises*, headed by Pierre Daix, warmly welcomed the book. Raymond Bellour had interviewed Foucault for the review as early as March 1966; he renewed his questioning the following year in a second interview. [19]

Catholics also joined in the debate. Jean-Marie Domenach, head of the review *Esprit*, examined this "new passion" and commented: "The provocative interview given by Michel Foucault in *La Quinzaine littéraire* has the ring of a new school's manifesto, and we shall continue to consult it . . . What a lot of questions there will be to ask! What a lot of questions we will ask! In the meanwhile we must hail the event." [20] Domenach, in fact, would ask Foucault these questions, and Foucault would fix on this one, the eleventh and last: "Does not a thought introducing constraints of system and discontinuity into the history of the mind remove any foundation for progressive political intervention?

Does it not lead to the following dilemma: either acceptance of the system, or an appeal to brute events, to the eruption of an external violence, as the only thing capable of overthrowing the system?" Foucault answered by clarifying his view of "progressive politics": "a politics recognizing the historical conditions and the stated rules of a practice, in which other politics acknowledge only ideal necessities, univocal determinations, or the free interplay of individual initiatives."[21] This important statement went unpublished until May 1968. Foucault took up the main elements of this answer in *L'Archéologie du savoir* (*The Archaeology of Knowledge*) in 1969.

François Mauriac also commented on the general infatuation with Foucault's theses in his famous "Bloc-notes" in *Le Figaro littéraire*: "But if this consciousness did exist, what could possibly make it not exist anymore? You end up making me feel brotherly toward Sartre, who was the enemy."[22]

And what about Sartre? Sartre was then wrestling with innumerable difficulties in writing the second projected volume of his *Critique de la raison dialectique* and in demonstrating the effectiveness of the synthesis he was trying to work out between existentialism and Marxism. But in an interview in a special issue of the review *L'Arc*, Sartre answered with a ferocity matching that of Foucault's attacks. The question, from Bernard Pingaud: "Do you see some common inspiration in the attitude of the younger generation toward you?" Sartre's answer:

At least some dominant tendency, because the rejection of history is not a general phenomenon. The success accorded Michel Foucault's last book is characteristic. What do we find in *Les Mots et les choses?* Not an "archaeology" of human sciences. An archaeologist is someone who studies the traces of a vanished civilization and tries to reconstruct it . . . What Foucault presents us with is—and Kanters saw this very well—a geology, the series of successive layers that make up our "ground." Each of these layers defines the conditions of possibility of a certain type of thought prevailing throughout a certain period. But Foucault does not tell us the thing that would be the most interesting, that is, how each thought is constructed on the basis of these conditions, or how mankind passes from one thought to another. To do so he would have to bring in praxis, and therefore history, which is precisely what he refuses to do. Of course his perspective remains historical. He distinguishes between periods, a before and an after. But he replaces cinema with the magic lantern, motion with a succession of motionless moments. The very success of this book is enough proof that it was expected. But truly original thought is never expected. Foucault brought people what they needed:

an eclectic synthesis in which Robbe-Grillet, structuralism, Lacan, *Tel Quel*, one by one, are all used to demonstrate the impossibility of historical reflection.

And of course Sartre made the connection between this dismissal of history and the rejection of Marxism: "Marxism is the target. It is a matter of establishing a new ideology, the final dam that the bourgeoisie can erect against Marx."[23]

It seems clear that *Les Mots et les choses* was initially seen by many as a "right-wing" book. Robert Castel, who would become a close friend of Foucault's in the 1970s, presented it as such in the introduction he wrote in March 1968 for the French edition of Marcuse's *Raison et révolution*. In Foucault's words opposing silent and philosophical laughter to "all those who still want to talk about man, his reign, and his liberation . . . all these warped and left-wing forms of reflection," Castel detected a direct attack on Marcuse.[24]

"Poor old bourgeoisie!" Foucault would later say ironically. "With only my book for its ramparts!" And when he was questioned early in 1968 by Jean-Pierre Elkabbach for a radio broadcast, Foucault observed to him that history had an odd stutter—that when Sartre had attacked him, he had simply reproduced the vocabulary used by the Communists fifteen years before to excommunicate existentialism. Foucault also had a curt reply to Sartre's attacks: "Sartre is a man with too-important work to do—literary, philosophical work—for him to have time to read my book. He hasn't read it. Consequently, what he says cannot possibly seem pertinent to me." When Elkabbach mentioned Sartre's phrase "rejection of history," Foucault answered:

No historian has ever reproached me for this. There is a sort of myth of History that philosophers have. You know, philosophers are, in general, extremely ignorant of any discipline that is not their own. There is a mathematics for philosophers, a biology for philosophers. Well, there is also a history for philosophers. History for philosophers is some sort of great, vast continuity in which the freedom of individuals and economic or social determinations come and get entangled. When someone lays a finger on one of those great themes—continuity, the effective exercise of human liberty, how individual liberty is articulated with social determinations—when someone touches on one of these three myths, these good people start crying out that History is being raped or murdered. In fact, it has been quite some time since people as important as Marc Bloch, Lucien Febvre, the English historians, and others put an end to this myth of History. They practice history in an entirely different way, and they do it so well that I am delighted if I have killed this philosophical myth of History—this philosophical myth they accuse me of killing. That is precisely what I wanted to kill, not history in general, not at all. One cannot kill history, but killing History for philosophers, yes, I absolutely want to kill that.[25]

The publication of this sensational conversation in its entirety in *La Quinzaine littéraire* aroused a great furor, and Foucault wrote the review to say that he had not authorized its publication and did not acknowledge any of it.[26] Maybe he felt it was necessary to defuse the polemics.

A year before, in January 1967, *Les Temps modernes* had published two very harsh articles about *Les Mots et les choses*, written by Michel Amiot and by Sylvie Le Bon. Canguilhem abandoned his usual reserve to react to this mobilization of Sartreans. He published a long article on Foucault—undoubtedly one of the best pieces ever written about him—in *Critique*. "Should one lose one's head, as some of those we consider to be among the finest minds of our time apparently have?" the historian of science wondered. He was astonished at the attitude of Sartre, who had been his schoolmate at the ENS. "Should one, after having refused to live according to an academic routine, behave like an academic embittered by his imminent replacement as the authority?" After these *ad hominem* remarks, he launched a counterattack on the basic issue. "Despite what most of Foucault's critics have said, the term 'archaeology' means exactly what it says. It is the condition for another history, in which the concept of event is preserved, but in which events affect concepts, not men." Canguilhem ended with a discussion of the political aspect of polemics. Foucault was said to be reactionary because he wanted to replace man with "system." But was not this the task set by the logician Jean Cavaillès, the eminent epistemologist, twenty years earlier, for philosophy: "to substitute for the primacy of a lived, or reflected, consciousness the primacy of concept, system, or structure"? Cavaillès, who, a member of the Resistance, had been shot by the Germans. Cavaillès, "who did not believe in history in the existential sense" and who nonetheless "refuted in advance, by his participation in a history tragically lived to the point of death, the arguments of those who are trying to discredit what they call structuralism, by sentencing it to engender (among other ravages) passivity in the face of what is accomplished."[27]

The historical importance of Canguilhem's article should not be underestimated. It made public this philosopher's underground but major importance in French thought. Basically, by forcing things slightly, one could say that the real opposition running through specialized areas of philosophy during the 1950s and 1960s formed around the two poles embodied by Sartre and Canguilhem. Canguilhem had a considerable number of disciples who forged their instruments precisely in opposition to existentialism and personalism. The centrality of the former inspector general was obvious when Althusser's and Lacan's students organized a "Cercle d'Epistémologie" (constituting an entire program) at the Ecole Normale Supérieure and in 1966 began to publish *Cahiers pour l'analyse*. Each issue of this review presented a quotation from Canguilhem as an epigraph.[28]

Though dismissed as right-wing by many on the left, structuralism thrived in several groups formed around Louis Althusser. These groups frequently served as the seeds around which Maoist movements crystallized just before 1968 and in the years following. Today it is hard to conceive of the extent of Althusser's influence on every class at the ENS during the 1960s and 1970s. Upon the publication of *Pour Marx* and *Lire le Capital* in 1965, Althusser became, as Jeannine Verdès-Leroux has written, the object "of a passion, an infatuation, and an imitation evoked by no other contemporary figure."[29] This passion was simultaneously theoretical and political, and was firmly situated on the extreme left. Foucault stressed this point in an interview published in Sweden in March 1968. He contrasted the "flabby, dull, humanistic" Marxism defended by Garaudy with the dynamic, rejuvenating Marxism practiced by Althusser's students, who, he said, represented "the left wing of the Communist party" and who enthusiastically supported the structuralist theses. 'You can understand what the maneuver by Sartre and Garaudy was all about," Foucault explained to his interviewer, "when they claimed that structuralism is a typically right-wing ideology. That allows them to designate people who are actually on their left as being complicitous with the right. Which also allows them to present themselves as the sole representatives of the French Communist left. But it is nothing but a maneuver." Foucault also tried to redefine in a more general way the connection between political action and theoretical reflection conducted in structural terms: "I think that a rigorous, theoretical analysis of the way in which economic, political, and ideological structures function is one of the necessary conditions for political action, insofar as political action is a way of manipulating and possibly changing, drastically disrupting, and transforming structures . . . I do not consider that structuralism is exclusively an armchair activity for intellectuals; I think it can and must be integrated with practice." A bit later in the interview he said: "I believe structuralism should be able to provide all political action with an indispensable, analytical instrument. Politics is not necessarily doomed to ignorance."[30]

Before long Foucault would refuse to be called a structuralist, and he ended up considering it an attack simply to be so labeled. What are we to think of all the polemics that unfolded around this loosely applied term, this *appellation mal controlée*, or of Foucault's implication in these controversies that were as violent as they were elusive? Was he or was he not a structuralist? Claude Lévi-Strauss today says that Foucault was right to reject being so classified, because there was no connection between their work, and that all the public uproar surrounding a bunch of scholars was only something temporarily fashionable. What is certain is that all the commentators blithely integrated Foucault with the "structuralist tribe." The famous drawing by Maurice Henry in *La Quinzaine littéraire*, showing Lévi-Strauss, Lacan, Barthes, and Foucault wearing "tribal" costume and conversing, is only one expression of a general phenomenon.[31] The papers and reviews used the terms *structuralism* and *structuralists* even, and especially, when they asked what it was that linked them or differentiated them. Basically, then, how did things stand? Of these things at least we may be sure:

First, Foucault does seem to have acknowledged this term as applying to himself. In an interview in a Tunis newspaper, on April 2, 1967, he discussed the question at length. When asked "Why does the general public consider you the priest of structuralism?" he answered: "At the most, I am structuralism's 'altarboy.' Let's say that I shook the bell and the faithful fell to their knees and the nonbelievers cried out. But the mass had begun long ago." More seriously, he went on to define two forms of structuralism: on the one hand a method that was very productive in specific realms, such as linguistics, the history of religion, or ethnology; on the other hand, "an activity whereby theoreticians who are not specialists strive to define the current relations that may exist between some element or another in our culture, between such-and-such a science, a certain practical domain, and a certain theoretical domain, and so on. In other words, this would be a sort of generalized structuralism, one no longer limited to a precise scientific domain." It would also be a structuralism that "would concern our own culture, our present-day world, the practical or theoretical relations as a whole that define our modernity. This is where structuralism has value as a philosophical activity, if one acknowledges that diagnosis is the role of philosophy." The structuralist philosopher, therefore, would be someone who performs the diagnosis of "what today is." Predictive words. This statement heralds many of the definitions that Foucault would propose for the role of the intellectual when his path once more intersected with politics. But in any case, in this text he defines himself very clearly as a "structuralist." [32]

Second, Foucault was widely considered to be one, and not just by his "enemies." For example, in a text in 1967 in which he attempted to answer the question "what is structuralism?" Gilles Deleuze mentioned not only Lévi-Strauss and Lacan but also Althusser and Foucault. He knew very well that there were huge differences among them. That is why the central theme of his article was "how is structuralism recognizable?" He defined several formal criteria permitting one to discover, in works whose orientations and preoccupations were very different, certain fixed lines that were grounds for belonging to this movement. [33]

Third, it is true that Foucault very quickly, and more and more strenuously, refused the label. "It is up to those who use this label to designate diverse work," he answered in a 1969 interview, "to tell us what makes us 'structuralist.' You know the riddle: what is the difference between Bernard Shaw and Charlie Chaplin? There isn't any, because they both have beards, with the exception of Chaplin, of course!" [34] In 1981 he would tell Hubert Dreyfus and Paul Rabinow, who were working on a book about him, that not only had he never been a structuralist, but that he had considered giving his work the subtitle "An Archaeology of Structuralism" to situate himself more as an outside observer than as a practitioner of the human sciences. The most he would concede to these two American authors was that he had not sufficiently "resisted the seduction of the structuralist vocabulary." None of which prevented Dreyfus and Rabinow from devoting a whole chapter to his structuralist period and the "failure" resulting from it. [35]

Around the time of these interviews with some distance on the structuralist controversies, Foucault analyzed the hostility aroused by the structuralist movement in France. Turning Sartre's expression around, he saw it as Marxism's final bid to resist the inexorable prog-

Instruction religieuse

ᵉ P. : Jacques Pellion 1
" Yves Pouvreau 1
" Pierre Rivière 1
ᵉ Ac. : Yves Pouvreau 1

Excellence

ᵉ P. : Pierre Rivière 2
" Yves Pouvreau 2
" Paul Foucault 2
ᵉ Ac. : Jacques Pellion 2
" Michel Léger 2
" Robert Prieur 2
" Claude Ranger 2
" Patrick Chaumet 2
" Jean Goupy 1

Diligence

ᵉ P. : Pierre Rivière 3
" Yves Pouvreau 3
" Paul Foucault 3
" Jacques Pellion 3
ᵉ Ac. : Claude Ranger 3
" Michel Léger 3
" Robert Prieur 3
" Louis Dupuis 3
" Paul Puichaud 2
" Patrick Chaumet 3

Examens

ᵉ P. : Pierre Rivière 4
" Yves Pouvreau 4
" Paul Foucault 4
ᵉ Ac. : Jacques Pellion 4
" Robert Prieur 4
" Michel Léger 3
" Claude Ranger 4
" Louis Dupuis 2
" Jean Goupy 2

Composition française

ᵉ P. : Pierre Rivière 5
" Jacques Pellion 5
" Paul Foucault 5

2ᵉ Ac. Patrick Chaumet 1
3ᵉ " Paul Puichaud 1
" Claude Ranger 1
4ᵉ " Robert Prieur 1
5ᵉ " Pierre Marsal 1
6ᵉ " Maurice Grelet 1

1ᵉʳ Ac. : Claude Ranger 5
2ᵉ " Jean Sorin 5
3ᵉ " Michel Léger 4
4ᵉ " Yves Pouvreau 3
5ᵉ " Yves Pouvreau 1
6ᵉ " Christian Hornbostel 1

Histoire de la littérature française

1ᵉʳ P. : Pierre Rivière 6
2ᵉ " Paul Foucault 6
3ᵉ " Claude Ranger 6
1ᵉʳ Ac. : Jean Goupy 4
2ᵉ " Michel Léger 5
3ᵉ " Patrick Chaumet 6
" Jacques Pellion 6
4ᵉ " Yves Pouvreau 5
5ᵉ " Robert Prieur 5
6ᵉ " Christian Hornbostel 2

Version latine

1ᵉʳ P. : Pierre Rivière 7
2ᵉ " Paul Foucault 7
1ᵉʳ Ac. : Jacques Pellion -7
2ᵉ " Jean Sorin 2
3ᵉ " Robert Prieur -6
4ᵉ " Paul Mitteault 1

Thème latin

1ᵉʳ P. : Pierre Rivière 8
2ᵉ " Michel Léger 6
1ᵉʳ Ac. : Patrick Chaumet 8
2ᵉ " Jacques Pellion -8
3ᵉ " Charles Hugon de Scœux 1
4ᵉ " Paul Puichaud 3

Littérature latine

1ᵉʳ P. : Paul Foucault 8
2ᵉ " Pierre Rivière 9

Left: Academic records of the junior class at Collège Saint-Stanislas in Poitiers for the 1940–41 school year.

(Archives of Collège Saint-Stanislas)

Below: Academic records of the final year at Collège Saint-Stanislas for the 1942–43 school year.

(Archives of Collège Saint-Stanislas)

Bottom: Primary classes at the Lycée Henri IV at Poitiers, 1935–36 school year. Foucault is in the back row, fifth from the left.

(Private papers of Mme. Foucault)

Philosophie	Trait. Rele. Philosophie	de Physique	de Nat.	F	Trait. Rele. Philosophie	Histoire	Géographie	Math.	de Physique	de Nat.	Explan. orale	O	Hygiène	Total	R
	20 20	5	5	50/25	20 30	15	15	10	10	10	10	120/60		170/85	
P. Becker	14½ 9	6½	5/20	— 28	10 12	6	7	9	5	8	7½	— 64½		— 92½	7
P. Benguet	6 3		15		4 12	8	5	3	9	9	5	55		70	13
P. Bousquet	10 8	6½	24½		8 15	8	4	4	7	9	6	— 64		— 85½	39
P. Clergent	2 8	4½	14½		0 12	4	6	3	7	2		48		62½	14
P. Prore	4 7	5	16		7 13	7	5	3	8	9		— 64		77	12
E. Delhorange	6½ 12	3½	28½		" " "	"	"	"	"	"	"	— 82		— 103½	3
P. Foucault	3 10	6½	19½		12 18	12	9	6	9	9	8	— 82		— 103½	1

Below: The *hypokhâgne* class in Poitiers, 1944. Foucault is at the very top. *Right:* On the back of this photo Lucette Rabaté describes Foucault as "the number one whiz kid."

(Private papers of Lucette Rabaté)

L'inconscient.

In preparation for his exams for the *agrégation*, Foucault wrote out dozens of outlines on every possible subject. Here: "The Unconscious."

(Private papers of Jean-Paul Aron)

1re p. Inconscient et représentation.

A) Le pb st présence sans représentation. or + elle - que implique l'inconscient :
↓ moins de conscience; et ↑ + de réalité.
A mettre ass association libidinale : petite perception...

1/ Bergson et l'inconscient y mémoire
— réalité spatiale de l'inconscient
— l'effort spirituel.

2/ Durkheim et la représentation collective.

B dimension du conflit.

2ième p. Inconscient et conflit

1/ Janet et la csce. y conduite. D'où caractère relatif de la csce.

2/ Freud : — la csce est elle aussi relative
— l'inconscient y résultat de conflit.
— le surmoi est aussi l'inconscient.

3/ D'où critiquer cette l'inconscient freudien : l'inconscient y chose.

3ième p. L'Inconscient et le cogito

S il put envisager la réalité humaine à la 1ère personne, c/w admettre l'inconscient.

1 L'inconscient chez Descartes et Kant.
Apparition de la réflexion.

2 La csce thétique et non thétique.
Pb de la mauvaise foi. Conscience inconsciente

3 Merleau Ponty : l'implicité de la réflexion.

Left: Foucault in Sweden with his Jaguar, 1958.

Below: Foucault at the Maison de France in Uppsala, 1957.

(Photos: J.-C. Oberg)

Left: Georges Dumézil in 1949.
(Private papers of Claude Dumézil)

Below: Louis Althusser in 1976.
(Photo: Keystone)

Bottom: Georges Canguilhem in January 1988, during the colloquium "Foucault Philosophe."
(Photo: Gérard Uferas/Agence Vu)

Left: Letter from Foucault to Henri Gouhier, May 4, 1961. On the upper left are notes taken by Gouhier during Foucault's dissertation defense.

(Photo: D. R.)

Below: A copy of *Folie et Déraison* printed for the dissertation defense, 1961.

(Photo: D. R.)

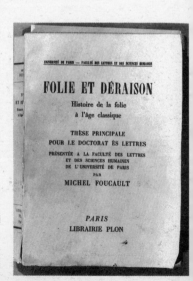

UNIVERSITÉ DE PARIS — FACULTÉ DES LETTRES ET DES SCIENCES HUMAINES

FOLIE ET DÉRAISON

Histoire de la folie
à l'âge classique

THÈSE PRINCIPALE
POUR LE DOCTORAT ÈS LETTRES
PRÉSENTÉE À LA FACULTÉ DES LETTRES
ET DES SCIENCES HUMAINES
DE L'UNIVERSITÉ DE PARIS
PAR
MICHEL FOUCAULT

PARIS
LIBRAIRIE PLON

Above: The structuralist picnic on the grass: Michel Foucault, Jacques Lacan, Claude Lévi-Strauss, and Roland Barthes. The drawing, by Maurice Henry, was published in *La Quinzaine Littéraire*, July 1, 1967.
(Photo: D. R.)

Below: Foucault after publication of *Les Mots et les choses*, 1966.
(Photo: Marc Garanger)

Above: Foucault with Jean Genet at a demonstration following the death of Pierre Overney, February 1972.
(Photo: Xavier Martin/Sipa Press)

Below: Foucault and Sartre demonstrate in the Goutte d'Or in support of immigrants, November 27, 1972.
(Photo: Gérard Aimé)

A la suite d'une interpellation

M. MICHEL FOUCAULT PORTE PLAINTE CONTRE DES POLICIERS

MM. J.-M. Domenach et Michel Foucault, et une douzaine de membres du groupe d'information sur les prisons, ont été interpellés respectivement le 1er mai aux portes des prisons de Fresnes et de la Santé, alors qu'ils distribuaient un texte sur l'abolition du casier judiciaire. Ils ont été relâchés vers 17 heures. M. M. Foucault a porté plainte pour arrestation illégale, atteinte aux libertés publiques, injures publiques et violences légères avec préméditation.

M. Michel Foucault, professeur au Collège de France, nous a fait le récit suivant :

« *Au poste de police où j'ai été emmené avec mon groupe, un policier, après avoir remarqué que plusieurs de nos noms n'étaient pas de consonance française, nous a demandé quels étaient parmi nous «ceux qui portaient* » *des noms vraiment gaulois». Quelques instants après, faisant la mimique de quelqu'un qui tire au revolver, il a crié : «Heil* » *Hitler !» Enfin, un autre d'entre eux m'a frappé dans le dos alors que je quittais le commissariat et que j'étais déjà dans la rue.* »

Left: Le Monde, 1971.

(Photo: D. R.)

Below: Alain Jaubert, Claude Mauriac, Michel Foucault, Jean-Paul Sartre, Michelle Vian, Gilles Deleuze, and Daniel Defert on their way to a press conference at the Ministry of Justice on the Place Vendôme, January 18, 1972.

(Photo: Elie Kagan)

Foucault and Yves Montand at Roissy, September 22, 1975. Intellectuals had been expelled from Spain after holding a press conference in Madrid to protest the death sentences of eleven militants.

(Photo: Pascal Lebrun)

Above: Ivry Gitlis, Claude Mauriac, Simone Signoret, Michel Foucault, and Patrice Chéreau at a demonstration in support of the Polish people, at the Paris Opera. December 22, 1981.

(Photo: Laurent Maous/Gamma)

Below: Foucault at the TUNIX meeting in Berlin, January 1978.

(Photo: Raymond Depardon/Gamma)

Above and below: Foucault at home, 1983.
(Photo: Martine Franck/Magnum)

Above: Foucault at Berkeley in October 1983, wearing the cowboy hat his students gave him. With the students is Paul Rabinow (second from the right).

(Private papers of Paul Rabinow)

Below: An article by Georges Dumézil in *Le Nouvel Observateur* (June 1984) on the death of Foucault.

(Photo: D. R.)

UN HOMME HEUREUX

PAR GEORGES DUMÉZIL

Au printemps de 1954, mes amis de l'université d'Uppsala me demandèrent de leur désigner un lecteur français. Procédure peu orthodoxe qu'ignoraient nos Relations culturelles. Mais depuis que j'avais occupé le poste, de 1933 à 1935, des liens étroits m'attachaient à Uppsala, où j'allais presque chaque année travailler un mois ou deux dans l'admirable bibliothèque qu'est la Carolina Rediviva. J'étais fort embarrassé de ma mission, quand Raoul Curiel, qui rentrait d'Afghanistan, me dit qu'il avait mon homme. Il venait de rencontrer un jeune normalien, agrégé de philosophie, encore incertain de sa carrière, qu'il n'hésitait pas à qualifier : « *l'être le plus intelligent qu'il eût connu* ». Je n'en demandai pas plus et j'écrivis à Michel Foucault, avec un éloge sincère de la vie uppsalienne. Il accepta. Comme je passais l'été au pays de Galles, je ne le vis pas avant son départ.

L'année suivante, dès la fin de mes cours du Collège, je repris le chemin de ma laborieuse Uppsala. Ses cours publiés faisaient du bruit. Les mères lui amenaient leurs filles pour l'entendre parler de « *l'amour en France de Sade à Jean Genet* ». Et lui-même avait trouvé rassemblée dans trois salons de la Carolina une riche bibliothèque médicale du XVIIe et du XVIIIe siècle. Un vieux legs qui dormait dans l'attendant : l' « Histoire de la folie » progressait ! Bref, un homme heureux. C'est alors que je le découvris. De trente ans mon cadet, il se trouva, dès ces premières journées, fraternel, ouvert, dévoué, confiant. Il se forma tout naturellement entre nous une amitié qui, pendant les trente autres années qui suivirent, ne devait connaître ni ombre ni déchirure. Je le retrouvai en 1956 à Uppsala, puis il quitta la Suède pour Hambourg, pour Varsovie, pour Clermont-Ferrand. Je n'eus plus à intervenir dans sa carrière sauf quand, un peu plus tard, en 1970, on pensa à lui pour le Collège de France. Ce fut Jules Vuillemin qui le présenta, à la mort de Jean Hyppolite. Je n'étais plus moi-même que professeur honoraire et je découvrais tardivement les Etats-Unis : mon rôle se borna à écrire de Chicago à six collègues électeurs que, quoi qu'on dît, Michel Foucault n'était pas le Diable. Plutôt le contraire. Il fut plus qu'honorablement élu.

D'autres présenteront son œuvre. Je ne reprendrai que le mot de Raoul Curiel. L'intelligence de Foucault était, littéralement, sans borne, même sophistiquée. Il avait installé son observatoire sur les zones de l'être vivant où les distinctions traditionnelles du corps et de l'esprit, de l'instinct et de l'idée paraissent absurdes : la folie, le crime, la sexualité. De là son regard tournait comme un phare sur l'histoire et sur le présent, prêt aux découvertes les moins rassurantes, capable de tout accepter, sauf de s'arrêter dans une orthodoxie. Une intelligence à foyers multiples, à miroirs mobiles, où le jugement naissant se doublait aussitôt de son contraire sans cependant se détruire ni reculer. Tout cela, comme il est usuel à ce niveau, sur un fond d'extrême bienveillance, de bonté. Les attachements qu'il a éveillés dans la jeunesse intellectuelle, en France, aux Etats-Unis, au Japon même, la résonance des quelques essais qu'il aura eu le temps de publier s'expliquent autant par cette générosité que par la puissance de sa dialectique et la séduction de son art. Notre amitié fut une facile réussite. Après Pierre Gaxotte il y a deux ans, après l'uppsalien Stig Wikander l'hiver dernier, Michel Foucault en se retirant me laisse un peu plus démuni, et non seulement des ornements de la vie : de sa substance même.

G. D.

Foucault in 1977. *(Photo: Michèle Brancilhon)*

ress of ideas. Structuralism rang the alarm for Marxist dogmatism, and French culture, being under Communist influence, certainly felt its corrosive power. Which was not surprising, Foucault explained. In the first place, structuralism was a movement that came to us from the East (via Jakobson, who was Russian; via the formalists; and so on), and the entire Stalinist tradition had worked to repress it and destroy it at its birthplace. To back up this claim, Foucault told the following anecdote: in 1967 he went to give some lectures in Hungary. Everything went just fine, and there were plenty of people in the audiences, until the day he proposed to talk about structuralism. The head of the university told him the lecture had to be given in his office, for a select group, because the subject was too difficult for the students. This reaction made Foucault wonder what was so frightening about this word, these themes, this idea, and in 1978 he came up with the analysis above for Ducio Trombadori.[36]

SUCCESS WAS FOUCAULT'S. Everyone who met him during the spring of 1966 described a happy man, visibly delighted with his success and his nascent celebrity. But when the euphoria had evaporated he seemed to think it was the worst book he had written. At one point he even more or less disowned it, asking Pierre Nora not to print it anymore. But this reaction was nothing new. As we have seen, he had already stopped distribution of *Maladie mentale et personnalité*, completely rewritten a second version, and ended up banning that also. With *Folie et déraison* Foucault's self-criticism took another tack. When the second edition came out under the title *Histoire de la folie* eleven years after the book had first appeared, he excised the first preface, which put too much emphasis on a "primeval experience" of madness. Now *Les Mots et les choses* required another whole book to clarify things. In response to the bad readings to which he thought he had been subjected, to dispel certain misunderstandings, to explain notions that caused problems, to dissociate himself from "structuralism," Foucault would write *L'Archéologie du savoir*, which was published in 1969. And in 1972, when *Naissance de la clinique* was reissued, he made some lexical changes there. For example, he changed the phrase "I should like to attempt here a structural analysis of a signified—that of medical experience—in one period" to "I should like to attempt here the analysis of a type of discourse—that of medical analysis—in one period." He also removed the notion of a structural study from the next page.[37]

At each stage, then, Foucault seemed to proceed by successive re-writings. He worked and he changed. He claimed the right to do so in his preface to *L'Archéologie du savoir*:

> What, do you imagine that I would take so much trouble and so much pleasure in writing, do you think that I would keep so persistently to my task, if I were not preparing—with a rather shaky hand—a labyrinth into which I can venture, in which I can move my discourse, opening up underground passages, forcing it to go far from itself, finding overhangs that reduce and deform its itinerary, in which I can lose myself and appear at last to eyes that I will never have to meet again. I am no doubt not the only one who writes in order to have no face. Do not ask who I am and do not ask me to remain the same: leave it to our bureaucrats and our police to see that our papers are in order. At least spare us their morality when we write.[38]

But one thing is certain: when it was time to look back over his work, the "formalist" books he wrote during this period. *Les Mots et les choses* and *L'Archéologie du savoir*, were not his favorites.

Among all the reactions aroused by *Les Mots et les choses*, there was one that went straight to Foucault's heart. This was a letter he received from René Magritte, in which the painter made some comments about notions of resemblance and similarity. He included a series of his drawings with the letter, one of which was a reproduction of *Ceci n'est pas une pipe*. Foucault thanked him and asked for some information about one of Magritte's paintings that obliquely appropriated Manet's *Le Balcon*, a picture that particularly interested Foucault. This exchange of letters was the source of a study that Foucault did on Magritte, also titled "Ceci n'est pas une pipe," published first in *Cahiers du chemin* and later as a small volume. As for Magritte's reply concerning Manet, Foucault intended to use it in a book he was beginning to write.[39]

13

~~~

The Open Sea

Foucault, wreathed in glory as a result of *Les Mots et les choses*, arrived in Tunis. How did it happen that he again found himself far from France? Of course, he had no desire to work in Clermont-Ferrand anymore. But, as we have seen, it was no easy task to find a position elsewhere. And why Tunis? Once again, it was the result of an odd combination of circumstances. Gérard Deledalle, a specialist in English and American authors, had come to the University of Tunis in 1963 and established its first degree program in philosophy. In 1964 he invited his former professor, Jean Wahl, to give a series of lectures on Wittgenstein, and while he was there asked if he would stay in Tunis to teach. Wahl accepted, but as a result of family reasons and because he felt very homesick he returned to Paris after six months. When he learned that Foucault was looking for a position abroad, he wrote to Deledalle to ask if the job was still open. It was, but several formalities had to be taken care of. First the Tunisian authorities had to be applied to. Then, when they had given their approval, Foucault had to present his candidacy officially. As far as the French were concerned, there was no problem: Jean Sirinelli took care of everything. Thanks to the Ministry of Foreign Affairs, Foucault would be "on administrative leave" from Clermont-Ferrand, with a three-year contract. But Foucault saw his new voluntary exile as simply another place in which to wait; what he really wanted was a job in Paris.

He arrived in Tunisia at the end of September 1966. "A country blessed by history, one that deserves to live forever because it was where Hannibal and St. Augustine lived," he told Jelila Hafsia as they strolled through the vestiges of Carthage, an archaeological site of breathtaking beauty;[1] its open sea and blinding sun gave an irrepressible sense of plunging into the depths of time and of the world. But before Carthage, Foucault discovered the splendor of another landscape. Gérard Deledalle and his wife met him at the airport and took him to the village of Sidi Bou Saïd, where they lived. Perched on a hillside overlooking the bay, just a few kilometers from Tunis it was the kind of place one dreams of. Foucault stayed first at the Dar Saïd, a small hotel whose rooms surrounded a courtyard flooded with the fragrance of jasmine and orange trees. He remained in the village throughout his two years in Tunisia, living successively in three almost identical houses with white walls and blue blinds. "In this village where he was happy," recalls Jean Daniel, who met Foucault at this time,

> he was best known for his habit of working from daybreak on at the windows of his villa that overlooked the bay, and for his greedy appetite for living and loving in the sun. On each of my trips there, I would go to find him so we could take a walk, which he liked to be long, fast, and energetic. He would invite me into a room carefully kept cool and dark, at the end of which was a sort of big, raised slab where he put the mat he used for a bed, a mat that, like the Arabs and the Japanese, he rolled up during the day . . . My stay in Tunis happened to coincide with that of Daniel Defert, his companion. All three of us went to a beach that was shaped like a peninsula and protected by dunes from the rest of humanity. In this imaginary desert there was a light, simultaneously ocher and lunar, that reminded Foucault of *Le Rivage des Syrtes*. The last time I was in that place, Foucault talked about Julien Gracq and Gide, whom his friend Roland Barthes was fondly rereading. In this setting he seemed to flee philosophy; literature was a refuge.[2]

It was, however, to teach philosophy that Foucault had come to Tunisia, and he devoted himself to it with great success. The *faculté des lettres et sciences humaines* is located in the large old city lycée, built in the 1950s, on the Boulevard du 9-Avril. It overlooks the Casbah and Lake Sijoumi. At the beginning of his stay, Foucault took the train from Sidi Bou Saïd to Tunis, then walked from the station, crossing the Médina and going up Avenue Bourguiba. Later he bought a car, a white convertible Peugeot 404.

The students attended his courses avidly. The subjects were all very different, because he taught at all three of the levels preparing for the *license*. He discussed Nietzsche with some, and Descartes, whom he read in conjunction with Husserl's *Cartesian Meditations*. He gave a course on aesthetics, in which he showed slides and analyzed the evolution of painting from the Renaissance to Manet. Even so, he did not neglect psychology. He lectured on "projection" and explained the basic elements of psychology, psychiatry, and psychoanalysis all at once. Of course he inevitably lingered over Rorschach theory. Then there were the famous public lectures, still admiringly spoken of today by his former students, on "man in Western thought." Not far from *Les Mots et les choses!* The audience was very large—more than two hundred people every Friday—and extremely varied. As in Uppsala, this lecture series was highly appreciated by the city's cultured society, and every age, every profession was represented.

Although the young people who attended Foucault's courses were enthusiastic about his teaching, they had reservations about his political views. According to their testimony today, he was long perceived as a pure "representative of Gaullist technocracy," "too Western to understand Tunisia," and so on. His hostility to Marxism disconcerted his students, who were even more willing to label him "right-wing" because they did not particularly like hearing him quote Nietzsche at every turn and sometimes felt he was deliberately provoking them.

Foucault actively participated in university and intellectual life in Tunis. He rubbed shoulders with the French faculty whose jobs brought them to the city, of course, and became friends with Gérard Deledalle and his wife, and with Jean Gattegno, whom he would meet again at Vincennes. He worked with the philosophy club organized by the students, and he lectured at the Club Tahar Hadad on Boulevard Pasteur, whose head, Jelila Hafsia, had a passion for the French philosopher. Foucault lectured there on "structuralism and literary analysis" in February 1967, and on "madness and civilization" in April of that year.

Also in 1967 he had Jean Hyppolite invited to the university. Fatma Haddad, who was Foucault's assistant at the time, remembered how emotionally he introduced his former teacher to the audience. Hyppolite was supposed to discuss "Hegel and modern philosophy." About to begin his lecture, he indicated Foucault, who was seated beside him: "There must have been some mistake when you invited me, because modern philosophy is sitting right there." Foucault had just introduced the subject of the lecture in these terms: "All philosophical reflection today is a dialogue with Hegel, and creating the history of Hegel's philosophy is to practice modern philosophy."

The "encounter" with Paul Ricoeur left the Tunisians with a less glorious memory. At the height of the structuralist controversy, they had expected a fascinating confrontation between the two thinkers. Ricoeur had been invited by the cultural center in Carthage for a series of lectures on the philosophy of language. Foucault and Gérard Deledalle attended one of these together: "He was sitting right next to me," said Deledalle, "and he kept on making funny remarks. Ricoeur noticed it." But when it came time for discussion, after the lecture, Foucault never said a word. Deledalle understood at that moment that perhaps inviting the two philosophers to join him for dinner that evening had not been such a good idea. He never forgot the tense, unpleasant atmosphere and how it spoiled the evening. Impossible to bring up any intellectual subject at all. When Ricoeur left Tunis shortly afterward, he saw Foucault preparing to take the same flight as he. He told the head of the cultural center of Carthage, who had taken him to the airport: "We will talk in the plane." He wrote her several days later to thank her for her welcome and told her that the predicted discussion had never taken place. Foucault, pretending not to see him, had taken a seat at the other end of the plane. But although he refused to play the game of "the debate of ideas," Foucault had no trouble telling his students what he thought. "I am going to summarize what Ricoeur said," he told them. After each point he asked them whether or not it was a faithful summary. And when they acquiesced, he told them: "Well, now we're going to tear it all apart."

Perhaps the reason Foucault spent so much time on the history of painting in his lectures was that he intended to write a book about Manet. On June 15, 1966, before leaving for Tunis (and only a few months after the publication of *Les Mots et les choses*), he had signed a contract with Jérôme Lindon, the editor-in-chief at Minuit, for an "essay on Manet" with the title "Le Noir et la surface." The book was never published, but in several of his lectures Foucault explained what it was about Manet's paintings that caught his attention. The creator of *Bal à l'Opéra*, *Bar des Folies-Bergères*, and *Le Balcon* interested him not as the painter who made Impressionism possible, but as the painter who made all of modern painting possible. Manet broke with rules that had been in effect since the Quattrocento. The painter had been forced to mask, to evade, to make people forget the fact that the paint was applied and inscribed on a certain fragment of space, a wall or a picture. Manet broke this set of conventions and invented the picture-object, the painting that represents its own materiality. He brought the fundamental material elements of painting into the representation. He integrated pictorial physics into the scene represented: the light from outside, the strong vertical and horizontal lines repeating the format of the painting and the weave of the cloth. He did away with depth, and the picture became a concrete space before which the spectator can and must shift. Manet never went beyond representational painting. But he freed painting from conventions burdening representation. Thanks to Manet, painting would be able to play with spatial properties, with its pure, material properties, used for their own sake.

Most of Foucault's time was taken up with writing *L'Archéologie du savoir*. He wrote furiously and struggled violently with notions of enunciation, discursive formation, regularity, and strategy. He was trying to establish and pin down an entire vocabulary, to define and articulate an entire set of interacting concepts. These were the terms in which he presented his work on the book jacket:

> What was my aim in writing this book? Did I wish to explain what I had wanted to do in my earlier books, in which so many things still remained obscure? Not altogether, not exactly. By going a little farther in the same direction, and coming back, as if by a new turn in the spiral, just short of what I set out to do, I hoped to show the position from which I was speaking; to map the space that makes possible these investigations and others that I may never accomplish; in short, to give meaning to the word *archaeology*, which I had so far left empty . . . And where the history of ideas tried to uncover, by deciphering texts, the secret movements of thought (its slow progression, its conflicts and retreats, the obstacles that it has overcome), I would like to reveal, in its specificity, the level of things said: the condition of their emergence, the forms of their accumulation and connection, the rules of their transformation, the discontinuities that articulate them. The domain of things said is what is called the *archive*; the role of archaeology is to analyze that archive.[3]

Foucault knew that the stakes were considerable. He had been introduced as Sartre's successor, and the challenged master had launched a harsh counterattack. The fight was on, and if he wanted to make off with the winnings, Foucault must not disappoint the expectations of an eager crowd awaiting the next heated exchange. Foucault was hard at work: at his desk at home early in the morning, in the Bibliothèque Nationale in Tunis in the afternoon. He also spent a lot of time talking with Deledalle because the book dealt with problems that were related to the latter's interest in linguistics and the philosophy of language.

Foucault consulted him as an expert on English and American philosophy, which he did not know well. Deledalle talked with him almost daily during his walks through Sidi Bou Saïd, and he watched the stack of papers, black with notes, grow higher with every visit. Foucault chiseled his phrases as meticulously and fervently as a goldsmith. The book was finished when Foucault left Tunisia and was published early in 1969.

But Tunisia, for Foucault, was not simply divided between the pleasures of the sun and the asceticism of philosophy. Since the day he had stepped back from politics it had been just a matter of time before he was sure to become caught up in it again. Existence fated that this would happen in Tunis just when French intellectuals were on the brink of plunging into the whirlwind events of May 1968. Foucault saw little of these, having returned to Paris only briefly at the end of May. He was there long enough to attend the meeting in Charléty stadium, among the leftist groups who shared with Pierre Mendès France the hope that the Gaullist regime would soon fall. Walking with Jean Daniel, the editor of *Le Nouvel Observateur*, in the streets one day, and watching the students march, he told Daniel: "They are not making a revolution; they are a revolution." Foucault returned to Tunis certain that the end of the Gaullist era was near, that the left would take power, and that Mendès France or François Mitterrand would be called upon to play an important role.

But although he was persuaded that there would be a swing in the French government, he knew that the same thing would not happen in the Tunisian regime. Agitation had begun at the University of Tunis in December 1966. A student had been beaten up by the police for refusing to pay for a bus ticket. In response to this incident, the rebellion spread through the university. By June 1967 the problems were far worse. Following Israel's rout of Arab armies during the Six-Day War, violence flared and spread in the Tunisian capital. Pro-Palestinian demonstrations degenerated into anti-Semitic riots. Foucault was appalled by these events. He expressed his disgust to Georges Canguilhem on June 7, 1967:

> Last Monday we had here a day (a half-day) of pogrom. It was far worse than reported in *Le Monde*—at least fifty fires. A hundred and fifty or two hundred shops—the poorest, of course—were ransacked, the age-old sight of a ransacked synagogue, carpets dragged into the streets, trampled, and burned, people running through the streets, taking refuge in a building the crowd wanted to set on fire. And since then—silence, the metal curtains down, no one, or almost no one, in

the quarter, children playing with broken trinkets. The government's reaction was quick and firm, apparently sincere. But it [the violence] was obviously organized. Everybody knows that for weeks, no doubt months, it was working underground, unbeknownst to the government and against it. In any case, nationalism plus racism adds up to something ghastly. And when one also adds the fact that the students, because they are leftist, lent a hand (and more) to all that, well, it makes one deeply sad. And one wonders through what strange trick (or stupidity) of history Marxism could provide the occasion (and vocabulary) for that.

Foucault did not hide from his students his disgust at such acts. But the riots of June 1967 were merely the beginning of a wave of unrest that would keep the university in a state of tension for more than a year. The Marxist students grouped around the movement "Perspectives" were at first primarily Trotskyites but increasingly shifted toward Maoism. They mobilized on behalf of their "Palestinian brothers," but at the same time they engaged in more and more radical forms of opposition to the government and to President Bourguiba's regime. From March to June 1968, after a revival of unrest provoked by Vice-President Hubert Humphrey's visit to Tunisia, there was a harsh clampdown. Among those put in prison were several of Foucault's students. The French teachers joined in protest against the arrests and torture. But some of them advocated more visible and vigorous action to demonstrate their solidarity. A general meeting of French teachers was called, and Foucault and Jean Gattegno were put in the minority by their colleagues, who felt an obligation to be cautious in a foreign country. Foucault also went to see the French ambassador to ask him to intervene. The diplomat replied that it was obviously impossible for him to get mixed up in the internal affairs of Tunisia.

Foucault, Gattegno, and several others did not resign themselves to being passive. They helped the students who had escaped the roundup, sheltered them in their homes. Foucault, for example, hid the group's duplicating machine, and several tracts were printed in his garden. After the 1968 summer vacation, when Foucault returned to Tunisia, he tried to testify at the students' trial. He had prepared a statement to read on behalf of Ahmed Ben Othman. But he was not given permission; all the proceedings took place behind closed doors. Foucault's stubbornness earned him threats on several occasions by plainclothes policemen—or stand-ins for the police? Once he was even seriously manhandled and struck, after having been stopped on the road to Sidi

Bou Saïd. These were warnings sent with a minimum of protocol by the Tunisian authorities. Officially, however, he was never disturbed. His prestige was too great, and it would have been extremely difficult for the government to take him on. Georges Lapassade was expelled from the country and reproached Foucault for having acted too feebly. But Foucault preferred discreet and effective action to what he considered irresponsible behavior, doomed above all to failure. As for Gattegno, his contract was terminated at the end of July 1968, and he would be sentenced in absentia to five years in prison. The students received alarmingly heavy prison sentences. When he went back to Tunisia in 1971, Foucault tried once again to intervene with the minister of the interior and was even granted an interview, but it was a waste of time. Foucault then decided not to set foot in the country until the political prisoners were freed.

One thing is certain: Foucault was extremely shaken by these events. He expressed this strongly in his interviews with Ducio Trombadori in 1978, as he went back over his political itinerary and experiences.

I had some luck during my life: in Sweden I saw a social-democratic country that functioned "well" and, in Poland, a people's democracy that functioned "badly." I saw Germany during the 1960s, at the moment it began its rapid economic development. Then a Third World country, Tunisia. I lived there for two and a half years. It made a real impression. I was present for large, violent student riots that preceded by several weeks what happened in May in France. This was March 1968. The unrest lasted a whole year: strikes, courses suspended, arrests. And in March, a general strike by the students. The police came into the university, beat up the students, wounded several of them seriously, and started making arrests. There were trials, during which some students were given eight, ten, as many as fourteen years of prison. I had an immediate and precise notion of what was at stake with all the things happening in the universities of the world. Being French constituted a certain protection as far as the authorities were concerned and allowed me to do (as many of my colleagues did) a number of things, to see what was going on, and also to see how the authorities, the French government reacted to all this—not all of it was pretty.

I have to say that I was tremendously impressed by those young men and women who took terrible risks by writing or distributing tracts or calling for strikes, the ones who really risked losing their freedom! It was a political experience for me. My brief time spent with the Communist party, what I had been able to see in Germany, the way things worked out for me when I returned to France, in relation to problems I had wanted to raise concerning psychiatry—all of this had left me with a rather bitter experience of politics, and a thoroughly speculative skepticism. I make no secret of that. But there, in Tunisia, I came around to offering some concrete aid to the students . . . I had to enter into the political debate somehow.

For Foucault one of the most striking aspects of the Tunisian revolt he watched unfolding was the role played by political ideology. His students "all claimed to be inspired by Marxism, with a violence, intensity, and passion that was altogether remarkable. It constituted for them not merely a better analysis of things, but at the same time a kind of moral energy, a kind of altogether remarkable existential act." And he added (this was at a time when he was excited about the effect of the Iranian revolution):

> What is there in today's world that is able to give you the desire, the taste, the capacity for, the possibility of an absolute sacrifice? with no possible hint of profit, ambition, or thirst for power behind it? That was what I saw in Tunisia. It was the evidence that myth is necessary. A political ideology or a political perception of the world, of human relations and situations was absolutely necessary to begin the struggle. The precision of theory and its scientific value, on the other hand, were entirely secondary and, in discussions, constituted more of a dead end than a real principle of just and proper conduct.

One can see why Foucault felt amazement, when he returned to France at the end of 1968, at the "hyper-Marxization" of what was being said: "An unleashing of theories, discussions, anathema, expulsions, splintered splinter groups, that completely confounded me . . . What I saw in France in 1968–69 was exactly the opposite of what I had found interesting in Tunisia in March 1968."[4] This was how he explained his intention always to be involved in concrete, limited, specific struggles, at a distance from all the verbiage, the innumerable quibbles.

IN THE FALL OF 1968 Foucault was back in France. He kept his house in Sidi Bou Saïd, but he knew he was an undesirable in Tunisia. And he had found a way to get back to Paris—or rather, near Paris. Didier Anzieu had asked if he would join the psychology department that he had recently created at Nanterre. Foucault hesitated, for a number of reasons: first, he felt rather embarrassed about competing for the position against the Lacanian psychoanalyst Pierre Kaufmann, who was well-known as a member of the Resistance during the war. In his letter to Canguilhem where he described the anti-Semitic riots he had witnessed in Tunisia, Foucault ended by saying that it was "physically unbearable for him to oppose a Jew," even if this opposition took place merely in a "regular academic game." And there were other reasons. Foucault did not particularly want to teach psychology anymore. "Psychology is not for me," he told Robert Francès, then a professor at the department at Nanterre, who described Foucault's behavior as a veritable "hesitation waltz." And above all, Foucault had several irons in the fire: there was a new professorship opening up at the Sorbonne; there was a possibility of something at the École Pratique des Hautes Etudes; and most important, at the Collège de France, Vuillemin's and Hyppolite's efforts were slowly but surely having some effect. In the end he did accept Anzieu's offer and was elected and appointed to the faculty at Nanterre.

But he never went. He chose, instead, to join the group establishing a university at Vincennes. On November 18, 1968, he notified the dean at Nanterre that he was giving up his "leave" at the faculty (authorized only three days before by the ministry) because the Centre Expérimental at Vincennes had just offered him "the newly created position as tenured professor of philosophy." This move occasioned an odd bureaucratic and financial problem: who was supposed to pay Foucault for the period from October 1, 1968 (when his appointment in Tunis expired), to December 1, 1968 (the effective date of his appointment at Vincennes)? The Ministry of Education sent a very official letter to the dean at Nanterre, informing him that he had to pay Michel Foucault's salary because he had held the position at that institution during the time in question, even though he had never performed the functions.

Certainly one reason Foucault chose as he did was that things were not going well as far as the Sorbonne was concerned. His latest attempt to be appointed there had been no more successful than the earlier one. Georges Canguilhem, ever faithful, confided about the matter to Raymond Aron, who was one of his colleagues in philosophy. Aron had invited Foucault to speak in his seminar a few months earlier. "I would be delighted," Aron wrote him on February 27, 1967, "to offer you an audience of about fifty, of a generally high level, to whom you can speak freely about anything you are interested in, for example, your conception of the human sciences as knowledge. I promise in advance to abstain from any polemics and to turn you over peacefully to the young turks, if there are any." On March 7 Foucault replied: "Since you were kind enough to be willing to let me speak, I very gratefully accept the risk. I shall try to remove some of the ambiguities from 'knowledge,' as I have tried to describe it. And, by god, if your young turks cut me into pieces, it will in any event give me great pleasure to hear them." The session took place on March 17 and went very well. "Foucault behaved like a little boy in the presence of Aron," one witness says.

Aron, therefore, seems to have been predisposed to lend a sympathetic ear to Canguilhem's request. And on April 28, 1967, he sent the following letter to Foucault in Sidi Bou Saïd:

> Dear friend, Georges Canguilhem and I have been talking about your chances of getting a tenured position in Paris next year. As he must have told you, the possibilities at the Sorbonne are slight. I have therefore thought of a director's position at the École Pratique des Hautes Etudes. Heller has told me that [Fernand] Braudel would be entirely disposed to hire you, but that he is afraid it would compromise any later chances at the Collège de France if you went into the sixth section (of the École des Hautes Etudes], of which, apparently, the Collège de France has a low opinion, because of the predominance of the fourth section there.[5] Of course, the choice is up to you, and I will take no initiative before you let me know what your feelings are and where things stand. I do not take academic careers very seriously, but I hope, in the interest of your work, that you are able to ignore this sort of worry and not experience the active hostility of colleagues antagonized by too brilliant a talent and success. Of course, I believe you are capable of taking this sort of hostility lightly. But, for one's inner balance and for the peace required by scientific work, it is better not to have to overcome one's defensive reflexes.

He ended by alluding to the discussion in February: "I took great pleasure in our dialogue and I hope that you do not hold my teasing against me. Hoping to see you soon, yours in friendship."

Foucault saw this letter, which does seem very friendly, as a verdict that he was not admissible. He wrote Canguilhem on May 2: "I'm sorry to waste your time and to bring you into this mess. It seems simplest to include the letter I got from Aron this morning. It seems very clear, and, well, very straightforward, because it asks me to choose, yes or no, Sorbonne or Collège." He went on: "The Collège seems far too much for me; I have not done enough work to have any claims there. As for the Sorbonne, if the great majority of the philosophers don't support me, clearly I don't have a chance. Whence a certain temptation to stay where I am—where things aren't bad, really, as

Hyppolite may have told you." Clemens Heller, in any event, confirms Aron's version of Braudel's position: the latter admired Foucault very much and did not want to ruin his chances at the Collège de France. Moreover, Braudel very actively supported his candidacy. Foucault, once successfully elected, wrote a letter to him on December 27, 1969, thanking him for his help.

1968 ended. Foucault left Tunisia. He left Sidi Bou Saïd and the hillside university overlooking the Casbah. He left behind the sunshine and sea he loved so much. He returned to France and did not leave it again except for rather brief trips. Shortly after his return he moved into a large ninth-floor apartment in a modern building on Rue de Vaugirard, in the fifteenth arrondissement, facing Adolphe-Chérioux Square. Large bay windows offered a magnificent view of all of western Paris. He often sunbathed on the large balcony running the length of the livingroom and study. Instead of the heights of Sidi Bou Saïd, at his back there now stood a wall of shelves of books and reviews.

Part III

＊＊

"MILITANT AND PROFESSOR AT THE COLLÈGE DE FRANCE"

14

A Vincennes Interlude

Night had fallen on January 23, 1969, when dense groups of riot police—the CRS (Compagnies Républicaines de Sécurité)—advanced upon the odd mass of buildings that had sprung up in just a few months on the outskirts of the Bois de Vincennes. The new university had opened its doors only a few days before—just time enough for organizing the first strike, the first occupation of the premises, and the first fight with the police. January 23, 1969. That was the night on which Michel Foucault joined the active ultra-left—a latecomer, for it already had a history, traditions, and prominent figures. When he joined, it was more a matter of rubbing shoulders and intersecting with it than belonging without reservation. But he did do it. He joined and went on to inscribe within it a good deal of his own itinerary during the 1970s.

After its great fright in May 1968, the government sought to make itself less vulnerable and very quickly went about "reforming higher education." An omnibus reform bill was presented at the beginning of the school year by Edgar Faure, the brand-new minister of education, and passed in October. Henceforth the universities would be governed in accordance with principles of autonomy, interdisciplinarity, and participation by those using them. But Faure did not wait for a vote on the law that would bear his name: in August he decided to construct new buildings to house "experimental centers" near Porte Dauphine, on land vacated by NATO, and in the Bois de Vincennes, on the outskirts of Paris, on property that had belonged to the military for more than a hundred years. There, on about eleven acres, groups of modern, prefabricated structures would shelter the "Centre Expérimental de Vincennes." Faure appointed the dean of the Sorbonne, Raymond Las Vergnas, a well-known specialist in English, to organize the launching of this new university. At the beginning of October 1968 he assembled an Orientation Commission (its official name) composed of about twenty people, including Jean-Pierre Vernant, Georges Canguilhem, Emmanuel Le Roy Ladurie, Roland Barthes, and Jacques Derrida. It was their job to choose the team of teachers who would be responsible for selecting the group of professors, junior lecturers, and lecturers who would actually work at the new university. Scarcely was the commission in place before popular newspapers and the right-wing press denounced it as being a collection of leftists. "A majority of the recruiters for the experimental faculty at Vincennes are ultra-leftist" proclaimed one headline in *Paris-Presse*.[1] They cheerfully categorized them all, from Roland Barthes, "one of the leaders of the structuralist school and a member of the extreme left," to Vladimir Jankélévitch, "important signatory of manifestos of the ultra-left." The polemical tone was established at the very outset. In the meantime, however, despite this hostile climate, the commission met to settle on a list of teachers who would form the "co-opting core," the selection committee.

Everything proceeded with great fanfare. A dozen people were chosen during the next few weeks: Jean-Claude Passeron and Robert Castel in sociology, Jean Bouvier and Jacques Droz in history, Jean-Pierre Richard in French. And in philosophy, at Georges Canguilhem's request, the choice fell on Michel Foucault. This news created a sensation, for Foucault was already very famous, and his name provided a focus for attention—particularly that of the leftists, among whom his reputation was not exactly brilliant. Foucault was not seen as a man who was very engaged—the supreme sin in the eyes of activists of every stripe flocking in to invest what would become the "red bastion" in the years after 1968. He was "Gaullist," they said. He hadn't "done anything" in May 1968—a major reproach. It was true; he hadn't even been in France. And when a huge general assembly convened on November 6, on the premises of the Sorbonne because the buildings at Vincennes were not yet open, to project the ways and means for getting the Centre Expérimental on the road, Foucault was directly confronted by his accusers. He muttered to Jean Gattegno, charged by Las Vergnas with organizing enrollment for the new school: "I'm going to tell them: 'While you were having fun on your Latin Quarter barricades, I was working on serious things in Tunisia.'" But his former colleague in Tunis dissuaded him from responding: "It won't do any good." Foucault kept silent. From then on he knew what was in store for him. He knew even better because the "student organizing committee," uniting the most extremist elements (among them Jean-Marc Salmon and André Glucksmann, one of Raymond Aron's former pupils, who had embraced the most excessive and sectarian form of ultra-leftism), had just published its "platform" in the November issue of the journal *Action*. The text was preceded by an introductory paragraph with these words: "Edgar Faure begins by trying to impress us: 'the new school will be a pilot university,' a 'university of the twentieth century.' Appointments of famous professors are announced, among them Michel Foucault, one of the stars of 'structuralism,' who is to be head of the philosophy department. The ministry hopes to distract public attention with these quarrels among cliques and schools. Just as it discussed doing away with Latin in the seventh grade but never mentioned anything about freedom in the lycées, *France-Soir* will headline its support for or opposition to structuralism, in the hope of making people forget the rest." The diatribe ended with these words: "This is not what the student movement is interested in." [2] What interested the student movement was rather simple. During the general assembly, one of those who had written the platform made a statement that was reported in *Le Monde:* "We must require that education at Vincennes develop political reflection and formation in such a way that it will become a base for external action." [3]

But Foucault had already set to work. He wanted to gather around him people who, in his view, represented "the best in French philosophy today," as he told several of his friends. A bit like what Vuillemin had wanted to do ten years earlier at Clermont-Ferrand. He began by asking Deleuze. But once again Deleuze was very ill and could not accept Foucault's offer; when he went to Vincennes two years later, Foucault had already left. Michel Serres, on the other hand, agreed immediately. He was even an official member of the selection committee, but he preferred to stay out of the nominating process. Foucault then tried to recruit from the younger generation: the students of Althusser and Lacan, including the group that had founded *Cahiers pour l'analyse*. A number of those he would have liked to recruit, such as Alain Grosrichard, were performing their military service. Judith Miller, Lacan's daughter, laughed about it: "It was because I didn't have that problem that I was appointed!" In addition to Miller, Alain Badiou, Jacques Rancière, François Regnault, and several others joined the faculty. But political criteria were constantly being superimposed on intellectual ones. To teach at Vincennes, at least in philosophy, one had to have "done" May 1968. And one had to belong to one of the little groups that proliferated and confronted one another after the great wave of freedom began to ebb. In fact, it was to keep the philosophy department from being entirely absorbed by Maoists, who were in a large majority among his recruits, that Foucault called upon Henri Weber, who was head of the Trotskyites. Etienne Balibar was also recruited and did not have an easy time of things, because he belonged to the Communist party. And finally, to play the part of moderator in this aggressively militant milieu, Foucault called upon a sage, François Châtelet, known for his pedagogical abilities as well as for his ability to create alliances.

Foucault was not involved only in his own department. He participated in the meetings preparatory to the opening of the center. These were held at the Sorbonne by Las Vergnas or by Jean-Baptiste Duroselle, a historian who had been chosen as a "delegate" to the selection committee but who had swiftly resigned in alarm over the leftist turn of events. Meetings were also held at the home of Hélène Cixous, a specialist in English, who was close to Las Vergnas and played an important role in the formation of the university at Vincennes. One of Foucault's greatest concerns was how to exclude the psychologists and psychology, so that he could allocate positions and credit to a section of psychoanalysis. With the support of Castel and Passeron, he argued in favor of Serge Leclaire's appointment. The discussions ended in compromise. Two departments, psychology and psychoanalysis, would be created. And everybody noticed Foucault's talents as a "strategist" in these discussions, the "art" with which he "maneuvered," and what some saw as his "manipulation."

Once again, however, Foucault himself would have to be officially appointed. Whereas everything went along smoothly in other disciplines, the philosophy section of the University Consulting Committee (the government body officially in charge of the careers of university educators) asserted that Foucault could not be recruited as a tenured professor of philosophy, because he himself was a recruiter. On November 9, 1968, Dean Las Vergnas wrote to the minister of education:

> On the advice of the Orientation Committee at its meeting on October 25, 1968, I had suggested that you ask Michel Foucault to be a member of the selection committee for Vincennes and asked that you appoint him a tenured professor of philosophy. Following the unfavorable decision taken by the CCU in its meeting on November 5, 1968, Michel Foucault informed me of his decision to resign from

the selection committee so that he could be voted on by his future colleagues. This vote took place on November 16, 1968. Eleven professors had received notification of their appointment to the University of Vincennes as of November 11, 1968. These are the results:

Voting, ten (one absent). Michel Foucault, ten votes.

I have, therefore, the honor of repeating my suggestion that Michel Foucault be designated as tenured professor of philosophy at . . . Vincennes, and request that you please submit his case once again to the CCU.

This time it went off without a hitch. Foucault's appointment took effect on December 1.

The University of Vincennes opened its doors, administratively speaking, in December 1968. The first classes began in January 1969, but things did not really get fully underway until February and March. "The atmosphere at Vincennes is like that of a noisy beehive, each one seeking his place," wrote *Le Monde* on January 15. But the humming hive would soon give way to absolute chaos. The climate of tension was not restricted to the Bois de Vincennes. At the beginning of the school year in the fall of 1968 and throughout the winter of 1968–69, *Le Monde* devoted one, two, sometimes three whole pages daily to "university agitation." Strikes and meetings, incidents involving more or less violent confrontations with the police, submerged lycées and universities in Paris and the provinces. Vincennes did not take long to join in the fun. On January 23 the student organizing committee of Lycée Saint-Louis in Paris had decided to hold a meeting at which films about May 1968 would be shown. The Bureau of Education had forbidden the meeting and had the electricity turned off. But three hundred lycée students entered the building with a generator, showed their films, and afterward marched out as a group to avoid questioning. They then proceeded to another meeting close by, in the courtyard of the Sorbonne, on the other side of Boulevard Saint-Michel. Soon the watchword was: Occupy the Bureau of Education, located in the buildings of the old Sorbonne. No sooner said than done. But the police intervened and cleared the premises. At the same time fighting broke out in the Latin Quarter. To express their solidarity, several hundred students at Vincennes and a number of professors decided to occupy their university. They entrenched themselves behind makeshift barricades—tables, chairs, desks, cabinets, television sets—all the brand-new equipment that had just been installed. And when the police intervened—two thousand strong—Vincennes had its first battle: teargas grenades versus stones and various other missiles. Gradually the police rounded up the students and professors into the large amphitheater. Michel Foucault and Daniel Defert, their eyes red with tears from the gas, were among the last to be questioned. Foucault told Passeron: "They broke everything in your office." Then all 220 people were put into buses and taken to Beaujon, the central administrative offices of the Paris police. They were released in the wee hours of the morning.

The government and the press reacted harshly. Faure denounced the "absurdity" of the incidents and deplored the extent of damage and plundering at the university. Conservatives reproached Faure for his "liberalism" and charged him with responsibility for the disorders and the "breakage." That day's graffiti, damaging Philippe de Champaigne's famous portrait of Richelieu at the Sorbonne, became an unremitting symbol of "leftist vandalism." Following these incidents, 34 students were expelled from the Vincennes and 181 others were threatened with prosecution. On February 10, 1969, there was a large meeting in the Latin Quarter at the Mutualité (site of all the leftist meetings in 1968) to protest these measures. Both Sartre and Foucault spoke before a huge crowd. According to Le Monde, Foucault was one of the most virulent speakers, denouncing police provocation and "calculated repression."

After this thundering inauguration, university existence continued to a rhythm of general meetings, demonstrations, clashes with the police, pitched battles between Communists and leftists or among leftist cliques. Classes were held, although they often took the form of psychodrama, verbal sparring, endless discussion, and the exchange of manic quibbles about the revolution, class struggle, the proletariat. Michel Serres, who left Vincennes immediately after this first year, had rather sinister memories of that time: "I had the impression," he said, "of being plunged into the same atmosphere of intellectual terrorism as the one imposed by the Stalinists when I was a student at the Rue d'Ulm." However, he made it his duty to continue with his course and to give exams.

Foucault was "director" of the philosophy department, even though the idea of directing was almost meaningless in such a context. In any case, a course program was posted. Its entries shed light on the prevailing intellectual climate and the worldview of the "Vincennois." Here are some of the course titles for 1968–69: "revisionism-leftism" by Jacques Rancière; "sciences of social formations and Marxist philosophy" by Etienne Balibar; "cultural revolutions" by Judith Miller;

"ideological struggle" by Alain Badiou. Of course, there were some who persisted with more traditional academic subjects: Michel Serres discussed positivist theories of science and the relationship between Greek rationality and mathematics; François Châtelet taught "Greek political thought." Foucault analyzed "The discourse of sexuality" and "the end of metaphysics." In 1969–70 courses were similarly mixed in tone and content: "theory of the second stage of Marxism-Leninism: Stalinism" by Jacques Rancière; "third stage of Marxism-Leninism: Maoism" by Judith Miller; "introduction to twentieth-century Marxism: Lenin, Trotsky, and the Bolshevik movement" by Henri Weber; "Marxist dialectics" by Alain Badiou. François Châtelet stoically continued with "critique of Greek speculative thought" and "epistemological problems in the historical sciences." Foucault offered "the epistemology of the sciences of life" and Nietzsche. The latter would provide the material for "Nietzsche, la généalogie, l'histoire" in the 1971 volume paying tribute to Jean Hyppolite. The first year there were so many in Foucault's class—more than six hundred—that he tried to limit enrollment. "No more than twenty-five," he told Assia Melamed, who was secretary of the section, and chose a rather small room. Even so, about a hundred showed up for his classes.

On January 15, 1970, Olivier Guichard, who had replaced Edgar Faure as minister of education, deplored the quality of philosophy instruction in 1968–69. He quoted several examples of course titles over the radio, denounced the "Marxist-Leninist" content of the courses given, and refused national accreditation of degrees awarded in philosophy at Vincennes. As a direct result, the students could no longer be candidates in the recruitment competitions for secondary school teaching. Foucault responded on January 24 during a press conference organized by the instructors: since Vincennes had as its goal the study of the contemporary world, how could the philosophy department avoid being a "reflection on politics"? Several days later he again defended "his" department. "How can one provide developed and diversified instruction when there are 950 students for eight professors?" he said in an interview published in *Le Nouvel Observateur*. "Would someone tell me clearly what philosophy is, and in the name of what, what text, what criterion, what truth, the things we are doing are being rejected?" Then he counterattacked: "It is not the reasons the minister gives that are the main issue, but rather the decision he intends to take. This is clear: students from Vincennes will not have the right to teach in the secondary schools. Now it is my turn to ask questions. What is the reason for this quarantine? What is so dangerous about philosophy (philosophy class) that so much care must go into protecting it? And what is so dangerous about people from Vincennes?" He then denounced the "trap" set by academic and political authorities for the Vincennes philosophy department: the promised absolute freedom was repressed the moment anyone wanted to exercise it.[4]

But Foucault's troubles were not over. Soon another matter flared up, drawing attention once again to the philosophy department. The methods of pedagogical supervision and exam procedures, as much as the courses themselves, had angered authorities at the ministry. Course credits had been awarded in an extremely unorthodox way. There was no requirement that professors give exams. The former secretary of the philosophy department described it this way: the first year, the professors shut themselves up in a room and the students slipped a little piece of paper, with their name written on it, under the door. They were listed as having passed. The second year, a list of those who had passed was typed up; it included anyone who asked to be on it. Judith Miller caused another eruption of scandal: in an interview for their book, she told Madeleine Chapsal and Michèle Manceaux that she passed out credits on the bus, and added that "the university is a piece of capitalist society" and that she would do her best to make it function "worse and worse." When an extract of this interview was published in *L'Express*, it was too much for the ministry.

On April 3, 1970, Miller, the daughter of Jacques Lacan and a prominent militant for the Maoist movement, received a missive from the minister informing her that he was compelled to "end her appointment in higher education" and was returning her to the position in secondary school instruction that she had left. Naturally, this decision increased tensions at Vincennes. The buildings were occupied, then emptied by the police.

This incident was just one of many that kept Vincennes in the news and fed the polemics surrounding the university and its very existence. On October 8, 1969, the president of the university, Jacques Droz, had issued this warning: "If irresponsible intrigues do not meet with opposition from students, I fear that Vincennes is headed for catastrophe and that we will be obliged to close it." The press returned to this question monotonously for several years. Depending on their political viewpoint, the papers asked: are they going to (or should they) close Vincennes? Month after month, headlines announced: "Vincennes reprieved," "Vincennes must live," like a litany trotted out on the heels of every incident. Vincennes would live. But for a long time it would live in the climate of violence created at the very beginning.

According to all the witnesses, the philosophy department was in the front line of these constant disturbances. A professor who took part in founding the university was of the opinion that this department was "from the beginning overcome by a self-destructive vertigo." And this all took place, if not with Foucault's complete concurrence, at least with his participation or backing. He moved with a certain amount of ease in this milieu of ultraleftist opposition, and in the beginning he seemed to participate wholeheartedly in the various demonstrations it devised daily. But it also seems that he tired of it quickly. There are even some who think he was traumatized by his experience at Vincennes, by the constant challenges to which the professors were subjected. He had been seen with an iron rod in his hands, ready to do battle with militant Communists; he had been seen throwing rocks at the police. But the climate at Vincennes was unlikely to suit him on a long-term basis. "I had had enough of being surrounded by half-madmen," he told a friend shortly after his departure. In any case, he did not particularly like contact with the students. And he arranged to spend the least possible time on campus in order to continue his research at the Bibliothèque Nationale. Basically, he would be very happy to leave this place, knowing as he had all along that his presence there was only temporary. Because at the same time he was campaigning for election to the Collège de France. He rewrote his application papers, visited with influential professors, and submitted himself to the rituals that this prestigious institution required of anyone hoping to be admitted.

Foucault remained at Vincennes for two turbulent years that would have important effects. It was there that he truly returned to politics and that he encountered history, "like a deep-sea diver lying at the bottom of the sea and picked up and brought to shore by a sudden storm," as he described it himself in an image that Jules Vuillemin recalled in his funeral address at the Collège de France.[5] This rising to the surface, this entry into politics undoubtedly owed a great deal to Daniel Defert, who moved in Maoist spheres and had been hired as a lecturer in sociology at Vincennes. In fact a whole new Foucault was born at this crucial time. By the time he left Vincennes he was far from the academic who served on ministerial committees or administered the oral exam for the Ecole Normale d'Administration. That man would gradually vanish and be forgotten. From the alembic at Vincennes emerged an engaged philosopher, one who intervened on every front, whether in action or reflection. In 1969 Foucault began to embody the very figure of the militant intellectual. This is when the Foucault whom everyone knows was created—the Foucault of demonstrations and manifestos; the Foucault of "struggles" and "critique," for whom a professorship at the Collège de France then provided an even firmer and more powerful base. Moreover, this "entrance into politics" did not for the moment make a deep impression on the strictly intellectual register. At Vincennes Foucault gave a course on Nietzsche, and the ideas expressed in his inaugural lecture at the Collège de France in December 1970 were closer to the preoccupations of *L'Archéologie du savoir* than to his later ideas on power. His articles and lectures from this period still bear surprising marks of his earlier theoretical preoccupations and style. Consider the lecture he delivered before the Société Française de la Philosophie on February 22, 1969: "What is an author?" It was based, of course, on Beckett's words: "What does it matter who speaks, someone said, what does it matter who speaks." In this indifference, said Foucault, "the most fundamental principle, perhaps, of contemporary writing is asserted." Foucault added a second theme to this indifference: "the kinship between death and writing." A memorable discussion followed the lecture, beginning with a rather lively exchange between Lucien Goldmann and Foucault. Goldmann criticized "structuralism" and ended by quoting this sentence written by a student in May 1968 on a blackboard in a room at the Sorbonne: "Structures do not take to the streets." And he added: "It is never structures that make history; it is men." Foucault replied rather curtly: "I have never, myself, used the word 'structure.' So I would like to be spared facile remarks about structuralism." Then he went on to discuss "the death of man": "This is a theme that allows me to bring to light the ways in which the concept of man has functioned in knowledge. It is not a matter of asserting that man is dead; it is a matter of seeing in what manner, according to what rule, the concept of man was formed and has functioned. I have done the same thing for the notion of the author. So let's hold the tears." Another speaker came to Foucault's aid: Jacques Lacan. "I do not believe," said the psychoanalyst, "that it is at all legitimate to have written that structures do not take to the streets, because, if there is one thing demonstrated by the events of May, it is precisely that structures did take to the streets. The fact that those words were written at the very place where people took to the streets proves nothing other than, simply, that very often, even most often, what is internal to what is called action is that it does not know itself."[6]

What were the lasting effects of the time Foucault spent at Vincennes? For him it was a chance to arrange things in a way that would forever alter the French intellectual landscape. For, despite all the turmoil, Vincennes would finally come into its own, and its philosophy department would have a definite influence. Gilles Deleuze, Jean-François Lyotard, and René Scherer were there; so Foucault's ambition to bring in "the best" was not altogether futile. The department of psychoanalysis rapidly became one of the centers of Lacanian influence. In July 1969 Foucault had invited Lacan himself to come and carry on his seminar at Vincennes, at the time when the ENS had refused to keep it there anymore. In the end the seminar took refuge at the law school, on the Place du Panthéon, but Lacan accepted the invitation to Vincennes to give a series of lectures. This series was cut short at the first session, on December 3, 1969. Baited by students, Lacan uttered the now famous words: "What you long for, as revolutionaries, is a master. You will get one." Then he got up and left the room. He simply phoned the philosophy department to inform them he was "Mardi-Gras-ing" the next lecture, which had been scheduled for early February, and was canceling all the rest.

When he left the philosophy department at Vincennes in the hands of François Châtelet, Michel Foucault knew he was leaving a somewhat unmanageable legacy: both a center of conflict and a source of intellectual effervescence.

15

The Solitude of the Acrobat

Mr. Director, my dear colleagues, ladies and gentlemen . . ."
There was silence in the room, and a voice began to be heard,
muffled, strained with emotion, almost distorted by stage
fright, words more murmured than projected: ". . . in this speech that
I must give today, and in those I shall have to give here, for years, perhaps . . ." It was December 2, 1970. Michel Foucault was delivering his
inaugural lecture at the Collège de France.

Several hundred people had crammed into the large amphitheater at
the Sorbonne where this ceremony had traditionally taken place for
centuries. It seemed that nothing had ever changed—this was before it
was modernized—the old wooden seats, the rather somber atmosphere. That particular day, as was often the case during those years of
agitation, the Latin Quarter was in a state of siege. Everyone in the
audience had had to pass through barricades formed by police cars and
lines of CRS, the visors of their helmets down and clubs in hand. They
provided a strange setting for the discourse soon to reverberate, evoking "confinements," "powers," and "norms." The police had not come
on Foucault's account, of course; but everyone made that connection.
When, a few days later, Pierre Daix described in *Les Lettres françaises*
the "great crowd" jostling to hear philosophy, he made sure to mention the "rows full of people standing, mostly young people, as if May
'68 had sent its loyal delegations into a more stale and sober assembly."[1] When Etienne Wolff, director of the Collège de France, delivered his brief speech of welcome to the new arrival in this "land of
freedom"—the imposing building on Place Marcelin-Berthelot that
housed the Collège—those delegations immediately made themselves
known, greeting his words with a mutter of derision.

Then Foucault began to read his text under Bergson's fixed gaze, whose bronze profile dominated the room: "Behind me I should have liked to hear, behind me, a voice speaking thus: 'I must go on, I can't go on; I must go on; I must say words as long as there are words; I must say them until they find me, until they say me—heavy burden, heavy sin; I must go on; maybe it's been done already, maybe they've already said me; maybe they've already borne me to the threshold of my story, right to the door opening onto my story; I'd be surprised if it opened.'" Foucault's audience was captivated as he slipped into this close paraphrase of Beckett's *L'Innommable*.[2] Among those who heard him: Georges Dumézil, Claude Lévi-Strauss, Fernand Braudel, François Jacob, and Gilles Deleuze.

Michel Foucault had just made his entrance into the holy of holies in the French university system. The same ceremony had taken place the day before with a somewhat different audience, to welcome Raymond Aron. On December 4 the Collège received Georges Duby. It was not entirely by chance that Foucault's and Aron's lectures were scheduled so close together. They had been elected on the same day, during the same meeting of professors. And, although it was never explicitly spelled out, more than one person has suggested that there was some sort of arrangement—tit for tat—between the partisans of each man.

But we must go back a few years to account for Foucault's election. First, to his friendship with Dumézil. Because he had reached retirement age, Dumézil had left the Collège by the time the vote took place. Nevertheless, he sent from the United States, where he had gone to teach, five or six letters to former colleagues whom he perceived as reluctant or a little worried about the candidate's sulfurous reputation, to lobby in Foucault's behalf. Dumézil's great store of prestige undoubtedly made his interventions extremely useful. Also, above all, he had begun mentioning, and then supporting, Foucault's candidacy long before his departure.

As early as 1966, Jean Hyppolite had taken advantage of the huge success of *Les Mots et les choses* to put election of Foucault on the agenda. He had begun the procedures necessary to make his plan succeed, speaking to this person or that about the possibility of such a candidacy, testing reactions. The reactions were diverse. Jules Vuillemin, who held the other chair in philosophy, supported him in this undertaking. Dumézil, Hyppolite, Vuillemin: a trio of supporters who were not to be ignored. Fernand Braudel also spared no pains. Hyppolite never saw what came of his undertaking; he died on October 27, 1968. When the question arose of filling the chair left vacant by his death, Foucault naturally came to mind. Thus Vuillemin would officially present the candidacy of his former colleague at Clermont. More precisely, he would propose to a meeting of professors the creation of a chair that would then be awarded to Foucault. Because elections to the Collège de France are in two stages: first comes the vote on a professorship, without any mention of whoever may hold it, even if in fact everyone knows who it will be; then there is a vote on the person who will hold this chair.

On November 30, 1969, the professors gathered to decide on the creation of two chairs: one in sociology, the other in philosophy. For the latter there were three competing proposals. Two other philosophers, Paul Ricoeur and Yvon Belaval, had entered the lists for Hyppolyte's position. Foucault had written, as was required, a pamphlet listing his books and projects, roughly describing his teaching program, and justifying the title he had chosen for the chair he hoped to occupy: "history of systems of thought." This pamphlet was about ten pages long and was addressed to all the professors of the Collège. Foucault first stated his academic identity: his studies, his diplomas, the posts he had held. Next he listed his publications: books, articles, prefaces, translations. Then he summarized his earlier research, from *Folie et déraison* to *L'Archéologie du savoir*.

In this exceptionally interesting document Foucault presented the logic behind his research. It is worth quoting at length not only for that reason but also because it is hard to come by today, having been printed privately and in small numbers.

In *Histoire de la folie à l'âge classique*,[3] I wanted to determine what could be known about mental illness at a given period. Such knowledge, of course, is manifested in the medical theories naming and classifying the different pathological types, and attempting to explain them. They can also be seen in phenomena of opinion—in that ancient fear aroused by madmen, in how the forms of credulity surrounding them interact, in how they are represented in theater or literature. Here and there analyses made by other historians could serve me as guides. But there was a dimension that seemed unexplored to me: it was necessary to study how madmen were recognized, set aside, excluded from society, interned, and treated; what institutions were meant to take them in and keep them there, sometimes caring for them; what authorities decided on their madness, and in accordance with what criteria; what methods were set in place to constrain them, punish them, or cure them; in short, what was the network of institutions and practices in which the madman was simultaneously caught and defined. Now, this network, when its functioning and the justifications given for it at the time are examined, seems very coherent and very well adapted. It involves an entire, precise, and articulated system of knowledge. Consequently, my object became apparent. It was the knowledge invested in the complex systems of institutions. And a method imposed itself. Rather than perusing the library of scientific books, as one so happily does, I had to visit a group of archives including decrees, regulations, hospital or prison registers, judicial precedents. Working at the Arsenal or the National Archives, I began the analysis of a knowledge whose visible body is neither theoretical or scientific discourse nor literature, but a regular, daily practice.

The example of madness, however, did not seem sufficiently pertinent. In the seventeenth and eighteenth centuries, psychopathology was still too rudimentary for one to be able to distinguish it from the simple interaction of traditional opinions. It seemed to me that clinical medicine, at the moment of its birth, put the problem in more rigorous terms. At the beginning of the nineteenth century it was in fact linked to established sciences, or those in the process of becoming established, such as biology, physiology, and pathological anatomy. But on the other hand it was also linked to a group of institutions such as hospitals, establishments providing care, and teaching clinics, as well as to practices, such as administrative inquiries. I wondered how it was that, between these two markers, a knowledge could have arisen, could have changed and developed, offering scientific theory new fields of observation, original problems, and objects that until that point had gone unnoticed; but how, in return, scientific learning had been imported into it, and had taken on prescriptive value, and a quality of ethical norms. The practice of medicine makes up an unstable mixture of rigorous science and uncertain tradition, but it is not limited to this; it is constructed like a system of knowledge with its own equilibrium and coherency.

It could be generally conceded, therefore, that there are realms of knowledge that cannot exactly be called sciences and yet are more than mere mental habits. Consequently, I attempted in *Les Mots et les choses* the opposite experiment: to neutralize the entire practical and institutional aspect (without giving up my intention to get back to it some day) and to consider, at a given period, several of these realms of knowledge (natural classifications, general grammar, and the analysis of wealth in the seventeenth and eighteenth centuries), examining them one by one to define the kind of problems they posed, the concepts they used, and the theories they tested. Not only was it possible to define the internal "archaeology" of each of these domains in turn; but identities, analogies, and groups of differences could be perceived from one to the next, needing to be described. A global configuration emerged. Of course, it was far from characterizing the classical spirit in general, but it organized in a coherent manner an entire region of empirical knowledge.

I was, therefore, in the presence of two very distinct groups of results. On the one hand, I had determined the specific and relatively autonomous existence of "established realms of knowledge" [*savoirs investis*], and on the other, I had noted systematic relationships within the characteristic architecture of each. A clarification became necessary. I sketched it out in *Archéologie du savoir*: between opinion and scientific understanding, one can recognize the existence of a particular level, which we propose to call knowledge [*savoir*]. This knowledge takes shape not only in theoretical texts or experimental instruments, but in a whole system of practices and institutions. Nevertheless, it is not the pure and simple result of this semiconscious expression. It comprises, in fact, rules that are its own, and that thus characterize its existence, its functioning, and its history. Certain of these rules are specific to a single domain; others are shared by several. It is possible that, for a particular period, there are others that are generalized. Finally, the development of this knowledge and its transformations bring into play complex causal relations . . ."

Having thus explained his "earlier work," Foucault went on to present his "teaching project." This teaching, he said, would be subjected to two requirements: "never to lose sight of reference to a concrete example that can serve as experimental ground for the analysis; to elaborate theoretical problems that I may have already or may yet come across."[5]

The concrete example that was to occupy him "for some time" was the "knowledge of heredity." And these would be the theoretical problems: "To attempt to give this knowledge a status—to locate it between certain limits, and to choose instruments to describe it." Then it would be necessary to ponder the "elaboration of this knowledge in scientific discourse," that is, to ponder what "constitutes a science when one wants to analyze it not in transcendental terms but in terms of history." And the third theoretical register would concern "causality in the order of knowledge: to determine how—through what channels or what codes—knowledge records, not without choice or modification, the phenomena that until then were external to it, how it becomes receptive to processes that are foreign to it."[6]

Foucault concluded his presentation thus: "Between the sciences already constituted (whose history is frequently recorded) and the phenomena of opinion (which historians know how to treat), the history of systems of thought remains to be undertaken." At a more general level, this task would involve "reexamining knowledge, the conditions of knowledge, and the status of the knowing subject."[7] But Foucault did not pursue the program that he outlined here. Another "concrete" problem began to occupy him in 1971: prisons, not heredity. It was in fact a very concrete problem, for it would involve not just archives, but also political actions that would lead to his direct engagement with social movements that were to shake up the penal system.

For the moment, however, this was unimportant. The report was written, printed, and sent to all the professors. It fell to Jules Vuillemin to argue before them for the creation of the chair. To prepare his speech he invited Foucault on several successive evenings to the little apartment where he then lived in the Marais. They debated which aspects should be emphasized. And, since Vuillemin wanted to present a report that was very clear to colleagues in all the disciplines, he asked Foucault to elaborate on several points that he felt were not clearly defined. Everything went wonderfully until they came to the notion of enunciation (*énoncés*) as it appears in *L'Archéologie du savoir*. There the candidate and his sponsor were at loggerheads: no matter how much Foucault explained what he meant, Vuillemin continued to find this notion obscure. Foucault got angry, accused Vuillemin of insincerity, and left, slamming the door behind him. A "ceremony of reconciliation" had to take place before the two could return to work and Vuillemin could complete his report.

Vuillemin's report, seven closely typewritten pages, was very rigorous and effective. It surveyed Foucault's thought, indicating its main points and its evolution. The report ended with a definition of Foucault's undertaking as it could be construed from *Les Mots et les Choses* and *L'Archéologie du savoir* (though without ever naming the books or their author, since the objective was only to spell out the general principles defining the professorship). "The history of systems of thought is, therefore, not at all the history of the man or the men who think these thoughts. In the last analysis, it is because the conflict between materialism and spiritualism is still caught in the terms of this latter alternative that the opposition is between brothers more than between enemies. They are divided but share the same question: as the subject of thoughts one chooses individuals or groups, but one always chooses a subject. Anyone attempting to doubt this should reread the often-quoted allusion to Marx, that one must distinguish the bee from

the architect, however uninspired he may be, because the latter first
builds the house in his head. Abandoning dualism and constituting a
non-Cartesian epistemology clearly require something more: eliminating the subject while keeping the thoughts, trying to construct a history without human nature."[8]

The meeting of professors began at two-thirty on Sunday, November 30, 1969. Two other chairs were being proposed at the same time
as Foucault's: one in the philosophy of action, which was argued for by
Pierre Courcelle, a professor of Latin literature, and intended for Paul
Ricoeur; and one in the history of rational thought, supported by
Alfred Fessard, a professor of neurophysiology, intended for Yvon
Belaval. The latter was actively supported by a retired professor, Mar-
tial Guéroult, who had come expressly for this occasion. The three
"presenters" had drawn lots to determine the order in which they
would speak: first Pierre Courcelle, then Jules Vuillemin, then Alfred
Fessard. Finally it was time for a ballot. There were forty-six voting.
The results were:

> For a chair in philosophy of action: 11 votes
> For a chair in history of systems of thought: 21 votes
> For a chair in history of rational thought: 10 votes
> Blank ballots marked with an *x* (that is, specifically refusing the
> present candidates): 4

An absolute majority, plus one vote, was required—in this case,
twenty-four votes—for approval of a professorship. Therefore, another ballot was necessary. The results of this vote were:

> Philosophy of action: 10
> History of systems of thought: 25
> History of rational thought: 9
> Blank ballots marked with an *x*: 2

Vuillemin had won. Foucault was chosen. He was forty-three years
old. He who had envisaged his career as a perpetual voyage from job to
job, a wandering from city to city—there he was now, in the heart of
Paris, in its most glorious temple of learning.

On April 12, 1970, the professors assembled again, this time to
designate Foucault officially as occupant of the chair just created. Vuillemin gave another long report, this time analyzing each of Foucault's
books and indicating the main directions of his projected research as

Foucault himself had described it in his pamphlet.[9] Immediately afterward, thirty-nine professors cast their votes. Foucault got twenty-four; fifteen ballots were marked with an x—an indication of the active hostility of a strong minority.

Before submitting its choice to the minister of education, the Collège still had to request approval from one of the academies constituting the Institut de France. It fell to the Académie des Sciences Morales et Politiques to give an opinion on this election. This step was a mere bow to tradition, since the minister always approved the vote of the Collège. Luckily for Foucault—because, of thirty-one who could vote and twenty-seven who did, not one supported him: twenty-two ballots were marked with an x, and five were left blank. In his report to the minister, the permanent secretary of the Academy explained this strange vote in the following way: "The Academy took note of the fact that there were fifteen ballots marked with an x, or more than a third of those voting [in the second ballot at the Collège] . . . Under these conditions it decided not to present any candidate for this chair." The minister appointed Foucault despite the Academy's refusal.

Therefore, on December 2, 1970, before a very prestigious audience composed of the professors of the Collège de France and numerous important individuals in the cultural and academic world, but also before a crowd of young, anonymous admirers, Michel Foucault began to speak, his muffled and restrained voice stunning the audience. Shortly afterward Foucault would publish this inaugural lecture with the now famous title, *L'Ordre du discours* ("The Discourse on Language"), restoring some passages that he had omitted so as not to exceed the time allowed. The theme of this discourse was discourse itself, and Foucault began, in a sort of ironic reminder of the situation, by evoking the fear of speaking, the anxiety before one begins, and the institution that is there to reassure, "to solemnize beginnings," and to calm the speaker's fears: "But what is so perilous, then, in the fact that people speak," asked Foucault, "and that their speech proliferates? Where is the danger in that?" And he proposed an answer: "I am supposing that in every society the production of discourse is at once controlled, selected, organized, and redistributed according to a certain number of procedures, whose role is to avert its powers and its dangers, to cope with chance events, to evade its ponderous, awesome materiality."[10] Foucault passed in review all the devices for controlling and mastering discourse. He was not talking about history, except contemporary history:

What civilization, in appearance, has shown more respect towards discourse than our own? Where has it been more and better honored? Where has it been more radically freed from its restraints and universalized? But, it seems to me, a certain fear hides behind this apparent supremacy we accord, this apparent logophilia. It is as if there were taboos, barriers, thresholds and limits deliberately set in place so they would reduce the most dangerous elements of its wealth and so its disorder would be organized according to figures that dodge what is most uncontrollable. It is as if people had wanted to efface even so much as a trace of its irruption into the play of thought and language. There is undoubtedly in our society, and in all societies I imagine, but with different forms and rhythms, a profound logophobia, a sort of dumb fear of these events, of this mass of spoken things, of these statements suddenly appearing, of everything about them that might be violent, discontinuous, aggressive, even disordered and dangerous, of the great, incessant and disorderly buzzing of discourse.[11]

Foucault regrouped the systems of constraint, erected by society to pacify all this seething discourse, into three categories. First were the external processes of *exclusion: prohibition* and *taboo* (not all may be said), *division* and *rejection* (relegating, for example, the speech of madmen), and finally the *will to truth*, "a prodigious machinery whose intent is to exclude," which has reinforced itself down the centuries and yet is the constraining device least talked about. "All those who, at one moment or another in our history, have attempted to get around this will to truth, calling it into question precisely at the point at which truth undertakes to justify a taboo and to define madness; all those, from Nietzsche to Artaud and Bataille, must now serve as (probably haughty) signposts for the work we have to do."[12]

The second group of principles of delimitation: those that work within discourse itself. *Commentary*, reduplicating the text or speech to nullify its fortuitousness; the notion of the *author*, which reduces the strange singularity of discourse to the recognizable identity of an *I*, and *individuality*; finally, the *disciplines*, whether scientific or otherwise, which arrange and classify knowledge and push back to the margins anything they cannot assimilate.

The final group: the rules of execution required of the discourse. Rituals of how it is set in play in the society, requirements that must be satisfied before one has the right or is in a position to speak: "think of technical or scientific secrets; of the forms of diffusion and circulation in medical discourse, of those who have appropriated economic or political discourse." Or think of the role of schools: "Every educational system is a political means of maintaining or of modifying the appropriation of discourses, with the knowledge and powers they bring with them."[13]

The task that Foucault set himself, perhaps, was to restore full rights to disorder, and he intended to wage battle against the tight web of constraint that set "the order of discourse" in place. And, if he could not undo and defeat this order, at least he would analyze it and make it visible, removing the mask of obviousness it hid behind. And since philosophies, especially those dominating the postwar period, only intensified and reinforced the ways exclusion worked, through the idea of an originating subject, an originating experience, or even a universal mediation, Foucault appealed to a real reversal of philosophical values. To accomplish this work, he intended to use a double method: first the *critical* process, to untangle the web of taboos, exclusions, and limitations in which discourse found itself confined; then the *genealogical* process, to uncover discourse in the very moment it springs up, at the very point where it makes an appearance either despite or with systems of constraints.

The program Foucault proposed for his research was organized along several lines. The first stage was to analyze one of the strong links in these principles of exclusion: the will to truth and the will to knowledge; and, in this framework, to study also "the effect of a discourse claiming to be scientific—medical, psychiatric or sociological—on this group of practices and prescriptive discourses of which the penal code consists. The study of psychiatric skills and their role in the penal system will serve as a point of departure and as basic material for this analysis." That was the critical aspect of it. For its genealogical aspect, even though it was a hard distinction to establish, he evoked the analysis of a "discourse concerning heredity," which he had already mentioned in his candidacy papers, and "the taboos in discourse on sexuality," a study that was genealogical as much as it was critical, because "it would be difficult and abstract to carry out this study, without at the same time analyzing literary, religious, and ethical, biological and medical, as well as juridical discursive ensembles, wherever sexuality is discussed, wherever it is named or described, metaphorised, explained or judged."[14]

Foucault ended with his tribute to Jean Hyppolite: "I know now what was so awesome about beginning to speak; for it was here, where I speak now, that I listened to that voice, and where its possessor is no longer, to hear me speak."[15]

In *Le Monde* the next day, Jean Lacouture gave an account of this "initiation ceremony" to which the philosopher submitted "as easily as a deacon in the days of heresy."

The inaugural lecture was, as its name indicates, the overture to a course of instruction. Until 1984 the course that Foucault gave every week for twelve weeks was one of the events of Parisian intellectual life. Every Wednesday, at first in late afternoon and then (in a vain attempt to cut down on the crowds) at nine in the morning, Foucault would display all the resources of his knowledge, his labor, and his pedagogical talents before unfailingly large and avid crowds, who would squeeze into Room 8 and into the other rooms connected to the public address system. An article in 1975 on the great professors of the French university described it:

> When Foucault comes into the arena, briskly, cutting right through like someone plunging into the water, he steps over bodies to get to his chair, pushes aside the tape recorders so he can set his papers down, takes off his jacket, turns on the light, and takes off at a hundred miles an hour. A strong, effective voice, carried by loudspeakers (the only concession to modernity in a room that is poorly lit by basinlike stucco fixtures). There were three hundred seats and five hundred people piled in, taking up every last inch of space. A cat wouldn't dare to set foot there. I was imprudent enough to arrive only forty minutes before the lecture began. The result: I ache all over. Sitting for almost two hours on the guardrail of a window is hard. Moreover, it was stifling . . . None of this had any effect on Foucault's oratory. It was lucid and terrifically effective. There wasn't the slightest concession to improvisation. Foucault has twelve hours a year to explain in a public lecture the direction of his reasearch during the past year. Consequently, he condenses as much as possible and fills the margins like those correspondents with still too much to say when they reach the bottom of the page. At 7:15 Foucault stops. The students rush up to his desk—not to talk to him, but to turn off their tape recorders. No questions. In the crush Foucault is alone.

Foucault admitted to the journalist after this lecture: "We ought to be able to discuss what I have proposed. Sometimes, when the lecture has not been good, it would take very little to make it all fall into place. But there never is a question. In France, the effect of such a large group is to make real discussion impossible. And, with no feedback, the lecture turns into a show. My relation with the people there is like that of an actor or an acrobat. And when I have finished speaking, there is a sensation of total solitude." [16] For the Collège de France, as an institution, has its peculiarities. The professors do not have students, strictly speaking. They have listeners, to whom they award no diplomas, to whom they give no exams, and consequently, with whom they have no dialogue, no contact. There is only this strange, weekly confrontation between the tightrope walker and the spectators who come to applaud his feats.

The course he gave at the Collège was the basis of Foucault's books from that time on. The tradition of the Collège required it. One was supposed to lay out one's work in progress, "science creating itself," according to Renan's phrase. And there was an obligation to do something new every year. Foucault therefore used the material he was working on, formulating hypotheses and reflecting on them. Thus did *Surveiller et punir*, *La Volonté de savoir*, and the last two parts of *Histoire de la sexualité* come into being. This professorial activity required an enormous amount of preparation. And Foucault often said, in the final years of his life, how much he wanted to be done with this burden, whose weight oppressed him more and more each year. But on December 2, 1970, the moment was one of triumph, not yet one of weariness.

16

~~~

A Lesson from the Darkness

The pamphlet had an odd vertical format. Its title: *Intolérable*. On the back cover was a list of its announced targets:

> These are intolerable:
>   courts
>   cops
>   hospitals, asylums
>   school, military service
>   the press, television
>   the State.

But its real target was the prison. This forty-eight-page booklet was published in May 1971 as the first in a series to be produced by a new movement called the Groupe d'Information sur les Prisons (GIP).[1]

Michel Foucault brought this movement into being. He announced its birth on February 8, 1971, in Saint-Bernard Chapel, beneath the Gare Montparnasse:

> There is no one among us who is certain of escaping prison. Today less than ever. Police control is tightening on our everyday life, in city streets, and on the roads; expressing an opinion is once again an offense for foreigners and young people, and antidrug measures are increasingly arbitrary. We live in a state of "custody." They tell us that the system of justice is overwhelmed. That is easy to see. But what if the police are the ones who have overwhelmed it? They tell us that the prisons are overcrowded. But what if the population is over-imprisoned? There is very little information published about prisons; it is one of the hidden regions of our social system, one of the dark compartments of our existence. It is our right to know. We want to know. That is why, with magistrates, lawyers, journalists, doctors, and psychologists, we have created an association for information about prisons.

We propose to let people know what prisons are: who goes there, and how and why they go; what happens there; what the existence of prisoners is like, and also the existence of those providing surveillance; what the buildings, food, and hygiene are like; how the inside rules, medical supervision and workshops function; how one gets out and what it is like in our society to be someone who does get out.

This information is not going to be found in the official reports. We will ask those who, for one reason or another, have some experience with prison or a connection with it. We ask them to contact us and tell us what they know. We have composed a questionnaire they can request. As soon as we have a sufficient number of results, we will publish them.[2]

The text of this appeal was signed by Foucault; by Pierre Vidal-Naquet, a historian who specialized in ancient Greece and who had become known during the Algerian War for his denunciation of the French army's use of torture; and by Jean-Marie Domenach, who was at that time the editor of the Catholic review *Esprit*. The address given as the GIP's "mailbox" was 285 Rue Vaugirard, Foucault's residence. Moreover, the appeal was written mostly by Foucault. It is easy to see what made him interested in it. Just as in the case of madness, the dividing line separating "normal" men from incarcerated men is not as certain as one would think, and that line was where he had to establish his observation post to detect how mechanisms of power are deployed. However, Foucault's involvement in this issue would not be theoretical. He at once leapt into action, the day-to-day battle. How distant this text founding the GIP seems from the inaugural lecture at the Collège de France given just two months before!

The waves of unrest following May 1968 were often translated into violent demonstrations, and they provoked numerous arrests and convictions of ultra-leftist militants. People were prosecuted for incitement to violence, breaches of state security, or publication of banned newspapers such as *La Cause du peuple*. Among those who were imprisoned were Alain Geismar, Michel Le Bris, and Jean-Pierre Le Dantec. In September 1970 twenty-nine of these incarcerated militants started a hunger strike to obtain "special conditions" as political prisoners. Until then they had been considered as "common-law" prisoners and subjected to the same conditions of detention as everyone else. The strike lasted almost a month but achieved only very partial results. Those whose case was explicitly political—that is, the militants who had to be judged in the State Security Court, were allowed more visits, books, and newspapers. The others, those designated in the vocabulary of the time as simply *casseurs*—property damagers—had a law enacted against them and remained subject to common-law statutes. But for the time being the hunger strike was called off.

It resumed in January 1971, this time with outside support. More hunger strikers moved into the Saint-Bernard Chapel and other groups participated at the Sorbonne and the Halle-aux-Vins. Several well-known individuals, among them Yves Montand, Simone Signoret, Vladimir Jankélévitch, and Maurice Clavel, offered their support as well. At the same time, in the National Assembly François Mitterrand, the deputy from Nièvre, questioned the minister of justice, René Pleven, denouncing the treatment of political militants, "whose actions, though perhaps open to criticism, are no less the result of an ideological choice." On February 8 Pleven showed signs of retreat: he announced the establishment of a commission to study the easing of conditions demanded by the strikers. Despite all this, Secours Rouge (Red Aid), an organization created to fight repression, called for a demonstration the next day. The meeting was immediately prohibited and, when it took place, on February 9, violently repressed. Dozens of people were taken in for questioning, and many were wounded; one young man was disfigured by a teargas bomb exploding in his face. At a press conference on February 8 at Saint-Bernard Chapel the militant leftists' lawyers, Georges Kiejman and Henri Leclerc, emphasized that their "clients" had obtained satisfaction on the essential matters. Then Pierre Halbwachs, the spokesman for Secours Rouge, passed the microphone to Michel Foucault, who read the manifesto of the GIP.

In effect, the movement by the ultra-leftist prisoners had aroused a more general debate about prison conditions. As early as September, during their first strike, conscious of how paradoxical it might seem that leftist militants were demanding special status, the hunger strikers had published a statement "written inside the prisons of France." It said: "We demand effective recognition of the political nature of our imprisonment. We do not lay claim, however, to any privileges in relation to the other, common-law prisoners. As we see it they are victims of the social system, which, after having produced them, refuses to re-educate them but is content with rejecting them. Even more, we want our struggle, our denunciation of the present scandalous prison system, to serve all prisoners."

For Foucault this sort of statement must have awakened a vision of those voices he had heard through the thick dust of the archives, across the even thicker screen of psychiatric, economic, and juridical concepts. Basically, everything that would interest him during the 1970s was already simmering in *Folie et déraison*. Foucault's work, including his vocabulary and his themes, underwent radical transformations from the early 1960s to the 1980s. Yet everything new that arose through his labor, research, and action seemed to spring from some internal necessity. The volume *Résumés des cours du Collège de France*, collecting Foucault's annual summaries of his work from 1970 to 1982, makes this process apparent. The themes are all linked, and each reworking seems demanded by the one that preceded and provides a premonition of the one to come.[3] Ruptures, difficulties, and regrets all played their part in an oeuvre whose organization seems essentially coherent.

Shortly after its initial appeal, the GIP began its investigation. Questionnaires were distributed to the families of prisoners as they stood in line for visiting hours. Foucault sought out this direct contact, collecting testimony about the prisoners' conditions and their past life. He was fascinated by these fragments of individual history, by these moving trajectories, by all the brutal reality of this existence on the margins of society. The questionnaire was accompanied by a brief commentary denouncing the situation: "Prisoners are treated like dogs. The few rights they have are not respected. We want to bring this scandal to the light of day." There was only one solution: to conduct this investigation and gather testimony. "To help us collect information the attached questionnaire should be filled in with the help of prisoners and ex-prisoners."

The first pamphlet, published by Champ Libre, proclaimed the objectives of the movement:

> The GIP does not propose to speak in the name of the prisoners in various prisons: it proposes, on the contrary, to provide them with the possibility of speaking themselves and telling what goes on in prisons. The GIP does not have reformist goals; we do not dream of some ideal prison: we hope that prisoners may be able to say what it is that is intolerable for them in the system of penal repression. We have to disseminate as quickly and widely as possible the revelations that the prisoners themselves make—the sole means of unifying what is inside and outside the prison, the political battle and the legal battle, into one and the same struggle.

The introduction to the pamphlet explained the objectives of the GIP at greater length.

> Expressed through courts, prisons, hospitals, psychiatric hospitals, occupational medicine, universities, the press, and informational organs—through all these institutions, under different disguises,

exists a form of oppression that is deeply rooted in the political. The exploited class has always known how to recognize this oppression; it has constantly resisted it but has been thoroughly subjected to it. Now it has become intolerable to new social strata—the intellectuals, technicians, lawyers, doctors, journalists . . . Those responsible for distributing justice, health, knowledge, and information are beginning to feel a political power's oppression in things they do themselves. There is a new intolerance now joining forces with the proletariat in its long struggle. Instruments created by the proletariat in the nineteenth century are being rediscovered. First are investigations of working conditions by the workers themselves. This is where the "investigations for intolerance" that we now undertake come in.

1. These investigations are not intended to ameliorate, alleviate, or make an oppressive system more bearable. They are intended to attack it in places where it is called something else—justice, technique, knowledge, objectivity. Each investigation must therefore be a political act.

2. They aim at specific targets, institutions with a name and place, administrators, people who are responsible, directors—who create victims and give rise to revolts, even among those in charge of these institutions. Each investigation must therefore be the first episode in a struggle.

3. They group together around these targets various social strata that the ruling class had kept separate through social hierarchies and divergent economic interests. They have to break down these barriers that are indispensable to power by bringing together prisoners, lawyers, and magistrates; or doctors, patients, and hospital personnel. Each investigation must, in every important strategic point, constitute a front, one prepared to attack.

4. These investigations are not made from the outside by a group of technicians. Here the investigators and investigated are the same. It is up to them to speak, to dismantle this compartmentalization, to formulate what is intolerable and to tolerate it no longer. It is up to them to take charge of the struggle that will prevent the exercise of oppression.[4]

Among the pamphlet's concrete proposals was one to start a campaign to "abolish police records."

Four pamphlets in all were published. The second, also printed by Champ Libre, was a study of a "model prison," the one at Fleury-Mérogis. The next two were published by Gallimard. The third dealt with the "assassination of George Jackson" on August 21, 1971, in San Quentin prison. The fourth and last pamphlet, in January 1973, was devoted to prisoner suicides during 1972. Its objective was to show

how a desperate burst of collective actions had been succeeded by the most dramatic form of individual insubordination. Among the many cases mentioned, the most remarkable reproduces the letters written by a thirty-two-year-old man who had spent fifteen years in prison. Kept in solitary confinement for homosexuality, he had hanged himself. The letters, written under the influence of sleeping pills, are astonishing and disturbing. They are introduced by a brief, unsigned commentary written by Foucault. He considered the body of letters "exemplary because, through the quality of his soul and thought, it tells us exactly what a prisoner thinks about. And this is not at all what we usually believe it is. Even prison," Foucault went on, "has a yet more secret prison, one harsher and more grotesque, solitary confinement, which Pleven's 'reform' takes pains not to mention." In a later section Foucault stated: "What is in question is not just a social system in general with its exclusions and convictions, but the ensemble of deliberate provocations that are embodied in it, by means of which the system functions and guarantees its order and with which it creates those whom it excludes and convicts, in conformity with politics that are the politics of the power of police and administration. A certain number of people are directly and personally responsible for the death of this prisoner."[5]

Foucault, in passing, touched on a theme that would become central to his reflections about the penal system. The prison produces delinquency and establishes it as the destiny of people who once have spent time behind its bars: "Through a very specific police system, police records and monitoring, taking away any chance to escape the consequences of a first conviction, young people are quickly driven back to prison soon after leaving it." Michelle Perrot, quoting these lines in a 1986 article, wrote: "The production of delinquents, the management of what is unlawful: some of the themes from *Surveiller et punir* are recognizable here. It is possible to measure here the direct and concrete experience sustaining this book. A great book about society's dark side, it fed on this lesson from the darkness."[6]

The GIP was Foucault's major concern at the beginning of the 1970s. It was really his movement—his and Daniel Defert's. A good many people from Vincennes joined them rather informally (since it was not a party, there was no membership or identification card), including Jean-Claude Passeron, Jean Gattegno, Robert Castel, Gilles Deleuze, Jacques Rancière and his wife, Danielle, and Jacques Donzelot. Slightly later, there would be Claude Mauriac.

Claude Mauriac, the son of François Mauriac, had been General de

Gaulle's personal secretary immediately after the war. In 1971, when Foucault was already active in the far left, Mauriac was a journalist at *Le Figaro*. Mauriac describes their first meeting in his journal, *Le Temps immobile*, and devotes several hundred pages to recounting its consequences on his life. This journal is both a chronicle of friendship and a day-by-day account of the militant activities of a handful of intellectuals during the 1970s.[7] It all began with an incident of the sort that frequently occurred during demonstrations. On May 29, 1971, Alain Jaubert, a journalist at *Le Nouvel Observateur* accompanying a wounded demonstrator to the hospital, was severely beaten up while riding in the police car. Jaubert was then charged with rebellion and using violence against the police. Since he was a journalist, this episode caused quite an uproar. Foucault, Deleuze, a lawyer, Denis Langlois, a Dr. Timsitt, and several journalists met to conduct a "counterinvestigation" that would establish the real truth. Claude Mauriac attended their first press conference as a representative of *Le Figaro*, and his presence caused considerable comment. Foucault phoned him afterward to ask if he would like to join the investigative commission. Mauriac accepted. He reports having told Foucault several days later, in a café in the Arab section of Paris: "'If someone had shown me this café just a week earlier, and told me that today I would be seen sitting here talking to Michel Foucault, I would have had a hard time believing it.' And he [Foucault] replied, 'I hope you will forgive me for having dragged you into this mantrap.'"[8] A mantrap in which Mauriac was caught for years and which he still remembers with emotion.

The Jaubert affair also had other consequences. The GIP's imperative to collect and to circulate information, along with the difficulty of gaining any opening with the large editorial and newspaper agencies, led Maurice Clavel to create the APL, the Agence de Presse—Libération (Liberation News Agency), which in turn played an important part in the creation of the daily paper *Libération*.

The GIP frequently held its meetings in Hélène Cixous's apartment near Parc Montsouris. She remembered that their discussions were "totally action oriented." "Foucault was really a very pragmatic person; his aim was always to be effective." Everyone in the small group acknowledged him as their "head." And Jean-Marie Domenach spoke of the incredible amount of energy expended by Foucault and his constant availability: "I don't know how he managed to organize everything," he said. "He, along with Daniel Defert, took care of everything. He sent the mail, made the contacts, made thousands of phone calls; he was always there when necessary." And it was often necessary, because there were plenty of occasions for action. Starting in November 1971, a series of revolts spread throughout the French prison system. The situation quickly became explosive and culminated in prisoners' setting fire to the central prison in Toul on December 5 and 13, 1971. The police stormed the prison, and about fifteen prisoners were wounded. The GIP mobilized to denounce the repression and the conditions of detention that were at the origin of the revolt. A "Committee for Truth and Justice" was established in Toul and organized information meetings. The sessions were occasionally tumultuous, particularly when the prison guards wanted to have their say. Foucault participated in several press conferences. The first of these was held on December 16, two years after the minister of justice had appointed an investigative commission to examine the events, their causes, and possible remedies. A high point in the polemics was the report by the medical psychiatrist at the prison, Dr. Edith Rose, to the minister of justice and the president. It was a damning text, describing in detail the prisoners' conditions of existence, such as the way they were treated when they were sick. It was, quite simply, terrifying. The reading of this document at the meeting in Toul caused a sensation. Several days later Foucault presented extracts from it in *Le Nouvel Observateur*:

> In the simple facts she lays out, what is concealed, or rather, what bursts forth? Somebody-or-other's dishonesty? Someone else's dubious performance? Hardly ever. Rather, it is the violence of relationships of power. The administration speaks only through statistical charts and curves, the unions only in terms of working conditions, budgets, and recruitment funds. Here and there, one only wants to attack the evil at its "roots," that is, where no one sees or feels it—far from the event, far from the forces in confrontation and the act of domination. But now the psychiatrist at Toul has spoken. She has disrupted the game and broke the great taboo. She was inside a power system, and, rather than criticize its functioning, she denounced what has just happened, on a particular day, a particular place, under particular circumstances . . . What was said at Toul will, perhaps, be an important event in the history of penal and psychiatric institutions.[9]

On January 5, 1972, Foucault spoke again. After giving the results of the investigation the GIP had conducted among the prisoners, he insisted on "the necessity to keep public opinion informed about what goes on in the prisons" and challenged "M. Pleven to tell the truth." At the next meeting a message from Sartre was read from the podium, describing the revolt at Toul as "the beginning of the struggle against the repressive regime that keeps us all in the atmosphere of a concentration camp."

Other insurrections broke out at Lille, Nîmes, Fleury-Mérogis, and Nancy. René Pleven denounced the actions of the GIP and other ultra-left groups. "It is obvious," he said, "that certain subversive elements are presently trying very hard to use the prisoners, who risk having to bear the consequences, to provoke dangerous unrest, or start it up again, in various penal institutions." At the same time the Communist newspaper, *La Marseillaise de l'Essonne*, was demanding that authorities put an end to the intrigues of this "association of thugs." But the GIP forged ahead. To protest the brutal intervention of the police at Nancy's Charles III prison, it decided to organize a press conference at the Ministry of Justice. And on January 18, 1972, Claude Mauriac, Jean-Paul Sartre, Michelle Vian, Gilles and Fanny Deleuze, Michel Foucault, Daniel Defert, and twenty or thirty others assembled on Rue Castiglione in front of the Intercontinental Hotel. The group moved toward the Place Vendôme and went as far as the arches of the ministry, where a barrier prevented them from going any farther. Michel Foucault then read a report written by prisoners in Melun. When the demonstrators began to chant "Pleven resign" and "Pleven assassin," the CRS arrived and, according to Claude Mauriac, "with no further ado, pushed all these people back outside, where I was, and I could see how they resisted the pressure, Foucault at the front, all red and his muscles bulging with the effort."[10] On the square there was a brief crush, and some members of the crowd were arrested: Alain Jaubert and Marianne Merleau-Ponty. Sartre and Foucault intervened in vain. Mauriac, stating his identity and his connection to *Le Figaro*, had more success. He promised that the group would disperse as soon as the two demonstrators were released. This was done. Then the press conference moved to the premises of the APL, where Foucault once again read the report from Melun and mentioned the confrontations in Nancy. Three days later the GIP called for a demonstration on the Boulevard de Sébastopol, and more than a thousand people turned out.

There were other, less spectacular actions organized by the GIP: meetings in front of prisons on Christmas night and Saint Sylvester's night, with firecrackers and flares; messages and shouting, amplified by loudspeakers to let the prisoners know they were not cut off from the world. Foucault took part in one of these at Fresnes on December 31, 1971. Little sketches, lasting only minutes before the police dispersed them, were performed at prison gates by members of the Théâtre du Soleil troupe, directed by Ariane Mnouchkine. Police clubs rained down their hail of blows on the GIP militants in Paris, Nancy, or anywhere else. "At Nancy, I was literally knocked unconscious by the police," said Hélène Cixous. Foucault and Domenach were brutally questioned with a dozen others on May 1, 1971, when they distributed tracts calling for the abolition of police records in front of Santé prison in Paris. Foucault lodged a formal complaint for "illegal arrest, breach of public freedoms, public insult, and rash violence with premeditation." No grounds were found for his lawsuit, which was settled in favor of the police.

The GIP endlessly invented new forms of action. When six of the insurgents at Nancy went on trial in June 1972, the GIP wanted to publicize the proceedings. Following performances of *1793*, Ariane Mnouchkine's theater production, the audience was invited to remain in the theater for a brief recreation of the courtoom events. The stenotyped court record was used for a text. Foucault played the role of a police guard or a courtroom judge.[11] To guarantee legal assistance for prisoners, Foucault and Gilles Deleuze persuaded Paul Eluard's widow to sponsor and shelter the short-lived Association for the Defense of Prisoners' Rights, whose president was the writer Vercors.

The GIP had considerable success, establishing committees throughout France. And, although the initiative came mostly from Maoist militants, its membership extended far beyond left-wing circles. Lawyers, doctors, and members of religious orders swelled the numbers to as many as two or three thousand. But it was not an enduring success. Foucault, faithful to his principle of departure, wanted to leave the prisoners and former prisoners their say. Already the Prisoners' Action Committee (CAP) had published its first pamphlet, in December 1972. One leader of this committee was Serge Livrozet, who had spent several years in prison at Melun. Foucault wrote a foreword to his book, *De la prison à la révolte*. "Serge Livrozet's book," he wrote, "is a part of this movement that has been working on the prisons. I do not mean to say that it 'represents' what all, or even most, prisoners think. I am saying that it is one element in this struggle, that it was born from this struggle and will play a role in it. It is the individual and powerful expression of a certain popular experience and a certain popular thought concerning the law and illegality. A philosophy of the people."[12]

The CAP did not take long to declare its independence from its prestigious sponsors. In response to an interview about criminality and illegality, published anonymously by Foucault in *Libération*, Livrozet wrote on February 19, 1974: "These specialists in analysis are a pain. I don't need anyone to speak for me and proclaim what I am."[13] By that point the GIP had already disbanded. In an article in 1976 Daniel Defert and Jacques Donzelot took stock of the movement, commenting bitterly about the CAP militants: "They are going on with it, but what response are they getting?"[14]

Bitterness and a sense of failure were, no doubt, what Foucault felt after the GIP broke up. "Michel thought it had accomplished nothing," said Gilles Deleuze in an interview in 1986. Deleuze also stressed the importance of this "adventure," this "experience" for Foucault, which was testing a new idea of intellectual engagement: no longer as an action conducted in the name of higher values, but as a focusing of attention on realities that have gone unnoticed, showing what is intolerable and what it is in an intolerable situation that makes it truly intolerable. But the GIP, Deleuze added, was also a way of "producing statements." That is why, in his view, contrary to whatever Foucault himself might think, the GIP was a success. "Today something is being said about prisons, by the prisoners naturally, but sometimes by non-prisoners, something that would previously have been impossible to formulate."[15]

∾

IN HIS COURSE AT THE COLLÈGE DE FRANCE, Foucault focused on penal justice and law. With a small research team in 1973 he published a book on Pierre Rivière, a youth tried and sentenced at the beginning of the nineteenth century for having killed his mother, brother, and sister. "We had in mind a study of the practical aspects of the relations between psychiatry and criminal justice. In the course of our research we came across Pierre Rivière's case," he wrote in his foreword.[16] The volume contained Rivière's own written account of his crimes, along with the entire file containing the judicial hearings, the medical and legal consultations, the sentencing, the imprisonment, and the account of the suicide. He explained why this interested him:

Documents like those in the Rivière case should provide material for a thorough examination of the way in which a particular kind of knowledge (e.g., medicine, psychiatry, psychology) is formed and acts in relation to institutions and the roles prescribed in them (e.g., the law with respect to the expert, the accused, the criminally insane, and so on). They give us a key to the relations of power, domination, and conflict, within which discourses emerge and function, and hence provide material for a potential analysis of discourse (even of scientific discourses) which may be both tactical and political, and therefore, strategic. Lastly, they furnish a means for grasping the power of derangement peculiar to a discourse such as Rivière's and the whole range of tactics by which we can try to reconstitute it, situate it, and give it its status as the discourse of either a madman or a criminal.[17]

How closely these words resemble his inaugural lecture at the Collège de France—except that the analysis has now moved from the order of discourse to social practices. Other publications would follow: prefaces, articles, interviews, debates, and colloquia on the subject of justice and prisons. Foucault was also actively engaged in combating the death penalty. For example, in 1976 he refused to have lunch with Valéry Giscard d'Estaing because the latter had refused to pardon Christian Ranucci, who had been convicted of murder.

ONE OF FOUCAULT'S FINEST BOOKS, perhaps the finest, *Surveiller et punir*, came out in 1975. It was subtitled *Naissance de la prison*. Foucault had shifted the grounds of his intervention. No longer are we at the gates of the prison; instead, the action consists in historical research, which Foucault sets in opposition to habits and tendencies of thought. The book, he explained at the beginning, was a product of the present more than of history; and his project consisted in "writing the history of the present." What was in question, in the struggle surrounding the prisons, was the entire technology of power exercised on bodies. What was prison? How did we get from flagrant torture in earlier times to the silence of present-day reclusion?

An ancient inheritance from the dungeons of the Middle Ages? Rather, more of a new technology: the perfection from the sixteenth to the nineteenth centuries of an entire group of procedures for covering, controlling, assessing and shaping up individuals, making them both "docile and useful." Surveillance, exercises, maneuvers, notations, ranks and positions, classifications, examinations, registrations. Discipline: a whole way of subjecting bodies, mastering human multiplicity, and manipulating their forces was developed through the centuries of classicism in hospitals, in the army, in schools, colleges or workshops. The eighteenth century invented freedoms, no doubt, but it provided them with a deep, solid substratum—the disciplinary society from which we still derive. The place of the prison in the formation of this surveillance society must be located.[18]

Foucault was determined to demonstrate the role played by the "human sciences" in this process:

> Modern penalty systems no longer dare speak of punishing crimes; they claim rather to readapt criminals. It will soon have been almost two centuries since these systems began to be connected with "human sciences." It gives them something to be proud of, or at least something not to be too ashamed of: "Maybe I am not yet completely just, but be patient, see how I am in the process of becoming learned." But how would it be possible for psychology, psychiatry or criminality to justify today's justice? Since their history demonstrably shares the same technology, so that they have really shaped each other. There lies, beneath men's knowledge and beneath humane punishments, a certain disciplinary investment in bodies, a form mingling constraint and objectification, the same "power-knowledge." Is it possible to create the genealogy of modern morality starting from a political history of bodies?[19]

Just as he had done in *Histoire de la folie* and *Naissance de la clinique*, Foucault deserted the canonical texts of traditional philosophy to "nose around" in police files or reformist projects. "It is not in Hegel or Auguste Comte," he explained in an interview in 1975, "that the bourgeoisie speaks openly. Alongside these texts that are regarded as sacred there is an absolutely conscious strategy, one that is organized and well thought out, that can be read clearly in masses of unknown documents constituting the effective discourse of a political action."[20]

Surveiller et punir was very well received. The pages on the torture at Damiens and the savagery of punishments in the eighteenth century, with which the book opens, have been quoted often. The key idea concerning the role of prisons in producing delinquency as a self-enclosed milieu, which the power structure does its best to control, has also been frequently cited. Jeremy Bentham's Panopticon, which Foucault describes at length, was designed so that it was possible to see everything constantly from around a central point. Its architectural organization became the symbol of this "eye of power," the institutional surveillance that movements formed around a variety of specific issues (prisons, women's rights, immigration, and so on), would denounce endlessly throughout the 1970s. *Surveiller et punir* was developed and thought out during the ups and downs of these struggles and, in return, was to be useful in the fight. "All my books," said Foucault in the same 1975 interview, "whether *Histoire de la folie* or this one, are little toolboxes, if you will. If people are willing to open them and make use of such and such a sentence or idea, of one analysis or another, as they would a screwdriver or a monkey wrench, in order to short circuit or disqualify systems of power, including even possibly the ones my books come out of, well, all the better."

On page 308 the book abruptly stops with: "At this point I end a book that must serve as a historical background to various studies of the power of normalization and the formation of knowledge in modern society."[21]

17

~~~

*Popular Justice
and the Workers' Memory*

"Look, it's Foucault!" Everyone turned to watch him go by. Foucault's silhouette, his physique recognizable in a crowd of thousands, became an image that stuck in memories and photographs of the demonstrations. Starting in 1970, Foucault became a public figure. He was known, recognized, and his name mentioned frequently in newspapers, memoirs, and histories. These abundant sources focus on the public figure, the militant—on the person, in fact, that Dumézil never "believed in."

Foucault's life in the 1970s was, one could say, "fragmented." The circle of his relationships became much larger and, above all, so diverse that it embraced the absolute opposite poles of the intellectual and cultural milieu. Foucault kept the different people and groups that he associated with rather strictly compartmentalized. And, as Jean Daniel remarked once, Foucault had the ability to make everyone he spoke with think that he or she was the only one to have such a special relationship. This trait has frequently led to distorted perspectives in accounts of this period. But keeping these different groups impervious to each other was the condition of their continued existence in Foucault's life. This dispersion and fragmentation make a purely chronological account of these years impossible. From this point on, we must look at Foucault's life facet by facet, in relation to dominant themes or problems.

~~~

PARIS, NOVEMBER 27, 1971. The setting is the Maison Verte, a place run by Pastor Hedrich in the eighteenth arrondissement, a working-class neighborhood with an enormous population of immigrant workers. Foucault and Jean Genet, "unshaven, the stubble thick and white," were already in the room. Claude Mauriac describes it: "And, in this room on Rue Marcadet where we met around two in the afternoon to arrange the final details of our demonstration, an old man, small and unassuming, arrived. It was Jean-Paul Sartre, who would say very little. He sat opposite me, and I was between Genet and Foucault." This scene was not lacking in grandeur. "It was thus that I saw Jean-Paul Sartre and Jean Genet face to face, the hagiographer and the saint. And thus I was present at the first meeting between the old great philosopher and the young great philosopher, Jean-Paul Sartre and Michel Foucault."[1] It was perhaps the first time they had spoken, but not the first time they had seen each other; both Sartre and Foucault had participated at the meeting on February 10, 1969, at the Mutualité, after the evacuation of Vincennes. But the setting and the crowd there had made any contact between the two philosophers impossible.

It had been five years since the violent polemics that had brought these two thinkers into conflict and focused the attention of the intellectual world. The events of May 1968 had blown through French society, a wind turning everything upside down, making all the earlier points of reference obsolete. Indeed, Claude Mauriac could never have been the one to write this group's memoirs if this had not been the case. The former Gaullist was now taking part in demonstrations with leftist students. He found himself in the front ranks of the struggle, the *front des luttes*, as it was called at the time, side by side with intellectuals who advocated radical subversion of the established order.

Given all these changes, the meeting between Sartre and Foucault was not surprising. It took place in connection with a demonstration "against racism." Djellali Ben Ali, a young Algerian, had been rough with a woman who was caretaker at an apartment in Goutte d'Or, the Arab quarter of Paris. A man who was the woman's friend had grabbed a rifle, which went off accidentally, killing the young man. It was a banal and sad news item, as *Le Monde* described it a few years later when the trial took place. But when it happened, there was a different perception of the drama. Several thousand people demonstrated "against this racist crime," and Foucault launched an independent investigation to study living conditions in the quarter. Gilles Deleuze, Jean Genet, Claude Mauriac, Jean-Claude Passeron, and several others served on this Djellali committee.

A few moments after this first meeting between Foucault and Sartre, small groups were assembling at the corner of Rue Polenceau and Rue de la Goutte-d'Or. The quarter was besieged by police. But, as usual, the police were under orders not to touch Sartre, so the demonstrators could put up signs pretty much as they wanted. They reproduced their "appeal to the local workers," denouncing the threats from "organized networks of racists supported by the power structures" that burdened the Goutte-d'Or. The text was signed by Deleuze, Foucault, Genet, Sartre, Michel Drach, Simone Signoret, Claire Etcherelli, Monique Lange, Michel Leiris, Michèle Manceaux, Marianne Merleau-Ponty, Thierry Mignon, Yves Montand, and Jean-Claude Passeron. Some of those who had signed and a large number of Maoists milled about in the almost deserted streets, under the eye of riot squads. There is a famous series of photographs showing Sartre and Foucault, a mega-phone in his hand, announcing that they were setting up office in the fellowship room at Saint-Bruno Church the next day. They hoped to offer legal assistance to anyone who needed it, or simply to help them fill out the administrative papers and forms, all the files that immi-grants constantly had to provide.

Very tired, already ill, Sartre left almost immediately; the rest of the group returned to Maison Verte for a meeting. The next day Foucault told Mauriac: "Yesterday evening I stayed to have dinner in one of the restaurants in the quarter, and when I went into the restaurant some-one shouted: 'There's Jean-Paul Sartre.'" Foucault added: "I'm not sure it was a compliment."

Passeron, Mauriac, Foucault, and Genet took turns running the office. It was not long before the Djellali committee grew large enough to spawn a Committee for the Defense of the Rights of Immigrants, which then organized several demonstrations. For example, on March 31, 1973 several thousand people marched on Boulevard de Belleville and Boulevard de Ménilmontant to protest the "Fontanet circular," which limited possibilities for obtaining visiting or working permits. Foucault and Mauriac led the march.

Committee meetings were occasionally tense. Most of the Arab workers taking part in them were members of "Palestine committees" who hoped that the denunciation of racism would be extended to the denunciation of Israel. But Foucault, like Sartre, had always been pro-Israel. And he would remain so. This was, no doubt, one of the main points on which he differed from the actively pro-Palestinian Maoist movement, which often manipulated the committee and the direction taken by its protests.

This mobilization against racism was also the occasion for Foucault and Genet's brief association. Foucault had long admired the writer; he had discussed Genet's sulfurous writing in his lectures at Uppsala.

Genet had always supported racial minorities and felt a violent disgust at anything resembling racism. In 1970 he spent two months in the United States with the Black Panthers. He was very much involved in support for the Palestinians and had spent some time in the refugee camps; this was the subject of his last book, *Un captif amoureux*, published a few weeks after his death. Genet became a member of the Djellali committee through Catherine Von Bülow, a German woman who had been for many years a dancer in the New York Metropolitan Opera ballet. She moved to France and found a job at Gallimard, where she met both Foucault and Genet. For a while she was very close friends with Genet and looked after him whenever he came to Paris. She was active in the Secours Rouge and La Cause du Peuple and was thus on the spot when the protests surrounding the Djellali committee began. She wrote an extraordinarily moving memoir recounting her part in the events.[2]

Foucault and Genet used to take walks in the streets of Goutte d'Or, stopping to sit in the cafés, where Genet was perhaps more comfortable than Foucault. According to Von Bülow, "the only thing that interested him was the Palestinian struggle." His fascination with the Arab world probably accounted for his withdrawing soon from the turbulent world of demonstrations in Paris. No one ever knew where he lived—whether in Paris, in Morocco, or anywhere else. He appeared; he disappeared. One never knew when he would do so, or for how long. Sometimes he would be there, wearing his inevitable leather jacket; then he would "take a dive," and no one knew where he had gone or if he would return. Although Foucault and Genet never had much to say to each other, according to Catherine Von Bülow, and very little in common outside their militant action, in those days there was a certain complicity between them. Foucault liked Genet. He wanted him to meet Dumézil—the highest token of his esteem. Genet agreed, but Dumézil did not: he did not like the individual or his books, he told Foucault; so why meet the man?

᭡

AT FOUR IN THE AFTERNOON on Saturday, December 16, 1972, in the broad boulevards, in front of the Hotel Rex, shouts rang out: "Cops! Racists! Murderers!" Several dozen people were trying to gather in front of the Bonne-Nouvelle metro stop. An Algerian worker, Mohamed Diab, had been killed under particularly suspicious circumstances a few days earlier in a police station; 136 intellectuals had called for a demonstration "in mourning and protest" for him. Police headquarters had forbidden the gathering, and there was an instant onslaught by the CRS to disperse the marchers as they attempted to assemble; a tornado of violence, lasting only moments. The police avoided taking on any of the important people who were present. But Foucault and Claude Mauriac would not stop intervening, rescuing those who had been arrested by pulling them from the hands of the police; so they were subjected to the same fate as the rest. Beaten, insulted, roughed up, arrested, Mauriac, Foucault, and Genet were taken to headquarters at Beaujon for an identity check. Mauriac describes it in his journal: "After passing several other cells jammed full of young comrades, we were put in a cell, Michel Foucault and I, no one else. Jean Genet went by, well guarded on his way who knows where, and we spoke briefly with him."[3] At midnight they were all freed, but for the next few days the papers were full of this affair.

M

FOUCAULT DID NOT BELONG to any political movement. But throughout this period he had close connections with the Maoists involved with La Cause du Peuple, with whom Daniel Defert was closely linked. Whenever Foucault led a demonstration, whether the issue concerned the GIP or the Djellali committee, the Maoists were very much a presence. He also took part in meetings of the "Truth and Justice Committees" that the Maoists had set up all over France. For example, he was present at the meeting of the Grenoble Committee for Truth and Justice at the end of November 1972. Fifteen hundred people gathered to charge the administration with responsibility for a 1970 fire at a dance club, "the 5/7," in Saint-Laurent-du-Pont, that had taken the lives of almost a hundred and fifty people. Foucault spoke about the situation of young workers, whose only possible jobs were menial labor, handling and packing, at ridiculous wages. He added: "This young man has nowhere to live, so of course he has to go out. And when he goes out, once again he takes a beating. He needs twelve or fifteen francs just to go into the dance club. He orders an orange juice, and that costs eight or ten francs; and so on. Well, I say these young men and women are being exploited and robbed." And after denouncing the racketeering to which night clubs were subjected, he attacked the connections between politicians and these forms of corruption. He concluded:

All over the country, discreetly or indiscreetly, noisily or quietly, an entire system of control is being set in place: the elected officials with their badges, the cadres of the UDR [Union des Démocrates pour la Vème République], the SAC [Service d'Action Civique], official or unofficial police. The populace is in the process of being surrounded and limited by a system responsible for keeping it in step or reducing it to silence. As for the administration, what does it do in all this? It has only one thing to do, and it does it well. It shuts its eyes and lets it happen. It lets the 5/7 be built and opened and burned down. Any time and anywhere that there is a profit to be made, its attitude is *laissez-faire*.[4]

In February 1972 Foucault published a long dialogue with Pierre Victor on the subject of popular justice in a special issue of *Les Temps modernes* "put together by militant Maoists," including André Glucksmann, Jean-Pierre Le Dantec, and Alain Geismar. Pierre Victor, whose real name was Benny Lévy, was one of the leaders of the Maoist movement. He was not only Sartre's secretary from 1973 on; he was also Sartre's interlocutor, along with Philippe Gavi, in the book titled *On a raison de se révolter;* and he published a series of interviews with Sartre in 1980, shortly before the latter's death. These interviews stunned Sartre's friends and pained and angered Simone de Beauvoir, who saw his thought heading in directions she no longer recognized. After leaving the fighting phalanxes of French-style Maoism, Pierre Victor converted to orthodox Judaism and today devotes himself to studying Jewish religion and thought.[5]

But in 1972, by all accounts, Victor was still the "charismatic leader" of a small army of "resistants," as Maoist militants then thought of themselves. They were resistants in an occupied country. In power were the bosses, whose military force was the police. The idea of a dialogue with Foucault came to Victor in June 1971, after the *contre-enquête* concerning the Jaubert affair, in which Foucault had played a very important role. The Maoists wanted to create a people's court to judge the police, as they had at Lens in 1970, condemning the Compagnie des Houillères following the death of some miners. Sartre had been one of the protagonists in this well-publicized countertrial. In fact the idea of a people's court is the first one discussed in the dialogue between Victor and Foucault in *Les Temps modernes*. Foucault detested the very notion of a court. "We must ask," he said, "whether such acts of popular justice can or cannot be organized in the form of a court. Now my hypothesis is not so much that the court is the natural expression of popular justice, but rather that its historical function is to ensnare it, to control it and to strangle it, by reinscribing it within institutions which are typical of a state apparatus." He went on to speak of the massacres of September 1792:

The September executions were at one and the same time an act of war against internal enemies, a political act against the manipulations of those in power and an act of vengeance against the oppressive classes. Was this not—during a period of violent revolutionary struggle—at least an approximation to an act of popular justice; a response to oppression, strategically effective and politically necessary? Now, no sooner had the executions started in September, when men from the Paris Commune—or from that quarter—intervened and set about staging a court: judges behind a table, representing a third party standing between the people who were "screaming for vengeance," and the accused who were either "guilty" or "innocent"; an investigation to establish the "truth" or to obtain a "confession"; deliberation in order to find out what was "just"; this form was imposed in an authoritarian manner. Can we not see the embryonic, albeit fragile form of a state apparatus reappearing here? The possibility of class oppression: Is not the setting up of a neutral institution standing between the people and its enemies, capable of establishing the dividing line between the true and the false, the guilty and the innocent, the just and the unjust, is this not a way of resisting popular justice? A way of disarming it in the struggle it is conducting in reality in favor of an arbitration in the realm of the ideal? That is why I am wondering whether the court is not a form of popular justice but rather its first deformation.

Pierre Victor responded:

Yes, but look at examples taken not from the bourgeois revolution but from a proletarian revolution. Take China. The first stage is the ideological revolutionisation of the masses, uprising in the villages, acts of justice by the peasant masses against their enemies: executions of despots, all sorts of reprisals for all the extortions suffered over the centuries, etc. The executions of the enemies of the people spread, and we would all agree in saying that these were acts of popular justice. All this is fine: the peasant has a good eye for what needs to be done and everything goes just fine in the countryside. But a new stage in the process develops, with the formation of a Red Army, and then it is no longer simply a matter of the masses in revolt against their enemies, for now we have the masses, their enemies plus an instrument for the unification of the masses, namely the Red Army. At this point all of the acts of popular justice are supported and disciplined. And it is necessary that there be some legal authority so that the diverse acts of vengeance should be in conformity with law, with a people's law which is now something entirely different from the old system of feudal law. It has to be decided that this particular execution or that particular act of vengeance is not simply a matter of an individual settling of accounts, that is, purely and simply an individual revenge against all the oppressive institutions which had themselves equally been based on egoism. In this case it is true that there is what you call a neutral institution which stands between the masses and their immediate oppressors. Would you argue that at this point in the process a people's court is not only a form of popular justice but is a deformation of people's justice?

Then Foucault:

Are you sure that in this case a "neutral institution" came to intervene between the masses and their oppressors? I do not think so. I would say that, on the contrary, it was the masses themselves which came to act as intermediary between any individual who might become separated from the masses, from the aims of the masses, in order to satisfy an individual desire for vengeance, and some other individual who might well, in fact, be an enemy of the people but whom the former individual might be aiming to get at simply as a personal enemy.

Throughout this forty-page dialogue, Foucault proposed a history of the judicial system and of the physical form of courts. The most striking thing about this text is the profound opposition between the two men's attitudes: Pierre Victor appeared to be a man of order, of organization, of system, whereas Foucault seemed viscerally resistant to institutions and to the ways in which any movement, any uprising, is threatened with lapsing into the institution. Consider Foucault's description of what a court is physically and materially:

Look a bit more closely at the meaning of the spatial arrangement of the court, the arrangement of the people who are part of or before a court. The very least that can be said is that this implies an ideology. What is this arrangement? A table, and behind this table, which distances them from the two litigants, the "third party," that is, the judges. Their position indicates firstly that they are neutral with respect to each litigant, and secondly this implies that their decision is not already arrived at in advance, that it will be made after an aural investigation of the two parties, on the basis of a certain conception of truth and a certain number of ideas concerning what is just and unjust, and thirdly that they have the authority to enforce their decision. This is ultimately the meaning of this simple arrangement. Now this idea that there can be people who are neutral in relation to the two parties, that they can make judgments about them on the basis of ideas of justice which have absolute validity, and that their decisions must be acted upon, I believe that all this is far removed from and quite foreign to the very idea of popular justice. In the case of popular justice, you do not have three elements, you have the masses and their enemies.

In response to Victor's objections, in which he continued to refer to China and the idea of a revolutionary court, Foucault explained his position in the following way:

> In societies such as our own, on the contrary, the judicial apparatus has been an extremely important state apparatus of which the history has always been obscured. People do the history of law, and the history of economy, but the history of the judicial system, of judicial practices—of what has in fact been a penal system, of what have been systems of repression—this is rarely discussed. Now, I believe that the judicial system as a state apparatus has historically been of absolutely fundamental importance . . . There was a particular period when the penal system, of which the function in the Middle Ages had been essentially a fiscal one, became organized around the struggle to stamp out rebellion. Up until this point, the job of putting down popular uprisings had been primarily a military one. From now on it was to become taken on, or rendered unnecessary by a complex system of courts/police/prison . . . This is why the revolution can only take place via the radical elimination of the judicial apparatus and anything which could reintroduce the penal apparatus, anything which could reintroduce its ideology, and enable this ideology to surreptitiously creep back into popular practices must be banished.

This dialogue goes a long way toward describing the political and ideological horizon of the left wing in France at the beginning of the 1970s. It is equally evident from it that Foucault was far from totally adhering to the political thought of the group with which he was allied. For example:

Foucault: When you say that this happens under the leadership of the ideology of the proletariat, then I want to ask you what you mean by ideology of the proletariat.

Victor: I mean by that the thought of Mao Tse-tung.

Foucault: Fine. But you will grant me that what is thought by the mass of the French proletariat is not the thought of Mao Tse-tung, and it is not necessarily a revolutionary ideology.

Foucault saw courts, in fact, as the reproduction of bourgeois ideology:

> The court implies, therefore, that there are categories which are common to the parties present (penal categories such as theft, fraud; moral categories such as honesty and dishonesty) and that the parties to the dispute agree to submit to them. Now, it is all this that the bourgeoisie wants to have believed in relation to justice, to its justice. All these ideas are weapons which the bourgeoisie has put to use in its exercise of power. This is why I find the idea of a people's court difficult to accept, especially if intellectuals must play the roles of prosecutor or judge in it, because it is precisely the intellectuals who have been the intermediaries in the bourgeoisie's spreading and imposing of the ideological themes that I'm talking about.

Then, when Pierre Victor summed up the discussion in words such as these: "At the first stage of the ideological revolution, I'm in favor of looting, I'm in favor of 'excesses.' The stick must be bent in the other direction, and the world cannot be turned upside down without breaking eggs," Foucault made the plain and simple objection: "Above all, it is essential that the stick be broken."[6]

In an interview published in 1973 Sartre commented upon Foucault's position concerning popular justice. Seven years after accusing the "structuralist" Foucault of being the last rampart of the bourgeoisie, Sartre disputed the theses of a Foucault who seemed to have gone too far to the left. Foucault's point of view led him to "conceive of popular justice as simple acts of violence when and where they are produced." Then he added:

> We do not agree, the Maos and I on one side, with him on the other. We consider that the people are perfectly capable of creating a court of justice . . . Foucault is the one who is radical. Any form of bourgeois or feudal justice assumes there is a tribunal, a court, with judges who are behind a table; consequently they are done away with. Justice implies first a huge movement that overturns institutions. But if, in the course of this great movement, the form of revolutionary justice appears, that is, if people are asked in the name of justice what prejudices they have been subjected to, I can't see that whether people are sitting behind a table or not causes any harm.[7]

Given the context and Foucault's preoccupations, it is not surprising that he became closely involved in an event that took place two months after his discussion with Pierre Victor and went on to monopolize the front page throughout 1972: the Bruay-en-Artois affair. In a small mining town in the north of France a sixteen-year-old girl had been murdered one night in a vacant lot. The judge in charge of investigation turned his suspicions toward a prominent person in the town, the lawyer in charge of real estate transactions for the Compagnie des Houillères. Consequently, he charged Pierre Leroy with the murder and sent him to jail. When the public prosecutor asked that the accused be released on bail, this "minor judge" refused the request of his superiors, and the whole workers' population of the town supported his resistance to the will of a "class justice." Judge Henri Pascal was accused of ignoring the requirement that ongoing investigations be kept secret and was removed from the case on July 20, 1972, by a final court of appeal.[8]

The Maoists, of course, had latched onto the affair well before this date. As early as May 4, a Truth and Justice Committee had been formed to denounce the "class evidence fabricated by the bourgeoisie," as the mimeographed newspaper *Le Pirate*, published by militants and journalists, described it. The committee organized demonstrations, marches, meetings, a hunger strike. Tracts written by Maoist militants in the north set the tone: "A worker's daughter, peacefully on her way to visit her grandmother, was cut to pieces. It is an act of cannibalism. No matter what verdict bourgeois justice hands down, Leroy will have to submit to that of popular justice." On May 1 *La Cause du peuple* headlined the affair on its cover: "And now they are murdering our children." Inside, this statement appeared: "Only a bourgeois could have done that." This text, signed (but not written) by "angry" residents of Bruay, reported with relish remarks heard in the streets: "He must be made to suffer by degrees" and "I'll tie him up and drag him behind my car at sixty miles an hour."[9] But Sartre, who was editor-in-chief at *La Cause du peuple*, did not want to accept responsibility for remarks like this. In the next issue he put the question: "Lynching or popular justice?" And after assuring readers of his profound adherence to the principles of "class hatred," "a basic feeling aroused by exploitation in anyone who is exploited," he put the situation clearly and firmly, rejecting the possibility of deciding guilt without proof. Sartre wrote "The article should have focused on the legitimate hatred of the people directed at the *lawyer*, as a characteristic class enemy, for his *social* activities, rather than at Leroy, the murderer of little Brigitte, for the reason that it has not yet been proved that he killed her." [10] Sartre's attempts to lead his "comrades" back to reason had no effect. Pierre Victor answered Sartre in a statement signed collectively by La Cause du Peuple, printed next to Sartre's text in the same issue: "It is our turn to ask the question: if Leroy (or his brother) is found out, does the populace have the right to size him bodily? Our answer is yes. To overthrow the authority of the bourgeois class, the humiliated people will be right in establishing a short period of terror and in bodily attacking a handful of detestable and hated individuals. It is difficult to attack the authority of a class without a few heads belonging to members of this class being carried around on the end of a stick." [11] Another issue devoted to Bruay would appear in August 1972, with no change in the journal's perspective on the case. Sartre, however, on the invitation of the Committee for Truth and Justice, went to the scene itself.

Foucault also went. He saw this mobilization of an entire city around problems of justice as an exemplary act of popular will. For the first time the people were politicizing a "trivial event." Political struggle was no longer concerned merely with claims; it now also questioned the entire judicial system.[12] It is very hard to determine exactly how deeply involved Foucault was in the Bruay affair. For example, according to François Ewald, who was teaching at the time at the lycée in Bruay and was one of the leaders of the Committee for Truth and Justice (photographs published in *La Cause du peuple* show him leading marches), Foucault was not connected with the affair at all; he, Foucault simply came to see the unhappily famous vacant lot, like Sartre and Clavel. Philippe Gavi confirmed this version. He saw a great deal of Foucault during this period and remembered Foucault's being extremely critical of the Maoists. Claude Mauriac mentions Foucault's position in his journal, in a conversation dated June 23, 1972. He had expressed surprise at Foucault's radicalism, and the latter replied: "I was there. Just seeing the place is enough—and the hedge, not hawthorns the way they say, but hornbeam, and very tall, cut back right in front of the spot they found the body." Mauriac objected that the issue was not one of determining whether the lawyer and his girlfriend were guilty ("it is possible that he, or she, or they are," he said), but rather of condemning the outside intervention that decided they were guilty without any proof. Foucault replied: "Without this intervention Leroy would have been released. Judge Pascal would have had to succumb to pressure from the public prosecutor. For the first time the northern bourgeoisie has ceased to be as sheltered as it has always been. That is why what happened at Bruay-en-Artois was so important." [13]

Mauriac also reports a much later conversation with Foucault about Bruay, in February 1976. Mauriac began:

"So, you no longer think the lawyer was guilty."
"No."
"But you do remember the conclusion you came to after visiting the place."
"Yes, and I immediately constructed a whole theory around it . . ." [14]

This exchange occurred during a discussion about François Ewald, who had left Bruay in 1975 and come to Foucault to work under him at the university, studying the Bruay affair. From then on he was one of the principal participants in Foucault's seminar. Today Ewald is head of the informal circle that calls itself the "Centre Foucault," established in 1987.

We may conclude, therefore, that although he was long persuaded of the lawyer's guilt, and although he followed the Bruay affair with close interest, Foucault, like Sartre, felt little sympathy for the articles published in *La Cause du peuple*. In fact he emphasized this point during preparations to launch the paper *Libération*. At a meeting one of the participants had said that their project was to write articles "under the control of the people." Foucault questioned the meaning of "control" and cited the articles on Bruay in *La Cause du peuple* as a counter-example. When people are being questioned they must be told honestly how the article will finally be written, he said. They have to know that they will be listened to with the intention of reproducing their words exactly: "everybody must know that he participates in the writing just by speaking, whereas at *La Cause du peuple* one has the impression that the editors reserve their rights to triage. But I say no to this." [15]

Why dwell at such length on the Bruay affair? Because according to witnesses, the dissensions that it created led to the end of a certain form of ultra-leftism. That is how Serge July sees it today. He was one of the Maoist militants most involved in the battle of Bruay, and he wrote one of the controversial articles in *La Cause du peuple*.

During the Jaubert affair, in June 1971, Foucault had set up an investigative commission that included Claude Mauriac. There was a vast mobilization of journalists to defend the rights of their profession. Some of them—Evelyne Le Garrec, Claude-Marie Vadrot, Jean-Claude Vernier—decided to establish a news agency, to be called Agence de Presse—Libération (which quickly became known as APL), and they asked Maurice Clavel to be its managing director. Clavel, like Mauriac, was a former Gaullist who joined the leftist movement after 1968. He had contributed to the review *La Liberté de l'esprit* in the postwar years, when Marxism-Stalinism reigned in intellectual circles. During this period, while Mauriac assailed the intellectuals of the left, "who bank on their reputations to indulge themselves in bad faith and stupidity," [16] in addition to articles Clavel wrote novels and plays. He also taught philosophy in the secondary schools until his lack of seriousness led the inspector general, Canguilhem, to have him dismissed. Clavel then made his way as best he could, finding refuge with an old friend from *khâgne* who was a technical counselor to General de Gaulle. In 1966, however, he broke with de Gaulle over the Ben Barka affair, joined the staff of *Le Nouvel Observateur* and soon became one of its star columnists. When *Les Mots et les choses* was published that year, he praised Foucault's work to the skies. In the aftermath of 1968, Clavel made a short leftist film for the television program "A armes égales" (Equally armed), broadcast on December 13, 1971. After the showing of the film he was to take part in a face-to-face discussion with Jean Royer, the ultraconservative deputy mayor of Tours. In the film itself, Clavel spoke of President Pompidou's "aversion" for the Resistance. His phrase had shocked the show's technical directors, who had cut it. Immediately after the film was shown, Clavel stood up on live television before an audience of millions and shouted: "Censors, good night!" He then left the set, causing quite a furor in the press for the next few days.

The objective of the APL was to collect and disseminate news about the struggles and movements, to circulate photographs and communiqués that other agencies usually prevented from getting into the newspapers. Foucault was connected with the APL from the outset. Along with Clavel and Sartre, for example, he wanted to launch an investigation into the death of Pierre Overney, a Maoist militant killed on February 25, 1972, in front of the Renault factories at Billancourt. But tensions at the time were so high that it was impossible even to talk with the workers.

The APL very quickly linked up with another project. The Maoists associated with La Cause du Peuple knew that they were too isolated and had to find alternative strategies to sectarianism and violence. The project they developed at the end of 1972 was both very simple and very ambitious: to launch a popular daily newspaper that would cover the struggles without being a mere mouthpiece of any one political current. Sartre, despite his poor health, agreed to be its director and was closely involved in the long and difficult gestation of what would become one of the major French dailies.[17] Sartre even agreed to be interviewed on Jacques Chancel's "Radioscopie" on February 7, 1973. He had not spoken on a state-owned radio station since the Manifesto of 121, in 1960, when leading intellectuals had called on soldiers to desert the French army during the Algerian War. But to publicize the paper's inception he was willing to play the game of questions and answers about his life and work for an hour—all the time pushing to talk about *Libération*.

Its founding manifesto proclaimed the newspaper as "an ambush in the jungle of information," a daily that finally would give "voice to the people." In the last months of 1972 and at the beginning of 1973, meetings were held on Rue de Bretagne, in the third arrondissement, to discuss what form would be given to a journalism that had yet to be invented. The Maoists were represented by Pierre Victor and Serge July. Philippe Gavi represented an opening up toward non-Maoist currents. And there was a group of intellectuals: Sartre, Mauriac, Foucault, and Alexandre Astruc. These intellectuals were not content merely to provide money; they also wanted to have some real part in the newspaper's development. Foucault, for example, proposed establishing "Libération committees" all over France. These committees would not only distribute the paper but also gather information and put it together, thus playing the role of a public writer. Above all, as he saw it, the much-touted "popular control" had to exert itself through marginal groups such as movements of delinquents, homosexuals, and women.

Foucault would also have liked to undertake a "Chronicle of the Workers' Memory." In one of the earliest issues—numbered 00[18]—in an interview with a worker from the Renault plant named José, he explained why he wanted to develop this column into a sort of regular series in the paper. "Workers have in their heads," he said, "fundamental experiences, the results of great struggles: the Popular Front, the Resistance. But the newspapers, books, and unions keep only what suits them, when they don't just forget about it altogether. Because of all this forgetting, it is impossible to profit from the knowledge and experience of the working class. It would be interesting to use the newspaper to collect all these memories, to recount them, and above all to make them the basis for defining potential instruments of struggle." [19] The series could go all the way back through the nineteenth century or even further, and thus reconstitute the history of popular struggles.

In a later interview with this Portuguese worker at Renault, Foucault was introduced as a "militant and professor at the Collège de France." Part of their discussion went as follows:

José: What an intellectual who works for the people can do is to reflect the light coming from those who are exploited and make it brighter. He acts as a mirror.

Foucault: "I wonder if you are not somewhat exaggerating the role of intellectuals. We are in agreement that workers have no need of intellectuals to know what it is they do. They know this perfectly well themselves. An intellectual, for me, is a guy hooked into the system of information rather than into the system of production. He is able to make himself heard. He can write in papers, give his point of view. He is also hooked into a former system of information. He has the knowledge, obtained from reading a certain number of books, that other people do not have directly available to them. His role, consequently, is not to form the workers' consciousness, since that already exists, but to allow this consciousness, this workers' knowledge, to enter the information system and be circulated. This will help other workers, and other people who are not workers, to become aware of what is happening. I agree with you when you speak of a mirror, if one takes the mirror to be a means of transmission . . . We can say this: the intellectual's knowledge is always partial in relation to the worker's knowledge. What we know about the history of French society is entirely partial in relation to all the vast experience that the working class has.[20]

Foucault had no desire to be merely a prestigious "patron" of the paper. Nor was he content with providing an article from time to time. He wanted to take an active part, reporting, attending meetings, participating in decisions. He quickly realized that this level of journalistic involvement could occur only if he was there every day. And obviously it was impossible for him to spend all his time in the editorial offices, as anyone responsible for publishing a newspaper must. Moreover, the founding journalists were not eager for the intellectuals to involve themselves so directly. So Foucault's contributions to *Libération* never went beyond the stage of preliminary proclamations. Aside from one or two articles, among them the anonymous text on illegalism that earned him a violent response from Serge Livrozet in 1974, he did not write for the paper. Moreover, existence at *Libération* was far from reposeful. As Maurice Clavel described it later: "I remember I played a modest part in the creation of a left-wing newspaper, *Libération*, with a united, courageous, and enthusiastic group of Marxists. They soon stopped being so fond of one another. At the end of a few months, had they had political power, they would have exterminated each other."[21] From 1975 to 1980 Foucault was far more likely to express himself in *Le Nouvel Observateur*; then he began contributing to *Libération* regularly again. In several conversations with Mauriac in 1975 and 1976, Foucault expressed sadness at seeing the paper lie every day, distorting facts as much as the most avid right-wing paper. It was during this period that a particular theme emerged in Foucault's remarks about politics: if one wants to be credible and effective, one must first know, and above all *speak*, the truth. Speaking-the-truth, *véridiction*, had to be the founding principle of any journalism of intervention.

Foucault maintained rather close ties with Maurice Clavel. When Clavel organized a television broadcast from his house in Vézelay in 1976, he asked Foucault to take part in it. Foucault accepted, along with Christian Jambet, Guy Lardreau, and André Glucksmann. A wide political swing had taken place. Leftism was dead and the former Maoists were pondering the subject of God or the nature of totalitarianism. But ties created during the leftist era, in the Maoist groups among others, would continue to function just as the ties formed by the Stalinists in the postwar years functioned and still continue to function, after their swing to the right: a whole network of friendships, mutual assistance, and appointments.

Clavel was utterly fascinated by Foucault. He talked about him endlessly. He devoted twenty or thirty pages to Foucault in his book *Ce que je crois*, published in 1975. In it he quoted a letter from Foucault in April 1968, thanking him for having understood so well what he was trying to do in *Les Mots et les choses*, and for having analyzed his theoretical work so well.[22] Clavel confessed to his obsession in an article he wrote in 1976, when *La Volonté de savoir* came out. "My monomania with regard to Michel Foucault is well known. I consider him to be Kant, the man, 'after whom it is impossible to think as before.' And more than that, I think I have shown that Kant fell back asleep, whereas

Foucault has never stopped sharpening our waking state, keeping us awake with ever-increasing jolts."[23] When Clavel died in 1979, Foucault wrote an emotional tribute to this companion in the struggles. In a short article in *Le Nouvel Observateur*, he compared Clavel to Maurice Blanchot—the highest praise: "Blanchot: diaphanous, motionless, waiting for a day more transparent than day, attentive to signs that leave a trace only in the movement erasing them. Clavel: impatient, jumping at the slightest noise, shouting into the twilight, calling the storm. These men—how can one conceive of two more different?—introduced into this bearingless world in which we live, the only tension that does not make us laugh or blush afterward: the tension breaking the thread of time." He concluded: "He was at the heart of what was undoubtedly most important in our era. By this I mean a vast and very profound change in the consciousness of history and of time as it had gradually been formed by the West. Everything organizing this consciousness, everything providing continuity for it, everything promising that it would reach completion, tore apart. There are those who would like to sew it back together. But Clavel told us that we must, today, this very day, live time differently. Today above all."[24]

❧

"WHAT HAVE WE DONE? Good God, what have we done?" In 1971 Georges Dumézil had a phone call from a professor at the Collège de France to say how appalled he was. He had played a large part in getting Foucault elected and was distinctly disconcerted to see what this newly elected member was up to. It was in all the papers: Foucault side by side with Sartre and the leftists; Foucault heading a march of immigrants; Foucault at the gates of prisons. "What have we done?" cried the professor, perhaps testing the opinion of this man considered by everyone to be a moral and scientific authority. Dumézil exerted himself to reassure his colleague: "We did very well," he answered. He was far from sharing Foucault's political ideas. He simply did not take his protégé's "excesses" to be such a tragedy. It might even be said that he did not take them seriously. As far as he was concerned this was one of those comedies that everyone acts out for himself or for other people. And then, he was more than seventy, and did not want to call such a deep friendship into question over political ideas. He had got beyond that a long time ago. When Foucault came to visit him they avoided the subject. At the very most Dumézil joked with him from time to time: "But what in the world were you up to at the gates of a prison?"

But nothing that would jeopardize the profound, essential agreement the two men had formed fifteen years earlier at Uppsala.

History has shown that Dumézil was right. Not only was Michel Foucault a very great teacher, but, above all, he participated in the life of the institution as much as any of his colleagues. "There were two Foucaults," says Emmanuel Le Roy Ladurie today, "the one who demonstrated and the one who attended the meetings of the Collège. Foucault took his academic role very seriously." Foucault played the academic game to the end, merely trying from time to time to persuade the institution to make some small departure, as when he suggested Pierre Boulez as a candidate. He took part in discussions, gave his views about the applicants who might be elected to the Collège. He knew how to eliminate candidates whom he absolutely did not want and how to mobilize support for the ones who would have his vote.

Foucault gave his course at the Collège on Wednesday. From 1970–71 through 1974–75 he lectured on the following topics in succession, one each year: "the will to knowledge," "penal theories and institutions," "punitive society," "psychiatric power," and "abnormality." In 1975–76, in a course suggestively titled "'society must be defended,'" he discussed the use of war models in political thought. In 1977–78, after a year's hiatus, an analysis of "population management" in a course called "security, territory, populations." From this point on, his research followed the direction laid out by *Histoire de la sexualité*, going ever further back in time. The final year that he taught, 1983–84, he tackled the relation of "truth-speaking" (*parrhesia*) to "self-concern" in ancient Greece.

Foucault also was responsible for a seminar hour on Mondays. He announced during his lecture that he expected to admit only those who in fact did the work. But at each session he found more than a hundred people before him. He tried hard to set a stricter limit on those entitled to be present, but he was called to order by the Collège administration. The establishment was founded on a single principle: instruction had to be open to everyone. Foucault resorted to ploys: in November he gathered a small group of students and scholars in his office and assigned each of them a report to prepare for January, when the lectures and seminar would begin. He ended up by combining the two and teaching for two hours on Wednesday morning. Some years he also met—sometimes in his office, sometimes in a café—with the small group of people with whom he wanted to conduct collective research. The membership of this little "Foucauldian tribe," like that of a royal court, varied considerably. Along the way, rivalry and contests for rank and precedence brought conflicts and arguments, which sometimes led to noisy breakups. Foucault was not unaware of the situation, and sometimes it bothered him. He talked about it with some of his friends. And he dealt with it explicitly in a letter in which he pondered the role played by one person or another, wondering in substance: what happens among them when I am not there?

At the end of each year Foucault wrote, as was required, a summary of his course for the Collège's *Annuaire*. In some years he mentioned the people who gave reports in the seminar and their subjects, but these lists are by no means exhaustive; and in some years there is no mention of anyone at all. In 1970–71 the seminar was on "penalty" in nineteenth-century France. In 1971–72 it was on the "case" of Pierre Rivière, and Foucault mentioned that Robert Castel, Jean-Pierre Peter, Gilles Deleuze, Alexandre Fontana, Philippe Riot, and Maryvonne Saison took part in the project. In 1972–73 the seminar prepared a volume consisting of material collected on Pierre Rivière. Foucault gave no names, but by referring to the list compiled in this volume one may add the following as participants: Blandine Barret-Kriegel, Patricia Moulin, Jeanne Favret, Gilbert Burlet-Torvic, and Georgette Legée. Deleuze did not work on this book. In 1973–74 the seminar was on two subjects: "medicolegal expertise in psychiatric matters" and "the history of hospital institutions and architecture in the eighteenth century." The latter led to another collective publication, *Les Machines à guérir* (Healing machines), in 1976, with contributions by Michel Foucault, Blandine Barret-Kriegel, Anne Thalamy, François Béguin, and Bruno Fortier.[25] In 1974–75 the seminar topic was medico-psychiatric expertise, in 1975–76 the notion of the "dangerous individual" in criminal psychiatry. In 1977–78 the seminar analyzed "everything that leads to increasing state power," and "principally, the maintaining of order, discipline, rules." Talks were presented by Pasquale Pasquino, Anne-Marie Moulin, François Delaporte, and François Ewald. The 1978–79 year was spent on legal thought at the end of the nineteenth century. Talks were given by François Ewald, Catherine Mevel, Eliane Allo, Nathalie Coppinger, Pasquale Pasquino, François Delaporte, and Anne-Marie Moulin. In 1979–80 the seminar was devoted to certain aspects of liberal thought in the nineteenth century, with talks given by Nathalie Coppinger, Didier Deleule, Pierre Rosanvallon, François Ewald, Pasquale Pasquino, A. Schutz, and Catherine Mevel.[26]

According to the administration of the Collège de France, "Michel

Foucault never had *stricto sensu* an 'appointed assistant.' Two researchers were successively put at his disposal to serve this function: from 1977 to 1980, François Ewald, who came from secondary school instruction and continued to work for Michel Foucault after he had left again for the CNRS; then, until 1983, Eliane Allo, who was one of the group of assistants at the Collège de France."

Foucault liked working in a team. Collective research was one of the most attractive aspects of the American university system for him—the possibility it offered for setting up seminars the way he liked them. He mentioned this frequently to Paul Rabinow.

◆

FOUCAULT KEPT A NUMBER OF FRIENDSHIPS that had been formed during this period of left-wing activity. But one of his oldest and certainly one of his truest friendships did not survive the political reorientations following 1975. There was never an actual rupture between Foucault and Deleuze; they simply stopped seeing each other. Foucault now kept at a distance the relationship that had been so important to him since 1962.

This friendship was born at Clermont-Ferrand, in the shadow of Nietzsche. It developed, continued, and, as the years went by, showed itself for all to see in a series of intersecting articles in which the two philosophers alternately praised each other's publications. Deleuze enthusiastically reviewed *Raymond Roussel* in 1963 and *Les Mots et les choses* in 1966.[27] In 1970 he wrote at even greater length on *L'Archéologie du savoir*, in an article whose title is now famous: "Un nouvel archiviste"; and in 1975 he reviewed *Surveiller et punir*.[28]

Foucault participated in this repartee with a review of *Différence et répétition* in 1969,[29] and in 1970 with a longer commentary on both *Logique du sens* and *Différence et répétition*. This article, titled "Theatrum philosophicum," begins: "I must discuss two books of exceptional merit and importance . . . Indeed these books are so outstanding that they are difficult to discuss; this may explain, as well, why so few have undertaken this task. I believe that these works will continue to revolve about us in enigmatic resonance with those of Klossowski, another major and excessive sign, and perhaps one day, this century will be known as Deleuzian."[30]

Foucault–Deleuze: a philosophical friendship. And a political friendship. In 1971, when Foucault created the GIP, Deleuze was one of the first to join. He served on the investigative commission on the Jaubert affair and was active on the Djellali committee. A long dialogue on the relation between intellectuals and power, published in *L'Arc* in 1972, shows the depth of their agreement. In it Foucault and Deleuze defined the new relationship of intellectuals to what the preceding generation had called "engagement." Henceforth it would no longer be relevant to "totalize" struggles, to create a theory about them, to say what their significance was. To the Sartre-style "total intellectual" they opposed a "specific intellectual"—one who would wage his battles only on precise points, and in well-defined places. These local struggles would not, however, be any the less "radical," according to Foucault. They would be "uncompromising" struggles, "not reformism, not trying merely to adjust the same power, changing, at most, the incumbents. And these movements have a connection to the revolutionary movement of the proletariat itself insofar as it must combat all the controls and constraints that everywhere provide a new version of the same power." What produced the unity and universality of these partial struggles, Foucault added, was "the system of power itself, all forms of the exercise and application of power." Deleuze responded: "One cannot touch anything at any point in practice without coming up against this diffuse ensemble. Consequently, blowing up the whole thing, on the basis of even the slightest protest, comes to be desirable. In this manner, every partial revolutionary defense or attack becomes part of the workers' struggle." [31]

By 1977 the political landscape had changed, and the two speakers in this dialogue no longer shared the same vocabulary. The books Foucault published during this time, particularly *Surveiller et punir*, seemed concerned with some of the same themes. But a book is the expression of what an author was thinking at the time he conceived and wrote it; there is a built-in delay between research and publication. This time lag may explain the "crisis" that Foucault underwent in 1976 and 1977, after the publication of *La Volonté de savoir*. And possibly this crisis accounts for the distance that arose then between him and Deleuze. For they ceased to associate with each other.

But the real reason is probably more political. In 1977 Deleuze and Foucault protested against the extradition of Klaus Croissant, the lawyer of the "Baader-Meinhof band," who risked being sentenced in Germany for having overstepped the prerogatives of a defense attorney by materially aiding the accused. He had requested asylum in France but was about to be extradited when Foucault spoke out. In a November 14 article in *Le Nouvel Observateur* he wrote: "There exists the right to a lawyer who speaks for you, with you, who allows you to be heard and to preserve your life, your identity, and the force of your refusal . . . This right is not a legal abstraction or a dreamer's ideal; this right is part of our historical reality and must not be erased from it." When Klaus Croissant was taken from his cell to be expelled from the country, Foucault was in front of the Santé prison with a few dozen others to bar the way symbolically. The police forcibly dispersed the crowd, and Foucault suffered a fractured rib. A few days later, again in *Le Nouvel Observateur*, he energetically addressed the leaders of the left and demanded that they take stronger positions, specifically, that they defend the two women being prosecuted for having "hidden" Croissant before his arrest in Paris.[32] When the minister of justice, Alain Peyrefitte, attempted to respond to his former schoolmate at the Ecole Normale, Foucault replied in the harshest terms.[33] After the extradition, Foucault, along with several other well-known personalities, including Sartre, Beauvoir, and Marguerite Duras, called for a demonstration on November 18 at the Place de la République.

It is perfectly clear that Foucault was going all out in his support for the German lawyer. He was truly engaged. But he wanted to limit his fight to a strictly legal problem. He was willing to support the lawyer, but not his clients. He had no intention of supporting people he considered to be "terrorists." And that is precisely what he seemed to reproach Deleuze for doing. Deleuze was also active in the defense of Klaus Croissant; but the two philosophers signed different texts. Foucault's protest was limited to the rights of defense and the refusal of extradition. The one signed by Deleuze and Felix Guattari represented West Germany as a country moving toward a police dictatorship. This, no doubt, was the crux of the "quarrel" between Foucault and Deleuze—or, more exactly, Foucault's quarrel with Deleuze. Because there was no explosion, no dispute, no explanation. Their longtime close association simply came apart.

A passage in Claude Mauriac's journal confirms this interpretation. On March 10, 1984, Mauriac and Foucault were trying to intervene in behalf of immigrant workers expelled from their lodgings in the Goutte d'Or. They were wondering whom they could get to sign the letter they were sending to the mayor of Paris: "X would be good," said Foucault. But no, he couldn't ask him. Mauriac expressed surprise, and Foucault replied: "We don't see each other anymore . . . Ever since Klaus Croissant. I couldn't accept terrorism and blood. I did not approve of Baader and his gang."[34] Mauriac, who always names names, this time preferred not to name the person Foucault was talking about. But "X" was obviously Gilles Deleuze.

Starting at the end of 1977 and the beginning of 1978, Foucault and Deleuze no longer saw each other. Their paths separated. Each continued to read the other's books and articles, but from then on this was their only contact.

Foucault had a very strange misadventure in Germany one month after Croissant was extradited. In December 1977 he was in Berlin with Daniel Defert. Trying to go to East Berlin, they were confronted by police who dug through their papers, photocopied their notes, and demanded that they explain why they mentioned certain books in their notebooks. It made a "frightening impression" on them, as Foucault described it. Two days later, in West Berlin this time, three police cars stopped in front of them as they were leaving their hotel. They were surrounded by police armed with machine guns, told to put their hands up, and searched. They had made the mistake at breakfast of mentioning a book about Ulrike Meinhof, and someone had denounced them. They were then taken to the police station for verification of their identity. We didn't do anything, said Foucault in *Der Spiegel*. We just looked like intellectuals, and therefore like potential suspects. Intellectuals: those people whom all powers considered to be "a filthy species."[35]

In late January 1978 Foucault was marching through the icy streets of Hannover in defense of Peter Bruckner, a professor summarily fired from the university for having defended a banned book. (Foucault later wrote a preface to the French edition of Bruckner's pamphlet, *Ennemi de l'Etat*.)[36] This time, however, he found a more agreeable Germany than the one of "professional interdictions" encountered so recently. He had come with Catherine Von Bülow to participate in the big TUNIX (meaning *ne fais rien*—"don't do anything") meeting in West Berlin. For three days, thirty thousand people enthusiastically debated all the possibilities for struggle that were opening up for "alternative" movements.

The different assessments by Deleuze and Foucault of the Croissant affair were only an expression of their radically divergent evolution on political questions in general. Their opposition became absolutely clear during a quarrel about the "new philosophers." Deleuze had taken Glucksmann and his fellows apart in a pamphlet in which he demolished the empty and hollow concepts of those whom he considered to be TV buffoons. He proclaimed his "horror" at their recantations, their "martyrology." "They are living on corpses," he said. His whole text teemed with similar expressions. These harsh words were published on June 5, 1977.[37] Deleuze was quite aware that a month earlier Foucault had praised Glucksmann's book *Les Maîtres-Penseurs* in the columns of *Le Nouvel Observateur*. Glucksmann, a former ultra-Maoist, had spectacularly reversed himself in 1974. From then on he systematically denounced gulags, forms of totalitarianism, and the philosophies leading in this direction. Foucault thanked him for finding a place in philosophical discourse where "these runaways, these victims, these indomitable ones, these dissidents still standing tall—in short, these 'bloody heads' and other white forms whom Hegel wanted to erase from the world's darkness" could be heard.[38]

There is no doubt at all that at this time Foucault's choice had been dictated more by political considerations than by philosophical ones. In the years that followed he frequently spoke of Deleuze to his friends, particularly to Paul Veyne. He often said that Deleuze was "the only philosophical mind" in France. And one of his fondest desires, shortly before his death, was to be reconciled with Deleuze. Daniel Defert knew this and asked Deleuze to speak at Foucault's funeral. Deleuze must also have hoped for reconciliation. He devoted a magnificent book to Foucault, one vibrant with intelligence and feeling. Why this book? "Out of my own necessity," replied Deleuze. "Out of admiration for him, out of emotion over his death, over this interrupted work."[39]

18

~~~

"We Are All Ruled"

September 22, 1975. In the bar of a large hotel in Madrid, Yves Montand read a statement:

Eleven men and women have just been condemned to death. They were given their sentence by special courts and they were denied their right to justice. They were denied the justice that demands proof before sentencing, that provides convicts with the right to defend themselves, that guarantees them the protection of law no matter how serious the accusation, that forbids ill-treatment of prisoners. In Europe we have always fought for this justice. We must still fight for it today each time it is threatened. We do not wish to claim innocence for these people; this is not within our power. We do not ask for belated leniency; past actions of the Spanish regime make such patience impossible. But we ask that the fundamental rules of justice be respected for men in Spain just as they are for those in other places.

The celebrated actor was joined by Régis Debray, Constantin Costa-Gavras, Jean Lacouture, the Reverend Father Laudouze (representing Témoignage Chrétien), Claude Mauriac, and Michel Foucault. Foucault had written the text.

A few days earlier, Catherine Von Bülow had telephoned: "Something must be done. We cannot allow the Franco dictatorship to execute these young militants." Foucault agreed: "Something must be done." But what? First they had to think—fast. A meeting was set for the next morning at Von Bülow's. Claude Mauriac, Jean Daniel, Father Laudouze, Régis Debray, and Costa-Gavras took part. The filmmaker suggested that they go to Spain, witnessing with their actual physical presence a solidarity that petitions, manifestos, and demonstrations did not express strongly enough. "Foucault was immediately seduced by this slightly crazy notion, and he quickly convinced me," said

Claude Mauriac. "Yves Montand agreed; he was not there, but he would join us."[1]

On the other hand, Foucault was not particularly enthusiastic about the suggestion made by Debray, Daniel, and Costa-Gavras to hold a press conference. "What is missing," he said, "is some idea that can make our protest more dramatic. Our physical presence in Spain, with all the risks implied (not that great, perhaps, but they do exist), is what is important. It is new, has never been done before. If this is just to end up with a press conference . . ."[2] Foucault preferred the idea of handing out tracts in the street. After a great deal of discussion and hesitation, the various protagonists reached an agreement. There would be a press conference, but they would also circulate a text signed by important individuals. They made a list: Sartre, of course. Aragon. Mauriac was charged with asking André Malraux. Von Bülow mentioned Simone de Beauvoir, drawing an angry outburst from Foucault. She smiles about it today, but it astonished her at the time. "Ah, no! Not that woman!" He was still sour about the attacks of Sylvie Le Bon, a close friend of the novelist, in *Les Temps modernes* in 1967.

Mauriac obtained Malraux's signature, and Foucault got Aragon's. There were, in the end, five names on the appeal: André Malraux, Pierre Mendès France, Louis Aragon, Jean-Paul Sartre, and François Jacob. And there were seven who would take the message to the Spanish people. Jean Daniel supported the protest, which required delicate organization from Paris, with all the logistic apparatus of *L'Observateur*. But he could not join the group—it was impossible for him to be free on a Monday, because it was the day they "put the paper to bed." Instead, Lacouture went along to report on this team's fleeting visit to a country where fascism was in its death throes but still murderous. They could stay only seven hours, but even that was no mean feat. They did not hope to save those condemned to death. But they wanted to express their indignation in the Spanish capital.

At the airport, just as they were getting on the plane, Foucault told Mauriac and his wife, Marie-Claude, who was accompanying them: "I admired André Malraux so much when I was a student that I knew pages and pages of his book by heart."

They arrived in Madrid without incident. The press conference began, and Montand had time to read the French text to the journalists. "We have come to Madrid," he concluded, "to bring this message. We were called by the gravity of these matters. Our presence is intended to show that we are shaken by an indignation that brings us, and many others, into solidarity with these threatened lives." When it was time for Debray to speak, reading the Spanish translation, plainclothes policemen burst into the room and ordered them to remain seated, not to move. Costa-Gavras served as interpreter. Foucault asked: "Are we under arrest?" The police replied: "No, but everyone must stay seated." Foucault had kept several copies of the appeal and refused to turn them over to a policeman who tried to take them. There was a brief confrontation between the rebellious philosopher and the representative of law and order. One of Foucault's thousand faces: "Pale, tense, trembling," in Mauriac's account; "ready to leap, to spring, go on the attack, the most useless, the most dangerous, and the finest attack, and all the more admirable in his refusal, his aggressiveness, and his bravery because one felt (one knew) that for him it was both a physical reaction and a moral principle: the bodily impossibility of being subjected to the contact of a police officer and taking an order from him."[3] A few days later Foucault commented on the incident in *Libération:* "I consider that it is the cop's job to use physical force. Anyone who opposes cops must not, therefore, let them maintain the hypocrisy of disguising this force behind orders that have to be immediately obeyed. They must carry out what they represent, see it through to the end."[4] Foucault gave in only after Mauriac urgently intervened. Violence had not made him lose his sense of humor; he whispered: "If there had been a machine gun I would have given in sooner, of course."[5] Foucault's physical bravery was also among Montand's strongest memories of this Spanish expedition. This trait appears again and again, in every account of Foucault's militant action—his force of refusal, his will to rebel against the repressive act, against police action; against "discipline."

Minutes later a squad of uniformed police, armed with machine guns, arrested all the journalists present, mostly foreigners. They were taken away in handcuffs. Some were released two hours later, the others at nightfall.[6] The seven French "mercenaries," as the pro-Franco newspaper *Arriba* called them, were led away, but minus the handcuffs. Foucault described the scene in *Libération:*

> Yves Montand was the last one out. He came to the top of the hotel steps, where armed police lined both sides of the staircase. Below, the police had emptied the square, and their buses were some distance away. Behind the buses were several hundred people watching the scene. It was like a repetition of the scene in *Z* in which Lambrakis, the left-wing deputy, is clubbed down. Montand, very dignified, his head thrown back a little, came down very slowly. At that moment we

really felt the presence of fascism. The way people have of looking, without seeing, as if they had witnessed this scene hundreds of times. And at the same time, this sadness . . . And this silence.[7]

The message bearers were taken back to the airport, and, after a thorough search, interminably long, they were once again on a plane, departing for Paris. Suddenly there was an incident. One of the police insulted Father Laudouze in Spanish. And Costa-Gavras shouted in reply: "Abajo fascismo, abajo Franco!" The policeman dashed toward him and ordered the filmmaker to follow him. Costa-Gavras refused. The plane was unable to take off. The waiting began again. Finally things worked out, the airplane taxied onto the runway, then took off for Paris, where dozens of journalists and photographers awaited.

A few days later, with the executions apparently imminent, Foucault, Defert, and Mauriac went to demonstrate together in front of the Spanish embassy, on Avenue Georges-V. When a young militant asked Foucault if he would be willing to visit his group and discuss Marx, Foucault lost his temper. "Don't talk to me about Marx any more! I never want to hear anything about that man again. Ask someone whose job it is. Someone paid to do it. Ask the Marxist functionaries. Me, I've had enough of Marx."[8] Admittedly it was not a good moment to make such a request. But this incident reported by Mauriac is far from being a simple anecdote. Marxism was at the heart of plenty of discussions among Parisian intellectuals. Solzhenitsyn's book *The Gulag Archipelago* was published in France in 1974, beginning a vast and unstoppable undermining process. In the mid-1970s French Marxism, omnipresent throughout the preceding thirty years, a conduit for all theoretical or political thought, the era's *horizon indepassable*, was quite simply crumbling away, disappearing from the intellectual scene.

On September 29, when the first executions had taken place, Foucault, Mauriac, and Defert participated (but this time separately) in the huge march that left the Place de la République for the Bastille. At the end of the demonstration, as teargas bombs began to explode, as the CRS began to charge, the former Gaullist Claude Mauriac, former secretary to General de Gaulle, joined thousands of militants from the far left and lifted his fist.

❧

Friendships are made in so many ways. The one now beginning between Foucault and Montand would last until the philosopher's death. And for Foucault, it soon would increase twofold by the addition of another relationship, even more intense, with Simone Signoret. They would meet frequently. They would talk to each other on the telephone a great deal. And more than once their names would be together at the foot of a petition. "My girlfriend," Foucault liked to call her. When he said, "I had lunch with my girlfriend" or "I have to phone my girlfriend," everyone knew he was talking about "la Simone," his other name for her. In 1982 Foucault and Signoret went to Poland with Bernard Kouchner to demonstrate, once again, their solidarity inside an oppressed country.

When Montand speaks today of his friendship with the philosopher, or when he shows the letter Foucault sent Signoret after the recital he gave at the Olympia theater in the fall of 1981, he has a hard time containing his emotion. The letter is warm. In it Foucault thanked them for the terrific evening and took advantage of the occasion to make a real declaration of his friendship. "So many perfections given to simple memories, it is extraordinary and overwhelming! And then," he went on, "there was all the friendship of yesterday: ours has been wonderful. For several years it has been extremely important to me. Starting yesterday, you and Montand have allowed me to love many more things in my past and in my present. My love to you."

From 1975 to 1984, together they would sign many petitions and manifestos. They would plan and organize protests with, among others, Bernard Kouchner, an activist in the organization Médecins du Monde.

Only once does Montand remember there being any disagreement. It came up at the end of the summer of 1983, "the day Glucksmann, Kouchner, and I wrote a text demanding that the French government show more strength against Kadhafi in Chad. Foucault did not want to sign it. And Signoret went along with him. They did not want people to have the impression that they were calling for war."

Yves Montand, Simone Signoret, Michel Foucault: always ready to denounce injustice, always prompt in mobilizing for a cause. When Roger Knobelspiess proclaimed his innocence from the depths of solitary confinement, they were moved to organize the prisoner's defense. He had been sentenced in 1972 to fifteen years in prison for a holdup that he flatly denied—a holdup in which the loot was eight hundred francs. It was something to get stirred up about. Given temporary leave from the prison, he took off, this time committing a series of holdups, to which he confessed and for which he was sentenced in 1981. But Knobelspiess was a rebellious prisoner; he made a lot of noise denouncing the legal system. He was a prisoner doomed to maximum security who wrote books to make his voice heard. One of them, *QHS: quartiers de haute sécurité*, appeared in 1980. It was announced on the first page that it had been published "at the request of a committee for defense made up, among others, of Michel Foucault, Jean Genet, André Glucksmann, Claude Mauriac, Yves Montand, Simone Signoret, and Paul Thibaud, and with the support of the Bar Association of France, the French Democratic Lawyers Association." In his foreword to the book in 1980 Foucault wrote: "This is a harsh document. For ten long years many voices have been raised in debate. There are those who are impatient with this. They would like the institution itself to propose its own reform, while those who are uninitiated remain silent. Luckily this is not how things are. Real, profound changes spring from radical criticisms, from the assertion of refusals, and from steady voices. Knobelspiess' book is part of this battle." Foucault then went on to tear apart the implacable logic of incarceration and solitary confinement. "He was sentenced for a crime that he fiercely denies. Could he get along in prison without acknowledging that he was guilty? But you see how it works. Because he resists, he is sent to maximum security. And if he is in maximum security, he is dangerous. 'Dangerous' in prison, so even more dangerous set free. Consequently, he is capable of having committed the crime of which he is accused. Small matter that he denies it; he could have done it. And the maximum security quarters bring new proofs. Prison demonstrates what the hearing, perhaps, established insufficiently." [9] A second book by Knobelspiess, *L'Acharnement*, had an introduction by Claude Mauriac. When he was sentenced in 1981 for the six holdups of 1976 and 1977 to which he confessed, *Le Monde* described it as an instance of repairing the mistake made by the legal system in 1972. He was sentenced to five years in prison, but the court of assizes asked that he be given a presidential pardon, which François Mitterrand did. When the freed prisoner was suspected in 1983 of having taken part in an attack on an armored van and was again arrested near Honfleur, the right-wing press was very ironic and announced it to be a lesson: where had those who had signed the manifestos, who had defended this bandit, gone? The answer was not long in coming. Signoret and Foucault mounted the battlements. In *Libération*, Foucault wrote:

> What happened? A man was condemned to fifteen years in prison for a holdup. Nine years later the court in Rouen declared that the sentence was clearly out of proportion. Freed, he has just been accused again for other acts. And suddenly the entire press is calling it a mistake, proclaiming that we have been duped and brainwashed. And

whom are they shouting about? About the people who had demanded a more measured justice, against the people who had asserted that prison is not likely to transform a convict. Let's ask a few simple questions. Where was the mistake made? Those who have tried seriously to state the problem about prisons have said it for years: prison was instituted to punish and to improve. Does it punish? Perhaps. Does it improve? Certainly not. There is no rehabilitation, no training, but rather the constitution and reinforcement of a "delinquent milieu." Someone who goes to prison for stealing a few thousand francs is far more likely to come out a gangster than an honest man. Knobelspiess' book showed this very well. The prison inside the prison, the maximum security quarters, was very likely to create furiously angry men. This is what Knobelspiess said, this is what we said, and it ought to be better known. The facts, to the extent that we are able to know them, seem likely to confirm it.

And Foucault had a harsh reply for all those who accused intellectuals of being irresponsible: "As for you, anyone who thinks a crime today is sufficient justification for a punishment yesterday, is incapable of reasoning. But worse, you are a danger to us and to yourselves, assuming that, like us, you do not want to find yourselves under a system of justice benumbed by its arbitrary aspects. You, too, are a historic danger. Because justice always must question itself, just as society can exist only by means of the work it does on itself and on its institutions."[10]

↟

IN THE SPRING OF 1975, *Surveiller et punir* received a tremendous welcome, including a two-page spread in *Le Monde* and a special issue of *Le Magazine littéraire*. Scarcely had the cheers died down when Foucault was back on the proscenium. A year and a half after this masterwork on the "birth of the prison," he published the first volume of *Histoire de la sexualité*. There is a clear relation between the two works, stated from the outset by Foucault: both are about "power" and the ways in which it is exercised. In *Surveiller et punir* he had demonstrated that power traverses society as a whole by means of "disciplinary" procedures that constrain bodies; now he was investigating the "devices" linking sexuality with mechanisms and networks of power.

Histoire de la sexualité originated in the intersection of an earlier project and "current events." In the preface to *Folie et déraison* in 1960, Foucault had announced his intention to produce a work on the subject. He had never stopped thinking about it. There was an echo of it in 1963, in his article on Bataille, "Préface à la transgression." During this period he was still thinking of sexuality in terms of the prohibition and the transgression constituting it. Foucault also discussed this with his friend Gérard Lebrun when he lectured in Brazil in 1965. When he showed the manuscript of *Les Mots et les choses* to Lebrun, he confided that next he would like to write a history of sexuality, adding: "It is almost impossible to do. One would never be able to find the archives." This idea regained all its original vigor in the aftermath of 1968. Ideologies of liberation proliferated, and what Robert Castel terms "psychoanalism"—the invasion of every mode of thought or action by a psychoanalytic vulgate—held sway. The two phenomena had one point in common: uninterrupted talk about sex. Everybody talked about sex, to say how it was frustrated and repressed by bourgeois morality and by the conjugal and familial model. There were some who claimed that Freud had freed us from this morality, at least a little. But so halfheartedly, said others, so prudently, in a way that was so conformist, that one ought also to denounce the normalizing functions of psychoanalysis itself. But everyone, no matter what their skill or what their method, wanted to talk about sex. Sex would unveil man's truth or offer him possibilities of happiness.

Foucault said of this "repression":

> We have found it difficult to speak on the subject without striking a different pose: we are conscious of defying established power, our tone of voice shows that we know we are being subversive, and we ardently conjure away the present and appeal to the future, whose day will be hastened by the contribution we believe we are making. Something that smacks of revolt, of promised freedom, of the coming age of a different law, slips easily into this discourse on sexual oppression. Some of the ancient functions of prophecy are reactivated therein. Tomorrow sex will be good again.[11]

From the very first pages, Foucault explodes this "repressive hypothesis" and all the theoretical and political formulations that thrive in its presence. His intention?

> To examine the case of a society which has been loudly castigating itself for its hypocrisy for more than a century, which speaks verbosely of its own silence, takes great pains to relate in detail the things it does not say, denounces the powers it exercises, and promises to liberate itself from the very laws that have made it function . . . The question I would like to pose is not, Why are we repressed? but rather, Why do we say, with so much passion and so much resentment against our most recent past, against our present, and against

ourselves that we are repressed? By what spiral did we come to affirm that sex is negated? What led us to show, ostentatiously, that sex is something we hide, to say it is something we silence? And we do all this by formulating the matter in the most explicit terms, by trying to reveal it in its most naked reality, by affirming it in the positivity of its power and its effects. It is certainly legitimate to ask why sex was associated with sin for such a long time . . . but we must also ask why we burden ourselves today with so much guilt for having once made sex a sin.[12]

But raising doubts about the "repressive hypothesis" does not mean merely reversing the hypothesis. Once again Foucault's work claims to be historical and critical, archaeological and genealogical: "The object, in short, is to define the regime of power-knowledge-pleasure that sustains the discourse on human sexuality in our part of the world . . . the essential aim will not be to determine whether these discursive productions and these effects of power lead one to formulate the truth about sex, or on the contrary falsehoods designed to conceal that truth, but rather to bring out the 'will to knowledge' that serves as both their support and their instrument."[13]

Foucault, who in *L'Archéologie du savoir* and then in *L'Ordre du discours* had examined principles of rarefying discourses, here reversed his perspective. What interested him now was the injunction to speak and the forms this assumed. He proposed to trace the history of this proliferation, the principles that formed its basis, and their application. Because from the sixteenth century on, the "putting into discourse of sex" has not been a victim of restrictions but rather "subjected to a mechanism of increasing incitement": "the will to knowledge has not come to a halt in the face of a taboo that must not be lifted, but has persisted in constituting . . . a science of sexuality." One is forced to admit: "Ours is, after all, the only civilization in which officials are apt to listen to all and sundry impart the secrets of their sex."[14]

La Volonté de savoir is a short book, scarcely more than two hundred pages, in a small format; but it addresses an impressive number of themes and problems. Foucault brought in the research on heredity that he had mentioned in the pamphlet for his candidacy at the Collège de France. There are also sketchy summaries of his work on liberalism and population management, on "biopolitics." Then there is, of course, the tireless questioning about what separates the normal from the pathological, the evocation of "perversity" subjected to the gaze of psychiatry. The few pages on rights, law, and norms are astonishing. There are shock formulas that elicited thousands of comments: "Power comes from below" is one. Because of all the misunderstandings arising from this phrase, Foucault had to emphasize that it could not be read without the sentences that followed. "Power comes from below; that is, there is no binary and all-encompassing opposition between rulers and ruled at the root of power relations, and serving as a general matrix— no such duality extending from the top down and reacting on more and more limited groups to the very depths of the social body. One must suppose rather that the manifold relationships of force that take shape and come into play in the machinery of production, in families, limited groups, and institutions, are the basis for wide-ranging effects of cleavage that run through the social body as a whole." [15] In the tradition of *Surveiller et punir*, Foucault wanted to disintegrate all the Marxist theories of power—dying hard when he began writing these books and just starting to totter when they were published.

But the book's point of departure and its force undoubtedly lie in the break Foucault made with psychoanalysis, particularly Lacanian psychoanalysis. Foucault knew this would stir up objections—accusations that he was mixed up about who the enemy was, confusing people who talk about censoring and repression and who think sexuality must be freed from these trammels, with people who talk in terms of "law" and think on the contrary that "the law is what constitutes desire and the lack instituting desire" (this is how Foucault formulated what everyone would have recognized as Lacan's theory). But in fact, Foucault explained, the two forms are interdependent. Although they reach opposite conclusions and options, they share the same "representation of power," a juridicopolitical conception, haunted by the monarchical model of a unique, centralized power.

How much territory had been covered since *Les Mots et les choses*! At that time there were three human sciences that had escaped Foucault's lethal attacks: ethnology, linguistics, and the Lacanian version of psychoanalysis. Foucault's entire archaeological enterprise in the work that had made him famous was really based on Lacan (and Lévi-Strauss). And now, in *La Volonté de savoir*, he was setting out on a genealogical quest against Lacan. He even went so far as to present the series of studies he was preparing as "an archaeology of psychoanalysis" [16]—a break with Lacan, but also with all those who opposed his analyses: freedom ideologies, Freudian-Marxism, theories of desire, spinoffs from Sade and Bataille. These are contradictory doctrines, but interdependent, Foucault explained. They are caught in the same "devices" of knowledge and power. [17]

Where did Foucault intend to go in history, to lead these opposing discourses to their common source? This return in time, he announced, would take us back to the Christian doctrines of confession. "The confession was, and still remains, the general standard governing the production of the true discourse on sex. It has undergone a considerable transformation, however. For a long time, it remained firmly entrenched in the practice of penance. But with the rise of Protestantism, the Counter Reformation, eighteenth-century pedagogy, and nineteenth-century medicine, it gradually lost its ritualistic and exclusive localization; it spread . . ."[18] Only the passage of centuries lies between the confessional and the psychoanalyst's couch, remarked Maurice Blanchot, and they have always shared the same eagerness to make people talk about sex.[19] Finally, there is, in *La Volonté de savoir*, this questioning of scientific concepts that seems to haunt all of Foucault's books from the very beginning. For the unique and simple practice of confession, as it is described in manuals for penance in the Middle Ages and in the sixteenth century, has given way before "an explosion of distinct discursivities which took form in demography, biology, medicine, psychiatry, psychology, ethics, pedagogy, and political criticism." Foucault considered that "we would do better to locate the procedures by which that will to knowledge regarding sex, which characterizes the modern Occident, caused the rituals of confession to function within the norms of scientific regularity: how did this immense and traditional extortion of the sexual confession come to be constituted in scientific terms?"[20] In this proposed examination of "all this equipment" of power, which made confession function in new, scientific forms, what was at issue was to show the tremendous subjection of men that had been accomplished by Western culture throughout the centuries—subjection, that is, the constitution of "subjects" in both senses of the word. Clearly we are not far from *Surveiller et punir*.

La Volonté de savoir is a very slim volume, but one in which all of Foucault seems to come together. In his view, however, it was only a prelude, a prologue to a series of historical investigations that would verify the basic hypothesis. When the book came out the following list was on the back of the cover:

HISTOIRE DE LA SEXUALITÉ
1. *La Volonté de savoir*

FORTHCOMING:
2. *La Chair et le corps*
3. *La Croisade des enfants*

4. *La Femme, la mère et l'hystérique*
5. *Les Pervers*
6. *Populations et races*

And to crown it all, in a note inside the book, he announced yet another forthcoming work, *Le Pouvoir de la vérité* (The Power of truth).

As always, Foucault meant to conduct these historical investigations himself. That was his practice as a historian. Never content with reading works already written on one question or another, on one period or another, he had to go see for himself. No doubt this was one of the greatest ruptures that Foucault effected in philosophical thought. "For a long time," he said in an interview, "'theoretical' or 'speculative' reflection has had a rather distant and perhaps somewhat disdainful relationship with history. One read historical works, which were often of very high quality, in search of raw material considered 'accurate.' Then all that was required was to reflect upon it, to provide it with a meaning and truth that it did not have on its own. Free use of others' work was permitted—so much so that no one even thought of hiding the fact that one was elaborating on work already done; this work was cited shamelessly. Things have changed, it seems." Perhaps this change was somehow a reaction to Marxism. It no longer seemed "sufficient to have confidence in knowledgeable people or to think in a detached manner about things others had been there to see." In any event, the same sort of change

> aroused the desire to accept no longer things to be reflected upon, ready-made from the hands of historians. One had to go find them oneself, to define them and approach them as historical objects. This was the only way to give real content to our reflection upon ourselves, our thought, and our behavior. Conversely, it was a way of not being unknowing prisoners of the implicit postulates of history. It was a way of providing new historical objects for reflection . . . It was not reflection on history but reflection in history. A way of testing thought with work in history; also a way of testing work in history by a transformation of conceptual and theoretical frameworks.

In any case, and this was perhaps the most important point, "it is work one must do oneself. One must go to the bottom of the mine. It takes time. It takes effort."[21] Faced with Foucault's incursions into their territory, historians responded variously with enthusiasm or skepticism, with cooperation or categorical rejection.[22]

The sequels to *Histoire de la sexualité* were laid out, the files already prepared. On his desk there was a voluminous folder for each of the titles planned, awaiting the hour of its definitive elaboration, the moment when Foucault's prose—beautiful and precise, meticulously worked—would take hold of the material inside, to transfigure it. An initial manuscript by Foucault is almost undecipherable handwriting, loaded with additions and scratched-out words. "Begin and begin again," as he said. But he told one friend that he hoped to finish one volume every three months.

La Volonté de savoir—the only one of his works with an explicitly Nietzschean title—is a sharp-edged, burning text, full of irony. It is, perhaps, the one in which Foucault, writing with astounding economy, "kept thought moving" the most. This is undoubtedly one of the reasons it had a reception that Foucault perceived as lukewarm and reserved. He had wanted to go against the flow, strike the dominant "current" ideas head-on, tell all people the historical truth of their acts and their words. He had succeeded beyond his hopes. But could he have expected the people he thus manhandled to thank him? The press gave the book quite a favorable reception: there were many interviews and articles. But Foucault felt that everyone around him was somehow disappointed and had not understood. He spoke about it to Gilles Deleuze at the beginning of 1977, when they were still close, and Deleuze wrote him a letter telling him all the new things the book had said, the things that made up its strength and richness. But Foucault kept on feeling upset. Of course, he still had enough energy to react strongly against the most overt polemics and to assassinate with one sentence the essayist who had thought that with fifty pages he could make people "Forget Foucault."[23] When Baudrillard's book with this title came out, he dismissed it with: "I would have more problems remembering Baudrillard." Still, Foucault seemed despondent.

What might have made Foucault feel so fragile? Perhaps there were some people close to him who had reservations. In any case, he was sorry that he had published this first volume without the studies for which it was intended to serve merely as an introduction. He said as much in the preface to the German edition in 1983:

> I know that it is imprudent to send out first, like a bomb meant to illuminate, a book that constantly alludes to things meant to be published in the future. There is a great danger that it will seem arbitrary and dogmatic. Its hypotheses can appear to be assertions settling the question, and analytical grids may lead to misunderstanding and be taken for new theories. This is what happened in France, where critics who had suddenly been converted to seeing the struggle against repression as beneficial (without going so far as to demonstrate any

great zeal in this department) reproached me for denying that sexuality had been repressed. But I certainly never claimed that there had been no repression of sexuality. I simply asked myself whether the analysis, as a whole, was obliged to be articulated around the concept of repression to decipher the relations among power, knowledge, and sex; or, indeed, whether one might not understand things better by inserting the taboos, the obstacles, the expulsions, and the dissimulations into a more complex, more global strategy that would not be fixed on repression as its principal and essential focus.[24]

Foucault had the bitter feeling that he had been ill-read and ill-understood. Ill-loved, perhaps. "Do you know why one writes?" he had asked Francine Pariente when she was his assistant at Clermont-Ferrand. "To be loved." Was he really so "ill-loved" in 1976? *La Volonté de savoir* was a huge success in the bookstores. It was one of Foucault's best-selling works: in June 1989 almost 100,000 copies had been printed. But success can also be harmful. This one led to a "crisis" for Foucault—a personal crisis and an intellectual crisis.

Not one of the titles announced by Foucault on the cover of *La Volonté de savoir* would ever appear. Perhaps, as Deleuze suggests, he was too wrapped up in his analyses of power and had to extricate himself from these before he could successfully provide a sequel to the first volume. He did, however, begin working on all the proposed themes; they surface in several of his texts. For example, he edited and wrote an introduction to the memoirs of a French hermaphrodite, Herculine Barbin, known as Alexina B.[25] For the American edition he wrote a long commentary, "Do We Need a True Sex?"[26] The memoirs appeared in France in 1978, in a new series that Foucault was starting at Gallimard, Les Vies Parallèles. This is how he introduced the series:

> The ancients liked paralleling the lives of famous men; one could hear exemplary ghosts speaking through the centuries. Parallels are created, I know, to join in infinity. Let us imagine other parallels that diverge indefinitely. No meeting point, no place to take them in. Often their only echo is that of the end to which they are condemned. One should grasp them in the force of the impulse that drives them apart. One should locate the momentary, dazzling trail they left behind in their violent haste to reach a darkness where "no one talks about it any more" and where "reputations" disappear. It would be like some reverse Plutarch: lives so parallel that nothing can join them.[27]

He also wrote an introduction to *My Secret Life*, the book by the nineteenth-century English libertine mentioned several times in *La*

Volonté de savoir.[28] And in *Cahiers du chemin* he published a long article, "La Vie des hommes infâmes," intended as the introduction to a book of the same title. He announced that one would see strange characters in it, "quasi-fictional" lives, "a few rudiments of which" he wanted to "assemble into a legend of obscure men."[29] The projected book was never published, at least in the form in which it was announced. But he would, nonetheless, find words for these pathetic ghosts in *lettres de cachet* taken from the Bastille archives, collected and introduced in collaboration with Arlette Farge in 1982 in *Le Désordre des familles*.[30] This volume was published twenty years after Foucault had proposed writing a book on prisoners at the Bastille for the same Archives series in which *Le Désordre* appeared.

Above all, Foucault began work on Christian doctrines of the sixteenth and seventeenth centuries. At the same time, in his lectures, he was examining the techniques of population management and forms of power in the eighteenth and nineteenth centuries.

ON DECEMBER 17, 1976, on the set installed at the Louvre specifically for a telecast of the program "Apostrophes," Bernard Pivot exclaimed in astonishment: "So, you really don't want to talk about your book?" "No," answered Michel Foucault. "First, one writes things in part because one thinks them but also so one won't have to think them any more. Finishing a book is also not wanting to see it any more. As long as one has some love for his book, one works on it. Once one no longer loves it, one stops writing it." And especially when there was another book deserving more attention: "a book of the sort I like: made up of fragments of reality, things said, deeds, documents, sadness, misfortunes . . ." The author? Don't even look for one. It is simply tapes from a trial in the Soviet Union that arrived in the West thanks to the courage of the children of the accused, Dr. Stern. An "ordinary trial," as it is called in the title of the collection. This man, Dr. Stern, had two sons who wanted to emigrate to Israel. The KGB asked him (he had been a Communist since the war) to forbid them to go into exile, and when he refused he was brought before the courts, if one can go so far as to call them that. He was accused of taking bribes. Dozens of witnesses for the prosecution were supposed to confirm this. But during the hearing they retracted, to establish that Dr. Stern was innocent. Nonetheless he was sentenced to eight years of forced labor.[31] This was the book Foucault wanted to talk about, an extraordinary document of "ordinary" reality in the Soviet Union. Wasn't the broadcast dedicated to "man's future"? Of course, it was important to discuss man's first footsteps on the moon, but one must not forget "the footsteps of those men and women who come to tell us what the truth is." Never forget that, faced with the power the state has over bodies, there is also the resistance of individuals who know how to say *no*.

When *La Nouvelle Critique* asked him to take part in a discussion of *Moi, Pierre Rivière*, Foucault replied that he did not want to discuss this book, but would be willing to write an article on the case of Dr. Stern. His suggestion never received a response.

Foucault was unstinting in his efforts to help "dissidents from the Eastern countries." In June 1977, when Leonid Brezhnev visited Paris, he wanted, as usual, to "do something." He and Pierre Victor decided to arrange a gathering of French intellectuals and Soviet dissidents. Foucault organized it all remarkably well. Twelve people signed the invitation, among them Sartre, François Jacob, and Roland Barthes. It read: "On the occasion of Leonid Brezhnev's visit to France, we invite you to a friendly meeting with dissidents from the Eastern countries, at the Récamier theater, on June 21, at 8:30 P.M." Ionesco had already arrived when, at the appointed time, Sartre arrived on the arm of Simone de Beauvoir. This scene was what most impressed all who saw: an old, sick man, almost blind, moving slowly forward and guided by that legendary woman. There were many dissidents present: Leonid Pliouchtch, Andrei Siniavsky, Andrei Amalrik, Vladimir Bukovski. And Mikhail Stern, who had finally succeeded in leaving the Soviet Union. Inside the theater, Foucault welcomed them all as a large crowd looked on and numerous television cameras recorded the event.

In March 1979 Foucault loaned his apartment for a colloquium between Israelis and Palestinians, organized by *Les Temps modernes* at the initiative of Pierre Victor. "Foucault's living-room was equipped with tables, chairs, and a tape recorder," wrote Simone de Beauvoir. "In spite of a few technical difficulties, the first meeting took place on March 14. Sartre opened the meeting with a brief talk."[32] But Foucault was not present. "He was willing to provide the space but not to take part in the discussions," according to Edward Said.[33] Both Beauvoir and Said describe the colloquium as a "disaster."

↬↬

FOUCAULT AND SARTRE. Together once again on June 20, 1979. This time it was to save the boat people. Bernard Kouchner and a team of physicians had anchored a boat named *L'Ile de lumière* off the island of Poulo Bidong to help Vietnamese who wanted to flee their country.

But Kouchner's group wanted to establish an airlift between the camps in Malaysia and Thailand and the processing centers for refugees in the Western countries. A press conference was held at the Hotel Lutétia. There, Glucksmann "introduced" Sartre and Raymond Aron on the podium. Classmates at the ENS, they had not associated with each other for thirty years, and Sartre had directed a torrent of abuse at Aron ten years earlier. Foucault was in the room, along with Yves Montand and Simone Signoret. He took the floor to demand that President Giscard d'Estaing increase the number of refugees allowed to move to France. It was also Foucault who welcomed Aron and Sartre at the Collège de France for another press conference a few days later, after they had gone as part of a delegation of intellectuals to see the president, who, according to Beauvoir, made them "promises that were just words in the air."[34] Foucault had a great investment in this protest. He had been part of the original committee, "Un Bateau pour le Vietnam," in November 1978. In 1981 he would go to Geneva for a press conference "against acts of piracy," for which he wrote and read a declaration, a sort of charter of human rights:

> There exists an international citizenry that has its rights, that has its duties, and that is committed to rise up against every abuse of power, no matter who the author, no matter who the victims. After all, we are all ruled, and as such, we are in solidarity.
>
> Because they claim to look after the happiness of societies, governments assume the right to put men's misfortune, caused by their decisions or allowed by their negligence, into a ledger of profit and loss. It is one of the duties of this international citizenry always to turn to good account, in the eyes and ears of the government, these misfortunes of men, for which it is not true that they are not responsible. Men's misfortune must never be the silent remnant of politics. It is the basis of an absolute right to rise up and address those who hold the power. We must refuse the division of labor that very frequently is proposed to us: it is the job of individuals to become indignant and to speak out; it is the job of governments to reflect and to act. It is true, good governments are in favor of the sacred indignation of those they rule, provided this remains in the realm of the lyrical . . . The will of individuals must be inscribed in a reality that the governments wanted to monopolize. This monopoly must be wrested from them bit by bit, each and every day.[35]

On the morning of Saturday, April 19, 1980, Catherine Von Bülow telephoned Foucault to ask if he was going to Sartre's funeral. "That goes without saying," answered Foucault. A few hours later the two marched together in a procession of twenty or thirty thousand people following the hearse to the cemetery at Montparnasse: "the final demonstration of May 1968," as it was frequently called. Foucault talked with Von Bülow and also with Claude Mauriac. "We talked about Sartre," said Von Bülow. "And he told me: 'When I was a young man, he was the one—along with everything he represented, the terrorism of *Les Temps modernes*—from whom I wanted to free myself.'"

19
~~

A Revolution of Bare Hands

On their flight to Teheran, Michel Foucault and Thierry Voeltzel began to be anxious. What would they find on their arrival? It was just days after "Black Friday," September 8, 1978, when the Shah's army had shot into a crowd. There were almost four thousand dead. The whole world was stunned and outraged by the massacre. In Paris a protest demonstration had been organized by the Ligue des Droits de l'Homme (Human Rights League), the unions, and the left-wing parties.

It was a journalistic project that took Foucault to Iran. In 1977 the editor of the Italian daily *Corriere della sera* had asked him to write a regular column for them. But Foucault had no desire to write cultural or philosophical articles. He proposed to do on-the-scene "investigations" instead. Was this a way for him to get around the request, as some have suggested? Or, as others believe, did he simply feel the need to move a little, to escape Paris following what he took to be the failure of *La Volonté de savoir*? In any case, *Corriere della sera* accepted his project as presented.

Journalism was nothing new for Foucault. He had been closely involved in launching *Libération*, and he had long been a regular contributor to *Le Nouvel Observateur*. And he had conducted many "investigations" during his leftist period, particularly in working with the Groupe d'Information sur les Prisons (GIP). The first thing he did, because he also wanted it to be a collective undertaking, was to assemble a small team. Then he put Thierry Voeltzel in charge of coordinating it. Foucault had met this young man one day when Voeltzel was hitchhiking. They became friends, and Foucault had even interviewed him about his past and his present, his life in general, for an astonishing little book that had been published several months earlier with a preface by Claude Mauriac. The interviewer's name never appears in the book, but Foucault, in the course of his questioning, mentioned some of his own experiences, to compare them with those of Voeltzel.[1] Foucault also called on André Glucksmann, Alain Finkielkraut, and several other friends. He described his notion of reporting in *Corriere:* "The contemporary world is teeming with ideas that spring up, stir around, disappear or reappear, and shake up people and things. This is not something that happens only in intellectual circles or in the universities of Western Europe; it also happens on a world scale, and it happens particularly among minorities that, because of history, have not up to now been in the habit of speaking or making themselves heard." And he added:

> There are more ideas on earth than intellectuals imagine. And these ideas are more active, stronger, more resistant, more passionate than "politicians" think. We have to be there at the birth of ideas, the bursting outward of their force: not in books expressing them, but in events manifesting this force, in struggles carried on around ideas, for or against them. Ideas do not rule the world. But it is because the world has ideas (and because it constantly produces them) that it is not passively ruled by those who are its leaders or those who would like to teach it, once and for all, what it must think. This is the direction we want these "journalistic reports" to take. An analysis of thought will be linked to an analysis of what is happening. Intellectuals will work together with journalists at the point where ideas and events intersect.[2]

Before leaving for Iran, Foucault met several times with Ahmad Salamatian, an Iranian exile who had been in Paris since 1965. He belonged to the National Front, a liberal, nonreligious party of the center-left—very "Third Republic." "Radical-socialist, in a framework of national liberation," is how Salamatian described it. It was Mohammed Mossadegh's party in the abortive democratic experiment of 1953. Foucault and Salamatian met through Thierry Mignon, a lawyer, and his wife, Sylvie. They had known Foucault while they were active in the GIP and immigrant defense. They also served on the committee formed by Sartre in 1966 for the defense of Iranian political prisoners, and in connection with this, Thierry Mignon had performed several investigative missions to Iran for the Ligue des Droits de l'Homme. Since 1971 Foucault had been signing petitions produced by this committee, although he did not participate in it directly. For example, he signed a protest published in *Le Monde* on February 4, 1976, against "the silence of French authorities in the face of flagrant human rights violations in Iran," in which nineteen "antifascist, militant revolutionaries" had just been executed. The list of signers ran the gamut from Jean-Paul Sartre and Simone de Beauvoir to François Mitterrand, Michel Rocard, Lionel Jospin, and Jean-Pierre Chevènement, to Yves Montand, Claude Mauriac, and Gilles Deleuze. The uprising against the Shah's regime had grown considerably during 1978, and by the beginning of September the repression had turned to carnage.

Ahmad Salamatian obtained books and documentation for Foucault. He provided him with addresses, contacts, and a list of people to see. Several days later Foucault was in Iran. "When you arrive at the airport after curfew, a taxi takes you at breakneck speed through the streets of the city. They are empty. The only things slowing the car down are the roadblocks set up by men with machine guns. Woe betide if the driver does not see them. They shoot. All up and down the Avenue Reza Shah, silent now, as far as the eye can see, red lights and green lights flash off and on in vain, like the watch ticking on the wrist of a dead man. This is the undivided rule of the Shah."[3] Foucault set to work the next day on his inquiry. Because it was very difficult to make any contacts within the religious opposition, he met first with militants from the democratic opposition; he also met with members of the military, to try to understand the role the army would play in any test of strength. "Friends," he wrote, "have arranged a meeting for me with several superior officers, all members of the opposition, in a completely sterile spot in the suburbs of Teheran. The more trouble that develops, they told me, the more the government is compelled to call up troops unprepared for the task of keeping order, and disinclined to do so. They are soon in a position to discover that they are not dealing with international communism but rather with the streets, the merchants in the bazaar, with employees and the unemployed, who are just like their brothers, or just like what they themselves would be if they were not soldiers."[4]

Foucault continued his reporting. Talking with leaders of the opposition who were denouncing the Shah's regime, that "ensemble of modernism-despotism-corruption," he remembered a walk he had taken two or three days earlier:

There was a detail that struck me when I visited the bazaar, which had just reopened after more than a week of strikes. There were dozens and dozens of incredible sewing machines lined up in the stalls, big and elaborate the way nineteenth-century newspaper advertisements show them. They were decorated with drawings of ivy, climbing plants, and flower buds, in crude imitation of old Persian miniatures. All these out-of-service Westernisms wearing the signs of an out-of-date East also bore the inscription: "Made in South Korea." I felt then that I understood that recent events did not represent a withdrawal of the most outmoded groups before a modernization that is too brutal. It was, rather, the rejection by an entire culture, an entire people, of a modernization that is an archaism in itself. It is the Shah's misfortune to be of one piece with this archaism. His crime is that he maintains through corruption and despotism this fragment of the past in a present that wants nothing to do with it any more.

Foucault then drew a lesson from everything he had seen and heard: "Modernization as a political project and as a principle of social change is a thing of the past in Iran ... With the current Iranian regime in its death throes, we are present at the final moments of an episode that began almost sixty years ago: an attempt to modernize Islamic countries in a European mode." Foucault concluded the article with these words: "Consequently, I beg of you, let's hear no more talk in Europe about the fortunes and misfortunes of a ruler who is too modern for a country that is too old. The Shah is what is old here in Iran. He is fifty, even a hundred, years behind. He is as old as predatory sovereigns. His is the antiquated dream of opening up his country by means of secularization and industrialization. His project of modernization, his despotic weapons, his system of corruption are what is archaic today."[5] Foucault was not content with meeting politicians and leaders of the opposition. He also wanted to hear from students, men in the street, Islamic youth proclaiming they were prepared to die. He went around the cemeteries, which were the only authorized places of meeting. He went to the universities and the doors of the mosques. He set off for Qum with Thierry Voeltzel to see Ayatollah Shariat Madari, whose residence there served as a refuge for many who were militantly involved with human rights defense committees.[6] He spoke with Madari, and also with Mehdi Bazargan, who would become prime minister after Ayatollah Khomeini's return to Iran. It was difficult to get through to Madari's house: soldiers with submachine guns guarded the street. For a whole week Foucault gathered information, listened, looked, always taking notes, walking everywhere. He wanted to see everything, understand everything. Voeltzel remembers them as exhausting days.

A few days before their arrival, there had been ceremonies of mourning in all the mosques in Iran to honor the victims of the repression. The mullahs' shouted imprecations had been recorded and were being broadcast everywhere. Foucault could hear the echo of their voices, "terrible as Savanarola's must have sounded in Florence, as the Anabaptists in Münster, or the Presbyterians in Cromwell's time."[7]

Foucault asked the same question of everyone he met: "What do you want?" And invariably he got the same reply: "An Islamic government." Foucault stayed in Iran for a week. Back in Paris, he wrote four splendid articles, mixing details and striking anecdotes with deep reflection, which appeared in *Corriere della sera* from September 28 to October 22, 1978.[8] On October 16 he published a condensed version in *Le Nouvel Observateur* that ended with these words:

> At the dawn of history, Persia invented the State, and it gave the formulas to Islam: its administrators served as the Caliph's officers. But from this same Islam Persia derived a religion that provided its people with infinite resources of resistance against the power of the State. Should we see, in this will for an "Islamic government," a reconciliation, a contradiction, or the threshold of something new? . . . What meaning is there for the men inhabiting this little corner of earth, whose ground and underground are stakes in world strategies, when they seek, even at the price of their own lives, something that *we* have forgotten, even as a possibility, since the Renaissance and the great crises of Christianity: a political spirituality. I can already hear the French laughing. But I know they are wrong.[9]

A RELIGIOUS DIGNITARY, an old man, came forward slowly and sat under the big apple tree in the middle of the garden. several dozen people formed a circle around him and listened to the words he uttered in a voice that sounded serene but that resonated, thousands of times over, to shake the world. The Ayatollah Khomeini moved to Neauphles-le-Château, a small city near Paris, on October 7, 1978, after fourteen years of exile in Iraq. From all over Europe Iranian students and exiles, embodying every oppositional tendency, came to see him. There were also a few Europeans, mostly journalists. Among the first to come were *Libération*'s Pierre Blanchet and Claire Brière, and with them Foucault. Abolhasan Bani-Sadr, one of the leaders of the exiled opposition and a "spiritual son" of Khomeini who had been living in France for a long time, had notified Blanchet and Brière as soon as the ayatollah had arrived in Paris. (Bani-Sadr would briefly become president of the Islamic republic and now once again lives near Paris.) Blanchet and Brière had met Foucault during his trip to Iran, where they too were working as reporters. They telephoned him right away and went with him to Bani-Sadr's home in Cachan to await the ayatollah. Foucault asked Bani-Sadr to explain to the ayatollah that it would be better to

avoid denouncing the Shah too violently because he would risk immediate expulsion. That evening Foucault got no closer to the ayatollah
than a glimpse of his silhouette. The journalists fared no better at
Neauphles. They had to wait several days before he would see them.

After what he had seen in Iran, Foucault was tremendously eager to
see Khomeini. His name alone set millions of Iranians into motion,
human tides that it seemed nothing could stop. But, as Foucault put it,
Khomeini quickly "wrecked everybody's plans." He said no: no attempt at reconciliation; no compromise; no election; no merged government. The Shah had to go. Period. And he threatened to exclude
from the movement any politician who supported any of the Shah's
plans to save his regime. All the stir at Neauphles, the comings and
goings of "important Iranians," showed that the ayatollah's intran-
sigence had not marginalized him. To the contrary, everyone believed
in the "power of the mysterious current passing between an old man
exiled for fifteen years and his people who are invoking him." The
situation in Iran "seemed to hang on a great duel between two person-
ages wearing their traditional emblems: the king and the saint. The
sovereign up in arms and the defenseless saint; the despot faced by a
man who held up his bare hands, who was acclaimed by his people.
This image has a great driving force of its own, but behind it lies a
reality that is signed by the deaths of thousands." [10]

During a visit to Neauphles with Ahmad Salamatian and Thierry
Mignon, Foucault witnessed a minor incident. A mullah from Khomeini's entourage wanted to prevent a German journalist from entering the yard because she was not veiled. Salamatian protested: "Is that
the image you want to give of your movement?" The ayatollah's son
and son-in-law intervened, reproaching the mullah for having been too
zealous. The German journalist was allowed to enter. During their return trip in the car, Foucault said how very impressed he had been,
while in Iran, to see that wearing the veil was a political gesture:
women who were not in the habit of wearing it insisted on putting it
on to participate in demonstrations.

Before returning to Iran a month later, Foucault consulted at length
with Bani-Sadr. Bani-Sadr recalls: "He wanted to understand how this
revolution was able to be produced, developing with no reference to
any foreign power, and stirring up an entire nation, despite the distance between towns and the difficulties of communication. He wanted
to reflect on the notion of power."

FOUCAULT ARRIVED AGAIN in Teheran with Thierry Voeltzel and resumed his investigation. He questioned striking workers from various backgrounds: "privileged" members of the middle class, such as a pilot from Iran Air, in his modern apartment in Teheran; and oil workers at the Abadan refinery a thousand kilometers to the south. From this trip came a new series of reports, four articles published in *Corriere* in November 1978.[11] In the final article Foucault pondered the role of Khomeini, this "almost mythic character":

> No head of state, no political leader, even with the support of all the media in his country, can claim today to be the object of so personal and so intense an affection. This attachment is, no doubt, the result of three *things:* Khomeini *is not there.* For fifteen years he has lived in an exile that he himself does not want to leave until the Shah is gone. Khomeini *says nothing,* nothing except no—no to the Shah, to the regime, and to dependency. Finally, Khomeini *is not a politician.* There will be no Khomeini party, there will be no Khomeini government. Khomeini is the point of fixation for a collective will.

He went on to define the Iranian movement: "It is an uprising of men with their bare hands who want to lift the tremendous weight pressing each of us down, pressing them down in particular, these oil workers and peasants on the frontiers of empires—the weight of the entire world. It is perhaps the first great insurrection against a planetary system, the most modern form of revolt. And the one that is most mad."[12]

The French newspapers had begun seething with controversy even before the second series of reports. On November 6 *Le Nouvel Observateur* published a letter from an Iranian woman who was indignant about Foucault's article on October 16: "After twenty-five years of silence and oppression, should the Iranian people have only the choice between the SAVAK (the secret police) and religious fanaticism?" She went on:

> Spirituality? A return to popular sources? Saudi Arabia is a country that drinks from the source of Islam. And the hands of thieves and the heads of lovers fall. It seems that the Western left is sufficiently lacking in humanism to find Islam desirable—for others! There are many Iranians, like myself, who are distraught and in despair over the idea of an "Islamic government." They know what they are talking about. Everywhere, all over Iran, Islam serves as a screen for feudal or pseudo-revolutionary oppression. Often, also, as in Tunisia or Pakistan, in Indonesia and in Iran, Islam, alas, is the sole means of expression for muzzled populations. The liberal left in the West ought to know what an iron mantle Islamic law is capable of becom-

ing, for societies who are eager for change. It should not let itself be seduced by a remedy that is worse, perhaps, than the illness.[13]

Foucault answered in the next issue of the weekly:

Since in Iran people have demonstrated and people have died, shouting "Islamic government," it was an elementary duty to ask oneself what was the content of these words and what force was behind them. I indicated, moreover, a number of elements that seemed not very reassuring to me. If Mme H's letter had contained only a mistaken reading, I would not have replied. But it contains two things that are intolerable: (1) It confuses and holds in a single contempt every aspect, every form, every virtuality of Islam, rejecting these en masse with the age-old reproach of "fanaticism." (2) It suspects every Westerner of being interested in Islam only out of contempt for Muslims (what would one say of a Westerner who had contempt for Islam?). The problem of Islam as a political force is one of the essential problems for our times and for the years to come. The first condition for approaching this problem with the slightest bit of intelligence is not to begin by adding hatred.[14]

Foucault continued to be interested in Iran. When Ayatollah Khomeini left Paris on February 1, 1979, Foucault was at the airport to be present at an event whose impact was truly worldwide. On February 13 he sent a new article to *Corriere della sera*. The Shah was gone, Ayatollah Khomeini had returned. Millions of Iranians jammed the road leading from the airport into downtown Teheran, millions of men and women shouting "Khomeini, you have finally returned!" Foucault mulled over the future. He had said in an earlier article: "I do not know how to write the history of the future. I am a maladroit forecaster of the past. I would, however, like to grasp *things as they are happening*, because these days, nothing is finished, and the dice are still rolling. That may be what a 'journalist''s work is, but it is true that I am just a neophyte."[15] In his final article, he raised questions about the movement he had watched take place before his very eyes:

Its historical importance does not, perhaps, result from its conforming to some recognized "revolutionary" model. It results more from the possibility that it will turn all the political facts in the Middle East upside-down—hence doing the same for the strategic balance worldwide. Its singularity, up to now its strength, risks later becoming a power for expansion. It is certainly as an "Islamic" movement that it can inflame the entire region, overturning the most unstable regimes and disrupting the most solid. On the scale of hundreds of thousands of men, Islam, which is not simply a religion but also a way of life, the belonging to a history and a civilization, is liable to constitute a gigantic powderkeg. As of yesterday, any Muslim state can be revolutionized from within on the basis of its secular traditions.[16]

Much has been said about Foucault's "pro-Iran" commitment. But very few people have read everything he wrote about the Iranian revolution, because the *Corriere* articles were never translated from Italian. And Foucault did not want them collected into a single volume in Italy. He saw them as news reports, not as texts for a book. Reading them today, one can see the extraordinary fascination the Iranian revolution had for him. It was a revolution that was exempt from politics, or in any case, from Western political categories. And it was a movement that fascinated every observer. On Foucault's death, Jean Daniel spoke of this "mistake we made together," and Serge July today still says that he thought—and wrote—the same things as Foucault. Yet, he added, "one felt already in the air all the signs of what was going to happen." The incredible repression that turned processions into bloodbaths had aroused profound revulsion against the Shah's regime and broad sympathy for the Iranian people. Everyone hoped the Shah would lose the fight and leave Iran. No one particularly asked what would happen afterward. Foucault clearly saw that the country would not easily return to traditional forms of politics and that the religious fervor providing the insurrection with all its force was not going to go away once victory was obtained. The mullahs were not going to return sensibly to their mosques.

Apart from this simple prescience that the connection between politics and religion creates unequaled power, Foucault undoubtedly had ill-founded hopes for the future he was heralding. But in journalistic reporting in the fever of the historical moment, it is a very delicate task to sort things out and render an acute political judgment. According to Thierry Voeltzel, Foucault wanted to be a simple journalist. He always went wherever the group of reporters went.[17] But he was not a simple journalist. If he had been, no one would dream of reproaching him today for what he wrote.

Others were very ready to remind him of that fact. As soon as the new power had shown its true face, that is, almost immediately after Khomeini's return in February 1979, when the arrests and executions began—the same litany of bloody acts of repression—Claudie and Jacques Broyelle, former Maoists who had gone over to sitting in judgment, went after him in the columns of *Le Matin*. In one of his articles

Foucault had pondered the question "A quoi rêvent les Iraniens?" (What are the Iranians dreaming?). The Broyelles asked in *Le Matin:* "What are the philosophers thinking?" Foucault had a harsh reply for them.[18]

A few weeks after this exchange Foucault published an open letter to Mehdi Bazargan, the prime minister of the "Islamic government." He recalled their meeting in Qom in September 1978:

> We talked about all the regimes that have been oppressive in the name of human rights. You expressed a hope that in the so widely asserted will of the Iranian people for an Islamic government, one could succeed in finding a real guarantee for these rights. You gave three reasons. First, a spiritual dimension, you said, ran through this people's revolt in which each one, for the sake of a completely different world, risked everything (and for many this "everything" was no more nor less than themselves); second, it was not the desire to be ruled by a "government of mullahs"—you did, I think, use that expression. What I saw from Teheran to Abadan was far from contradicting what you said. Finally, you said that Islam, as far as these rights were concerned, with its long history and its present dynamism, was capable of facing, on the matter of these rights, the formidable wager that socialism had not taken up any better (that being the least one can say) than capitalism.[19]

On May 11, 1979, Foucault sought to clarify things one last time, in a long article published on the front page of *Le Monde:* "Inutile de se soulever?" ("Is it useless to revolt?"). It was a superb outburst by a bitter, wounded man, standing up for things he had said, justifying his words with a disdainful elegance to anyone who felt authorized to give him lessons in political morality. The article ended, in fact, with a definition of the role of intellectuals and of the morality it is based upon:

> These days intellectuals do not have a very good "press." I think I can use this word in a rather precise sense. Therefore, it is not the moment to say that one is not an intellectual. People would just laugh anyhow. An intellectual I am. If someone should ask me what it is I think I am doing, I would answer: if the strategist is a man who says, "what importance does a particular death, a particular cry, a particular uprising have in relation to the great necessity of the whole, and of what importance to me is such-and-such a general principle in the specific situation in which we find ourselves?" then it is indifferent to me whether the strategist is a politician, a historian, a revolutionary, someone who supports the Shah or the ayatollah. My theoretical mo-

rality is the opposite. It is "antistrategic": be respectful when singularity rises up, and intransigent when power infringes on the universal. A simple choice, a difficult thing to do, because one must simultaneously be on the lookout for the things, just slightly below the surface of history, that break and trouble it, and watch for the things, just slightly behind politics, that must be its unconditional limits. That, after all, is my work: I am neither the first nor the only person to do it. But I chose it.

Foucault later did his best to support Ahmad Salamatian, who became vice-minister of foreign affairs in 1979 but had to flee Iran in 1981 after spending several months in hiding.

For a long time thereafter Foucault rarely commented on politics or journalism. Serge July remembers having made several proposals to him, all of which Foucault refused. The substance of his reply was that one can't ad-lib journalism; more work and a better understanding are necessary. The long article that Foucault was writing in early 1979 on Jean Daniel's *L'Ere des ruptures* was not simply a tribute to the ties of friendship. It resonates as a confession of an abortive vocation, an expression of admiration for those who master a skill that frequently consists in revising certainties without renouncing convictions, in managing to change one's opinion and at the same time remain faithful to oneself; admiration for those who daily live out Merleau-Ponty's urging that one "never consent to be completely at ease with one's own evidence." The title of the article was "Pour une morale de l'inconfort": For an ethics of discomfort.[20]

✦

THE CRITICISM AND SARCASM that greeted Foucault's "mistake" concerning Iran added further to his despondency after what he saw as the qualified critical reception of *La Volonté de savoir*. But he went on with his work. He launched an immense new undertaking: interpreting the literature of early Christianity. In order to do so he left what had been his favorite haunt, the Bibliothèque Nationale. Service there had deteriorated; he could no longer stand the endless waiting to get a book, the increasing obstacles and formalities to consult the slightest document. He had discovered a place where he was welcome and where he had access to all the books that interested him. This was the library of the Dominican order in Paris, the Bibliothèque du Saulchoir, on Rue de la Glacière, in the thirteenth arrondissement. Foucault had met its director, Michel Albaric, in June 1979 at dinner at Roger Stéphane's.

Soon afterward, Foucault ran into Albaric at the BN and complained of the conditions there. "Come to the Saulchoir, then," the monk told him. Foucault would spend entire days in that tiny reading room, ensconced next to one of the bay windows opening onto a square courtyard.

In the early 1980s Foucault was also preoccupied with publishing matters. These concerns were largely related to his belief that too wide a circulation for scholarly books was disastrous for their reception, because it brought with it a multitude of misunderstandings. The moment a book went beyond the circle of those to whom it was really addressed, that is, those scholars who knew the problems with which it dealt and the theoretical traditions to which it referred, it no longer produced "effects of knowledge," but "effects of opinion," as Foucault called them. In these years his principal concern seemed to be with avoiding effects of opinion. His watchword was seriousness. At one point he contemplated publishing from then on at Vrin, a thoroughly academic establishment on the Place de la Sorbonne that specialized in theses and scholarly books.

These issues became more acute and more central when Foucault abruptly broke his ties with Pierre Nora. They had had a friendly and understanding relationship ever since the publication of *Les Mots et les choses* in 1966. But early in 1980 Nora started a review called *Le Débat*. And his lead editorial in the first issue seemed to attack all the authors published in Gallimard's Bibliothèque des Sciences Humaines and Bibliothèque des Histoires series, which included Foucault. Indeed, Foucault felt that he himself was the target of several passages in the editorial. There was a violent argument between the two men, and Foucault decided to publish the rest of *Histoire de la sexualité* elsewhere. He contacted several editors, and, as the news spread, several editors contacted him. He soon concluded an agreement at Seuil with François Wahl, a friend of Barthes.

Seuil had already announced publication of his work when Claude Gallimard invited Foucault to come to see him. During that meeting he reminded Foucault that the publishing house had helped finance René Allio's film adaptation of *Moi, Pierre Rivière* . . . In exchange for a commitment from Foucault to publish all his books at Gallimard. Up to this point nothing had been able to sway Foucault. His decision to leave Gallimard was irrevocable. Was he bound by any contract? "Let them sue me," he told anyone who would listen. But on this matter he felt morally bound. He therefore continued to give his books to Nora, although he would never be truly reconciled with him. Once triggered, Foucault's anger was not easily placated. Foucault demanded absolute fidelity in friendship, and never pardoned anything he considered a betrayal or treachery. Nora was simply one of many friends with whom he broke. There were many names one did not mention in Foucault's presence.

Foucault, then, continued to be published at Gallimard, and in 1983 he even contributed to *Le Débat*, in a dialogue with Edmond Maire. But he also embarked on an important project at Seuil with Wahl and Paul Veyne. They launched a new series aimed at restoring rigorous research, now stifled by the publishing situation, to its rightful position: "Des Travaux. It has the sound of a proclamation: Some Works. Foucault wrote the announcement describing the series' objectives:

> French publishing does not at this time adequately reflect the work that can be done in universities and in other places where research takes place. It also does not reflect anything of this sort undertaken abroad. There are economic reasons for this—production costs, translation costs, and hence the selling prices of such books. There is also the position that books of opinion occupy and the way they are reported in the press. The aim of this series . . . is not to put scholarly books into circuits of mass consumption. It is to establish relations between homogeneous elements—between those who work and those who work . . . There will be three orders of text published here: long and exacting works that editors often shrink from; short works that, in a few dozen pages, spell out a research project so it can be developed as a series; translations of foreign works that we need in order for research in France to break out of its enclave.

The first title, published in February 1983, was Veyne's *Les Grecs ont-ils cru à leurs mythes?* At the end of the volume there was a list of books "forthcoming in the same collection." Two works were announced: *La Reine et le Graal*, by Charles Méla, and *Le Gouvernement de soi et des autres*, by Foucault. The latter would become one of the volumes of *Histoire de la sexualité*.

Everyone close to Foucault at the beginning of the 1980s remembers hearing him talk almost obsessively about the conditions of intellectual research, the role of newspapers in circulating ideas, and, above all, the widespread confusion of values. "Hastily written books saying almost anything about the history of the world from its beginnings, dashing off a reconstitution of more recent histories by means of slogans and ready-made phrases," were put on a level with serious, rigorous books. Or even worse: these less serious works filled up the front of the window, pushing the others into the background, bit by bit depriving them even of the possibility of seeing the light of day.[21]

Foucault especially deplored the decline of the "critical function":

There is no longer any place where exchanges, discussions, perhaps a rather lively debate among different ideas can be expressed. Think about the reviews. They are all cliquish or else a medium of bland eclecticism. It is the very function of critical work that has been forgotten. During the 1950s criticism was a form of work. To read or to discuss a book was an exercise one engaged in somehow for oneself, for one's own profit to change oneself. Speaking well of a book that one did not like or trying to take enough distance in speaking of a book one liked a bit too much, was an effort ensuring that something happened between one writing and another, between one book and another, between a book and an article. Blanchot and Barthes introduced something significant into French thought in the 1950s. Now it seems that criticism has forgotten this function and fallen back upon politicojuridical functions: denouncing the political enemy, judging and condemning, or else judging and singing praises. Those are the most meager and least interesting functions of all. I don't blame anyone. I know all too well that the reactions of an individual are tightly combined with institutional mechanisms, so I cannot say: this is who is responsible. But clearly there no longer exists today any sort of publication that can assume a real critical function.[22]

What remedies might there be for this impoverished situation? "There are several things connected," replied Foucault, in the same interview. "One must rethink what the university can be, or at least that part of the university with which I am best acquainted, where literature, human sciences, philosophy, and so on are studied. Very significant work has been done there during the past twenty years. This must not be allowed to become sterile. Second, the question of university publications has to be rethought, the publication of research and studies. Third, one must work to create places of publication, reviews, pamphlets, and so on." In passing, Foucault also denounced the absurdity of the training dispensed by universities, which was linked to the system of competitions: "The university is still stuck in schoolish exercises that are frequently absurd or antiquated. It is enough to make you cry to see the work a candidate for an *agrégation* in philosophy does. It is fake work, absolutely foreign to what research could be, what it should be. I know a certain number of students who could definitely train themselves by editing texts, making critical editions, translating foreign books, introducing foreign, or even French works. That is, by doing work that could be useful to themselves and to others." Foucault confided in conclusion: "Do you know what my dream is? It would be to start a publishing house for research. I am frantically in pursuit of these possibilities of showing work in motion, in its problematic form; of a place where research could be presented in its hypothetical, provisional aspect."

20

~~~

Missed Appointments

The Place de la Bastille was filled with people singing the "Internationale" and waving red flags. The *peuple de gauche* (people of the left, a phrase that would be much in vogue) noisily celebrated the victory of their candidate for president of the republic. François Mitterrand had defeated Valéry Giscard d'Estaing. Foucault had refused to sign petitions for the Socialist candidate: "People must be considered grown-up enough to decide by themselves when it is time to vote, and to rejoice later if that's what is called for."[1] And indeed, there he was, on May 10, 1981, in the mild Parisian spring, walking with some friends in the midst of the joyous crowd that had surged into the streets as soon as victory was announced. Several days later, considering that "the time has come now to react to what is beginning to be done," he gave public and spectacular support to the new government in an interview that appeared in *Libération*. "I am struck by three things," he said:

> For a good twenty years, a series of questions has been raised within society itself. And for a long time these questions have not had any status in "serious," institutional politics. The socialists seem to have been the only ones to grasp the reality of these problems and take them up—which, no doubt, is not irrelevant to their victory. Second, relating to these problems (I am thinking especially about justice, or the immigrant question), the first measures or first statements are completely in keeping with what one might call a "logic of the left." The logic behind Mitterrand's election. Third, and most remarkable, these measures do not move in the direction of majority opinion. Neither on the death penalty nor on the immigrant question do the choices follow the most commonly held opinion.[2]

As if inspired by some astounding foresight, he added:

It seems to me that this election was felt by many to be a sort of victorious occasion, marking, that is, a change in the relationship between those who rule and those who are ruled. Not that those who are ruled have taken the place of the rulers. After all, this was about a shift in political class. We are entering into a party government, with all the dangers entailed by that, which is something we must never forget. But once this change has occurred, what is at issue is knowing whether it is possible to establish a relationship between the rulers and the ruled that is not a relationship of obedience, but one in which work would play an important role . . . We must escape the dilemma in which one is either for or against. After all, one can stand—face to face. Working with a government does not imply either subjection or total acceptance. One can simultaneously work and stubbornly resist. I even think these two things go together.

But the socialist government would not propose to "work" in common with Foucault. Of course, there were possible posts for him: cultural adviser in New York, or perhaps even director of the Bibliothèque Nationale. It seems clear that in the first instance it was Foucault who declined. No doubt he would have accepted the post of ambassador, but he thought that he was no longer of an age to be cultural adviser; in any event, such a job did not correspond to what he might expect from a government that wanted to honor him. On the other hand, he certainly would have accepted the position as director of the BN. He was already talking—joking, of course, but it proves he was thinking it was a possibility—about the superb apartment that went with the job and the impressive office that would have been at his disposal. But a friend of François Mitterrand's was appointed. And when the post was available again two years later, there was no longer any question of naming Foucault to fill it. His colleague from the Collège de France, André Michel, would be chosen.

Why did the relationship between Foucault and the socialist government deteriorate so rapidly? Because Foucault, who had stood a little off to the side ever since the Iranian affair, made a thundering return into the world of petitions when the coup d'état in Poland took place. He provided a blatant demonstration of what he referred to as his "stubborn resistance" toward power, even left-wing power.

On December 13, 1981, the whole world was dumbfounded to learn that the Polish dream was falling apart; General Wojciech Jaruzelski had just put a brutal end to several months of ferment and expansion in the Solidarity movement. The opposition leaders had been arrested, and tanks were patrolling the streets of the big cities. The reaction of the French foreign minister, Socialist Claude Cheysson, was a harsh shock for all those who had watched hopefully as democratic processes were instituted at Warsaw and Gdansk. Cheysson stated, in effect, that this was a purely internal affair concerning Poland, and that the French government had no intention of getting involved.

The phone rang very early the next day at Foucault's apartment. It was Pierre Bourdieu, proposing some form of reaction to Cheysson's statement, which seemed outrageous to him. Foucault immediately agreed, and minutes later the sociologist and the philosopher were on Rue Vaugirard writing a call for protest. The two had been at the Rue d'Ulm together after Bourdieu's arrival there in 1951. Since then they had not had much to do with each other; their careers and major interests had kept the two somewhat apart. But they had a number of things in common, including great respect for Canguilhem; both claimed to be his disciples. Moreover, Foucault had helped with Bourdieu's election to the Collège de France at the beginning of 1981. Their collaboration on this document marked the beginning of a closer relationship between these two leading lights of the French university. This protest was undoubtedly the first they had ever started together. Bourdieu had not been particularly involved in politics. He had kept his distance from the Communist party in the 1950s and from ultra-left-wing groups in the 1960s and 1970s. On December 14, however, Foucault and Bourdieu were instantly on the same wavelength. They very quickly prepared the text of their appeal, whose tone was quite violent. Foucault also agreed with Bourdieu that they should contact the trade union CFDT (Confédération Française des Travailleurs Démocratique). They hoped to develop ties between a workers' union and the intellectuals similar to those that had existed in Poland between Solidarity and the cultural and university milieus.

But they still had to collect some signatures for the text they had just written, and get it published. They dealt briskly with this business, and a few hours later the appeal was transmitted to *Libération* and to the AFP with the supporting signatures of a number of people considered to be symbols of the French left: Marguerite Duras, who was known to be a friend of François Mitterrand; director Patrice Chéreau; Simone Signoret and Yves Montand and two people who were having lunch with them that day, filmmaker Claude Sautet and writer Jorge Semprun, who enthusiastically joined in signing. Gilles Deleuze was contacted but preferred to abstain, not wanting to put the new Socialist government in a difficult position. On December 15 the appeal, titled

"Les Rendez-vous manqués" (Missed appointments), appeared in *Libération*.

> The French government must not, like Moscow and Washington, make us believe that setting up a military dictatorship in Poland is an internal affair leaving the Polish people with the ability to decide their destiny themselves. This is an untrue and immoral assertion . . . In 1936, a socialist government found itself confronted with a military putsch in Spain; in 1956, a socialist government found itself confronted with repression in Hungary. In 1981, a socialist government is confronted with the coup in Warsaw. We do not want it to take the same attitude as its predecessors. We remind it of its promise to assert the obligations of international moral standards against the obligations of *Realpolitik*.

Then came the list of the first signers—very short, but very prestigious: "Pierre Bourdieu, professor at the Collège de France; Patrice Chéreau, director; Marguerite Duras, writer; Bernard Kouchner, Médecins du Monde; Michel Foucault, professor at the Collège de France; Claude Mauriac, writer; Yves Montand, actor; Claude Sautet, producer; Jorge Semprun, writer; Simone Signoret, actress."[3]

Libération printed the appeal far down in one corner of the front page. The editors certainly had not tried to make it obvious. But these few lines followed by these few names had an enormous impact. Ivan Levaï, the anchor on Europe I radio during the peak morning hours, immediately invited Foucault and Montand to appear on his news program on December 16 and explain their ideas. On December 17 *Libération* reprinted the protest with new signatures: comedian Guy Bedos, sculptor Ypoustéguy, filmmaker Jean-Louis Comolli, historian Pierre Vidal-Naquet. An address was given: more signatures and expressions of support could be sent to sociologist Jeannine Verdès-Leroux. *Libération*, which had announced that it would publish new lists of signers every day, soon had to give up, the influx of mail was so great. There were well-known names from the world of the arts and the university: Claude Roy and Loleh Bellon, Suzanne Flon, René Allio, Emmanuel Le Roy Ladurie, Georges Canguilhem, Jean Bollack, Paul Veyne. Dozens of scholars, university and lycée students, and members of the trade unions sent pages filled with signatures that they had collected in lecture halls, classes, labs, and offices. There were letters, too, ranging from simple expressions of support to offers of help in whatever needed to be done.

The petition seemed to express perfectly the current of sympathy that brought fifty thousand people into the streets of Paris to protest the coup in Poland. During this demonstration the Socialist leaders were booed and hissed, greeted with cries of "Chacun chez soi, merci Cheysson." There was, in fact, a considerable mobilization in France surrounding the events in Poland, and the press as a whole devoted a great many pages to it every day. Sales of *Libération* skyrocketed; it acted as the mouthpiece of the entire movement, and even published in a special issue all the articles and commentary that had appeared on a daily basis.

The Socialist party's reaction was on the same scale as the support for Foucault and Bourdieu's appeal. Lionel Jospin, the party's first secretary, violently attacked Montand during a radio broadcast, recalling that the singer-actor had toured the Soviet Union in 1956. The next day Montand replied in a public letter: "It is because I went to the USSR in 1956 that no one has ever again made me swallow words such as 'counterrevolution' or 'noninterference in the affairs of sister parties' or 'there is nothing to be done.'"[4] Jack Lang, the minister of culture, joined in the counterattack. "What clowns, what dishonesty," he choked out indignantly in *Les Nouvelles littéraires*. In an interview in *Le Matin* he went on to describe this group of intellectuals as proof of a "typically structuralist fecklessness . . . One is obliged to note that the first wish of the signers, before being of any help to the Polish people, is to break up the French political majority."[5]

It is true that the so-called united left was on the verge of implosion and that the right was clamoring for the resignation of the government's Communist ministers. But Lang's virulence can probably be more easily explained by the fact that he saw himself as the minister of the intellectuals, accountable for their actions. Above all, he had been too quick to believe that everyone with leftist views was going to unite in supporting this new power that had just swept away the right. Using the rhetoric of the new government, the minister of culture liked to describe the left's accession to power as a passage from "darkness" to "light." In this context, any petition written by well-known people on the left and addressed to a power that, as he saw it, they should consider to be theirs, seemed inadmissible, unthinkable, impossible. And yet that was certainly what had just happened. Therefore, he would use all the resources at his disposal to organize a "backfire," as a woman who had long worked with him described it, and show that the intellectuals en masse were behind him and the president.

This campaign first took the form of another petition, published— as an advertisement, paid for by the ministry—on an entire half-page of *Le Monde*. Lang paid one of his friends, the writer Jean-Pierre Faye, to collect signatures for a text both denouncing the repression in Poland and supporting Mitterrand's action. Many important individuals signed this letter, but few knew about the strategy behind it. François Jacob, Jean Lacouture, Alfred Kastler, Vladimir Jankélévitch, Antoine Vitez, and Jean Daniel were there; also Pierre Vidal-Naquet, who denied having agreed to add his name; and Gilles Deleuze.

Lang and Faye also organized a huge demonstration of support for the Polish people at the Paris Opera on December 22, with two thousand people invited. Foucault, Signoret, Montand, and Patrice Chéreau decided to go together and met at a nearby café beforehand. Unlike the others, Foucault had not received a written invitation. "Costa-Gavras and I tried in vain to give him one of our invitations," Claude Mauriac recalls. "Not on your life, he exclaimed, there's no way. If anyone demanded he show them an invitation and if they refused to let him in, he would immediately leave (and we would leave with him, we all said, Simone Signoret, Costa-Gavras, Chéreau, and I) and make a phone call. Where would he call? *Libération*, of course. Imagine the uproar. He wouldn't miss it for the world. He was gloating in advance, but although we had certainly decided to act in solidarity with him, we were not really very sure, on the contrary, that it was advisable."[6] But there was no incident. Foucault had no problem entering the Opera.

The polemics continued. Bourdieu, speaking for those who had protested, pinned Lang and Jospin brutally against the ropes. He claimed that intellectuals were independent in relation to any government in power, then argued for a return to the tradition of a "libertarian left" that had been stifled by a left of party machinery and "apparatchiks."[7] As a result there was a complete break between the Socialist government and several of the most important representatives of French culture. The Socialists, however, despite appearances and despite their virulent reaction, had not been deaf to the protests. When Foucault and Montand were interviewed on the radio, the Elysée sent a policeman on a motorcycle to pick up a tape of the broadcast. And at the same time that they were aggressively replying to the intellectuals who had signed the protest, both Jospin and Lang were doing their best to set things straight; they refused responsibility for the things Cheysson had said, insisting that they were the views of their author only, not of all Socialists.

But the harm had been done, and it would be some time before Foucault let this episode rest. He would never make up with the Socialist party and its government, despite many overtures from the latter. When Jack Lang invited him to his office to talk, Foucault went in and straight back out, telling his friends: "I called him an idiot." No doubt the exchange was less harsh, but one thing is certain: the bridges were almost completely broken. True, Foucault did attend a lunch in September 1982 organized by François Mitterrand, with Beauvoir, Vidal-Naquet, and Daniel. But, as he told his friends, it was something he "couldn't get out of." With a few important exceptions, Foucault had no further relations with the Socialists. He also announced that he would never again read *Le Monde*, because Jacques Fauvet, the editor-in-chief, had criticized the intellectuals who "found it so hard to accept the tenth of May." He never missed a chance to urge all his friends and students to follow his example.

Foucault and Bourdieu's "missed appointments" appeal had one positive and immediate result: Bourdieu's idea was realized and a connection with the CFDT immediately established. In fact Bourdieu telephoned the colleagues of Edmond Maire, the secretary-general of the union, the very day the signatures were being collected. Maire mentioned these conversations in an interview published in *Libération* on December 15—that is, in the same issue that contained the Foucault-Bourdieu protest: "This morning we were contacted by a number of intellectuals who have previously had no specific connection with CFDT. They hope that the worker-intellectual link that provided one of the frameworks and one of the strengths of Solidarity will manifest itself in France." A first meeting was held on December 16 at the CFDT offices on Rue Cadet, in the ninth arrondissement. Several leaders of the group of affiliated trade unions attended, including Maire, who had to leave early for a meeting with the prime minister. Foucault, Bourdieu, and the mathematician Henri Cartan were present, as well as several academics who had had some connection with CFDT: Alain Touraine, Jacques Julliard, and Pierre Rosanvallon. Bourdieu urged the creation of a permanent liaison between the union and the group of intellectuals meeting on this occasion, so that they could react quickly in case of emergency. Foucault urged that an information center or a press agency be established to collect, filter, and recirculate every sort of information (political, legal, and so on) about the situation in Poland.

A jointly written text was prepared at another meeting the next day and made public on December 22 at the main union headquarters, in Square Montholon. A hundred people were present. Side by side on the podium were Maire, Bourdieu, Foucault, and CFDT leader

Jacques Chérèque. The mathematician Laurent Schwartz read the prepared text: "It is not enough to condemn the bid for power . . . We
must join forces with the Polish people in their struggle." Then badges
were given out. Soon small white rectangles with Solidarity's symbol in
red letters were adorning jacket and coat lapels; Foucault wore his for
several months. He spoke at some length during this meeting: "We
have to work for the long haul and constantly. The first problem is one
of information. The voice of Solidarity must not be stifled. We must
therefore stress the importance of establishing a press agency, able to
provide news on a daily basis, at the disposal of Solidarity." He also
proposed sending a mission of lawyers and physicians to Poland and
mentioned the projects of Médecins du Monde and its "Varsovivre"
operations.

This event at CFDT headquarters was followed by a series of meetings at the Jussieu *faculté* leading up to a "study day" about Poland on
February 20. Foucault attended all the preparatory sessions and the
study day itself, at which there were several hundred people.

But some participants in these study groups questioned the nature of
their relationship with CFDT. Shortly before the study day there was
a brief explosion. "We do not want to become fellow travelers with
CFDT," they said. "You are there as an organization," they told the
union representatives, "and we are there as individuals. We are going
to be made into satellites." Foucault went to work to calm people down
and offered some conciliatory words: "It is not a matter of becoming
fellow travelers. It is not a matter of walking alongside, but of working
with." Soon after the study day, he abandoned the meetings at Jussieu;
he was somewhat weary of their "folkloric" aspect, especially their complete lack of effectiveness or usefulness. Bourdieu had long before
fallen by the wayside, for the same reasons. The movement did not
long survive their silent departure.

For several months, however, he continued to work with the Solidarity committee formed by a Polish group in Paris. Seweryn Blumsztajn, the head of the committee, recalled that Foucault, "with
exceptional devotion, devoted hours on end to helping with the most
bureaucratic and repetitive tasks. He could always be counted on. I had
the impression that I was making him waste precious time. For example, he was a member of our finances committee. I remember his
long accounts, complete with all the figures. I couldn't help thinking he
had better things to do."[8]

Foucault evidently thought otherwise. He spared no efforts in behalf
of the Polish people. In September 1982, for example, he and Simone

Signoret accompanied Bernard Kouchner and two other physicians, Jean-Pierre Maubert and Jacques Lebas, on the last "Varsovivre" mission organized by Médecins du Monde. For three thousand kilometers they took turns at the wheel of the small van carrying the Polish people medicine that Kouchner admitted "they did not really need." For Kouchner these treks were "the only way we had of not abandoning those who bore the hopes of this great caged-in half of Europe."[9] The van was also carrying, much more discreetly, printing materials. In Warsaw they met with militants, intellectuals, and students. They wanted to visit Walesa in prison but were never given authorization. A visit to Auschwitz evoked intense emotion. "We separated to go down," wrote Kouchner, "and all took turns waiting alone for a moment, for a long, long second, standing before the crematorial oven until it became perfectly clear in its thermal simplicity."[10]

Upon his return from Poland, Foucault explained the reasons for the trip:

> The Polish people need us to talk to them and to go there. But they also need us to talk about Poland when we get back. At the present time there is no discussion in France about Poland, about the aid we provide it and the financing of its debts. Poland poses a permanent problem, the problem of Europe's relations with the Soviet bloc, the problem of the division of Europe. And, except for very short periods—times of invasions or coups d'état—no one talks about it. "Not only are you letting us down," say the Poles, "but you are letting yourselves down," as if by letting them down we were renouncing a part of ourselves.[11]

This action in behalf of Poland was Foucault's last political demonstration. It took him back over traces of his own past in Warsaw, where he had lived and worked twenty-five years before. To this country he had had to leave so suddenly, he now returned to pay his respects once more to "the great stubborn sun of Polish freedom," as he had called it in the preface to *Folie et déraison*.

Foucault maintained his ties with CFDT and with Edmond Maire. With the latter he published a long dialogue titled "La Pologne et après . . . ," a joint reflection on unionism, popular movements, politics, the left and its history. "The problem, therefore, was Poland," said Foucault at the beginning of this interview.

> What was happening there provided the example of a movement that was a union movement through and through but all of whose aspects, all of whose actions, all of whose effects, had political dimensions.

What was happening there posed (not for the first time, but for the first time in a very long time) the problem of Europe; and here [in France] it was, at the same time, a test to know how much weight the Communist presence in the government carried. This is, of course, the point at which the meeting with CFDT came about, as you know. We did not "seek out" each other; an "alliance" with a handful of intellectuals had no strategic value for you; and the weight of a union with a million members was not necessarily reassuring for us. We met up with each other at the same point, and were only surprised that it had not happened sooner—considering how long certain intellectuals had been hashing over this sort of problem and considering how long CFDT had been one of the places where political, economic, and social thinking was most active.[12]

This "working with," something that had not happened with the traditional left, was what Foucault was trying to achieve with CFDT. One result was his participation in a volume edited by the union about the problems with the social security system.[13] CFDT remembered this collaboration and paid homage to Foucault shortly after his death by organizing an exposition and publishing a collection of articles by Maire, Kouchner, and Bourdieu.[14]

In further fallout from this militant fervor, during the summer of 1983 Foucault planned to write a short book on—against—the Socialists. He had been astounded and irritated by all the uproar orchestrated during July and August on the subject of "the silence of left-wing intellectuals." A broad discussion had been organized in the columns of *Le Monde* about the disappearance of the left-wing petition signers. An article by Max Gallo, a mouthpiece for the government, had been its point of departure. This article was extremely levelheaded and seemed very much like an offer of reconciliation. Gallo responded to those who wondered where were the Gides, the Malrauxs, the Alains, the Langevins of yesteryear, and to those who searched the podiums at meetings to count the number of intellectuals there, with an attempted analysis:

> May and June '81, whose connection with May '68 is nonetheless obvious, may seem to be a victory for the left in which intellectuals as a group participated relatively little, at least actively. Which explains some of the difficulties arising between this group of intellectuals and the new government: reciprocal misunderstandings, frustrations, and appeals by institutions to the artists and intellectuals who had been formally involved in political support and who were not the most

"advanced" in terms of the work involved. Whence the feeling on the part of many intellectuals of having been forgotten or misunderstood, or called upon merely to celebrate and praise. This situation is fraught with consequences.

The article ended with this sentence, seeming to side with the intellectuals whom the Socialist party had attacked a year and a half before: "It is not big names on the platforms of political engagement that the country needs most, but concrete involvement in thought, completely independent, completely honest."[15] A long series of articles and a long controversy followed. But Foucault said nothing. In private he was ironic: "When I wanted to talk in December 1981, they told me to shut up. When I shut up, they are surprised at my silence. Which means just one thing: they give me the right to speak only when I agree with them." More seriously, he advanced his work with CFDT: "While people are mulling over the silence of the intellectuals, I was thinking about health care with members of the union." But he was not particularly happy with what he interpreted as a veritable injunction, a call to order, and the expression of "latent Pétainism," as he put it on numerous occasions. "Mitterrand is Pétain," he told anyone who would listen. He talked about this controversy in an interview published one month before his death:

> When we urged you to change your discourse, you condemned us with your most worn-out slogans. And how you are changing direction, under pressure of a reality that you are incapable of perceiving; you are asking us to provide you, not with the thought that might enable you to confront it, but with a discourse that would conceal your change. The trouble lies not, as has been said, in the fact that intellectuals ceased to be Marxists as soon as the Communists came to power; it lies in the fact that the scruples of your alliance prevented you, when it would have been useful, from carrying out with the intellectuals the work of thought that would have made you capable of governing.[16]

Foucault, then, planned to write a small book on "governing in a different way," as a reply to the things said about his silence. In it he hoped to analyze the underlying reasons for the successive failures of leftist governments in France. What the Socialists lacked, he thought, was precisely the "art of governing," and this he wanted to demonstrate by going back in history. He had started reading Blum's texts. He had even thought of a title, "La tête des socialistes," because he intended to explore the mental structures of members of the party. He was exasperated with all the cursory analyses that had sprung up on the totalitarian phenomenon: "This notion of totalitarianism is not a pertinent concept. With such a crude instrument nothing can be understood. What has to be studied is the parties, the party function." The book was supposed to take the form of an interview with me. Paul Otchakovsky-Laurens, the editor of the small press where it was to be published, had even sent him a researcher to help him with the library work. The book, of course, never came to be; it would hardly be begun. From the moment the discussion began Foucault saw it was not possible to approach such a complex and burning issue, on which many books had already been written, without putting in several years of work. There were other, more essential jobs awaiting him. *Histoire de la sexualité* was once again on track, and he still had hopes of finishing it in the months to come.

In the fall of 1983 Foucault organized a study group with Bernard Kouchner, André Glucksmann, Pierre Blanchet, Claire Brière, and Michelle Beauvillard, and several others. They somewhat self-mockingly called it Tarnier Academy, after the hospital where they held their meetings. This was an attempt to bring together, outside the political parties, people who wanted to take up again the tasks that Foucault had envisaged during his involvement with Poland: providing information and at the same time seeking possibilities for action. Each meeting focused on a specific problem, such as Lebanon, Afghanistan, or Poland. Foucault also wanted someday to devote a meeting to the left wing in France. Foucault and Kouchner planned to publish their reflections and their discussions in a review with the straightforward name *Académie Tarnier*. The group broke up soon after Foucault's death. "It was really around him that we were meeting," said Brière. "He was the intellectual and moral authority around whom we wanted to meet. After his death there was no longer any sense in continuing. Anyhow, for me, there wasn't even any question of it."

Other plans arose from Foucault's long conversations with Bourdieu during this period. "If we do nothing we will be severely reproached if the right wing returns to power," Foucault remarked constantly, according to Bourdieu's account. They agreed that they should explore a "logic of the left," emphasizing all the things the Socialists did nothing about, or did too little, or did so badly. The result would be a kind of "white paper" written by a collective of specialists, who would describe the unrest and the problems in several spheres, offer possible solutions, and propose forms of action. The focus would be on culture, education, and research. This project, too, was never realized.

Michel Rocard, the minister of planning, wanted to establish a study commission to examine these same questions. Simon Nora was to be the head, and Bourdieu and Foucault agreed to serve. Rocard was one of the few men in the Socialist government with whom they had not broken their ties. Jean Daniel organized several lunches in a restaurant near the Place des Victoires, bringing together Rocard, Foucault, Maire, Bourdieu, and people from *Le Nouvel Observateur*, such as Franz-Olivier Giesbert and Jacques Julliard. For that matter, it was only after Rocard became prime minister in May 1988 that a real reconciliation came about between the 1981 "petitioners" and the Socialist government. Bernard Kouchner became government secretary for humanitarian action, and Pierre Bourdieu was made president of a study commission on the content of instruction, set up by Lionel Jospin, the education minister. Perhaps, as Bourdieu thinks today, this happened because, for those at the head of the Socialist party, the whole story of "missed appointments" marked a painful rift in their consciousness and profoundly changed their image of the relationship a government could have with intellectuals; because they were able to understand the lesson they had been given. Who can say if Michel Foucault today might not have been the head of a commission on reform of the penal code?

In 1984 Foucault asked Bernard Kouchner to entrust him with a mission. They discussed it and came up with several possibilities. Finally the physician suggested that he organize and be responsible for the next "boat for Vietnam." Foucault accepted. He intended to leave as soon as he had finished *Histoire de la sexualité*.

21

Zen and California

The cardinal, in his red robe, led the ceremony," said Michel Foucault. "He stepped before the faithful and greeted them with cries of 'Shalom, shalom!' All around the square there were armed police, and inside the church plainclothes police. The police drew back; it had no power against this. I have to say that there was a grandeur to this, a power; it carried immense historical weight." Foucault was in Brazil in October 1975 for a series of lectures when a journalist, a member of the clandestine Communist party, was killed at police headquarters. He was a Jew, "but the Jewish community," said Foucault, "did not dare hold a funeral. And it was the archbishop of São Paulo who wanted a ceremony—interdenominational, moreover—to be held in the Cathedral of Saint Paul in memory of the journalist. It drew thousands and thousands of people to the church, to the square . . ."[1] It was a period of repression, with successive arrests and acts of violence. Foucault did not want to continue giving his course in this atmosphere, and he made a public statement at the university to make it understood that he refused to teach in this country in which freedom did not exist. "At that time we were under police surveillance," recalls Gérard Lebrun, with whom Foucault was staying. Foucault almost immediately left the country.

He had already spent some time in São Paulo: in 1965, in 1973 at the invitation of the Catholic University of Rio de Janeiro, and in 1974 at the Institute for Social Medicine at the medical school in Rio. He had made trips into the interior as far as Belo Horizonte. Foucault certainly loved Brazil, delighted in it. After the incidents in 1975, however, he knew he had become an undesirable. No doubt it was to defy this unofficial ban that, in 1976, he agreed to give a series of lectures for the

Alliance Française in Salvador, the capital of the state of Bahia, in Recife, and in Belém. But there were no incidents or difficulties.

Although Foucault moved back to France for good when he returned from Tunisia, he by no means gave up traveling. His courses at the Collège de France took up a great deal of his time and energy; they required immense preparation. But the professors of the college were obligated to give only twenty-four hours of teaching a year (twelve hours of lecture and twelve of seminar). If they taught two hours a week, they could discharge their responsibility in approximately three months. Foucault, then, had time to travel. From 1970 to 1983 he spent several short periods in Brazil, Japan, Canada, and, of course, the United States.

In Japan in April 1978, hoping to be initiated into the practice of Zen, he made a strange experiment. His master, Omori Sogen, who was head of the international center for Zen meditation at Seionji temple, at Uenohara, suggested that he spend several days participating in the life of the monks. Christian Polac, the cultural attaché at the French embassy and a journalist for the review *Shunjuu*, accompanied Foucault. Afterward they published a report on the philosopher's voyage into the world of religion. "I am very interested in the Buddhist philosophy," Foucault told the *bonze* who greeted him, "but that is not the reason I have come. What is most interesting to me is life in a Zen temple itself, that is, the practice of Zen, its driving forces and its rules." When the *bonze* asked him what he thought the relationship between Zen and Christian mysticism was, Foucault answered: "The interesting thing in Christian spirituality is that one is always in search of further individualization. One is attempting to grasp what is at the basis of the individual soul. 'Tell me who you are': that is the spirituality of Christianity. In Zen, it seems to me that all the techniques connected to spirituality tend, on the contrary, to obliterate the individual." After this preliminary discussion and the visit to the buildings, it was time to actually do it. The *bonze* explained to him how to sit, how to breathe, until the little bell rang to signal the end of the meditation exercise.[2] Foucault later said, "It's very hard." Foucault was clearly very interested in Japan. How could he avoid investigating a civilization that, with respect to Western rationality and its limits, constitutes a sort of "enigma, very hard to decipher"? But although he was intrigued by what he saw of Japan, it never became a lover's passion, as it did for Barthes and Lévi-Strauss.

The country with which Foucault established the most intense relationship was the United States. His first visits, to the University of Buffalo at the invitation of its French department, occurred in 1970 and 1972, when he was just becoming known on American campuses; no more than a hundred people attended his lectures—in French—first on exchange and money, and in 1972 on the history of truth, based on an analysis of justice in ancient Greece. During his first visit he stayed at the faculty club, a rather stiff place where he was asked to wear a tie for dinner—a request scarcely guaranteed to please: he always preferred turtlenecks, the eternal white turtleneck made famous by dozens of pictures.

In 1972 John K. Simon in the French department engaged the help of a law professor who specialized in prison reform to arrange a visit to Attica, forty miles from Buffalo. The year before, this penitentiary had been the scene of extremely violent riots and a bloody repression; almost a hundred people had died. Foucault was very impressed by this enormous fortress, whose exterior resembled a medieval castle. He was struck, he told Simon later, by the "Disneyland" aspect of the entrance, behind which was hidden a "huge machine," "a machinery" of clean, neat corridors that determined, for those who went down them, trajectories that were direct, effective, and observable. Foucault also discussed his interest in the penitentiary system:

> Traditional sociology put the problem more in these terms: how can a society make individuals live together? . . . I was interested by the opposite problem, or, if you will, by the opposite answer to this problem: through what system of exclusion, eliminating whom, creating what division, through what workings of negation and rejection, is society able to function? But the question I will ask myself in the future is turned around: prison is too complex an organization to be reduced to the negative functions of exclusion. Its cost, the care taken with its administration, the justifications that one attempts to give it, seem to indicate that it possesses positive functions.[3]

Thereafter Foucault traveled to the United States more often. He lectured in New York in 1973. In the spring of 1975 he went to Berkeley for the first time, at the invitation of Leo Bersani, head of the French department. There he laid out for a hundred listeners the broad outline of what would become *La Volonté de savoir*.

In November 1975 Foucault participated in a "countercultural" colloquium in New York sponsored by the review *Semiotext(e)*, headed by Sylvère Lotringer. The meeting was moved from the Columbia University campus to Teachers College to accommodate the thousand participants. Foucault gave a lecture about sexuality and held a dialogue with Ronald Laing, one of the founders of the antipsychiatric movement. The left-wing composition of the audience perhaps accounts for the tone and content of what he said. He made thundering pronouncements, but always in order to maintain the rights of analysis and the theoretical gaze:

> I think that what has happened since 1960 is the simultaneous appearance of new forms of fascism, new forms of consciousness of fascism, new forms of description of fascism, and new forms of struggle against fascism. And the role of the intellectual since the 1960s has been, precisely, to situate oneself according to one's experiences, one's skills, one's personal choices, one's desire—to situate oneself at a certain point that will be such that one can simultaneously make visible forms of fascism that unfortunately are not seen or are too easily tolerated, describe these forms of fascism, try to make them intolerable, and define what specific form of struggle can be undertaken against fascism.

Foucault took psychiatry and the prison as examples and concluded: "I think that the question 'are you a writer or a militant?' is an old question that is now completely out of date, and in any case the specifics of what has recently been undertaken exclude the separation of theoretical or historical analysis from the particular struggle."[4] One incident put Foucault in a black rage: someone stood up after his lecture on sexuality (read in English by its translator) and accused Foucault of belonging to government bodies in charge of the prisons and of having come to New York to inform the French authorities about radical activity in America. Later, in the middle of the discussion with Laing, someone shouted: "Laing and Foucault are both paid by the CIA!" This time Foucault remained coolheaded and replied: "Yes, everybody is paid by the CIA except me. I'm paid by the KGB." This colloquium marked an important breakthrough for the French philosopher in America.

Another great moment followed a more classic, academic model. Foucault gave the Tanner Lectures at Stanford in October 1979, discussing "pastoral power." The title of the lecture series was "Omnes et Singulatim: Toward a Critique of Political Reason." More than three hundred people came to hear him, but most of the philosophy professors were absent—not because they refused to have anything to do with Foucault, but because they were not particularly interested in "French thought," which they felt to be insufficiently "argumentative." At this time Hubert Dreyfus and Paul Rabinow, two professors at Berkeley who were writing a book on his work, telephoned Foucault and asked to meet him, which he immediately agreed to do. "Here are my assassins," he said to them when they came to see him in his San Francisco hotel. But he worked with them for eight hours, beginning a regular collaboration based on friendly intellectual exchange. The resulting book contains several interviews with Foucault.[5] Additional interviews, along with extracts from books, articles, lectures, and unpublished prefaces, were published later in *The Foucault Reader*, edited by Rabinow.[6]

In October 1980 Foucault was a visiting professor at Berkeley, again at the invitation of the French department. He also gave the prestigious Howison Lectures, titled "Truth and Subjectivity." The lectures were widely discussed on campus, where already his welcome had reached "fanfare" level, according to Keith Gandal and Stephen Kotkin.[7] So many people attended that the police had to intervene to close the doors. The next month Foucault lectured at the Humanities Institute of New York University before a crowd of six or seven hundred people, in tandem with the sociologist and novelist Richard Sennett. *Time* magazine devoted two pages, filled with ironic comments on his "opaque" theories, to the "cult" developing around the French philosopher. It emphasized that Foucault had an abundance of bitter enemies in American universities, where his work was often severely judged and harshly attacked.[8] Conservatives reproached him for his radical positions, Marxists for his hopeless "nihilism." He was even reproached for being responsible, through his analysis of the asylums, for the presence of bag ladies in New York's streets. More than once Foucault had to draw weapons to set facts straight, to oppose aberrant readings, to protest against "monstrosities in criticism."[9]

By now Foucault drew huge crowds—at UCLA in 1981, at the University of Vermont for six weeks in 1982, and again at Berkeley in the spring of 1983. More than two thousand people attended his public lecture, "The Culture of the Self"; only Lévi-Strauss would draw larger audiences. By now Foucault was speaking in English. But he preferred to spend his time setting up work teams and research groups.

He returned to Berkeley—his last trip to the United States—in the fall of 1983, at the invitation of both the French and philosophy departments, although he was still completely ignored by most American philosophers. Specialists in logic or language theories saw no need of this "literature," which they ranked in the very French tradition of Bergson and Sartre. Foucault's audience consisted primarily of historians, such as the students of Peter Brown, whose book on St. Augustine Foucault knew almost by heart; or Rabinow's students from the anthropology department. Foucault gave a course on liberalism and a more restricted seminar on the "arts of governing" in the 1920s. His students divided up the periods and countries: Germany, England, the United States, the USSR, and so on. In another lecture series on the importance of "truth-speaking" in ancient Greece, he analyzed the problem of "veridiction" in relation to "care of the self" and to ethics, tracing the evolution of the notion of truth. These lectures came out of his course at the Collège de France and undoubtedly represented one of the major directions in which his last research was heading.

Students loved this prestigious professor who enjoyed talking with them. He was always available during office hours at Dwinelle Hall, always ready to hear questions or requests, always ready to give advice or clear something up. "At first, we didn't dare go," David Horn recalled. "But then when we brought ourselves to do it, everything went terrifically well. We even went to lunch or dinner with him."

Foucault also spent many hours in the library. Each time he returned to France, he was full of praise for American libraries—what wonderful places they were to work in, with their extraordinary wealth, marvelous organization, and abundant and competent staffs. Berkeley's library was like the Carolina Rediviva to the tenth power. Foucault spent hours there, reading, taking notes, filling up index cards. He was finishing *Histoire de la sexualité*, but he had other projects. He meant to pursue his work on liberalism and get back to work on a book that would focus on sexual morality in the sixteenth century and the role of "the techniques of self," the examination of one's conscience and the care for the soul in Catholic and Protestant churches.

Foucault's influence remains considerable in the United States. After his death, colloquiums on his work in New York and Berkeley were attended by dozens of scholars and hundreds of students. The work group that Foucault set up in Berkeley is still functioning, publishing its results regularly in a newsletter, *History of the Present*; every issue also contains previously unpublished work by Foucault or articles about him. In 1981 *Time* called it a cult. Ten years later, Americans' passion for Foucault's work has lost none of its fervor.

⚡

FOR FOUCAULT the United States represented not only the pleasure of work but also, quite simply, pleasure. He savored the freedom available in New York and San Francisco, where reviews and newspapers thrive along with bars and nightclubs in homosexual neighborhoods. There, a vast gay community is organized and determined to establish its rights. And there, too, homosexuality is not limited to the young—unlike France, where a homosexual has to be young and beautiful if he wants to assert his sexual preference.

Discovering that homosexuality, which he had had so much trouble acknowledging and accepting, was an open and visible way of life and culture in New York and San Francisco, Foucault now wanted to live it to the full. In an interview with the gay newspaper *The Advocate* in Los Angeles, he said: "Sexuality is a part of our behavior. It's part of our world freedom. Sexuality is something that we ourselves create. It is our own creation, and much more than the discovery of a secret side of our desire. We have to understand that with our desires go new forms of relationships, new forms of love, new forms of creation. Sex is not a fatality; it's a possibility for creative life. It is not enough to affirm that we are gay but we must also create a gay life." He also talked about the "subculture of sado-masochism." "The practice of S/M is the creation of pleasure . . . And that's why S/M is really a subculture. It's a process of invention. S/M is the *use* of a strategic relationship as a source of pleasure (physical pleasure)." This "possibility of using our bodies as a possible source of very numerous pleasures is something that is very important." He went on to speak of the role of drugs: "Drugs have now become a part of our culture. Just as there is bad music and good music, there are bad drugs and good drugs."[10]

It seems that Foucault's experience of "good drugs" was not limited to the few "marijuana plants" that *Time* mentioned as growing on his balcony in Paris. Claude Mauriac reports a conversation he had with Foucault in 1975: "LSD, cocaine, opium, he tried them all, except of course heroin, but mightn't he even try that in his present dizzy state?"[11] And Foucault told Paul Veyne that he was under the influence of opium when he was hit by a car in July 1978, on the Rue de Vaugirard in front of the building where he lived. When he was taken to the hospital he asked someone to tell Simone Signoret, because he was supposed to give her the text of a petition. To the actress's great astonishment, a policeman phoned and, after excusing himself for bothering her, said: "There is a Monsieur Foucault who wants us to tell you he's had an accident." "You don't know who he is?" she exclaimed. "He's the greatest French philosopher!"

The most important thing in the interview in *The Advocate* is, perhaps, how the history of homosexual friendship has become a theme.

One thing that interests me now is the problem of friendship. For centuries after Antiquity, friendship was a very important kind of social relation: a social relation within which people had a certain freedom, a certain kind of choice . . . as well as very intense emotional relations . . . I think that in the sixteenth and seventeenth centuries we see these kinds of friendship disappearing, at least in the male society . . . One of my hypotheses . . . is that homosexuality became a problem—that is, sex between men became a problem—in the eighteenth century. We see the rise of it as a problem with the police, within the justice system, and so on. I think the reason it appears as a problem, as a social issue, at this time is that friendship had disappeared. As long as friendship was something important, was socially accepted, nobody realized men had sex together. You couldn't say men *didn't have* sex together—it just didn't matter . . . But once friendship disappeared as a culturally accepted relationship, the issue arose, "What is going on between men?" . . . I'm sure that the disappearance of friendship as a social relation and the declaration of homosexuality as a social-political-medical problem are the same process.[12]

The joy of America for Foucault was that he had finally achieved a reconciliation with himself. He was happy in his work. He was happy in pleasures of the flesh. Starting in the early 1980s he gave very serious thought to leaving France—it was harder and harder for him to deal with Paris—and moving to the United States. He dreamed aloud of living in the Californian paradise. Sunny, magnificent . . .

But that was precisely where the new plague began to spread its agonizing devastation.

22

Life as a Work of Art

This series of studies is being published later than I had antici-
pated and in an altogether different form."[1] Eight years had
gone by between the appearance of *La Volonté de savoir*, which
was supposed to serve as an introduction to a five-volume work, and
the publication in June 1984 of *L'Usage des plaisirs* and *Le Souci de soi*.
During these years Foucault had reworked and reorganized his undertaking several times to take into account the problems he had encountered along the way. At first he had sought the bedrock of his proposed
"archaeology of psychoanalysis" in the beginnings of the "discourse on
sexuality" in Christianity and in the doctrine of confession. He began
reading confession manuals and plunged into Christian literature. His
course at the Collège de France in 1979–80, called "the government of
the living," was "devoted to the procedures of soul-seeking and confession in early Christianity." The central issue was "how a type of
government of men is formed in which what is required is not simply
to obey but also to reveal, by saying it, what one is." In the course
Foucault analyzed the "history of the practices of penitence" and the
codification of the "examination of conscience" in monasteries, combined with the duty to tell everything about oneself to the elder or
to the master.[2] Using this research, Foucault completed a book that
he called "Les Aveux de la chair" (Confessions of the flesh). But during
this encounter with Christian morality, he found that it was impossible
to consider early Christianity without also considering what had gone
before—without locating the provenance of these "forms of relationship to oneself" that the Christian "doctrine of the flesh" used and
transformed into a theory of sin and transgression. And what Foucault
discovered, in his analysis of early Christianity, was not the emergence
of a new way of life, more "austere" and "rigorous," but a new form of

the "technique of the self." He therefore had to jettison his introduction to "Les Aveux de la chair," because here he contented himself with reproducing certain "commonplaces" found in books of this period, which attributed to the pagan culture a freer and more tolerant sexual morality than evidence allows us to see. On the contrary, the Christian theme of "austerity" was already present, to a great extent, in earlier cultures. But also because, above all, he found that the principal concern in pagan culture was not with rigorous rules of austerity but with a "technique of self," the "formation of self." So he went on a new search: a search for themes of "the care of the self" and "the use of pleasure" in ancient philosophy, to see how pagan moralities had constituted these "modes of subjection" just before Christianity developed its doctrines. His course at the Collège de France for 1980–81, "subjectivity and truth," "studied, in the work of philosophers, moralists, and physicians of the period from the first century B.C. to the second century A.D., the development in Greek and Roman cultures of the 'technique of life,' the 'technique of existence.' These techniques of life were considered only as they applied to the sort of acts that the Greeks called *aphrodisia;* a word for which, clearly, our notion of 'sexuality' is a thoroughly inadequate translation." Foucault added: "We can see how far we are from a history of the sexuality that was to be organized around the good old repressive hypothesis and its usual questions (how and why is desire repressed?). It is a matter of acts and pleasures, not of desire. It is a matter of the formation of self through techniques of life, and not through repression, taboo, and law. It is a matter of showing not how sex has been kept separate, but how this long history linking sex and the subject in our societies was begun." [3]

In 1981–82 Foucault went back a little further in a course called "the hermeneutics of the subject": "The point of departure for a study devoted to care of the self is, quite naturally, Plato's dialogue *Alcibiades.* In it three questions arise, concerning the relationship between care of self and politics, pedagogy, and self-knowledge." Foucault compared Socrates' recommendations to Alcibiades with the later texts of Stoic ethics, describing the change that had taken place between Plato and Stoicism: "Alcibiades had realized that he must care for himself, if he subsequently wanted to care for others. Now it became a question of caring for oneself, for the sake of oneself. One must, throughout one's entire life, be one's own object." [4]

Clearly, Foucault's project was transformed over the years by the ups and downs of a "logic of discovery," in which hesitations and mistakes, bad habits, and moments of repentance played their role, before being overcome and surpassed by new intuitions and new discoveries. *Histoire de la sexualité* became a history of techniques of self, a genealogy of the "subject" and of the ways in which it was constituted at the dawn of Western culture. In the spring of 1983 Foucault told Hubert Dreyfus and Paul Rabinow that there would be two volumes of his history of sexuality. The first, to be called "L'Usage des plaisirs," would deal with the morality of paganism and the techniques of self prescribed by this morality in relation to sexual ethics just before the rise of Christianity. The second volume, to be called "Les Aveux de la chair," would be devoted to early Christianity. Another book, not to be part of *Histoire de la sexualité*, would be a collection of studies on the self. It would include an article on *Alcibiades*, the first ancient text to develop the theme of care for the self. For this reason Foucault intended to call the volume "Le Souci de soi." It was to come out at Seuil, while the two others were to be published at Gallimard.[5] Clearly, they were talking about the book listed as "forthcoming" in the Des Travaux series with the title "Le Gouvernement de soi et des autres." The first version of the preface that Foucault wrote for *L'Usage des plaisirs*, which he gave to Paul Rabinow for his *Foucault Reader*, bears traces of this program. *L'Usage des plaisirs* was to study "late antiquity," that is, the pagan culture of the early centuries of our era. Ancient Greece is not mentioned in this general presentation of the sequels in *Histoire de la sexualité*.

Shortly afterward Foucault decided to integrate his two projects. And he made a shift in the titles. The study on Plato was amplified— so much so that *Alcibiades* was left on the sidelines (it was mentioned only once)—and this reflection on Greek antiquity became the center of *L'Usage des plaisirs*. Plutarch, Epictetus, Seneca, and Galen ended up in the next volume, which became *Le Souci de soi*. Then came the last volume, whose title remained unchanged: "Les Aveux de la chair." Having reached this stage, Foucault pondered the necessity of dividing the study into volumes. He wondered if it would not be simpler to bring it all together in one big book, which would be more than eight hundred pages long. But then publication would have to be delayed until the project was completely finished. The volume that was now intended to be the conclusion for the whole had been written long before the others, during a period when the project had not been conceived in this form at all. Foucault would therefore have to rework the conclusion. And, since he wanted to publish as quickly as possible, he decided on a "simple distribution" in three volumes, respecting the chronological order of the periods covered. In May 1984, when he had finished correcting proof for the two volumes to be published in June, he told his friends that he still had one or two months of work to do on "Les Aveux de la chair" before the whole thing would be finished. He thought that the final volume could be published at the beginning of the academic year, in October.

The final organization of *Histoire de la sexualité* therefore took this form, according to the advertising "insert" distributed in June 1984:

Volume 1: *La Volonté de savoir* (published in 1976)
Volume 2: *L'Usage des plaisirs*
Volume 3: *Le Souci de soi*
Volume 4: *Les Aveux de la chair* (forthcoming)

The insert, written by Foucault himself and almost impossible to find today, describes the survey of sexuality that had given him so much trouble:

The initial project of this series of studies, described in *La Volonté de savoir*, was not to constitute a historical review of sexual conduct and practices, nor to analyze the ideas (scientific, religious, or philosophical) through which these behaviors have been represented; it was to understand how, in modern western societies, something like an "experience" of "sexuality" had been constituted, since this familiar notion hardly appeared before the beginning of the nineteenth century.

To speak of sexuality as a historically constituted experience presupposed attempting to create the genealogy of the desiring subject, going back not merely to the beginnings of the Christian tradition, but to ancient philosophy.

As Michel Foucault went back from the modern era, beyond Christianity all the way to antiquity, he came up against a question that was very simple and, at the same time, very general: why are sexual behavior and the activities and pleasures derived from it an object of moral preoccupation? Why is there this ethical concern, which, depending on the moment, appears more or less important than the moral attention paid to other realms of individual or collective existence, such as feeding behaviors or the discharge of one's civic duties? This problematization of existence, when applied to Greco-Roman culture, seemed linked in turn to an ensemble of practices that might be called the "arts of existence" or the "techniques of self" which were sufficiently important to have an entire study devoted to them.

With the result, in the end, that this vast study on the genealogy of the man of desire from classical antiquity to the early centuries of Christianity, underwent a complete refocusing. And was divided into three volumes that are part of a whole:

L'Usage des plaisirs studies how sexual behavior was conceived of in classical Greek thought as a realm of appreciation and moral choices, and it studies the modes of subjectification referred to by this realm: ethical substance, types of subjection, forms of elaboration of the self, and the moral teleology. How medical and philosophical thought, as well, elaborated this "use of pleasures"—*chresis aphrodision*—and formulated several recurrent themes of austerity that would then center on four great axes of experience: the relation to one's body, the relation to one's wife, the relation to boys, and the relation to truth.

Le Souci de soi analyzes how this is problematized in Greek and Latin texts of the first two centuries of our era, and the shift it undergoes in an art of living dominated by the preoccupation with oneself.

Les Aveux de la chair, finally, will treat the experience of the flesh in the early centuries of Christianity and the role played by hermeneutics and the purifying process of deciphering desire.

Foucault worked long and hard to put the finishing touches on this series that had been announced for so long. His lengthy silence had fed any number of rumors: Foucault was finished, he had nothing more to say, he was at an impasse . . . Newspapers and magazines, always ready to look for the flaw, to flush out any weakness, to proclaim failure; jubilant enemies, impatient admirers or worried friends—everyone was obsessed with the question: so, when are we going to read the rest? Foucault had the impression that they were on his heels. A real "mind hunt (rather like a manhunt)," said Blanchot.[6] The feeling dominated him in this period, during which he wanted to leave the Collège de France. "One thing is certain, I won't give my course again next year," he told Pierre Bourdieu at the beginning of 1984. Foucault also spoke on numerous occasions about abandoning writing. Basically, he told Paul Veyne and several other people, one begins writing by chance and then continues by force of circumstances. He reiterated that writing was not an activity he had really chosen. He was the complete opposite of Sartre, who recounted in *Les Mots* that he had felt from his earliest youth that it was his calling. Then, above all, Foucault thought one had to pay far too high a price for *la gloire*—for fame and glory. But what was to be done? How could someone almost sixty change his life? He thought about journalism. He would like to do a column on geopolitics. But the past undoubtedly has its own strong inertia. And then, he wanted to finish these books to which he had devoted ten years of his life, ten years of unremitting labor. "He had to finish his books," wrote Hervé Guibert, one of Foucault's closest friends, in a magnificent novella evoking the agony and death of a philosopher. "This book he had written and rewritten, destroyed, disowned, destroyed again, rethought, reinvented, shortened and lengthened over ten year's time, this infinite book of doubt, of rebirth, of grandiose modesty. He was tempted to destroy it forever and to offer his enemies their idiotic victory, so they could spread the rumor that he was no longer able to write a book, that his mind had been dead for a long time, that his silence was only an admission of failure."[7]

But there it was. The undertaking had reached its conclusion. The incredible ambition to decipher the birth of modern man and his self-consciousness had borne fruit. The books would soon be published and Foucault did not hesitate to take a few good swipes at everybody who had made ironic comments on his silence. "As to those," he wrote at the beginning of L'Usage des plaisirs, "for whom to work hard, to begin and begin again, to attempt and be mistaken, to go back and re-work everything from top to bottom, and still find reason to hesitate from one step to the next—as to those, in short, for whom to work in the midst of uncertainty and apprehension is tantamount to failure, all I can say is that clearly we are not from the same planet."[8]

Foucault would undoubtedly have savored his revenge: in 1986 the rigorous, prestigious, and highly academic British review *Journal of Roman Studies* devoted a long, detailed, well-argued, and very favorable article to his last books.[9]

Paul Veyne played a large part in directing Foucault's attention toward increasingly distant times. Foucault had known the historian of antiquity ever since his days teaching psychology at the Ecole Normale. Veyne was one of his students and, with Passeron and several others, one of his friends. Since then they had lost track of each other. In 1975 Veyne was elected to the Collège de France. Gradually they again became close until, by the end of the 1970s and early 1980s, they had become intimate friends and intellectual accomplices. In 1978 Veyne wrote a long essay on Foucault's historical method, with the emphatic title "Foucault révolutionne l'histoire."[10] When Veyne, who lived in the south of France, was in Paris to give his course, Foucault put him up in the little studio connected to his apartment, which he usually used as a study. They would dine alone together when Veyne was there, or with one or two members of Foucault's little "family." Veyne and Foucault had long conversations on a multitude of topics, including their shared past and the years during which they had not seen each other. When Foucault completely changed his plan after finishing *Les Aveux de la chair*, he consulted Veyne often while writing *L'Usage des plaisirs* and *Le Souci de soi*. Foucault paid homage to him in his preface: "Paul Veyne has given me constant assistance throughout these years. He knows what the true historian's search for truth is about, but he also knows the labyrinth one enters when one sets out to trace the history of the games of truth and error. He is one of those individuals (rare nowadays) who are willing to face the dangers that the history of truth poses for all thought. His influence on what I have written here is pervasive." [11] Veyne's and Foucault's encounter was not merely on the terrain of antiquity. It was lit by "the great sun of a Nietzschean search," as Foucault called it in *Folie et déraison*. One of Foucault's main preoccupations in the last years of his life was to conceive of history in terms of "'games of truth,' the games of truth and error through which being is historically constituted as experience; that is, as something that can and must be thought." Foucault described the connection between his latest research and all that had gone before. All his books had basically asked the same question: What are the games of truth by which man proposes to think his own nature when he perceives himself to be mad, when he conceives of himself as a living, speaking, laboring being; when he judges and punishes himself as a criminal?" And finally: "What were the games of truth by which human beings came to see themselves as desiring individuals?" [12]

Foucault went to work again on "Les Aveux de la chair." One month, two, and it would be done. There were other projects waiting, in his files, in his drawers, in his Berkeley seminars. Then, above all, he wanted to take a rest: "What will I do when I finish my books? First, take care of myself," he told Dreyfus and Rabinow in April 1983. But the dreadful illness was doing its ghastly work, and Foucault had to be hospitalized at the beginning of June 1984. He struggled. He would struggle to the end. But this time the battle had been lost from the start. And this final volume of *Histoire de la sexualité* remains unpublished. In an interview in September 1986 Pierre Nora described the situation.

In a private letter that dates from before his illness, he expressed his wish that there be no "posthumous publication." Michel Foucault's heirs, knowing how much he cared for perfection, are therefore extremely hesitant. It is a matter of interpretation. Mine is quite clear. There are three parts. First, unfinished or abandoned texts, such as a manuscript on Manet, or his correspondence. There is no doubt about this part: no publication. Second, the courses at the Collège de France. That is open to discussion, and he himself hesitated. I can still hear him telling me: "There is a lot of throwaway material, but also plenty of work and ways to take it that might be useful to the kids." On the other hand, about this fourth volume, it seems unequivocal to me. It is part of *Histoire de la sexualité*, even the key to it, and it is obviously the part most important to Foucault. That he would completely rewrite it the minute he sat down to it again, and that this rewriting (usual with him) would have taken him further than even he thought, I am absolutely convinced. All the same, as it is, with a minimum of editorial tidying up . . . the manuscript exists and reflects a state of Foucault's thought, one that is perfectly coherent. In this case it seems to me that it is a heavy responsibility not to publish it. But I have no choice but to respect it.[13]

Paul Veyne and Georges Dumézil, unlike Nora, would put no limits on publication of Foucault's unpublished work. An old text by Foucault would seem to support their view. In a general introduction to Nietzsche's *Complete Works*, written in 1965 and published in 1967, Gilles Deleuze and Foucault make a case for the publication of all the posthumous writing and free access to manuscripts and notes: "No one can prejudge the form or contents the great book would have had (nor the other forms that Nietzsche would have invented if he had renounced his project). At the most, the reader can dream; even so, he has to be given the means."[14]

ON JUNE 2, 1984, Foucault felt dizzy and fainted in his apartment on Rue de Vaugirard. He was taken to a clinic in the fifteenth arrondissement, where he stayed until being admitted, on June 9, to the Salpêtrière, the hospital whose evolving roles he had described at such length in *Histoire de la folie*.

For several months Michel Foucault had complained continually about a nasty flu that was making him extremely tired and getting in the way of his work. He couldn't stop coughing; he sometimes had violent migraines. At the beginning of 1984, the illness made itself felt more and more. "It's like being in a fog," he said. However, he kept reworking "Les Aveux de la chair" and correcting proof for *L'Usage des plaisirs* and *Le Souci de soi*.

They would be his last books. His impatience, his rush, his determination to see them published, going to check his notes at the library despite the fact that he was frequently dizzy and dogged by lassitude, his absolute refusal to rest, to take a vacation, even just a short break, all point to the likelihood that he knew. These would be his last books, and he wanted to do all he could to make them complete.

Did he know, then, that he was at death's door? That he had AIDS? No, say most of his friends. He never knew the nature of this suffocating illness. Even in the hospital he was making enthusiastic plans for a trip to Andalusia, which he had visited the year before with Daniel Defert. That is what he said. He was hoping finally to take a rest there and to throw off his illness. Did he really believe it? Or did he want to reassure his friends? There is some evidence that the latter is the case. During the winter before his death, he telephoned Dumézil and told him: "I think I have AIDS." "I think . . ." This does not say he was sure. But in this confidence, quietly murmured to his old friend who was then eighty-six, one of the people who had been closest to him for thirty years, must we not hear the voice of truth acknowledging itself? Foucault knew, but, above all, he did not want to tell the people around him. He simply told the man whom he considered in a way to be his "spiritual master," the one who so often had played the part of "director of conscience" for him. Foucault knew. And he did not want to know.

In an article written for *Critique*'s special issue on Foucault in 1986, Paul Veyne reported a conversation with Foucault in February 1984, which Jean Piel decided not to publish. In these pages, Veyne described Foucault's attitude in the face of death. Had not Foucault himself said, in his book about Raymond Roussel, that the relationship of an author to his death is not a matter of anecdote? Here is Veyne's account:

> Foucault was unafraid of death, as he sometimes told his friends, when conversation turned to suicide, and events have proved, albeit in a different manner, that he was not bragging. In yet another way, ancient wisdom became a personal matter for him. Throughout the last eight months of his life, writing his two books played the same part for him that philosophical writing and personal journals played in ancient philosophy—that of work performed by the self on the self, of self-stylization. There was an incident connected with this, the memory of which is burnt into me, a sudden, heroic revelation. Throughout these eight months Foucault, then, had been working at writing and rewriting these two books, at settling this long-term debt to himself; he talked endlessly to me about these books, sometimes asking me to check one of his translations, but he complained of a

cough that wouldn't go away and a constant low-grade fever slowing him down; he asked me please to ask my wife for some advice. She is a doctor, but there was nothing she could do.

"Your doctors are bound to think you have AIDS," I told him jokingly one day. (One of the rituals of our friendship was to joke with each other about the difference between our tastes in lovers.)

"That is exactly what they think," he responded with a smile, "I realized it from the questions they asked me."

Today, readers will find it hard to believe that in February 1984 a fever and a cough were not yet enough to arouse suspicions. This illness was still enough of a distant and unknown scourge to be something legendary, even perhaps imaginary. None of his friends suspected anything. We only found out afterward.

"You ought to take a good rest," I went on. "You have been doing too much Latin and Greek and you're drained by it."

"Yes," he answered, "but afterward. First I want to get done with these two books."

"By the way," I asked him, merely out of curiosity (because the history of medicine is not a major passion for me), "does it really exist, AIDS, or is it a legend with a moral?"

"Well," he answered calmly, "listen," after thinking a minute, "I've studied the matter closely, I've read a lot of things about it. Yes, it exists. It isn't a legend. The Americans have studied it very closely." And he gave me the precise methodological details, which I have forgotten, in two or three sentences. He, after all, was a historian of medicine and, as a philosopher (I thought), was interested in what was going on today. Because the newspapers regularly carried brief paragraphs from American sources about the "homosexuals' cancer" (as they called it then). In retrospect, his coolheadedness over my stupid question takes my breath away. He himself must have thought that one day it would be this way, and he must have pondered the answer he gave me, and, as the most minute and bitter consolation, counted on my memory. Giving living *exempla* was another tradition in ancient philosophy.[15]

Foucault's friends visited him in his little hospital room. Daniel Defert, Hervé Guibert, Mathieu Lindon, and a number of others came to spend a bit of time with him. Summer was shining down on Paris, and the hospital building was surrounded by a vast park. It was rather a long walk to get there. Foucault laughed and joked. He commented on the first articles being published about the two books that had just come out. He seemed to be getting better. The newspapers, too, picked up the news that his health was improving. Foucault asked to see Georges Canguilhem. But it was too late. On June 25, in the middle of the afternoon, a dispatch from the national press agency stunned everyone in the editorial offices, and then throughout the intellectual community. The radio and television gave out the news: "Michel Foucault is dead."

Le Monde published the doctors' statement:

Professor Paul Castaigne, head of the neurology service at the Salpêtrière hospital, and Dr. Bruno Sauron, with the agreement of Michel Foucault's family, have issued the following statement: "Michel Foucault entered the clinic for illnesses of the nervous system at the Salpêtrière on June 9, 1984, where he was to receive further examinations necessary as a result of neurological complications following a septicemic condition. These explorations revealed the existence of centers of cerebral suppuration. Initially, treatment with antibiotics was effective; during this remission Michel Foucault was able to see the first reactions to the publication of his last books. An abrupt worsening made any hope of effective therapy impossible and death took place on June 25 at 1:15 P.M."

The next day the papers carried the headline "Michel Foucault is dead." *Libération* gave his photograph its entire front page and devoted eight more to the death of the philosopher: an editorial by Serge July, articles written in homage, a series of personal testimonials by Edmond Maire, Pierre Boulez, Jack Lang, Robert Badinter. And there was also an astounding statement, which all these years later everyone is still talking about with disgust and revulsion. A small item at the bottom of a page tried to challenge a "rumor" already making the rounds that Foucault had died of AIDS: "We are still astonished at the virulence of this rumor," said the unsigned article. "As if it were necessary for Foucault to have died in shame."[16] Over the next few days the paper was deluged by letters of protest. How, readers asked indignantly, could a journal calling itself *Libération* speak of "shame" in connection with dying of AIDS? Dozens of people, in Paris, New York, Berkeley, and elsewhere, have asked me to denounce this "disgraceful" article. Certainly it was an ill-considered text. Its author knew Foucault, liked him very much, and, according to one of his friends, "thought he was doing the right thing." He thought he was defending Foucault against a campaign aimed at discrediting the thinker. And no doubt, above all, he wanted to keep Foucault's friends from being bombarded with questions. I know that every day of his life he regrets the blunder, and I do not want to be among his attackers.

Several days later, *Libération* returned at length to the loss of Foucault. Among other pieces there was a four-page article whose announced purpose was to "recount" his life. It is a testimonial to the difficulty of carrying out such a project. It is a tissue of errors and absurdities, written in grandiloquent prose, that ends up repeating every legend, all the mythology, that was passed around about Foucault.[17] There were, on the other hand, articles of real quality: Robert Maggiori discussed the relations between Sartre and Foucault, and Roger Chartier those between the philosopher and historians.

Le Monde carried an article by Pierre Bourdieu on its front page. "There is nothing more dangerous," wrote Bourdieu, "than to reduce a philosophy, especially one so subtle, complex, and perverse, to a textbook formula. Nonetheless, I would say that Foucault's work is a long exploration of transgression, of going beyond social limits, always inseparably linked to knowledge and power." The sociologist ended with these words: "I would have liked to have said this better—this thought that was so bent on conquering a self-mastery, that is, mastery of its history, the history of categories of thought, the history of the will and of desires. And also this concern for rigor, this refusal of opportunism in knowledge as well as in practice, in the techniques of life as well as in the political choices that make Foucault an irreplaceable figure."[18] Inside were two pages filled with testimonials and analyses; here Veyne discussed the work of his lost friend: "Foucault's work seems to me to be the most important event of thought in our century."[19]

On June 29 Foucault's anxious face occupied the entire cover of *Le Nouvel Observateur*. Jean Daniel's editorial, "La Passion de Michel Foucault," was full of contained emotion, recalling their first meetings in Sidi Bou Saïd, their political complicity, their discussions, and their occasional differences in the years that followed. The final homage to a friend struck down. The weekly published several articles and testimonials. Fernand Braudel spoke of "national mourning": "France lost one of the most dazzling minds of the epoch, one of its most generously productive intellectuals."[20] Above all, this issue contained the most moving essay ever written about Foucault. Georges Dumézil had been in the habit of remarking, "When I am gone, Michel will write my obituary." But the ages of life had not required their payment in order, and the mythologist's prediction found itself reversed. The old man, broken and distraught, hastily wrote out a few pages in which he told of getting to know Foucault, how they had become confederates in a relationship that had been able to last for decades without clouding over, never threatened by the least of storms or wisp of cloud. Then he spoke of the work of the philosopher, who had taken his first steps in his company, in the library at Uppsala:

> Foucault's intelligence literally knew no bounds, even sophisticated ones. He set up his observatory on the regions of living being where the traditional distinctions between body and soul, between instinct and idea, seem absurd: madness, sexuality, and crime. His gaze from there moved like a lighthouse beam, turning onto history and onto the present, ready for even the least reassuring discoveries, capable of accepting anything except that of coming to rest at an orthodoxy. An intelligence with innumerable focuses, with movable mirrors, where nascent judgment was instantly doubled by its opposite, and yet without being destroyed or pulling back. All of this, as is usually the case at this level, with a profound kindness and goodness.

And Dumézil concluded: "it was easy for our friendship to succeed. Michel Foucault's withdrawal leaves me the poorer, lacking not only the ornaments of life, but its very substance."[21]

One of Foucault's last lectures at the Collège de France, in February 1984, was on "the courage of truth." In it he contemplated Plato's texts on the death of Socrates to show how the practice of truth-telling (*parrhesia*) and the "care of the self" can lead us to the truth of ourselves. He based his commentary on an essay by Dumézil that had just been published—on "the last words of Socrates."[22]

It was very early on a June morning, and the sun had not yet come up in Paris. But in the little courtyard behind the Salpêtrière there were already several hundred people who had come to pay their last respects to Michel Foucault. A long wait. Deep silence. Then a broken voice, husky in its grief:

> As for what motivated me, it is quite simple; I would hope that in the eyes of some people it might be sufficient in itself. It was curiosity—the only kind of curiosity, in any case, that is worth acting upon with a degree of obstinacy: not the curiosity that seeks to assimilate what it is proper for one to know, but that which enables one to get free of oneself. After all, what would be the value of the passion for knowledge if it resulted only in a certain amount of knowledgeableness and not, in one way or another and to the extent possible, in the knower's straying afield of himself? There are times in life when the question of knowing if one can think differently than one thinks and perceive differently than one sees is absolutely necessary if one is to go on

looking and reflecting at all . . . But then what is philosophy today—philosophical activity, I mean—if it is not the critical work that thought brings to bear on itself? In what does it consist, if not in the endeavor to know how and to what extent it might be possible to think differently, instead of legitimating what is already known?[23]

Foucault's words: a fragment of the preface to *L'Usage des plaisirs*. Gilles Deleuze read them, and the crowd listened. It was a motley crowd, in which all the different people who had crossed Foucault's thousand paths mixed—people who knew one of his thousand faces: at the university, in political struggles, or both at once, in friendship, in affection. In the very back were Dumézil and Canguilhem, as deeply moved as they were discreet. There were several professors from the Collège de France: Veyne, Bourdieu, Boulez. Everyone noticed the presence of Simone Signoret and Yves Montand, as well as of Robert Badinter, the minister of justice. Also present were Alain Jaubert, Jean Daniel, Bernard Kouchner, Claude Mauriac, and many many more, famous or anonymous: those who had signed petitions with him and those who simply attended his lectures every Wednesday.

A few hours later, in the afternoon of June 29, the casket was lowered into the ground in the little cemetery at Vendeuvre. This time far from crowds. Only the family was present. And a few friends. On the coffin lay a spray of roses that had not moved from its place during the long trip from Paris. Attached to it were three names: Mathieu, Hervé, Daniel. Since Mme. Foucault insisted that there be a religious service, it fell to the Dominican monk Michel Albaric, who was in charge of the Saulchoir Library, to give a brief homily. Then it was over.

You have to push open a creaking gate. Go down an *allée* lined with cypress trees. Just a few yards along there is a tombstone, a simple, grey marble slab. On it one can make out:

PIERRE GIRAUDEAU
EPOUX DE MARIE BONNET
1800–1848

And underneath, carved and gilded in the same way:

PAUL MICHEL FOUCAULT
PROFESSOR AU COLLEGE DE FRANCE
1926–1984

Across the road the large house, known hereabouts as the Chateau, can be seen—Piroir, the old structure that Michel Foucault visited one last time two months before his death, where he corrected his proofs for *Le Souci de soi*.

Foucault's writing changed a great deal in his last two books. It became calm, dispassionate, "appeased," according to Blanchot.[24] More sober, said Gilles Deleuze.[25] Almost neutralized. We are far from yesterday's "fiery" writing.[26] It is as if approaching death and the forebodings he had of it for several months had led Foucault onto the path of serenity. Seneca, whose works were among his favorite reading, would have praised such a model of "the philosophic life." Foucault seemed to have internalized the ancient wisdom to such a point that it became imposed upon his style itself—his style as a writer as well as his style as a man. Because the problem he had taken on was the "stylization of existence," the "aesthetics of life." This was a historical problem, of course, and one that he formulated as always by using historical records. But it was a problem that one feels (also, as always) very closely linked to what he was experiencing. Deleuze correctly emphasized that what interested Foucault at that particular moment was not a return to antiquity, but "us today."[27] Foucault himself told Dreyfus and Rabinow: "What strikes me is the fact that in our society, art has become something which is related only to objects and not to individuals or to life . . . But couldn't everyone's life become a work of art?"[28]

A small volume came out in the beginning of 1989: *Résumés des cours, 1970–1982*. In it were collected the summaries Foucault wrote for the *Annuaire du Collège de France*. The last one he wrote dealt with the course he taught in 1981–82, "the hermeneutics of the subject." At the end of it he evoked these Stoic precepts:

The particular value of meditation on death is not only that it anticipates what is generally considered as the greatest misfortune, it is not only that it makes it possible to convince oneself that death is not an evil; it offers the possibility of casting, in anticipation so to speak, a backward glance on life. In considering oneself as on the point of dying, one can judge each of the acts that one is in the process of committing according to its own worth. Death, said Epictetus, takes the laborer as he labors, the sailor as he navigates: "and you, what do you want to be your occupation when you are taken?" And Seneca imagined the moment of death as the one in which one might some-how become the judge of oneself and measure the moral progress that one had accomplished up to one's last day. In the twenty-sixth *Letter* he wrote: "Concerning the moral progress that I shall have been able to make, I will believe death . . . I am waiting for the day in which I will become my own judge and I will know if I have virtue on my lips and in my heart." [29]

What a strange echo these few words make today.

Notes
Selected Works of Foucault
Acknowledgments
Index

Abbreviations

NRF *Nouvelle Revue française*

PUF Presses Universitaires de France

Notes

1. "The City Where I Was Born"

1. Georges Canguilhem, remarks delivered at the opening of the colloquium "Foucault philosophe," January 9, 1988, Paris. This text remains unpublished and differs from the introduction written for the proceedings of the colloquium, *Actes du colloque: Michel Foucault philosophe* (Paris: Seuil, 1989).

2. James Bernauer and David Rasmussen give an account of the book's evolution in *The Final Foucault* (Cambridge, Mass.: MIT Press, 1988): first, *Folie et déraison. Histoire de la folie à l'âge classique*, principal thesis for the doctorate of letters (Paris: Plon, 1961), reissued in abridged form with the same title (Paris: Union General d'Editions, 1964). The original complete edition was reissued as *Histoire de la folie à l'âge classique* (Paris: Gallimard, 1972) with a new preface and two appendixes: "La Folie, l'absence de l'oeuvre" (reprinted from *La Table Ronde*, May 1964) and "Mon Corps, ce papier, ce feu" (reprinted from *Paideia*, September 1971); reissued in the Tel series without the appendixes (Paris: Gallimard, 1978). *Madness and Civilization*, trans. Richard Howard (New York: Pantheon, 1965), is based on the "drastically abridged edition of 1964 with some slight additions from the original edition"; Bernauer and Rasmussen, *Final Foucault*, p. 120. Most references to this work in the text will use the better-known title *Histoire de la folie*. *(Trans.)*

3. Gilles Deleuze, *Foucault* (Paris: Minuit, 1986).

4. *Critique*, August–September 1986; *Le Débat*, September–November 1986; *Actes. Cahiers d'action juridique*, Summer 1986; all special issues devoted to Foucault.

5. Gilles Deleuze, "La Vie comme une oeuvre d'art," *Le Nouvel Observateur*, August 29, 1986.

6. Postcard dated August 13, 1981.

7. I have used American secondary school terminology (grades seven through twelve) instead of French or British (sixth through first forms, respectively). *(Trans.)*

8. Quoted in *Les Collèges Saint-Stanislas et Saint-Joseph de Poitiers. Notes historiques et souvenirs d'anciens*, ed. Jean Vaudel (Poitiers: Librairie "Le bouquiniste," 1981).

9. The French system differs from the American in providing a final year

(terminale), which is equivalent to the first or second year of college. To graduate one must pass exams known as the baccalaureate, or *bac. (Trans.)*

10. Michel Foucault, interview, *Ethos*, Fall 1983, 5; translated as "The Minimalist Self" in Foucault, *Politics, Philosophy, Culture: Interviews and Other Writings, 1977–1984*, ed. Lawrence D. Kritzman (New York: Routledge, 1988), p. 7.
11. Quoted in Thierry Voeltzel, *Vingt ans et après* (Paris: Grasset, 1978), p. 55.

2. The Voice of Hegel

1. Emmanuel Le Roy Ladurie, *Paris-Montpellier, 1945–1963* (Paris: Gallimard, 1982), p. 29.
2. Ibid., pp. 27–29.
3. Jean d'Ormesson, *Au revoir et merci*, 2d ed. (Paris: Gallimard, 1976), p. 71.
4. Ibid., p. 76.
5. Michel Foucault, "Jean Hyppolite, 1907–1968," *Revue de mètaphysique et de morale*, April–June 1969, p. 131.
6. Jean-François Sirinelli, *Génération intellectuelle. Khâgneux et normaliens dans l'entre-deux-guerres* (Paris: Fayard, 1988).
7. See Chapter 1, note 2.
8. Michel Foucault, *Folie et déraison. Histoire de la folie à l'âge classique* (Paris: Plon, 1961), pp. x and xi.
9. Michel Foucault, *L'Ordre du discours* (Paris: Gallimard, 1971), pp. 80–81; translated by Rupert Swyer as "The Discourse on Language," appendix in Foucault, *The Archaeology of Knowledge*, trans. A. M. Sheridan Smith (New York: Pantheon, 1972).
10. *Les Temps modernes*, April 1948.
11. Vincent Descombes, *Le Même et l'autre. Quarante-cinq ans de philosophie française (1933–1978)* (Paris: Minuit, 1979), p. 24.
12. Elisabeth Roudinesco, *La Bataille de cent ans. Histoire de la psychanalyse en France*, vol. II (Paris: Seuil, 1986), p. 150.
13. Raymond Aron, *Mémoires* (Paris: Julliard, 1983), p. 94.
14. Georges Canguilhem, "Hegel en France," *Revue d'histoire et de philosophie des religions* (Strasbourg), 1948–49.
15. Jean Hyppolite, *Figures de la pensée philosophique*, 2 vols. (Paris: PUF, 1971), I, 196.
16. Maurice Merleau-Ponty, *Sens et non-sens* (Paris: Nagel, 1948), pp. 109, 110: translated by Hubert L. Dreyfus and Patricia Allen Dreyfus as *Sense and Non-sense* (Evanston: Northwestern University Press, 1964), p. 63.
17. Hyppolite, *Figures de la pensée*, II, 976.
18. Foucault, "The Discourse on Language," p. 235.
19. Foucault, "Jean Hyppolite," p. 136.

20. In *Hommage à Jean Hyppolite*, ed. Michel Foucault (Paris: PUF, 1969); translated by Donald F. Bouchard as "Nietzsche, Genealogy, History" in Foucault, *Language, Counter-Memory, Practice: Selected Essays and Interviews*, ed. Bouchard (Ithaca: Cornell University Press, 1977), pp. 139–164.

3. Rue d'Ulm

1. Bertrand de Saint-Sernin, "Georges Canguilhem à la Sorbonne," *Revue de métaphysique et de morale*, January–March 1985, p. 84.
2. Dominique Fernandez, *Le Rapt de Ganymède* (Paris: Grasset, 1989), pp. 291–292.
3. Ibid., p. 82.
4. Ibid.
5. Michel Foucault, "Préface à la transgression," *Critique*, August–September 1963, p. 762; translated by Donald F. Bouchard and Sherry Simon as "Preface to Transgression" in Foucault, *Language, Counter-Memory, Practice: Selected Essays and Interviews*, ed. Bouchard (Ithaca: Cornell University Press, 1977), pp. 29–52.
6. Michel Foucault, "Est-il donc important de penser?" interview, *Libération*, May 30, 1981; translated as "Practicing Criticism" in Foucault, *Politics, Philosophy, Culture: Interviews and Other Writings, 1977–1984*, ed. Lawrence D. Kritzman (New York: Routledge, 1988), p. 156.
7. *Roland Barthes par Roland Barthes* (Paris: Seuil, 1975); translated by Richard Howard as *Roland Barthes* (New York: Hill and Wang, 1977), p. 63.
8. Fernandez, *Le Rapt de Ganymède*, pp. 132–133.
9. Jean-Paul Aron, "Mon sida," *Le Nouvel Observateur*, October 30, 1987.
10. Michel Foucault, "Le Retour de la morale," interview, *Les Nouvelles littéraires*, June 28, 1984; translated as "The Return of Morality" in Foucault, *Politics, Philosophy, Culture*, p. 250.
11. The lectures were published as *L'Union de l'âme et du corps chez Malebranche, Maine de Biran et Bergson*, ed. Jean Deprun (Paris: Vrin, 1968).
12. All the lectures have been republished in *Merleau-Ponty à la Sorbonne* (Paris: Cynara, 1988).
13. A traditional nickname, referring to a crocodile of the Cayman Islands. *(Trans.)*
14. Emmanuel Le Roy Ladurie, *Paris-Montpellier, 1945–1963* (Paris: Gallimard, 1982), p. 44.
15. Jean-François Sirinelli, "Les Normaliens de la rue d'Ulm après 1945: une génération communiste?" *Revue d'histoire du monde moderne*, October–December 1986, pp. 569–588.
16. Maurice Agulhon, "Vu des coulisses," in *Essais d'ego-histoire* (Paris: Gallimard, 1987), pp. 21–22.
17. Jean Charbonnel, *L'Aventure de la fidélité* (Paris: Seuil, 1976), pp. 56–57.

18. From a letter quoted by Maria-Antonietta Macciochi in *Deux mille ans de bonheur* (Paris: Grasset, 1983), pp. 379–380.
19. Charbonnel, *L'Aventure de la fidélité*, p. 39.
20. Ibid.
21. Report by Paul Mazon, *Annuaire de la fondation Thiers. 1947–1952*, n.s., 41.

4. The Carnival of Madmen

1. Michel Foucault, "La Recherche scientifique et la psychologie," in *Des chercheurs français s'interrogent* (Paris: Privat-PUF, 1957), pp. 173–175.
2. René Char, "Partage formel," in *Oeuvres complètes* (Paris: Gallimard, 1983), p. 160. Quoted in Michel Foucault, "Introduction," in Ludwig Binswanger, *Le Rêve et l'existence*, trans. Jacqueline Verdeaux, intro. and notes by Michel Foucault (Paris: Desclée de Brouwer, 1954), p. 1; translated by Forrest Williams and Jacob Needleman as *Dream and Existence*, special issue of *Review of Existential Psychology and Psychiatry*, 19 (1984–85), 30.
3. Foucault, *Dream and Existence*, pp. 55, 74.
4. Ducio Trombadori, *Colloqui con Foucault* (Salerno: Cooperative editrice, 1981), p. 41.
5. Projected preface (unpublished in French) to *Histoire de la sexualité*, vol. II; translated in Paul Rabinow, ed., *The Foucault Reader* (New York: Pantheon, 1984), pp. 334 and 336.
6. Michel Foucault, interview, *Ethos*, Fall 1983, p. 5; translated as "The Minimalist Self" in Foucault, *Politics, Philosophy, Culture: Interviews and Other Writings, 1977–1984*, ed. Lawrence D. Kritzman (New York: Routledge, 1988), p. 7.

5. Stalin's Shoemaker

1. Ducio Trombadori, *Colloqui con Foucault* (Salerno: Cooperative editrice, 1981), pp. 27–29.
2. Ibid., p. 30.
3. Maurice Pinguet, "Les Années d'apprentissage," *Le Débat*, September–November 1986, pp. 129–130.
4. Ibid., p. 127.
5. Emmanuel Le Roy Ladurie, *Paris-Montpellier, 1945–1963* (Paris: Gallimard, 1962), p. 46.
6. Claude Mauriac, *Le Temps immobile*, vol. III: *Et comme l'espérance est violente* (Paris: Grasset, 1977), pp. 318–319.
7. Ibid., vol. IX: *Mauriac et fils* (Paris: Grasset, 1986), p. 290.
8. Trombadori, *Colloqui con Foucault*, p. 33.
9. Jean-Paul Aron, *Les Modernes* (Paris: Gallimard, 1984), pp. 65–66.

10. Trombadori, *Colloqui con Foucault*, p. 33.

11. Michel Foucault, *Les Mots et les choses. Une archéologie des sciences humaines* (Paris: Gallimard, 1966), p. 274; translated by Alan Sheridan as *The Order of Things: An Archaeology of the Human Sciences* (1970; reprint, New York: Vintage, 1973), p. 262.

12. Althusser quoted in *Le Magazine littéraire*, May 1984, p. 57.

13. Michel Foucault, interview, *Le Magazine littéraire*, July–August 1985; a slightly different version of "Postscript," in *Death and the Labyrinth: The World of Raymond Roussel*, trans. Charles Ruas (Garden City, N.Y.: Doubleday, 1986).

14. Maurice Blanchot, "Où maintenant, qui maintenant," *NRF*, no. 10 (1953); reprinted in Blanchot, *Le Livre à venir* (Paris: Gallimard, 1959). Blanchot's columns and critical essays are collected (with some changes) in *L'Espace littéraire*, *Le Livre à venir*, and *L'Entretien infini*. For a complete list, with dates and places of original publication, see Françoise Collin, *Maurice Blanchot et la question de l'écriture* (Paris: Gallimard, 1986).

15. Karl Jaspers, *Strindberg and Van Gogh: An Attempt at a Pathogenic Analysis with Reference to Parallel Cases of Swedenborg and Hölderlin* (Tucson: University of Arizona Press, 1977).

16. Maurice Blanchot, foreword to ibid., p. 12.

17. Michel Foucault, *Folie et déraison. Histoire de la folie à l'âge classique* (Paris: Plon, 1961), p. x.

18. Ibid., p. xi; from René Char, "Partage formel," in *Oeuvres complètes* (Paris: Gallimard, 1983), p. 160.

19. Maurice Blanchot, *Michel Foucault tel que je l'imagine* (Paris: Fata Morgana, 1986), p. 9.

20. Ibid., p. 10.

21. Paul Veyne, *René Char en ses poèmes* (Paris: Gallimard, 1990).

6. Discords of Love

1. Michel Foucault, "Introduction," in Ludwig Binswanger, *Le Rêve et l'existence*, trans. Jacqueline Verdeaux, intro. and notes by Michel Foucault (Paris: Desclée de Brouwer, 1954), pp. 9–10; translated by Forrest Williams and Jacob Needleman as *Dream and Existence*, special issue of *Review of Existential Psychology and Psychiatry*, 19 (1984–85), p. 31.

2. Foucault, *Dream and Existence*, p. 33.

3. Jean-Paul Aron, *Les Modernes* (Paris: Gallimard, 1984), pp. 64–65.

4. "Messieurs, faites vos jeux," *CNAC Magazine*, May–June 1983; reprinted in *Le Débat*, September–November 1986, pp. 178–188.

5. Jean Barraqué, "Propos impromptus," *Courrier musical de France*, no. 26 (1969), 78. For more on Barraqué, see the special issue of *Entretemps* de-

voted to him in 1987, especially the biographical sketch by Rose-Marie Janzen, to whom I am indebted for the references to Barraqué's texts quoted here.

6. Michel Foucault, interview, *Ethos*, Fall 1983, p. 7; translated as "The Minimalist Self" in Foucault, *Politics, Philosophy, Culture. Interviews and Other Writings, 1977–1984*, ed. Lawrence D. Kritzman (New York: Routledge, 1988), p. 13.

7. "Pierre Boulez ou l'écran traversé," *Le Nouvel Observateur*, October 2, 1982.

8. Michel Foucault, interview, *La fiera leteraria*, September 28, 1967.

9. Barraqué, "Propos impromptus," p. 80.

10. Michel Foucault, *Maladie mentale et personnalité* (Paris: PUF, 1954), p. 12; translated by Alan Sheridan from *Maladie mentale et psychologie* (Paris: PUF, 1962) as *Mental Illness and Psychology* (New York: Harper & Row, 1976), p. 10.

11. Foucault, *Maladie mentale et personnalité*, pp. 100–101.

12. Ibid., pp. 86, 104.

13. Foucault, *Mental Illness and Psychology*, p. 82.

14. Foucault, *Maladie mentale et personnalité*, pp. 23, 26.

15. For an analysis of the 1954 book and the changes from one edition to the other, see Pierre Macherey, "Aux sources de l'*Histoire de la folie*, une rectification et ses limites," *Critique*, August–September 1986, pp. 752–774; and Hubert Dreyfus' preface to the "California edition" of *Mental Illness and Psychology* (Berkeley: University of California Press, 1987).

16. Jean Hyppolite, *Figures de la pensée philosophique*, 2 vols. (Paris: PUF), II, 885–890.

17. See Elisabeth Roudinesco, *La Bataille de cent ans. Histoire de la psychanalyse en France*, vol. II (Paris: Seuil, 1986), pp. 310–311.

18. Michel Foucault, "La Recherche scientifique et la psychologie," in *Des chercheurs français s'interrogent* (Paris: Privat-PUF, 1957), pp. 201, 193.

19. Ibid., p. 201.

7. Uppsala, Warsaw, Hamburg

1. Michel Foucault, interview, *Ethos*, Fall 1983, p. 4; translated as "The Minimalist Self" in Foucault, *Politics, Philosophy, Culture: Interviews and Other Writings, 1977–1984*, ed. Lawrence D. Kritzman (New York: Routledge, 1988), p. 5.

2. Michel Foucault, *Folie et déraison. Histoire de la folie à l'âge classique* (Paris: Plon, 1961), p. x.

3. Interview, *Le Monde*, July 22, 1961.

4. Michel Foucault, *L'Ordre du discours* (Paris: Gallimard, 1971), p. 73; translated by Rupert Swyer as "The Discourse on Language," appendix in

Foucault, *The Archaeology of Knowledge*, trans. A. M. Sheridan Smith (New York: Pantheon, 1972), p. 98.

5. These courses were never published. Georges Dumézil's mention of "cours publiés" in his article in *Le Nouvel Observateur* at Foucault's death was a misprint; he had written "cours publics."

6. Quoted in Herbert R. Lottman, *Albert Camus: A Biography* (Garden City, N.Y.: Doubleday, 1979).

7. Michel Foucault, Proposal for the creation of a chair in semiology at the Collège de France; proposal of the candidacy of Roland Barthes for this chair (typescript, Collège de France, 1975).

8. Michel Foucault, "Roland Barthes, 1915–1980," *Annuaire du Collège de France*, 1979–80.

9. Étienne Burin des Roziers, "Une Rencontre à Varsovie," *Le Débat*, September–November 1986, p. 133.

10. Ibid., pp. 134, 136.

11. Michel Foucault, interview, *Bonniers Literära Magasin* (Stockholm), March 1968, p. 204.

12. Foucault, *Folie et déraison*, pp. i–v; translated by Richard Howard as *Madness and Civilization* (New York: Pantheon, 1965), pp. ix–xi.

13. *Folie et déraison*, p. v; translated in part in *Madness and Civilization*, p. xi.

14. *Folie et déraison*, p. ix; omitted from *Madness and Civilization*.

15. Michel Foucault, *Histoire de la folie à l'âge classique* (Paris: Gallimard, 1972), pp. 58–59.

16. Ibid., p. 100.

17. Ibid., p. 96.

18. Ibid., pp. 117–119.

19. Foucault, *Madness and Civilization*, pp. 269–272.

20. Ibid., pp. 281–285.

21. Ibid., p. 289.

8. The Talent of a Poet

1. Michel Foucault, *Folie et déraison. Histoire de la folie à l'âge classique* (Paris: Plon, 1961), p. xi.

2. Georges Canguilhem, "Sur l'*Histoire de la folie* en tant qu'évènement," *Le Débat*, no. 46, p. 38.

3. Michel Foucault, "La Vie: l'expérience et la science," *Revue de métaphysique et de morale*, January–March 1985, p. 3.

4. Georges Canguilhem, "Mort de l'homme ou épuisement du cogito," *Critique*, July 1967, pp. 599–618.

5. Canguilhem, "Sur l'*Histoire de la folie*."

6. Georges Dumézil, *Entretiens avec Didier Eribon* (Paris: Gallimard, 1987), pp. 95–97.

7. Claude Lévi-Strauss and Didier Eribon, *De près et de loin* (Paris: Odile Jacob, 1988), pp. 100–101.

8. Michel Foucault, "Le Style de l'histoire," interview, *Le Matin de Paris*, February 21, 1984.

9. Philippe Ariès, *Un historien du dimanche* (Paris: Seuil, 1982), p. 145.

10. Michel Foucault, "Le Souci de la vérité," *Le Nouvel Observateur*, February 17, 1984.

11. Ibid.

12. The quotations from Foucault's defense on the following pages are taken from the notes made by Henri Gouhier, president of the jury, now in the author's possession.

13. Reprinted in Daniel Lagache, *Oeuvres*, vol. I (Paris: PUF, 1977), pp. 439–456.

14. Michel Foucault, "La Folie, l'absence d'oeuvre," *La Table Ronde*, May 1964. Reprinted as an appendix to *Histoire de la folie à l'âge classique* (Paris: Gallimard, 1972), pp. 575–582.

15. In the sense in which Georges Canguilhem speaks of "l'*Histoire de la folie* as an event."

9. The Book and Its Doubles

1. Michel Foucault, interview, *Les Nouvelles littéraires*, March 17, 1975.

2. Michel Foucault, "Vérité et pouvoir," interview, *L'Arc*, no. 70 (1977), 16.

3. Maurice Blanchot, "L'Oubli, la déraison," *NRF*, October 1961, pp. 676–686; reprinted in Blanchot, *L'Entretien infini* (Paris: Gallimard, 1969); Roland Barthes, "Savoir et folie," *Critique*, no. 17 (1961), 915–922; reprinted in Barthes, *Essais critiques* (Paris: Seuil, 1964); Michel Serres, "Géométrie de la folie," *Mercure de France*, August 1962, pp. 683–696, and September 1962, pp. 63–81; reprinted in Serres, *Hermès ou la communication* (Paris: Minuit, 1968); Robert Mandrou, "Trois Clés pour comprendre l'*Histoire de la folie à l'âge classique*," *Annales: ESC*, July–August 1962, pp. 761–771.

4. Fernand Braudel, "Note," ibid., pp. 771–772.

5. Serres, *Hermès ou la communication*, pp. 167, 176, 178.

6. Barthes, *Essais critiques*, pp. 168, 172, 174.

7. Blanchot, *Entretien infini*, p. 291.

8. Mandrou, "Trois Clés," pp. 762, 771.

9. Reprinted in *Michel Foucault, une histoire de la vérité*, collective volume (Paris: Syros, 1985), p. 119.

10. Jacques Derrida, "Cogito et histoire de la folie," in *Ecriture et la différence* (Paris: Points-Seuil, 1967), pp. 52–53; translated by Alan Bass as *Writing and Difference* (Chicago: University of Chicago Press, 1978), p. 32.

11. Derrida, *Writing and Difference*, p. 31.

12. Ibid., p. 61.

13. Ibid., p. 57.

14. *Revue de métaphysique et de morale*, October–December 1963.

15. Michel Foucault, *Histoire de la folie à l'âge classique* (Paris: Gallimard, 1972), p. 602.

16. Michel Foucault, interview, *Le Monde*, July 22, 1961; Richard Howard, "The Story of Unreason," *Times Literary Supplement*, October 6, 1961.

17. Quoted in Claude Mauriac, *Le Temps immobile*, vol. III: *Et comme l'espérance est violente* (Paris: Grasset, 1977), p. 375.

18. See the special issue of *La Nef* on antipsychiatry, January–May 1971.

19. Robert Castel, "Les Aventures de la pratique," *Le Débat*, September–November 1986, pp. 42–44.

20. Foucault, *Histoire de la folie*, pp. 7–8.

21. Ducio Trombadori, *Colloqui con Foucault* (Salerno: Cooperative editrice, 1981), p. 39.

22. Castel, "Les Aventures de la pratique," p. 43.

23. Henri Ey, "La Conception idéologique de l'*Histoire de la folie* de Michel Foucault," *Evolution psychiatrique. Cahiers de psychopathologie générale* 36, no. 2 (1971).

24. See especially Henri Baruk, *La Psychiatrie sociale* (Paris: PUF, 1974).

25. Castel, "Les Aventures de la pratique," p. 47.

26. "La Folie encerclée. Dialogue sur l'enfermement et la répression psychiatrique," *Change*, no. 32–33 (1977).

27. Einaudi, *Crimini di paci* (Turin: 1975); translated into French by Bernard de Féminville as *Les Criminels de paix: recherches sur les intellectuels et leurs techniques comme préposé à l'oppression* (Paris: PUF, 1980).

28. Castel, "Les Aventures de la pratique," p. 47.

29. Foucault, "Vérité et pouvoir," p. 25.

30. Castel, "Les Aventures de la pratique," p. 45.

31. Trombadori, *Colloqui con Foucault*, pp. 77–78; the quotation is from the original French transcript.

10. The Dandy and the Reforms

1. The *liste d'aptitude* is divided into two categories: the *liste restreinte*, for positions as professor, meant for candidates who have already defended their thesis; and the *liste large*, for positions as instructor (*chargé d'enseignement*).

2. The reports by Bastide and the dean are in Foucault's *dossier de carrière*, Ministère de l'Education Nationale.

3. Etienne Burin des Roziers, "Une Rencontre à Varsovie," *Le Débat*, September–October 1986, pp. 135–136.

4. Jean-Claude Passeron, "1950–1980. L'université mise à la question: changement de décor ou changement de cap," in *Histoire des universités en France*, ed. J. Verger (Paris: privately published, 1986), pp. 373–374.

5. Luc Ferry and Alain Renaut, *La Pensée 68* (Paris: Gallimard, 1985).

6. In Gérard Courant, *Werner Schroeter* (Paris: Goethe Institut and Cinémathèque Française, 1981).

11. Opening Bodies

1. Michel Foucault, interview with Charles Ruas for "Postscript," in Foucault, *Death and the Labyrinth: The World of Raymond Roussel*, trans. Charles Ruas (Garden City, N.Y.: Doubleday, 1986), pp. 171–172.

2. In Raymond Roussel, *Comment j'ai écrit certains de mes livres*, ed. Jubert Juin (Paris: Pauvert, 1963); translated by Trevor Winkfield, without Juin's introduction, as *How I Wrote Certain of My Books* (New York: Sun, 1975).

3. Michel Foucault, "Pourquoi réédite-t-on Raymond Roussel? Un précurseur de notre littérature moderne," *Le Monde*, August 22, 1964.

4. Foucault, *Death and the Labyrinth*, p. 54.

5. To dissociate himself from Foucault's version of Roussel, Leiris has called the collection of his own articles *Roussel l'ingenu* (Paris: Fata Morgana, 1988).

6. Alain Robbe-Grillet, "Enigmes et transparence chez Raymond Roussel," *Critique*, December 1963, pp. 1027–33.

7. Maurice Blanchot, "Le Problème de Wittgenstein," *NRF*, no. 131 (1963); reprinted in Blanchot, *L'Entretien infini* (Paris: Gallimard, 1969), p. 493.

8. Michel Foucault, "Préface à la transgression," *Critique*, August–September 1963, p. 758; translated by Donald F. Bouchard and Sherry Simon as "Preface to Transgression" in Foucault, *Language, Counter-Memory, Practice: Selected Essays and Interviews*, ed. Bouchard (Ithaca: Cornell University Press, 1977), p. 38.

9. Foucault, "Preface to Transgression," pp. 43, 51.

10. Ibid., p. 50.

11. Michel Foucault, "Présentation," in Georges Bataille, *Oeuvres complètes*, vol. I (Paris: Gallimard, 1970), p. 5.

12. Michel Foucault, "La Pensée du dehors," *Critique*, June 1966; republished by Fata Morgana with the same title in 1987. The quotation is from the book, p. 15.

13. These letters were published in *Pierre Klossowski. Cahiers pour un temps* (Paris: Centre Georges-Pompidou, 1985), pp. 85–90.

14. Michel Foucault, "Nietzsche, Marx, Freud," in *Cahiers de Royaumont. Nietzsche* (Paris: Minuit, 1967), pp. 182–192. The discussion is on pp. 193–200, and the remarks quoted here on p. 199.

15. Michel Foucault, "Le 'non' du père," *Critique*, March 1962, pp. 195–209;

translated by Donald Bouchard and Sherry Simon as "The Father's 'No'" in *Language, Counter-Memory, Practice: Selected Essays and Interviews,* ed. Bouchard (Ithaca: Cornell University Press, 1977), pp. 68–86.

16. Michel Foucault, "Theatrum philosophicum," *Critique,* September 1970, p. 908; translated by Donald F. Bouchard and Sherry Simon in *Language, Counter-Memory, Practice,* p. 196.

17. Michel Foucault, *Naissance de la clinique. Une archéologie du regard médical* (Paris: PUF, 1963), p. v; translated by A. M. Sheridan Smith as *The Birth of the Clinic: An Archaeology of Medical Perception* (New York: Pantheon, 1973), p. ix.

18. Foucault, *Birth of the Clinic,* p. 146, 144, 196.

19. Ibid., p. 197.

20. Ibid., p. 198.

12. Ramparts of the Bourgeoisie

1. On this text by Merleau-Ponty, see Claude Lefort's introduction to *La Prose du monde* (Paris: Gallimard, 1969).

2. "Foucault comme des petits pains," *Le Nouvel Observateur,* August 10, 1966.

3. Jean-Luc Godard, "Lutter sur deux fronts," *Cahiers du cinéma,* October 1967.

4. Michel Foucault, "Introduction à l'*Anthropologie* de Kant," secondary thesis for the doctorate of letters, Université de Paris, Faculté des Lettres (typescript, Sorbonne Library), pp. 126–128.

5. Michel Foucault, *Les Mots et les choses. Une archéologie des sciences humaines* (Paris: Gallimard, 1966), pp. 396–397; translated by Alan Sheridan as *The Order of Things: An Archaeology of the Human Sciences* (1970; reprint, New York: Vintage, 1973), p. 385.

6. Gérard Lebrun, "Note sur la phénoménologie dans *Les Mots et les choses,*" in *Actes du colloque: Michel Foucault philosophe* (Paris: Seuil, 1989).

7. Foucault, *The Order of Things,* pp. 366–367.

8. Ibid., pp. 379–381.

9. Ibid., pp. 382–383.

10. Ibid., pp. 386–387.

11. Jean Lacroix, "La Fin de l'humanisme," *Le Monde,* June 9, 1966.

12. Robert Kanters, "Tu causes, tu causes, c'est tout ce que tu sais faire," *Le Figaro,* June 23, 1966.

13. Gilles Deleuze, "L'Homme, une existence douteuse," *Le Nouvel Observateur,* June 1, 1966.

14. François Châtelet, "L'Homme, ce Narcisse incertain," *La Quinzaine littéraire,* April 1, 1966.

15. Pierre Bourdieu, *Le Sens pratique* (Paris: Minuit, 1980), p. 8.

16. Michel Foucault, "L'Homme est-il mort?" interview, *Arts et loisirs*, June 15, 1966.

17. Jacques Milhau, "Les Mots et les choses," *Cahiers du communisme*, February 1968. For a discussion of how the Communist party greeted the "structuralist" theses, see Jeannine Verdès-Leroux, *Le Reveil des somnambules* (Paris: Fayard-Minuit, 1987).

18. Jeannette Colombel, "Les Mots de Foucault et les choses," *La Nouvelle Critique*, April 1967.

19. *Les Lettres françaises*, March 31, 1966, and June 15, 1967.

20. Jean-Marie Domenach, "Une nouvelle passion," *Esprit*, July–August 1966.

21. Michel Foucault, "Réponse à une question," *Esprit*, May 1968.

22. François Mauriac, "Bloc-notes," *Le Figaro littéraire*, September 15, 1966.

23. "Jean-Paul Sartre répond," interview, *L'Arc*, no. 30 (1966).

24. Robert Castel, "Introduction," in Herbert Marcuse, *Raison et révolution* (Paris: Minuit, 1968).

25. Michel Foucault, interview, *La Quinzaine littéraire*, March 1, 1968.

26. Michel Foucault, *La Quinzaine littéraire*, March 15, 1968.

27. Georges Canguilhem, "Mort de l'homme ou épuisement du cogito," *Critique*, July 1967. Canguilhem restated his position very clearly in a broadcast tribute to Jean Cavaillès on October 28, 1969: "It is not possible to speak of him without some sense of shame, because, if one survived him, it is because one did less than he. But if one does not speak of him, who will be able to differentiate between this unreserved commitment, this action with no attention to the rear, and the Resistance of those intellectual-resistants who talk about themselves so much because they alone are able to talk about their Resistance, it being so discreet? At the present time there are certain other philosophers who have formed the idea of a philosophy without a Subject. The philosophical work of Cavaillès can be invoked in support of this idea. His mathematical philosophy was not constructed with reference to any Subject that could possibly be precariously identified with Jean Cavaillès. This philosophy, from which Jean Cavaillès is radically absent, demanded a form of action that led him, through the narrow paths of logic, to the passage from which one never returns. Jean Cavaillès is the logic of the Resistance lived to the point of death. May philosophers of existence and of the individual person do as well next time, if they can."

28. The questions about *Les Mots et les choses* addressed to Foucault by the Cercle d'Epistémologie refer explicitly to Canguilhem's article. Foucault's replies, published in *Cahiers pour l'analyse* in July 1968, foreshadow *L'Archéologie du savoir*.

29. On Althusser see especially Verdès-Leroux, *Le Reveil des somnambules*, pp. 282–302.

30. *Bonniers Litterära Magasin* (Stockholm), March 1968.
31. *La Quinzaine littéraire*, July 1, 1967.
32. Michel Foucault, "Je suis tout au plus . . . ," interview, *La Presse de Tunis*, April 2, 1967.
33. Gilles Deleuze, "A quoi reconnait-on le structuralisme?" in *Histoire de la philosophie*, vol. IV: *La Philosophie au XXe siècle*, ed. François Châtelet (Verviers: Marabout University, 1967), pp. 293–329.
34. Michel Foucault, "La Naissance d'un monde," interview, *Le Monde*, May 3, 1969.
35. Michel Foucault, in Hubert Dreyfus and Paul Rabinow, *Michel Foucault: Beyond Structuralism and Hermeneutics* (Chicago: University of Chicago Press, 1983).
36. Ducio Trombadori, *Colloqui con Foucault* (Salerno: Cooperative editrice, 1981), pp. 49–60.
37. Michel Foucault, *Naissance de la clinique. Une archéologie du régard médical* (Paris: PUF, 1972), pp. xiv and xv. The English translation does not reflect these changes; see *The Birth of the Clinic: An Archaeology of Medical Perception*, trans. A. M. Sheridan Smith (New York: Pantheon, 1973), pp. xvii–xix.
38. Michel Foucault, *L'Archéologie du savoir* (Paris: Gallimard, 1969), p. 28; translated by A. M. Sheridan Smith as *The Archaeology of Knowledge* (New York: Pantheon, 1972), p. 17.
39. Michel Foucault, "Ceci n'est pas une pipe," *Cahiers du chemin*, January 1968; republished (with Magritte's two letters) by Fata Morgana in 1973; translated by James Harkness as *This Is Not a Pipe* (Berkeley: University of Califorina Press, 1982). Foucault's letter was published in René Magritte, *Oeuvres complètes* (Paris: Flammarion, 1979), p. 521.

13. The Open Sea

1. Jelila Hafsia, "Quand la passion de l'intelligence illuminait Sidi Bou Saïd," *La Presse de Tunis*, July 6, 1984.
2. Jean Daniel, "La Passion de Michel Foucault," *Le Nouvel Observateur*, June 29, 1984.
3. Michel Foucault, *L'Archéologie du savoir* (Paris: Gallimard, 1969), cover. This quotation also appears on the jacket of A. M. Sheridan Smith's translation, *The Archaeology of Knowledge* (New York: Pantheon, 1972). I have slightly modified the translation. *(Trans.)*
4. Ducio Trombadori, *Colloqui con Foucault* (Salerno: Cooperative editrice, 1981), pp. 71–75. This passage is taken from the initial transcript of the tape in French.
5. At the time of Aron's letter, the venerable Ecole Pratique des Hautes Etudes was divided into six sections. The fourth was devoted to "philolog-

ical sciences." The sixth section, created after World War II, was devoted to "economic and social sciences," but with a strong orientation toward history. Some years after the time of Aron's letter, the sixth section became an independent institution, the Ecole des Hautes Etudes en Sciences Sociales. In 1967 there may well have been oppositions between the sections, the sixth being very modernist, and the fourth being more conservative, or at least more traditional.

14. A Vincennes Interlude

1. *Paris-Presse—L'intransigeant*, October 8, 1968.
2. *Action*, November 1968.
3. *Le Monde*, January 12, 1968.
4. "Le Piège de Vincennes," *Le Nouvel Observateur*, February 9, 1970.
5. Jules Vuillemin, "Michel Foucault (1926–1984)," *Annuaire du Collège de France*, 1984–85.
6. Michel Foucault, "Qu'est-ce qu'un auteur?" and the discussion following, *Bulletin de la Société française de la philosophie*, July–September 1969, pp. 73–104.

15. The Solitude of the Acrobat

1. Pierre Daix, *Les Lettres françaises*, December 9, 1970.
2. Michel Foucault, *L'Ordre du discours* (Paris: Gallimard, 1971); translated by Rupert Swyer as "The Discourse on Language," appendix in Foucault, *The Archaeology of Knowledge*, trans. A. M. Sheridan Smith (New York: Pantheon, 1972), p. 215. For Beckett's actual text see *The Unnamable*, trans. Samuel Beckett (New York: Grove Press, 1958), p. 179.
3. The subtitle of Foucault's thesis *Folie et déraison*, which became the title of the 1972 edition. *(Trans.)*
4. Michel Foucault, *Titres et travaux*, pamphlet printed in fulfillment of requirements for candidacy at the Collège de France (Paris: privately printed, 1969), pp. 4–6.
5. Ibid., p. 7.
6. Ibid., pp. 7, 8.
7. Ibid., p. 9.
8. Unpublished text, Collège de France.
9. Unpublished text, Collège de France.
10. Foucault, "The Discourse on Language," p. 216.
11. Ibid., p. 228.
12. Ibid., p. 220.
13. Ibid., pp. 226, 227.

14. Ibid., pp. 232–233.
15. Ibid., p. 237.
16. Gérard Petitjean, "Les Grands Prêtres de l'université française," *Le Nouvel Observateur*, April 7, 1975.

16. A Lesson from the Darkness

1. *Intolérable*, no. 1 (Paris: Champ Libre, 1971).
2. "Création d'un groupe d'information sur les prisons," *Esprit*, March 1971, pp. 531–532.
3. Michel Foucault, *Résumés des cours du Collège de France, 1970–1982* (Paris: Julliard, 1989).
4. *Intolérable*, no. 1.
5. *Intolérable*, no. 4: *Suicides de prisons, 1972* (Paris: Gallimard, 1973), pp. 38–40.
6. Michelle Perrot, "La Leçon des ténèbres. Michel Foucault et la prison," *Actes. Cahier d'action juridique*, Summer 1986, pp. 76–77.
7. Claude Mauriac, *Le Temps immobile*, especially vol. III, *Et comme l'espérance est violente* (Paris: Grasset, 1977).
8. Mauriac, *Et comme l'esperance*, p. 334.
9. Michel Foucault, "Le Discours de Toul," *Le Nouvel Observateur*, December 27, 1971.
10. Mauriac, *Et comme l'espérance*, p. 334.
11. The text of this "play" was published in *Esprit*, October 1972.
12. Michel Foucault, foreword to Serge Livrozet, *De la prison à la révolte* (Paris: Mercure de France, 1973), p. 14.
13. Serge Livrozet, "Le Droit à la parole," *Libération*, February 19, 1979.
14. Daniel Defert and Jacques Donzelot, "La Charnière des prisons," *Le Magazine littéraire*, May 1976.
15. Gilles Deleuze, "Foucault and the Prison," *History of the Present*, no. 2 (Spring 1986).
16. Michel Foucault, "Présentation," in *Moi Pierre Rivière, ayant égorgé ma mère, ma soeur et mon frère . . . : un cas de parricide au XIXe siècle* (Paris: Gallimard-Julliard, 1973), p. 9; translated by Frank Jellinek as *I, Pierre Rivière, Having Slaughtered My Mother, My Sister, and My Brother: A Case of Parricide in the Nineteenth Century* (New York: Pantheon, 1975), p. vii.
17. Foucault, *I, Pierre Rivière*, pp. xi–xii.
18. Michel Foucault, *Surveiller et punir: naissance de la prison* (Paris: Gallimard, 1975), p. 35; translated by Alan Sheridan as *Discipline and Punish: The Birth of the Prison* (New York: Pantheon, 1977), p. 31.
19. Foucault, *Surveiller et punir*, jacket text.
20. Michel Foucault, "Des supplices aux cellules," *Le Monde*, February 21, 1975.
21. Foucault, *Discipline and Punish*, p. 308. The French edition ends on page

315; there, the statement quoted here, which appears as the final paragraph in *Discipline and Punish*, is presented as a footnote. *(Trans.)*

17. Popular Justice and the Workers' Memory

1. Claude Mauriac, *Le temps immobile*, vol. III: *Et comme l'espérance est violente* (Paris: Grasset, 1977), p. 291. Information about the history of the Djellali committee is taken from this volume and from vol. IX, *Mauriac et fils*. See also Catherine Von Bülow and Fazia Ben Ali, *La Goutte d'Or ou le mal des racines* (Paris: Stock, 1979), and issues of *Le Monde*.

2. Von Bülow and Ben Ali, *La Goutte d'Or*.

3. Claude Mauriac, *Le Temps immobile*, vol. II: *Les Espaces imaginaires* (Paris: Livre de Poche, 1985), pp. 293–294.

4. *La Vérité Rhône-Alpes*, December 1972. An excerpt from Foucault's speech was also quoted in *La Cause du peuple—J'accuse*, December 1, 1972, in a slightly different form.

5. For the relationship between Sartre and Pierre Victor, and for Simone de Beauvoir's reaction, see Annie Cohen-Solal, *Sartre, 1905–1980* (Paris: Gallimard, 1985), pp. 628–656; also Simone de Beauvoir, *La Cérémonie des adieux* (Paris: Gallimard, 1981).

6. Michel Foucault, "Sur la justice populaire. Débat avec les maos. Dossier: Nouveau Fascisme, nouvelle démocratie," *Les Temps modernes*, no. 310 *bis* (February 1972), 336–366. Translated in Foucault, *Power/Knowledge: Selected Interviews and Other Writings, 1972–1977*, ed. Colin Gordon (New York: Pantheon, 1980), pp. 1–32.

7. Jean-Paul Sartre, "A propos de la justice populaire," interview, *Pro justicia*, no. 2 (1973), 22–23.

8. On the Bruay-en-Artois affair, see Judge Henri Pascal, *Une Certaine Idée de la justice* (Paris: Fayard, 1973); also Jacques Batigne, *Bruay, un juge vous fait juge* (Paris: Plon, 1972).

9. *La Cause du peuple*, May 1, 1972.

10. *La Cause du peuple*, May 17, 1972.

11. Ibid. The reply that is signed collectively by La Cause du Peuple has been attributed to Pierre Victor by Hervé Hamon and Patrick Rotman, *Génération*, vol. II: *Les Années de poudre* (Paris: Seuil, 1988), p. 434.

12. Taped interview, Foucault Archives, University of California, Berkeley.

13. Mauriac, *Et comme l'espérance*, pp. 373–374.

14. Claude Mauriac, *Une Certaine Rage* (Paris: Robert Laffont, 1977), p. 73.

15. Mauriac, *Et comme l'espérance*, pp. 418–419.

16. *La Liberté de l'esprit*, February 1949.

17. On the birth of *Libération* see François-Marie Samuelson, *Il était une fois Libé . . .* (Paris: Seuil, 1979).

18. According to François-Marie Samuelson there were five of these.

19. Michel Foucault, "Pour une chronique de la mémoire ouvrière," *Libération*, February 22, 1973.

20. "L'Intellectuel sert à rassembler les idées," *Libération*, May 26, 1973.

21. Maurice Clavel, *Ce que je crois* (Paris: Grasset, 1975), p. 98.

22. Ibid., esp. pp. 122–148. Foucault's letter is on pp. 138–139.

23. Maurice Clavel, "Vous direz trois rosaires," *Le Nouvel Observateur*, December 27, 1976.

24. Michel Foucault, "Vivre autrement le temps," *Le Nouvel Observateur*, April 30, 1979.

25. *Les Machines à guérir. Aux origines de l'hôpital moderne*, collective volume, Dossiers et documents d'architecture, Institut de l'environnement (Paris, 1976).

26. *Annuaire du Collège de France*, 1970–71 through 1979–80. See also Michel Foucault, *Résumés des cours au Collège de France, 1970–1982* (Paris: Julliard, 1989).

27. Gilles Deleuze, "Raymond Roussel ou l'horreur du vide," *Arts*, October 23, 1963; idem, "L'Homme, une existence douteuse," *Le Nouvel Observateur*, June 1, 1966.

28. Gilles Deleuze, "Un Nouvel Archiviste," *Critique*, March 1970; idem, "Ecrivain non: un nouveau cartographe," *Critique*, December 1975; both reprinted in Deleuze, *Foucault* (Paris: Minuit, 1986).

29. Michel Foucault, "Ariane s'est pendue," review, *Le Nouvel Observateur*, March 31, 1969.

30. Michel Foucault, "Theatrum philosophicum," *Critique*, September 1972; translated by Donald F. Bouchard and Sherry Simon in *Language, Counter-Memory, Practice: Selected Essays and Interviews*, ed. Bouchard (Ithaca: Cornell University Press, 1977), p. 165.

31. Gilles Deleuze and Michel Foucault, "Les Intellectuels et le pouvoir," *L'Arc*, no. 49 (1972).

32. Michel Foucault, "Lettres à quelques leaders de la gauche," *Le Nouvel Observateur*, November 28, 1977.

33. "Alain Peyrefitte s'explique . . . Et Michel Foucault répond," *Le Nouvel Observateur*, January 23, 1978.

34. Claude Mauriac, *Le Temps immobile*, vol. IX: *Mauriac et fils* (Paris: Grasset, 1986), p. 388.

35. Michel Foucault, "Nous nous sentions comme une sale espèce," *Der Spiegel*, December 19, 1977.

36. Michel Foucault, foreword to Peter Bruckner and Alfred Krovosa, *Ennemi de l'Etat* (Paris: Claix, La Pensée Sauvage, 1979).

37. Gilles Deleuze, "A propos des nouveaux philosophes et d'un problème plus général," *Minuit*, supp., June 5, 1977.

38. Michel Foucault, "La Grande Colère des faits," *Le Nouvel Observateur*, May 9, 1977.

39. Gilles Deleuze, "La Vie comme une oeuvre d'art," *Le Nouvel Observateur*, August 29, 1986.

18. "We Are All Ruled"

1. Claude Mauriac, *Le Temps immobile*, vol. III: *Et comme l'espérance est violente* (Paris: Grasset, 1977), p. 540.

2. Ibid., p. 542.

3. Ibid., p. 561.

4. *Libération*, September 24, 1975.

5. Mauriac, *Et comme l'espérance*, p. 562.

6. Jean Lacouture, "Le Cadavre bafouille," *Le Nouvel Observateur*, September 29, 1975.

7. *Libération*, September 24, 1975.

8. Mauriac, *Et comme l'espérance*, p. 581.

9. Michel Foucault, foreword to Roger Knobelspiess, *QHS: quartiers de haute sécurité* (Paris: Stock, 1980), pp. 13–14.

10. Michel Foucault, "Vous êtes dangereux," *Libération*, June 10, 1983. Knobelspiess was acquitted of this charge in 1986 but was arrested again in 1987 after a gun battle with the police during a bank robbery.

11. Michel Foucault, *La Volonté de savoir*, vol. I of *Histoire de la sexualité* (Paris: Gallimard, 1976), pp. 13–14; translated by Robert Hurley as *The History of Sexuality, Volume I: An Introduction* (New York: Pantheon, 1978), pp. 6–7.

12. Foucault, *History of Sexuality: Introduction*, pp. 8–9.

13. Ibid., pp. 11–12.

14. Ibid., pp. 12–13, 7.

15. Ibid., p. 94.

16. Foucault, *La Volonté de savoir*, p. 172.

17. See, for example, Jacques-Alain Miller's paper presented at the colloquium "Foucault philosophe," in *Actes du colloque: Michel Foucault philosophe* (Paris: Seuil, 1989); and Denis Hollier's text in the same collection.

18. Foucault, *History of Sexuality: Introduction*, p. 63.

19. Maurice Blanchot, *Michel Foucault tel que je l'imagine* (Paris: Fata Morgana, 1986), p. 58.

20. Foucault, *History of Sexuality: Introduction*, pp. 33, 65.

21. Michel Foucault, interview, *Libération*, January 21, 1983.

22. A sample of these reactions and of Foucault's debate with historians can be found in the excellent volume edited by Michelle Perrot, *L'Impossible prison* (Paris: Seuil, 1980).

23. Jean Baudrillard, *Oublier Foucault* (Paris: Galilée, 1977); translated by Nicole Dufresne as *Forget Foucault* (New York: Semiotexte, 1987).

24. Preface to the German edition of *La Volonté de savoir* (Frankfurt: Suhrkamp, 1983).
25. *Herculine Barbin dite Alexina B*, ed. Michel Foucault (Paris: Gallimard, 1978).
26. Michel Foucault, "Do We Need a True Sex?" in *Herculine Barbin: Being the Recently Discovered Memoirs of a Nineteenth-Century French Hermaphrodite*, ed. Foucault, trans. Richard McDougall (New York: Pantheon, 1980). This introductory essay was published in French in the review *Arcadie* in November 1980.
27. *Herculine Barbin*, jacket text.
28. *My Secret Life*, ed. Michel Foucault (Paris: Les Formes du Secret, 1978).
29. Michel Foucault, "La Vie des hommes infâmes," *Cahiers du chemin*, January 15, 1977.
30. Arlette Farge and Michel Foucault, eds., *Le Désordre des familles. Lettres de cachet des archives de la Bastille* (Paris: Gallimard-Julliard, 1982).
31. *Un procès ordinaire en URSS*, clandestine tapes (Paris: Gallimard, 1976).
32. Simone de Beauvoir, *La Cérémonie des adieux* (Paris: Gallimard, 1981), p. 144.
33. Quoted in Annie Cohen-Salal, *Sartre, 1905–1980* (Paris: Gallimard, 1985), p. 650.
34. Beauvoir, *La Cérémonie*, p. 146. See also Raymond Aron, *Mémoires* (Paris: Julliard, 1983), pp. 711–712; and Claude Mauriac, *Le Temps immobile*, vol. VII: *Le Rire des pères dans les yeux des enfants* (Paris: Grasset, 1981), pp. 503–505.
35. Text published in *Libération*, June 30, 1984.

19. A Revolution of Bare Hands

1. Thierry Voeltzel, *Vingt Ans et après* (Paris: Grasset, 1978).
2. Michel Foucault, "Les Reportages d'idées," *Corriere della sera*, November 12, 1978. The text was written to introduce an article by Alain Finkielkraut on Carter's America.
3. These were to have been the final lines of an October 1 article in *Corriere*, but they were cut (with Foucault's consent) because they made the article too long. They remain unpublished.
4. Michel Foucault, "L'Armée. Quand la terre tremble," *Corriere della sera*, September 28, 1978. I have used Foucault's original unedited French text for all the *Corriere* articles.
5. Michel Foucault, "Le Shah a cent ans de retard," *Corriere della sera*, October 1, 1978. The title is the one chosen by the editors at *Corriere*. Foucault had used "Le Poids mort de la modernisation."
6. Michel Foucault, "A quoi rêvent les Iraniens?" *Le Nouvel Observateur*, October 16, 1978.

7. Michel Foucault, "Téhéran: la foi contre le shah," *Corriere della sera*, October 8, 1978. Foucault's title for this was "Iran. Dans l'attente de l'Imam."

8. Michel Foucault, "L'Armée," "Le Shah a cent ans," and "Téhéran"; and "Retour au prophète," *Corriere della sera*, October 22, 1978.

9. Foucault, "A quoi rêvent les Iraniens?"

10. Ibid.

11. Michel Foucault, "Une Révolte aux mains nues," *Corriere della sera*, November 5, 1978; "Défi à l'opposition," November 7; "La Révolte iranienne se propage sur les rubans des cassettes," November 19; "Le Chef mythique de la révolte," November 26.

12. Foucault, "Le Chef mythique." Foucault had titled this article "La Folie de l'Iran."

13. "Une Iranienne écrit," *Le Nouvel Observateur*, November 6, 1978.

14. Michel Foucault, "Réponse à une lectrice iranienne," *Le Nouvel Observateur*, November 13, 1978.

15. Foucault, "Le Chef mythique."

16. Michel Foucault, "Une Poudrière nommée Islam," *Corriere della sera*, February 13, 1979.

17. See Foucault's interview, "L'Esprit d'un monde sans esprit," in Claire Brière and Pierre Blanchet, *Iran. La révolution au nom de Dieu* (Paris: Seuil, 1979). Translated by Alan Sheridan as "Iran: The Spirit of a World without Spirit," in Foucault, *Politics, Philosophy, Culture: Interviews and Other Writings, 1977–1984*, ed. Lawrence D. Kritzman (New York: Routledge, 1988), pp. 211–224.

18. Claudie and Jacques Broyelle, "A quoi pensent les philosophes?" *Le Matin*, March 24, 1979; and Foucault's reply, *Le Matin*, March 26, 1979.

19. Michel Foucault, "Lettre ouverte à Mehdi Bazargan," *Le Nouvel Observateur*, April 14, 1979.

20. Michel Foucault, "Pour une morale de l'inconfort," *Le Nouvel Observateur*, April 23, 1979.

21. Michel Foucault, "Pour en finir avec les mensonges," interview, 1982, *Le Nouvel Observateur*, June 21, 1985.

22. Ibid.

20. Missed Appointments

1. Michel Foucault, "Est-il donc important de penser?" interview, *Libération*, May 30, 1981; translated as "Practicing Criticism" in Foucault, *Politics, Philosophy, Culture: Interviews and Other Writings, 1977–1984*, ed. Lawrence D. Kritzman (New York: Routledge, 1988).

2. Ibid.

3. "Les Rendez-vous manqués," *Libération*, December 15, 1981.

4. *Libération*, December 18, 1981.

5. *Les Nouvelles littéraires*, special issue on Poland, suppl., December 1981; *Le Matin*, December 21, 1981.

6. Claude Mauriac, *Le Temps immobile*, vol. IX: *Mauriac et fils* (Paris: Grasset, 1986), pp. 359–360.

7. *Libération*, December 23, 1981.

8. Seweryn Blumsztajn, in *Michel Foucault, une histoire de la vérité*, ed. Confédération Française des Travailleurs Démocratique (CFDT) (Paris: Syros, 1985), p. 98.

9. Bernard Kouchner, "Un Vrai Samouraï," ibid.

10. Ibid.

11. Interview with Bernard Kouchner, Simone Signoret, and Michel Foucault, *Le Nouvel Observateur*, October 9, 1982.

12. Edmond Maire, "La Pologne et après . . . ," dialogue with Foucault, *Le Débat*, May 1983, pp. 5–6.

13. CFDT, ed., *Sécurité sociale, l'enjeu* (Paris: Syros, 1983); translated by Alan Sheridan as "Social Security" in Foucault, *Politics, Philosophy, Culture*, pp. 159–177.

14. CFDT, *Michel Foucault, une histoire de la vérité*.

15. *Le Monde*, July 26, 1983.

16. *Le Magazine littéraire*, interview, May 1984. Translated by Alan Sheridan as "The Concern for Truth: An interview by François Ewald" in Foucault, *Politics, Philosophy, Culture*, pp. 266–267.

21. Zen and California

1. In Thierry Voeltzel, *Vingt Ans et après* (Paris: Grasset, 1978), p. 157.

2. "Michel Foucault et le Zen," interview, *Shunjuu*, no. 197 (1978).

3. "Michel Foucault on Attica," interview, *Telos*, Spring 1974, pp. 154–161.

4. The quotation is based on the original French text.

5. Hubert Dreyfus and Paul Rabinow, *Michel Foucault: Beyond Structuralism and Hermeneutics* (Chicago: University of Chicago Press, 1982).

6. *The Foucault Reader*, ed. Paul Rabinow (New York: Pantheon, 1984).

7. Keith Gandal and Stephen Kotkin, "Foucault in Berkeley," *History of the Present*, no. 1 (February 1985).

8. Otto Friedrich, "France's Philosopher of Power," *Time*, November 16, 1981.

9. Michel Foucault, "Monstrosities in Criticism," *Diacritics*, Fall 1971, in which Foucault replied particularly to an article by Georges Steiner, "The Mandarin of the Hour—Michel Foucault," *New York Times Book Review*, February 28, 1971. The controversy continued with Steiner's reply and a new clarification by Foucault (*Diacritics*, Winter 1971). See also the re-

sponse in the *New York Review of Books*, March 31, 1983, to the article by Lawrence Stone published on December 16, 1982.

10. Michel Foucault, "Sex, Power, and the Politics of Identity," interview, October 1982, *The Advocate*, August 7, 1984. Parts of this appeared as "Que fabriquent donc les hommes ensemble?" *Le Nouvel Observateur*, November 22, 1985.

11. Claude Mauriac, *Le Temps immobile*, vol. IX: *Mauriac et fils* (Paris: Grasset, 1986), p. 227.

12. Foucault, "Sex, Power, and Politics."

22. Life as a Work of Art

1. Michel Foucault, *L'Usage des plaisirs*, vol. II of *Histoire de la Sexualité* (Paris: Gallimard, 1984), p. 9; translated by Robert Hurley as *The Use of Pleasure* (New York: Pantheon, 1985), p. 3.

2. Michel Foucault, *Résumés des cours, 1970–1982* (Paris: Julliard, 1989), pp. 123–128.

3. Ibid., pp. 136–137.

4. Ibid., p. 150.

5. Transcript of an interview with Hubert Dreyfus and Paul Rabinow, April 19, 1983, Foucault archives of *History of the Present*, Berkeley. My thanks to Paul Rabinow, Hubert Dreyfus, and David Horn for having provided me the several hundred pages of all of these interviews. Rabinow and Dreyfus used part of them for the dialogue in *Michel Foucault, un parcours philosophique* (Paris: Gallimard, 1984), pp. 323–346. In this dialogue the division of *Histoire de la sexualité* into two parts, followed by a separate book, seems a given. This conception explains why Foucault, in a 1982 article, presented it as an "extract from the third volume of *Histoire de la sexualité*." Obviously, it is "Les Aveux de la chair" that he is talking about. See "Le Combat de la chasteté," *Communications*, no. 35 (1982).

6. Maurice Blanchot, *Michel Foucault tel que je l'imagine* (Paris: Fata Morgana, 1986), p. 62.

7. Hervé Guibert, "Les Secrets d'un homme," in *Mauve le Vierge* (Paris: Gallimard, 1988).

8. Foucault, *The Use of Pleasure*, p. 7.

9. Review of *L'Histoire de la sexualité*, *Journal of Roman Studies*, 76 (1986).

10. Paul Veyne, "Foucault révolutionne l'histoire," in *Comment on écrit histoire* (Paris: Seuil, 1979).

11. Foucault, *The Use of Pleasure*, p. 8.

12. Ibid., pp. 6–7.

13. Pierre Nora, interview, *L'Evénement du jeudi*, September 18, 1986.

14. Gilles Deleuze and Michel Foucault, "Introduction générale," in Friedrich

Nietzsche, *Le Gai Savoir*, vol. V of *Oeuvres complètes* (Paris: Gallimard, 1967), p. 11.

15. Paul Veyne's text, meant to conclude his article in *Critique*, August–September 1986. I am publishing these pages at Veyne's request.

16. "Hier à 13 heures . . . ," *Libération*, June 26, 1984.

17. Daniel Rondeau, "Le Canard et le Renard ou la vie d'un philosophe," *Libération*, June 30, 1984.

18. Pierre Bourdieu, "Le Plaisir de savoir," *Le Monde*, June 27, 1984.

19. Paul Veyne, "La Fin de vingt-cinq siècles de métaphysique," ibid.

20. "Le Témoignage de Fernand Braudel," *Le Nouvel Observateur*, June 29, 1984.

21. Georges Dumézil, "Un Homme heureux," ibid. In the book of interviews that I recorded with him in 1986, dedicated "to the memory of Michel Foucault," Dumézil returned at greater length to their friendship. See Georges Dumézil, *Entretiens avec Didier Eribon* (Paris: Gallimard, 1987).

22. Georges Dumézil, "Divertissement sur les dernières parôles de Socrate," in *Le Moyne noir en gris dedans Varennes* (Paris: Gallimard, 1984). Foucault discussed this text on February 15 and 22, 1984. See also Eliane Allo, "Les Dernières Parôles du philosophe. Dialogue entre Georges Dumézil et Michel Foucault sur le souci de l'âme," *Actes de la recherche en sciences sociales*, March 1986.

23. Foucault, *The Use of Pleasure*, p. 9.

24. Blanchot, *Michel Foucault*, p. 63.

25. Gilles Deleuze, "La Vie comme une oeuvre d'art," *Le Nouvel Observateur*, August 29, 1986.

26. Blanchot, *Michel Foucault*, p. 63.

27. Deleuze, "La Vie comme une oeuvre."

28. Hubert Dreyfus and Paul Rabinow, *Michel Foucault: Beyond Structuralism and Hermeneutics* (Chicago: University of Chicago Press, 1982), p. 237.

29. Foucault, *Résumés des cours*, pp. 165–166.

Selected Works of Foucault

Books (in chronological order)

Maladie mentale et personnalité. Paris: PUF, 1954.

Maladie mentale et psychologie. Paris: PUF, 1962. Translated by Alan Sheridan as *Mental Illness and Psychology.* New York: Harper & Row, 1976.

Folie et déraison. Histoire de la folie à l'âge classique. Paris: Plon, 1961. Abridged and translated by Richard Howard as *Madness and Civilization: A History of Insanity in the Age of Reason.* New York: Pantheon, 1965. Reissued with a new preface and two appendixes as *Histoire de la folie à l'âge classique.* Paris: Gallimard, 1972.

Naissance de la clinique. Une archéologie du régard médical. Paris: PUF, 1963. Translated by A. M. Sheridan Smith as *The Birth of the Clinic: An Archaeology of Medical Perception.* New York: Pantheon, 1973.

Raymond Roussel. Paris: Gallimard, 1962. Translated by Charles Ruas as *Death and the Labyrinth: The World of Raymond Roussel.* Garden City, N.Y.: Doubleday, 1986.

Les Mots et les choses. Une archéologie des sciences humaines. Paris: Gallimard, 1966. Translated by Alan Sheridan as *The Order of Things: An Archaeology of the Human Sciences.* 1970. Reprint, New York: Vintage, 1973.

L'Archéologie du savoir. Paris: Gallimard, 1969. Translated by A. M. Sheridan Smith as *The Archaeology of Knowledge.* New York: Pantheon, 1972.

Titres et travaux. Pamphlet printed in fulfillment of requirements for candidacy at the Collège de France. Paris: privately printed, 1969.

L'Ordre du discours. Inaugural lecture at the Collège de France. Paris: Gallimard, 1971. Translated by Rupert Swyer as "The Discourse on Language." Appendix to *The Archaeology of Knowledge.*

Surveiller et punir. Naissance de la prison. Paris: Gallimard, 1975. Translated by Alan Sheridan as *Discipline and Punish: The Birth of the Prison.* New York: Pantheon, 1977.

La Volonté de savoir. Vol. I of *Histoire de la sexualité.* Paris: Gallimard, 1976. Translated by Robert Hurley as *The History of Sexuality, Volume I: An Introduction.* New York: Pantheon, 1978.

L'Usage des plaisirs. Vol. II of *Histoire de la sexualité.* Paris: Gallimard, 1984. Translated by Robert Hurley as *The Use of Pleasure.* New York: Pantheon, 1985.

Le Souci de soi. Vol. III of *Histoire de la sexualité*. Paris: Gallimard, 1984. Translated by Robert Hurley as *The Care of the Self*. New York: Pantheon, 1986.
Résumés des cours au Collège de France, 1970–1982. Paris: Julliard, 1989.

Collected Essays and Interviews

Language, Counter-Memory, Practice: Selected Essays and Interviews. Edited by Donald F. Bouchard. Ithaca: Cornell University Press, 1977.
Politics, Philosophy, Culture: Interviews and Other Writings, 1977–1984. Edited by Lawrence D. Kritzman. New York: Routledge, 1988.
Power/Knowledge: Selected Interviews and Other Writings. Edited by Colin Gordon. New York: Pantheon, 1980.

Acknowledgments

A book such as this could not exist without the help, advice, and eye-witness reports of a great many people. I extend special thanks to: Maurice Agulhon, Michel Albaric, Eliane Allo, Louis Althusser, Gilbert Amy, Didier Anzieu, the late Jean-Paul Aron, Pierre Aubenque, Suzanne Bachelard, Michèle Bancilhon, Abol-Hassan Bani Sadr, Jean-François Battail, François Bédarida, Jacques Bellefroid, Renée Bernard, Leo Bersani, Tom Bishop, Pierre Blanchet, Maurice Blanchot, Howard Bloch, Olivier Bloch, Pierre Boulez, Jean-Marcel Bouguereau, Christian Bourgois, Paule Braudel, Yvon Brès, Claire Brière, Jacques Brunschwig, Catherine Von Bülow, Etienne Burin des Roziers, Robert Castel, Maurice Caveing, François Chamoux, Jean Charbonnel, Hélène Cixous, Maurice Clavelin, Francis Cohen, Annie Cohen-Solal, Michel Crouzet, Raoul Curiel, Pierre Daix, Jean Daniel, Marie-Josèphe Dhavernas, Régis Debray, Guy Degen, the late Jean Delay, Gérard Deledalle, Gilles Deleuze, Jean Deprun, Jacques Derrida, Jean-Toussaint Desanti, Jacques Dolly, Jean-Marie Domenach, Hubert Dreyfus, Claude Dumézil, Elisabeth Dutartre, Jean and Antoinette Erhard, Dr. Etienne, François Ewald, Michel Fano, James Faubion, Jean-Pierre Faye, Sylvie Ferrand-Mignon, the late Anne Foucault, Robert Francès, Norihiko Fukui, Keith Gandal, Maurice de Gandillac, Pierre Ganter, Jean-Louis Gardies, Jean Gattegno, Antoine de Gaudemar, Philippe Gavi, Gérard Genette, Bronislaw Geremek, Louis Girard, André Gisselbrecht, Henri Gouhier, François Gros, Georges Gusdorf, Fathma Haddad, Else Hammar, Ahmed Hasnaoui, Clemens Heller, Stenn-Gunnar Hellström, Malou Höjer, Denis Huisman, Marguerite Hyppolite, Rose-Marie Janzen, Jean-François Josselin, Madeleine Julien, Serge July, Gilbert Kahn, Jérôme Kanapa, Pierre Kaufmann, the late Hugues de Kerret, Pierre Klossowski, Jean Knapp, Bernard Kouchner, Arthur Krebs, Annie Kriegel, Sylvia Lacan, Agnès Lagache, Jean and Nadine Laplanche, Olivier Laude, Gérard Lebrun, Serge Leclaire, Victor Leduc, Bernard Legros, Michel Leiris, Emmanuel Le Roy Ladurie, Claude and Monique Lévi-Strauss, Marc Lévy, Jérôme Lindon, Sylvère Lotringer, Roberto Machado, Pierre Macherey, Alexandre Matheron,

Claude Mauriac, Robert Mauzi, Louis Mazauric, Essaied Mazouz, Assia Melamed, Suzanne Merleau-Ponty, Philippe Meyer, Jean Michon-Bordes, Jacques-Alain and Judith Miller, Jean-François Miquel, Jean Molino, Yves Montand, Jean-Pierre de Morant, Jacques Morel, Yann Moulier, Georg Nagy, Jacques Narbonne, Paule Neuvéglise, Marcel Neveux, Erik Nilsson, Pierre Nora, Jean-Christophe and Birgit Oberg, Jean d'Ormesson, Ahmed Othmani and Simone Othmani-Lellouche, Guy Papon, Jean-Claude and Francine Pariente, Jean-Claude Passeron, Michelle Perrot, Pierre Petitmengin, Françoise Peyrot, Pierre Pichot, Jean Piel, Dom Pierrot, Maurice Pinguet, Bernard Pivot, Raymond Polin, Jean-Bertrand Pontalis, Jacques Proust, Lucette Rabaté, Erik Rankka, Philippe Rebeyrol, Pierre Rivière, Alain Robbe-Grillet, Régine Roche, Daniel Rocher, Ahmad Salamatian, Jean-Marc Salmon, François-Marie Samuelson, Jean Sarvonnat, André Schiffrin, Jurgen Schmidt-Radefeldt, Dominique Schnapper, John Searle, Jacques Seebacher, Richard Sennett, Michel Serres, Lucien Sève, Margareta Silenstam, John K. Simon, Michel Simon, Jean Sirinelli, Jean-François Sirinelli, Roger Stéphane, Stig Strömholm, Emmanuel Terray, Anne Thalamy, Jacqueline Tomaka, Fathi and Rachida Triki, Jean-Louis Van Regemorter, Georges Vallet, Paul and Nelly Viallaneix, Jacqueline Verdeaux, Jeannine Verdès-Leroux, André Vergez, Etienne Verley, Guy Verret, Michel Verret, Thierry Voeltzel, Maurice Vouzelaud, Jules Vuillemin, Raymond Weil, Marc Zamansky, Jean-Marie Zemb, and Maciej Zurowski.

I thank the following institutions and depositories for access to documents: Alliance Française d'Uppsala, "Apostrophes" (Antenne 2), Archives Raymond Aron (courtesy of his daughter, Mme. Dominique Schnapper), Archives Jean Barraqué (Association Jean Barraqué, Paris), Archives de l'Institut National de l'Audiovisuel, Archives Départementales de la Vienne, Archives du Collège Saint-Stanislas, Archives du Lycée Henri-IV (Poitiers), Archives Nationales de France, Bibliothèque de la Sorbonne, Centre National de la Recherche Scientifique (Paris), Collège de France, Columbia University, *Corrieri della sera*, Ecole Normale Supérieure (Paris), Editions Flammarion, Editions Gallimard, Editions de Minuit, Editions Plon, Fondation Thiers, Institut de Psychologie, Carolina Rediviva Library (Uppsala), Lycée Henri-IV (Paris), Ministère des Affaires Etrangères, Ministère de l'Education Nationale, New York University, *Le Nouvel Observateur*, Rectorat de l'Académie de Paris, Université de Clermont-Ferrand,

ACKNOWLEDGMENTS

Université de Lille, Université de Paris VIII, Université de Tunis, University of California at Berkeley, and University of Uppsala.

I am also grateful for access to the personal papers of Pierre Bourdieu, Paule Braudel, Georges Canguilhem, Georges Dumézil, Anne Foucault, Henri Gouhier, Jelila Hafsia, Marguerite Hyppolite, Jean Knapp, Claude Lévi-Straus, Assia Melamed, Jean-Christophe Oberg, Jean-Claude Passeron, Jacqueline Verdeaux, Paul Veyne, and Jules Vuillemin.

Several individuals have been most cooperative in sharing information but have asked, for various reason, not to be acknowledged by name. This book owes a great deal to them, and I wish to express my gratitude.

I should also like to thank Marthe Burais, Corinne Deloi, and Thérèse Richard and the photo and documentation offices at *Le Nouvel Observateur*; the documentation services at the Fondation Nationale des Sciences Politiques; the Foucault Center at Berkeley and the review *History of the Present*; and the cultural services at the French embassies in Stockholm, Tunis, and Warsaw.

I am especially grateful to: Francine Fruchaud and Denys Foucault, for granting me authorization to publish extracts from their brother's correspondence; Françoise Verny and Monique Nemer, for their close attention during the writing of this book; David Horn and Dominique Seglard, for their generous and invaluable help; Mathieu Lindon, who knows how much I owe him; Pierre Bourdieu, Georges Canguilhem, Paul Rabinow, and Paul Veyne, who not only dredged up information from their memories and personal papers but also followed my work with tireless support and friendship, with unforgettable kindness and availability; and Marie Ymonet, who read, reread, and commented on each chapter as it was being written, and without whom this book could never have been completed.

Finally, I cannot conclude without fondly remembering Georges Dumézil, who was present at the inception of this book, who encouraged its very first steps, but who is no longer here to read it.

Index

~~~